Day of purcho

Age = 52 (OIC,

IRELAND IN
WORLD WAR TWO

This volume is dedicated
to the memory of
Comdt Peter Young
(1950–1999)

IRELAND IN WORLD WAR TWO

DIPLOMACY AND SURVIVAL

edited by

DERMOT KEOGH
*(Professor of History,
University College Cork)*

MERVYN O'DRISCOLL
*(Lecturer in Modern History,
University College Cork)*

MERCIER PRESS

First published in 2004 by
Mercier Press
Douglas Village, Cork
Email: books@mercierpress.ie
Website: www.mercierpress.ie

Trade enquiries to CMD Distribution
55A Spruce Avenue, Stillorgan Industrial Park
Blackrock, County Dublin
Tel: (01) 294 2560; Fax: (01) 294 2564
E-mail: cmd@columba.ie

ISBN 1 85635 445 8
10 9 8 7 6 5 4 3 2 1

A CIP record for this title is available
from the British Library

Mercier Press receives financial assistance from
the Arts Council/An Chomhairle Ealaíon

Printed in Ireland by ColourBooks, Baldoyle Industrial Estate, Dublin 13

CONTENTS

NORTHERN IRELAND, AND THE IRISH IN THE BRITISH ARMY

ACKNOWLEDGEMENTS

This collection of essays is the product of work done under the University College Cork Department of History's HEA-funded project, PRTLI 1. Entitled 'Culture Contact – Nation and State', the programme of research reviewed aspects of Irish history from the Middle Ages to the twentieth century. The work has resulted in a number of articles, monographs, and collections of essays of which *Ireland in World War Two: Neutrality and Survival* is the third in a series of five collections to be published by Mary Feehan and Mercier Press.

This book, *Ireland in World War Two*, began as a day-long conference held at UCC on 12 May 2001. Seventeen papers were delivered and three other members of the History department, Prof. J. J. Lee, Dr Donal Ó Drisceoil, and Prof. Geoffrey Roberts helped us to chair the numerous panels. We worked very closely with an able and experienced organisational team of past and present postgraduates including Ailish Cremin, Dr Laurence Fenton, Derek O'Flynn and Michelle O'Mahony. The diligent and dedicated administrative staff (Norma Buckley, Margaret Clayton, Veronica Fraser, Charlotte Holland, Geraldine McAllister, and Deirdre O'Sullivan) of the Department of History as always provided unremitting support and patience. We thank all those staff at UCC who helped in pre-publicity including Orla O'Callaghan, Ruth McDonnell and Marie McSweeney. The assistance of the *Irish Examiner* in providing several photographs for the pre-publicity literature should also be noted. In particular, we acknowledge the invaluable assistance of Suzanne Crosbie, Anne Kearney, Lilian Caverley and members of the *Irish Examiner* down through the years. A generous award from the Faculty of Arts Conference Fund also proved immensely helpful.

Following the conference, which attracted an audience of over 100 people, papers were commissioned from a number of the speakers. We also asked a number of academics and researchers to write on areas that had not been covered by the speakers. The published volume has seventeen essays covering a wide range of different aspects of neutral Ireland during the Second World War. We are extremely grateful to all contributors, but in particular to present and former postgraduates who help to make the Department of History such a vibrant intellectual and research-oriented place to work. They help make 'history'.

Eileen O'Carroll played a key role in helping to subedit the manuscript and to bring the book to its final form. One of our administrators, Margaret Clayton, herself a history doctoral student and former HEA studentship holder, generously contributed her bibliographical and subediting skills in the final race to the deadline. We are also thankful to Mary Feehan and the ever-helpful staff at Mercier Press, especially Aisling Lyons, for their patience and professionalism.

We are grateful to the HEA for providing resources to make a collection of scholarship of this kind possible. Our thanks, as ever, to the librarian, John FitzGerald, and the staff of the Boole Library at UCC, particularly those who work in the invaluable 'Special Collections': Helen Davis, Teresina Flynn, Catherine Horgan, Mary Lombard and Peadar Cranitch. Our thanks also to Catriona Crowe and the staff of the National Archives, Dublin; the staff of the 'Manuscripts Room' in the National Library of Ireland; Seamus Helferty, Archivist, University College Dublin Archives Department; and Brian McGee, Archivist, Cork Archives Institute. Generations of Irish historians and students owe them a debt of gratitude.

Finally, however, we must acknowledge the generous support of the late Comdt Peter Young, Comdt Peter Laing and all the staff of Military Archives, Dublin. This volume is dedicated to the memory of Comdt Young who undertook sterling work in practically single-handedly opening up a new vista in Irish historical research. Comdt Peter Laing and his staff continue in this great tradition. We would like to thank Mrs Annette Young and the Military History Society of Ireland for granting permission to republish Comdt Young's landmark essay 'Defence and the New Irish State, 1919–1939'. This was first published in a special 'Emergency' volume (vol. XIX) of the *Irish Sword* in 1995 on the fiftieth anniversary of the end of the Second World War. Peter is sadly missed by those generations of Irish historians who were fortunate enough to have experienced his passion for Irish military history and his voluminous knowledge of the archives.

Professor Dermot Keogh/Dr Mervyn O'Driscoll
Department of History, University College Cork.
June 2004

CONTRIBUTORS

Dr Jonathan Bardon, former Head of the Department of Academic and Continuing Education at the Belfast College of Business Studies, is a lecturer in the School of History in Queen's University Belfast. His publications include *Belfast: an illustrated history* (1982) and *A History of Ulster* (1992).

Dr Emma Cunningham is a graduate of UCC. In 2001 she completed her PhD on 'Irish–Canadian Relations, 1939–1950'.

Dr T. Ryle Dwyer is an historian and regular columnist with the *Irish Examiner*. He has written more than a dozen books on Irish historical subjects. His *Guests of the State: The Story of Allied and Axis Servicemen Interned in Ireland* (1994) was one of four books that he wrote on different aspects of the Second World War.

Dr Mark M. Hull, a former US army officer, earned his PhD at UCC, specialising in the history of wartime espionage. He currently teaches history at St Louis University. He is the author of *Irish Secrets: German Espionage in Wartime Ireland, 1939–1945* (2003), as well as several articles on military history.

Dr Niall Keogh was awarded a PhD from UCC for his thesis entitled 'Con Cremin and Irish Foreign Policy 1936–58' in 2003. He is currently writing a biography of Con Cremin.

Aoife Ní Lochlainn studied Irish and History at UCD and is currently completing a PhD at the European University Institute, Italy, in the area of Irish and British labour history.

Dr Andrew McCarthy was educated at UCC and the University of Sussex, completed his PhD thesis on Irish financial history in 1996, and teaches in Cork. He is currently writing a *Historical Dictionary of Modern Ireland* for the Scarecrow Press series, and editing with Professor Dermot Keogh a documentary reader on the Limerick Jews in 1904.

Dr Robert McNamara has a PhD from the National University of Ireland. He has held posts at UCC and NUI Maynooth. He is the author of *Britain, Nasser and the Balance of Power in the Middle East from the Egyptian Revolution to the Six Day War* (2003) and a number of journal articles on British and Irish history.

Dr Aengus Nolan graduated in History from UCC in 1991. In 1997 he was awarded a PhD for his thesis, 'Joseph Walshe and the management of Irish foreign policy, 1922–1946: A study in diplomatic and administrative history.' Aengus currently works for Intel Ireland Ltd., as an IT professional.

Dr Don O'Leary completed his PhD in the Department of History, UCC, in 1996. His book, *Vocationalism and Social Catholicism in Twentieth-Century Ireland* (2000), is based on his doctoral research.

Dr David O'Donoghue has worked as a journalist in many parts of the world. He has taught journalism at third-level, has worked for Europa Satellite TV (Brussels and Hilversum) and is currently a parliamentary reporter in Leinster House. He holds a PhD from the School of Communications at Dublin City University (1995) and is the author of *Hitler's Irish Voices: the Story of German Radio's Wartime Irish Service* (Belfast, 1998).

Dr Donal Ó Drisceoil lectures in History at UCC, and is joint editor of *Saothar: Journal of Irish Labour History*. He is the author of *Censorship in Ireland 1939–1945: Neutrality, Politics and Society* (1996), *Peadar O'Donnell* (2001), and joint author of *The Murphy's Story: the History of Lady's Well Brewery, Cork* (1997).

Dr Seosamh Ó Longaigh is UCC educated and has worked as a management consultant in both the private and public sectors for several years. He will publish *A Permanent State of Emergency: The Evolution and Use of Emergency Law in Ireland, 1922–1948* in early 2005.

Finbarr O'Shea is a graduate of, and holds an MA from, UCC. He is completing a doctoral thesis on adoption in twentieth-century Ireland. He is the author of *Writing Skills for History Students* (History Department, UCC, 2000) and is co-editor of *The Lost Decade: Ireland in the 1950s* (2004).

Professor Geoffrey Roberts teaches Modern History and International Relations at UCC. He is the author of *The Unholy Alliance: Stalin's Pact with Hitler* (1989); *The Soviet Union and the Origins of the Second World War* (1995); *The Soviet Union in World Politics, 1945–1991* (1998); and *Victory at Stalingrad: The Battle that Changed History* (2002).

Comdt Peter Young (b. 1950) was a military historian and the founding director of the Military Archives, Dublin. He died on 27 October 1999.

INTRODUCTION –
HISTORIOGRAPHY AND AUTOBIOGRAPHY
Dermot Keogh

This book represents research conducted between the 1980s and early twenty-first century – much of it by graduates of the History department at University College Cork. The Higher Education Authority's PRTLI 1 programme enabled the coordinators of the UCC History department's project of research, 'Culture Contact – Nation and State', to establish a thematic study on Ireland and the Second World War. I am grateful to the HEA for affording the History department the opportunity to undertake this research.

The volume is dedicated to the memory of Commandant Peter Young, military historian and the founding Director of the Military Archives, Dublin. His 'Defence and the New Irish State, 1919–1939', is the first article in the collection. It is fitting that a publication containing the work of so many younger historians should be dedicated to his memory. Commandant Peter Young has done so much to encourage a number of generations of historians to find their way through Irish military archives, identify files relevant to their research and will them on to completion and publication. His successor, Commandant Victor Laing, will not mind the singling out of Commandant Peter Young for his inspiration, dedication and perseverance in the building up of Military Archives. His role in the discussions leading up to the opening up of official archives was highly significant. Military Archives took the lead and the successful outcome allowed historians from the late 1970s onwards to complement the work they were doing abroad over the previous decades.

Ireland had a conservative and chequered record on access to official archives up to the 1970s. The files of the Department of the Taoiseach were available in part from the middle of that decade thanks to the Taoiseach and foreign minister of the National Coalition Government between 1973 and 1977, respectively Mr Liam Cosgrave and Dr Garret

FitzGerald. Those files helped greatly but they were fragmented and incomplete. Such a release was not uniform. While helpful for the study of Irish foreign policy, they also tantalised researchers who were then in a position to know the exact Department of Foreign Affairs references needed. But the Department of Foreign Affairs pursued a very illiberal policy, with the absence of legislation governing the release of files being given as their plausible reason for such a conservative policy.

Perhaps Iveagh House's experience in the 1950s helped condition that policy of conservatism. Professor T. Desmond Williams, History department, University College Dublin, had set a standard for the study of Irish diplomatic history. In the late 1940s and early 1950s, he published an important series of articles on Ireland and the Second World War. These appeared in the *Irish Press* and in *The Leader* in the early 1950s.[1] His work was not footnoted but the reader was left in no doubt that the studies were authoritative. They were based on a wide personal knowledge of Ireland in the war years and on the author's privileged access to relevant British government files. Professor Williams was also a friend of a number of senior Irish civil servants and diplomats. Had he continued to write more specialist articles on different aspects of his study in the 1950s, the historiography of Irish diplomatic history would now read very differently. He must be given great credit for publishing the articles and for writing so frankly about sensitive and controversial aspects of Irish diplomacy during the war years. But a combination of circumstances deflected him from continuing to publish on Irish wartime diplomacy. He transmitted his enthusiasm for further study in the area to his teaching of generations of history students at UCD. I was fortunate to be among those who heard his lectures and later enjoyed his friendship.

The pioneering work of Professor Patrick Keatinge, Department of Political Science, Trinity College Dublin, needs to be acknowledged here also. He approached the study of Irish foreign policy from the perspective of the political scientist. His first book served for many years as the text for the study of that subject among history students.[2] His later research also helped to establish Irish diplomatic history as a field of study in Irish universities.[3] Here it is important too to mention the work of the journalist, Joseph T. Carroll. His book on Anglo-Irish relations during the war years was one of the first to take advantage of the opening up – in however a limited fashion – of British official sources.[4]

The researcher in those distant days could also supplement that work by searching out collections of private papers that were gradually becoming available on request from the families of relevant politicians or diplomats. The former director of Irish Military Intelligence, Col. Dan Bryan, was very helpful to researchers.[5]

In the 1970s, much also depended upon the availability of official primary sources in Washington, Ottawa, Paris, Rome, etc. Dr T. Ryle Dwyer was among the first historians to use Irish files in the US archives.[6] It was also possible in the 1970s to write about Anglo-Irish relations. Professor Ronan Fanning, History department, UCD, worked in that field.[7] The British government operated under a 30-year rule even if the availability of files relating to Ireland was very restricted. Dr Deirdre McMahon was among the very first historians to use primary sources extensively for her innovative study, *Republicans and Imperialists: Anglo-Irish Relations in the 1930s*.[8]

Nevertheless, it remained virtually impossible to find a sustained run of official Irish documents in Dublin in the 1970s to complement what researchers were finding in London and in archives elsewhere.

Beginning to work on diplomatic history in the mid-1970s, paradoxically I found major Catholic ecclesiastical sources that threw light on the post-1916 period and the first two decades of the new Irish state. They were particularly important for the period of Dáil Éireann, 1919–21, and the 1920s and 1930s. It was possible to follow the leads provided in those papers to seek out other material in private hands or in state-run archives abroad – that is, usually not in Ireland. In that context, I was fortunate to find many new collections of papers that allowed me to pursue my studies of Irish foreign policy. The papers of the Italian Department of Foreign Affairs proved to be very relevant as did material in the National Archives, London.

Unfortunately, the Department of Foreign Affairs continued to oppose access to its archives during that decade. In contrast, Dr Garret FitzGerald, the minister between 1973 and 1977, was much more liberal in his approach. He made a clear and unambiguous decision to permit me access to relevant files. I was a doctoral student at the European University Institute, Florence. Disappointingly, that clear-cut policy decision was 'reversed' when Fianna Fáil returned to power in 1977 before I had an opportunity to consult the files. [I drove back from Italy only to arrive in Dublin to read the headlines in the evening papers – 'Fianna Fáil returned to power in election landslide'.] The following day, I was allowed to order down files that were of interest to me in the Public Record Office, Four Courts. However, in a surreal turn of events, the archivist had been given explicit and clear instructions that I should be allowed to see the files but not to read them. Thus, I untied the string of many brown-paper parcels, took out the files and reviewed the title pages of each of the files. Then, under supervision, I was compelled to replace each file, refold the brown paper and tie the string around the neat parcel. Notwithstanding the setbacks, I conducted my thesis research between 1976 and 1980 at the European University Institute, and successfully defended my doctorate in January 1980. The thesis has formed the basis of three monographs and many articles. I am not engaging in self-pity in recalling these events. It is simply to stress to younger scholars the degree and the radical nature of the change that has taken place in this country over 30 years. The positive research climate in the country in the early twenty-first century ought not to be taken for granted. There is always a danger of reversal. That came with the weakening of the Freedom of Information Act in 2003.

This volume of essays is a cause for personal celebration. The collection is both historiographical and autobiographical. My colleague and co-editor, Dr Mervyn O'Driscoll, was a graduate student in UCC where he completed his MA thesis in 1992 on 'Irish–German Relations 1922–1939'.[9] A radically revised version of this manuscript was published in 2004 by Four Courts Press, Dublin, entitled: *Ireland, Germany and the Nazis – Politics and Diplomacy, 1919–1939*.[10] Dr O'Driscoll, who received his doctorate from Cambridge University, is now an internationally recognised expert on diplomatic history and international relations, and is the supervisor of a new generation of talented students of foreign policy. In the intervening decade or so, between Dr O'Driscoll receiving his MA at UCC in 1992 and the publication of his classic study of Irish–German relations in 2004, the study of Irish diplomatic history has been transformed.

In the middle of the 1980s, the then Secretary of the Department of Foreign Affairs, Mr Seán Donlon, gave me unrestricted access to the archives of the Department of Foreign Affairs. The book, *Ireland and Europe, 1919–1948*, was the result. Other work followed.[11]

The primary factor prompting change in the climate of historical research in Ireland during those years was the establishment of the National Archives in 1988 and the introduction of a 30-year rule governing access to departmental files. The late Commandant Young and the Military Archives were ploughing a lone furrow for a number of years before those developments.

The National Archives now provides the historian with the material to study systematically Ireland in international affairs. Prior to the establishment of the National Archives, and unlike the situation in the early twenty-first century, the historian working on Irish diplomacy or Ireland in international affairs was severely hampered when attempting to fashion a topic for investigation. The relevant files were under lock and key in Dublin until the early 1990s.

Teaching in the History department at UCC, I was fortunate to encounter many graduate students willing to undertake studies in Irish foreign policy and international relations. The study of diplomatic history at UCC was put on a solid footing by a number of teachers in the early 1980s. These included Professor John A. Murphy, Professor Joseph J. Lee and Professor Denis Smyth, now working at the History department, University of Toronto. Dr Ged Martin increased the range of area studies by teaching British, Canadian, South African and Australian history. This was a very productive period in the opening up of new areas of research that included the use of official Irish archives. Postgraduate work grew under their supervision and flourished.

Joining the staff of the UCC History department in 1980, I was fortunate to encounter a number of generations of students very interested in the area of international relations, European studies and diplomatic history. It is a humbling experience to spend decades working in the archives and also keep pace with the increasing volume of high-grade theses research. The objective of such empirical research is to avoid facile moralising and the writing of history from the Olympian heights of the twenty-first century. The main task of any good thesis supervisor is to help train the student in the methods of empirical research. The bank of theses written by those new generations of historians is a testimony to the benefits of such training in the skills of historical analysis, documentation and investigation.

The list below, though not complete, highlights what was done under my supervision in this general area of diplomatic and intellectual history.

Type	Year	Name	Title
PhD	2001	Emma Cunningham	Irish–Canadian Diplomatic Relations, 1939–1950
PhD	2001	Paula Wylie	Diplomatic Recognition in Irish Foreign Policy, 1949–1963[12]
PhD	2000	Mark M. Hull	German Military Intelligence Operations in Ireland, 1939–1945[13]
PhD	1999	Seosamh Ó Longaigh	Emergency Legislation in the Irish State, 1922–1948: An analysis of its evolution and use
PhD	1999	Bronagh M. Allison	State Policy and the Revival of the Irish Language, 1922–1948
PhD	1999	Robert McNamara	Britain's Other Cold War: A Study of British

			Policy towards Nasser's Egypt 1957–1967[14]
PhD	1997	Angus Nolan	*Joseph Walshe and the management of Irish Foreign Policy, 1922–1946: A study in diplomatic and administrative history*
PhD	1996	Don O'Leary	*The Origins, Development and Decline of Vocationalism in Twentieth-Century Ireland*[15]
PhD	1994	Donal Ó Drisceoil	*Censorship in Ireland during the Second World War*[16]
PhD	1992	David J. Ryan	*An Examination of Diplomatic Relations between the United States and Nicaragua during the Reagan Presidency*[17]
PhD	1989	Bernadette Whelan	*Ireland and the Marshall plan 1947–51*[18]
PhD	1985	Edward G. Brockie	*Relations between Great Britain and the Holy See during the Pontificate of Leo XIII, 1878–1903*
MPhil	2000	Maria Maureen Daly	*Seán MacBride and the Management of Irish Foreign Policy during the first Inter-Party Government 1948–1951*
MPhil	2000	Mary O'Rourke	*George William Russell (AE): Practical Patriotism*
MPhil	1999	Geraldine O'Brien	*Ireland's Refugee Policy, 1932–1950*
MPhil	1999	Clive J. O'Sullivan	*Sentinel Towers: The Irish Treaty Ports 1914–45*
MPhil	1999	Coleman Doyle	*Industrial Relations in Post World War Two Ireland 1946–1959*
MPhil	1999	Gillian Deenihan	*Seán Lemass and Northern Ireland 1959–1966*
MPhil	1997	Maurice FitzGerald	*Irish–American Diplomatic Relations, 1948–1963*
MPhil	1997	Paul Logan	*Ireland's Diplomatic Links with Spain, 1920–1950*
MPhil	1997	Col. Maurice Walshe	*The politics of Irish defence: from the Civil War to the Congo, 1923–1964*
MA	1999	Gerard Burke	*The British Army and Fermoy, 1870–1922*
MA	1996	Collette Mary Cotter	*Anti-Semitism and Irish Political Culture, 1932–45*
MA	1996	Elizabeth Meaney	*Women in the Irish Public Service 1945–1958*
MA	1995	Cathal Condon	*An analysis of the contributions made by Archbishop John Charles McQuaid to the drafting of the 1937 Constitution of Ireland*
MA	1995	Denis M. Dineen	*The Carter Administration's Policy toward the Nicaraguan Revolution*
MA	1995	Damian Keane	*Irish–U.S. Relations During World War Two*
MA	1995	Nigel M. Moriarty	*Ireland's reaction to the cold war aspects of emergency planning, 1947–1963*
MA	1994	Michele Power	*European Political Cooperation, Ireland and Neutrality*
MA	1994	Finín O'Driscoll	*The Search for the Christian State – An Analysis of Irish Social Catholicism, 1913–1939*
MA	1993	Geraldine M. Barry	*Batista to Castro: Anglo–Cuban Relations in Transition, 1958–1959*
MA	1993	Helena B. Flynn	*Peasants and Diplomats: An Analysis of the 1932 Matanza in El Salvador*
MA	1993[19]	Nicola Franchi	*Italia e Irlanda Negli Anni Trenta Storia di Un'intesa Mai Decollata*
MA	1993	Carol E Leland	*The Christian Democratic Movement and European Integration 1945–1954*

MA	1993	Robert Patterson	*Ireland and France: An Analysis of Diplomatic Relations, 1929–1950*
MA	1992	Jonathan P. Hamill	*Republicanism and Socialism in Ireland 1923–1933: An Analysis of New Nationalism*
MA	1992	Mervyn O'Driscoll	*Irish–German Diplomatic Relations 1922–1939*
MA	1991	Ann Cronin	*Britain and Venezuela 1945–1958: A Study in Diplomacy*
MA	1991	Martina Hayes	*Anglo-Chilean Relations: 1952–1958; A Survey of British Diplomatic Attitudes towards the second Ibanez Regime*
MA	1990	Raymond Jennings	*Archbishop William J. Walsh's Influence upon the Political, Social and Higher Education Questions, 1885–1921*
MA	1988	Josephine Vaughan	*Britain and Nicaragua: An Analysis of Diplomacy and Attitudes 1926–1934*
MA	1988	Marita Foster	*The United States and El Salvador: An Analysis of United States Legation Reporting, 1930–44*
MA	1988	Finbarr J. O'Shea	*Government and Trade Unions in Ireland 1939–46: The Formulation of Labour Legislation*
MA	1987	Julia M. Crowley	*The Changing Catholic Church: An analysis of historiography and recent trends in the Latin American Church 1945–1983*
MA	1987	Martin J. O'Meara	*Sir Austen Chamberlain and the Dimensions of British Diplomatic Relations with Italy between 1924 and 1928*
MA	1985	Thomas Linehan	*The Development of Cork's Economy and Business Attitudes 1910–1939*
MA	1985	Treasa Landers	*The Politics of Coffee: Aspects of an Agrarian Revolution – El Salvador's Peasant Uprising of 1932*
MA	1984	Bernadette Whelan	*Europe: Aspects of Irish Foreign Policy, 1945–51*
MA	1983	Raymond C. Sun	*Social Catholicism and the Secularisation of the Working Class in France, Italy & Germany 1878–1914*

This is in no sense a comprehensive list of research on the Second World War completed at UCC. As I have already mentioned, other colleagues, including Professor Joseph Lee, Dr Denis Smyth, Dr Ged Martin, Dr Mervyn O'Driscoll, Dr Donal Ó Drisceoil, Dr Brian Girvin, Professor Geoff Roberts, etc., have all contributed research in the field.

The study of Irish foreign policy has grown extensively in the latter part of the 1990s. More theses on diplomatic history are being written in all Irish universities. There is also a growing body of thesis research in Canada, the United States, Australia, Britain, Germany, France, Italy and Spain.[20]

The publication of *Documents on Irish Foreign Policy* is further proof of the health of the new situation. This project was strongly supported by the former Irish Ambassador to London, Mr Ted Barrington. Then Head of Personnel in the Department of Foreign Affairs, he helped secure the necessary decisions to fund the project. The decision to an-chor the project in the Royal Irish Academy was a wise one. Four vol-umes have already been published.[21]

Notwithstanding the publication of important monographs and the bank of theses referred to above, research on Irish foreign policy in the Second World War is still relatively underdeveloped.[22] The Anglo-Irish relationship has been written about extensively as have also Irish–Ger-man and Irish–US relations.[23] Several articles have also been published in the same area and on more general aspects of Irish diplomacy.[24] How-ever, after over 30 years working in the field of Irish diplomatic history, it is satisfying to be in a position to say that many of the major historical issues relevant to Ireland and the Second World War can now be addres-sed in a systematic and comparative fashion.

This volume seeks to broaden the range of study on Ireland and the Second World War. Divided into five sections, part one examines the preparations and the planning for war by the Irish state in the late 1930s. The second part examines aspects of Nazi German involvement in Ireland and the role of its spies. This section also examines the Irish state's handling of the internment of Axis and Allied personnel. The third part provides new research on Irish diplomacy at home and abroad. The fourth part deals with life, politics and society on the Irish 'home front' while the final section examines the experiences of Northern Ireland, particularly during the 1941 blitz, and the role of the Irish in the British army.

The project permitted a wide range of researchers to transfer some of their findings on this subject into conference, colloquium and semi-nar papers. Coordinating this subject area then required each of the con-tributors to do further research and then revise their respective chapters for the volume. Work on other areas was commissioned in order to pro-duce a more comprehensive analysis of major topics and themes on Ire-land and the Second World War.

The questions addressed are complex, and the writers have risen to the challenge to reflect that complexity in their designated areas. Let me single out for example the two articles by Seosamh Ó Longaigh on the preparation and implementation of Emergency Law in Second World War Ireland. This is a very good example of the challenges facing the historian.

The cover for this book reflects the sombre nature of the contents

of the volume. It is entitled 'Study of a Head' and was painted by Seán
Keating. The despairing uncertainty of the war years is evoked by the
darkness and the gloom of the picture. It is the task and the craft of the
historian to examine the past in all its complexity. Keating's painting is
a strong image of the dilemmas confronting a wartime generation that
did not have the advantage of knowing the outcome of the conflict.
This volume is a contribution to a process of scholarship, dialogue and
academic debate, free hopefully from any hectoring tone of moral rec-
titude. It is based, as the reader will likely agree, upon hard work rooted
firmly in empirical research in archives – a strong and necessary antidote
to flights of fancy.

THE IRISH STATE
PREPAREDNESS AND PLANNING FOR WAR

DEFENCE AND THE NEW IRISH STATE, 1919–1939
Peter Young

In the early years of the twentieth century the struggle for freedom and independence from Britain ensured that the forces from which the Irish army eventually evolved were imbued with the belief that England's difficulty was Ireland's opportunity (Roger Casement's proposed Irish brigade in Germany being a case in point). Against that, of course, must be set the fact that 90% of the Irish Volunteers complied with John Redmond's appeal in 1914 to support the British in the First World War. However, opposition to the threat of conscription later united the whole spectrum of Irish political and military opinion and contributed in a major way to the success of Sinn Féin in the general election of December 1918. Given this background, the exploration of how a defence policy was developed in Ireland between the first Dáil Éireann (1919) and the outbreak of the Second World War in 1939, sheds some interesting political light, particularly during the difficult 1930s.

Statements made during the life of the first Dáil Éireann formed a basis for much of the thinking on defence policy for the following two decades. Neutrality was not then considered; rather, a pragmatic approach was put forward. De Valera understood that independence from Britain was not possible unless Ireland could give Britain certain security guarantees. In 1920, he stated 'mutual self-interest would make the peoples of these two islands, if both [were] independent, the closest possible allies in a moment of real danger to either'.[1] A proposal during the subsequent Anglo-Irish Treaty negotiations that Ireland be considered neutral never really saw the light of day.[2] In one memorandum it was noted that Ireland would be recognised as a free state and that the British Commonwealth would guarantee her freedom and integrity.[3] Lord Longford, in his study of the negotiations, claims that it was Michael Collins himself who changed the word 'neutral' to 'free'.[4] Arthur Griffith also accepted the point about mutual self-interest and, even when told that British possession of Irish harbours would mean that no other nation would consider Ireland neutral, stated that the Irish had no objections to 'taking the safeguards which are necessary for your [British] security'.

The articles of the Treaty, as finally agreed, which were to have the most significance for Irish defence policy in the years that followed, were numbers six, seven and eight. Article six gave Britain responsibility for the defence of the sea of Great Britain and Ireland, until Ireland could undertake her own coastal defence. This arrangement was to be reviewed after five years. Article seven in fact precluded Irish neutrality, as it offered Great Britain such harbours and other facilities in Ireland as might be required. Article eight, which is rarely mentioned, limited the size of the Irish defence forces as a proportion of population to the strength of the British forces in relation to UK population. During the debate in the Dáil, which followed the signing of the Treaty, little reference was made to either neutrality or defence policy. Even de Valera's Document No. 2 did not mention neutrality. An interesting clause in the subsequent Irish Free State constitution stated that, save in the case of actual invasion, the Irish Free State should not be committed to active participation in any war without Oireachtas assent. However, the phrase 'active participation' did not preclude passive participation without such assent, as was subsequently proved in the Emergency.

During the 1920s and 1930s, the general weakening of the centralised power of the Commonwealth enabled the Irish to consider themselves as not being obligated to Commonwealth commitments. Neutrality, even with Britain in control of the ports, began to assume a higher profile in the late 1930s as de Valera started to play off an Irish claim to neutrality with the possibility of agreeing to defence commitments if the question of partition were settled. The return of the ports in 1938 clearly had implications for Irish neutrality, although at the time it was the traditional concepts of freedom and independence that tended to be stressed. Nevertheless, in a speech to the Dáil in July 1938, de Valera hinted at significant nuances for the future, when he stated:

> assuming other things were equal, if there was any chance of our neutrality in general being possible, we would probably say that we wanted to remain neutral. I do not know that you can follow that up by saying in any war, but in general our desire would be neutrality as far as possible.[5]

He went on to refer to British and Irish mutual self-interest, especially because of their close geographical proximity, adding that in case of war, consultation with Britain might be necessary and advisable. Following this speech closer cooperation could be seen between Ireland and Britain, even to the extent of sending senior army officers to London. Ireland's wholehearted commitment to the League of Nations, at least up to the mid-1930s, also showed up the ambiguity of her neutrality. His biographers suggest that if the Second World War had come about from a joint decision of the League, de Valera's attitude might have been modified. However, the take-over of the ports and growing disillusionment with the League began to put neutrality on a more ideological level, although Ireland's economic dependency on Britain and extremely weak military capacity ensured that close contact with Britain would remain essential in time of war.

During these years of uncertainty the defence forces struggled against mighty odds to define their role. Although 1939 found the army chronically ill-prepared for war, events proved that by then it was at least able to furnish the personnel and the willpower needed to cobble together a defence capacity sufficient to give real meaning and credibility to Ireland's neutral status. The military leaders had faced enormous problems from the outset. The split in the Volunteers in 1914 was followed some years later by the divisions in the IRA in the wake of the Treaty. As the army explained in a 1927 memorandum on its difficulties to W. T. Cosgrave, president of the Executive Council, it had evolved from a revolutionary organisation that emerged from successful guerrilla warfare with the British, only to become embroiled in a civil war.[6]

At the end of the civil war the military leadership was faced with the tasks of reducing the strength of the forces under its command and reorganising those retained on recognised military lines as a regular army. The strength reductions led directly to the army crisis, or 'mutiny', of 1924, involving 250 resigned or discharged officers (out of a total of 3,300) whose actions profoundly affected the future of the defence forces. The power of the military versus that of civilian leadership had been a source of tension from the foundation of the Irish Volunteers in 1913, through 1916, the War of Independence and especially the civil war. The army crisis finally resolved this contest in favour of the civilian leadership, but to many on the military side it seemed that from then on control of military affairs became an end in itself for the civil servants, who judged any attempt by the defence forces to improve their lot as a challenge to their bureaucratic control. Whether correct or not, this belief was strengthened by the difficulties the defence forces encountered in the task of army reorganisation. In the initial reorganisation of 1924, the defence forces were not considered to have attained the full professional standards of other European armies and consequently pay was set at a lower level than might have been expected, a decision in which the general staff at the time acquiesced. However, in the absence of any reassessment, this temporary arrangement became permanent, and was an ongoing source of dissatisfaction.

In July 1925 the general staff made a submission to the government in which they sought a direction on defence policy.[7] Three alternative policies were discussed. The first was that Ireland have its own independent force, so organised that it would be unprofitable for any power to interfere with her in any way. This policy would be an integral part of state policy, be dependent on the economic position, and involve utilising the full resources – diplomatic, industrial and agricultural – of the state. The second policy was the organisation of a force that would be an integral part of the British imperial forces as a member of the Commonwealth. The general staff pointed out that internal disorder and the morale of the defence forces here would be vital factors if this policy were adopted. The third option was the abandonment to England of responsibility for defence against external enemies and the formation of a force to deal with internal disorders. The fact that the general staff made no comment on this suggestion appears to mean that it was not intended as a serious option. The submission identified three possible sources of internal aggression: (i) serious disturbances in the north-east of the country; (ii) an outbreak by the anti-Treatyites; and (iii) a serious riot or disturbance by anybody, such as the association of ex-army men, the communists, etc. It declined to comment on partition, beyond stating that the general staff was not *au fait* with the negotiations proceeding between the Irish and British governments, but that it recognised the weaknesses that partition imposed on any defence policy.

The government responded in October 1925 with a summary of its policy (which was to remain unchanged until 1946).[8] This stated:

1. The size of the standing army to be retained in normal times should not exceed 10–12,000 all ranks.

2. The organisation of this force would be such that it would be capable of rapid and efficient expansion in time of need to the maximum strength of the country's manpower. This would necessitate the training of all ranks in duties of a more advanced nature than those normally associated with each rank.

3. The army must be an independent national force capable of assuming

responsibility for the defence of the territory of Saorstát Éireann (Irish Free State) against invasion or internal disruptive agencies, but it must also be so organised, trained and equipped as to render it capable, should the necessity arise, of full and complete coordination with the forces of the British government in the defence of Saorstát territory whether against actual hostilities or against violation of the neutrality on the part of a common enemy.

Emphasising its earnest desire to avoid participation in any international struggle, the Executive Council nevertheless conceded:

We may be forced to act if any power decided to utilise our geographical position to launch an offensive against Great Britain or to disrupt seaborne traffic. Consequently we should be ready to cooperate with the British forces and if necessary assume control of mixed forces in Saorstát territory.

It directed that specialised preparation of plans to resist invasion from any quarter be prepared.

The chief of staff, General Peadar MacMahon, agreed that the strength of the standing army should, on economic grounds, be reduced to 10,000, but that a reserve of initially 4,500 (capable of expansion to 15,000), should be established. The figure 25,000 was the estimated requirement to put down internal disorder, but the chief of staff pointed out that a force of up to 100,000 would be required to resist a foreign invasion, with the full support of the resources of the country. The Executive Council then agreed to the formation of a reserve of 4,500 personnel. It made no mention of the forces required to resist foreign invasion, but did point out that the function of the reserve was dependent on the reduction of the standing army to 10,000 as soon as possible.

The general staff were appalled by the fact that what had originally been stated by the chief of staff had now been totally diluted. In a very strong letter to the Minister for Defence the chief of staff stated the following:

I have the honour to draw your attention to a very serious matter in connection with the formation of the army reserve. In my various communications to you in this matter I designedly avoided any mention of the ultimate strength of this force. The reasons for this are obvious. At the present time no official, military or civilian, could honestly attempt to estimate the ultimate strength of the reserve. In spite of this I am informed that the army finance officer supplied you with certain data for use during the estimates debates in the course of which he stated that the ultimate strength of the reserve would amount to 4,500 men. I would respectfully draw your attention to the following points:

a) I cannot accept responsibility for this statement. If I, or any other responsible military officer, advised you that this country could be defended
against anyone by an army of 10,000 men, plus 4,500 reservists, we would
deserve to be immediately deprived of our commissions on the grounds of
gross inefficiency and utter lack of responsibility to the country in the matter of national defence.

b) The responsibility of advising you on matters of military policy is mine,
not the army finance officer's; he is concerned solely with the financial implications of such policy. In this instance I consider that this action was
highly improper and cannot be allowed to pass unnoticed.[9]

This communication was the opening shot of an enduring conflict between the military and civilian branches of the Department of Defence
which was to work to the eventual detriment of the defence forces. The
first reserve to be established was the A reserve which was drawn from
former serving personnel. This was shortly followed by the establishment
of a B reserve in which initial training was given to personnel, followed
by annual camps and weekend training. These formations were matched
by corresponding reductions in the standing army which fell from 27
battalions in 1924 to 16 by 1927. An attempt to raise the question of
coastal defence at the imperial conference of 1927 was totally ignored.

From 1927–8 the resources of the army were concentrated in the
temporary plans division set up after the return of the military mission
from the US. In June 1928, this division submitted five very detailed
memoranda covering (i) preparation for war (ii) tactical organisation
(iii) territorial organisation (iv) reserves policy, and (v) military education. Although the recommendations were given general approval, the
directions necessary to put them into effect were not given. War equipment was to be provided only for permanent units, yet no programme
was adopted for its provision. In the meantime the standing army was
being further reduced: by 1930 the number of battalions had sunk to
five, and total strength to 5,300.

This reduction did not go unchallenged. A National Defence Association was established by serving officers to promote the cause of the
army and to protect their own positions. Its leadership included some of
the army's leading personalities, such as Hugo MacNeill, Michael J.
Costello, Liam Egan and Liam Archer. They took over publication of An
t-Óglach, the defence forces' magazine, and in issue after issue published
editorials berating Desmond Fitzgerald, the Minister for Defence, and
his department. The existence at that time of the 'hunt boards', which
went around the country selecting officers for demobilisation at short

notice, helped to increase membership. Curiously, the first official action taken against the association was on religious grounds. An editorial, written by Col. M. J. Costello, commented adversely on the then marriage establishments, by which only 12.5% of privates and corporals, 25% of sergeants and 50% of senior NCOs were allowed to draw marriage allowance.[10] The editorial quoted a statement in the Catholic *Standard* that such a restriction encouraged contraception in the army. Such a suggestion went beyond the bounds of what was acceptable. Costello was paraded before the chief of staff, warned as to future editorials and told that serving officers were to resign from executive positions in the association. It was then taken over by reserve officers, who included Col. Roger McCorley as secretary. The association survived until 1930 when it planned to publish a letter in the national newspapers, generally critical of government policy, which was to bear the signature of General Seán MacEoin who had recently resigned as chief of staff. At the last moment MacEoin withdrew his permission and the letter was never published. Pressure was put on the committee to resign and shortly afterwards the association was disbanded.

In the early 1930s, the army, in common with all other state agencies, was feeling the impact of the depression. Drastic cutbacks in public expenditure were implemented which, coupled with the apathy common amongst governments to their armies in peacetime, meant that the strength of the defence forces was soon at its lowest level, some 10–16% below establishment strength. It had to discharge time-consuming garrison, protective and routine duties, in addition to supplying training cadres for reserve formations. As a consequence no field training was carried out, and it was not until 1933 that the first brigade exercises since 1926 were held. Training of officers and NCOs suffered greatly as a result and combat efficiency was extremely low.

With a defence budget that never exceeded £1.5 million, lack of finance was a major contributory factor to the perilous state of the nation's defences. Although as a percentage of gross domestic product, this sum is not much less than that spent currently, the important point was that from 1924 to 1939 only 5% of total defence expenditure was used to purchase warlike stores, such as weapons, ammunition, armour, transport and aircraft. It took from 1929 to 1938 to equip the total of 14 battalions with infantry weapons only. The system of purchase led to huge delays in acquisition, as the following 1944 report of the chief of staff made clear:

This situation arose from the fact that a clear definition of defence policy was not at any time communicated to the army authorities and to the department of finance. These two bodies, the army authorities and the department of finance, held diametrically opposed views as to what defence policy was or what in fact it should be. There was no settled long-term programme for equipping the forces and such purchase plans as did exist were subject to change every few months. The estimate and purchase files at general headquarters show that the army authorities made continuous efforts to obtain equipment in the years in which it was procurable, but most of these efforts were nullified by civil service procedure.[11]

This lack of planning and the delay in acquiring equipment led directly to the situation in 1939 when the lack of vital stores was insurmountable.

Despite their deficiencies, the military in the 1930s began to evolve a defensive strategy against possible invasion. The first detailed plan was prepared in 1934, entitled 'Estimate of the situation that would arise in the eventuality of war between Ireland and Great Britain'.[12] It emphasised the moral and diplomatic importance of organised, regular-army resistance, rather than a system of guerrilla war. It acknowledged the overwhelming superiority of the British forces, but stressed that with the development of proper organisation, training and equipment, a force could be evolved to give true meaning to Ireland's neutral status. At a minimum, four (later amended to six) brigades would be required. Of the six, four would comprise a frontier force to blunt any British advance, and thereafter, in a series of delaying actions, retreat southwards. When organised resistance became finally impossible, guerrilla action would be resorted to. The hope was that by that stage diplomatic action would take precedence. An interesting aspect of the plan was for the gardaí to provide covering forces forward of the defensive positions and, following the British advance, to regroup behind the Irish lines to provide reserve units as required.

This basic plan was refined and altered over the next five years. By 1938 a four-brigade system was settled upon, even though the strength of the regular army did not exceed 6,000. The extra numbers were to be obtained from the A and B reserves which provided another 5,000 in total, and from the volunteer force which had formed in 1934. By 1935 the latter had already reached its maximum strength of 11,000 and even in 1938 it still totalled 9,500. Thus, approximately 20,000 men were available at short notice. However, these figures hide the fact that the combat efficiency of the defence forces as a whole was abysmally low. Training was sporadic and at unit level only. The day-to-day duties and lack of equipment meant that no large-scale manoeuvres were carried out after 1933. At no time were the leaders, the staffs or the troops exercised at brigade level, so it can fairly be said that the four-brigade system remained an aspiration rather than a reality.

In 1936 the director of military intelligence (G2), Col. Liam Archer, compiled a report for the chief of staff entitled 'Fundamental factors affecting Saorstát defence problems'.[13] It dealt in great detail with Ireland's geographical position in relation to war, its lack of defence resources and the general non-recognition in the country of defence problems. It also dealt with neutrality, particularly with the experience of small neutral states in the First World War. It discussed at length the position of the coastal ports, then of course still controlled by the British. Based on the use made of the ports by the British and US navies during the First World War, it argued that similar use could be made of them in any future conflict. It expressed great concern over the clause in the Treaty which stated that in time of war or strained relations with a foreign power, Britain would get such harbours and other facilities as she might require. G2 argued that Britain, if threatened in any way by another power, would take control of whatever facilities she required with or without Irish approval. Because of this and British control of the ports, Ireland would not be considered neutral in any conflict. The report estimated that the defence forces would at that time be unable to engage in organised resistance; but in a campaign of guerrilla warfare the British, if they took over port facilities by force, would require a huge garrison in Ireland to defend their gains. This observation was recognised by British military planners some time later. The handover of the ports in 1938 rendered much of the report obsolete, but its basic defensive premises were to remain the cornerstone of Irish military strategy up to and including the Emergency.

In the same year the director of intelligence also forecast that war was likely to break out in 1938 or 1939, and argued that the defence forces should re-arm in line with other European states and that a committee of national defence be established. No action was taken on these prescient observations. In a memorandum accompanying this report the chief of staff stated:

> The limitation of expenditure on defence to £1.5 millions annually and the restriction of the strength of the defence forces to approximately 5,000, providing in theory a highly trained cadre for expansion in war but in practice mainly employed in extensive guard and similar duties, seriously affects the effectiveness of the defence forces and our state of preparedness for na-

tional defence. Owing to lack of policy or objective the army is not prepared to resist external aggression. It has not the necessary organisation or
material and suffers from a lack of definite long-term policy. The time for
delay is now past and although the department [of defence] has little information on international affairs beyond that available to the public it is
nevertheless considered that there is a great danger of war in Europe.[14]

The reference to the lack of information on international affairs was a
thinly veiled criticism of the Department of External Affairs. The chief
of staff also pointed out that on mobilisation the army could produce
only the skeleton of four reinforced brigades and certain ancillary troops.
Existing units were far from complete in either personnel, material or
equipment; for example, only 9 out of 24 batteries of artillery required
were available. Existing wartime establishments of these four brigades
required a strength of 36,500 for all ranks, but they stood at under
20,000. There were deficiencies in training and an absence of adequate
anti-aircraft and air defences. He recommended doubling the existing
£1.5 million per annum defence expenditure for three years, together
with undertaking extra expenditure on the air corps and coastal defence.
Despite this, the Executive Council decided that normal provision only
be made in the 1937–8 estimates, and the following year the proposals
were again shelved. In September 1938 a general staff memorandum
informed the government that 'the actual strength, organisation and
equipment of the existing forces restrict their value to that of an instrument for the preservation of internal disorder only'.[15] It also pointed
out that in wartime, arms would only be obtainable from Britain or the
US. The possibility of arms procurement in the US, against British
wishes and in view of American neutrality laws, was remote.

In November the Taoiseach, then also acting Minister for Defence,
requested information on the plans and war organisation of the defence
forces. The four-brigade system was examined and found to be impractical due to shortages of men and equipment. Instead it was decided the
army should draw up an organisation which made the best use of what it
had. Rather cheekily the chief of staff responded with a scheme providing for one reinforced brigade only. After discussion with the Taoiseach,
a two-brigade scheme was eventually decided upon, providing a total
strength of 37,500. It was understood that the serious deficiencies in
equipment would have to be made up before any of the units could be
made effective. It was fully realised that the force to be provided was inadequate to defend the state. Its basis was not the military requirements
for defence, but purely the force that could be found within the limita-

tions of men and equipment. While the agreement with the Taoiseach represented a great advance on what had gone before, the problems of the defence forces were still far from over. On 16 January 1939, the Minister for Finance forwarded to the Minister for Defence a memorandum which stressed that the scheme envisaged was neither inevitable nor essential, although it was conceded that the attitude of Éire was one of peaceful intent and determination to preserve her sovereignty by all means at her disposal.[16] The document went on to state:

> It is assumed that provided we make it clear that we have no intention of allowing this country to be in any way antagonistic to the security of Britain, the possibility of any attack from Britain may be ignored. Even if such an attack were to be contemplated the consideration arises as to whether any attempt at formal resistance on our part would not be futile and whether it would not be better for us to make no organised resistance at all in order to avoid unnecessary bloodshed, suffering and economic destruction. It seems doubtful that the organisation of an army such as that put forward, which in actuality depended on British sources for the supply of necessary warlike equipment, could be accomplished without some understanding with Great Britain in relation to our future intentions. We must therefore contemplate being attacked even if such an attack were only intended as a measure of diverting British forces from the main spheres of conflict and of weakening our sources of essential supplies. We could then rely on the full protection of the Royal Navy, and complete protection by her air force would also be possible. The limits of our problem appear therefore to be confined to the provision of defence against a power or combination of powers likely to be at war with Britain and then only if it or they were in striking distance of our shores, i.e. from some Continental power.
>
> If the above conclusions were reasonably sound, our immediate problem seems to resolve itself mainly into a scheme of defence against air attacks. To guard against such air attack we seem to require a system of defence based on an adequate airforce, adequate means of information of threatened air-raids, adequate anti-aircraft armaments on land, with ancillary equipment such as searchlights and a full development of air-raid precautions. This scheme now submitted does not appear to have been framed on these lines; it provides for a miniature army, as armies go, equipped in all its branches.
>
> It is a miniature of an army that would be suitable for a country with land frontiers open to attack and invasion. It provides, for example, for increases in artillery, anti-tank weapons, armoured cars, etc. A large increase in ammunition and personnel is involved. Increases in aircraft, anti-aircraft guns and searchlights are also provided, but are more or less proportionate to the increases in the other branches of the army. No case whatever has been indicated for the necessity to create and maintain these two brigades and it is accordingly suggested that the defence scheme as put forward should undergo radical review.[17]

The attitude of total dependence on Britain and the suggestion of immediate surrender in the face of an attack from that quarter, made by the servants of a nation supposedly independent, is an unusual concept. However, the Department of Finance memorandum, in stressing the need for an air force, did expose a major weakness in the defence planning of the time. In the decade preceding the war the only figure of consequence to have appreciated the importance of air power was Col. Michael J. Costello, who as early as 1930 had sought a definite policy for the air corps, only to be thwarted by lack of finance. In 1938 he proposed yet another scheme, which was rejected by the chief of staff and the OC air corps. Subsequently the only concrete success of his belated mission to America in 1940, apart from the dispatch of Springfield rifles, was an offer of any amount of up-to-date US aircraft, with immediate delivery. The acquisition of American aircraft was agreed to by Frank Aiken, the Minister for Defence, but, as Costello himself said, the proposal encountered vehement opposition from the chief of staff and the OC air corps who insisted on the purchase of British aircraft (which of course it was never possible to obtain), and their argument won the day.

The Department of Finance memorandum was sent to the government in the same month (January 1939), accompanied by a reply from the Department of Defence. The latter[18] stated that the situations that had to be prepared for at that stage were:

1. Neutrality, in which we have announced to the world that we have no interest in the war and that we do not intend to take part in it.

2. Neutrality, with a friendly bias to Britain, in which, while not playing an active military part, our economic life is speeded up to give increased supplies to the British of everything we can produce and in which we allow no activities inimical to their interest to be carried out within our territory.

3. Cooperation with the British to defeat a mutual enemy.

4. Defence against a British attack.

The memorandum continued:

It is felt that in case the Dáil decided to take up either the attitude of complete neutrality or neutrality with a friendly bias to Britain, we might find ourselves very quickly at war against Britain's enemies or indeed against the British, if either of them felt that it was a simple and easy job to take over complete control of our country and its resources and to make what use of them they desired in their struggle for victory. In order to be left alone we must be prepared to resist attack from any quarter and so organise ourselves in time of peace as to be ready to throw our full weight against any enemy who might attack us.

Following submission of a further Department of Finance memorandum in which the views expressed in its earlier document were restated, the government considered the matter on 30 January. For once, the submission of the Department of Defence was accepted and sanction for the required defence expenditure granted. Officers were immediately sent to the British War Office to place orders for anti-tank weapons, anti-aircraft guns, searchlights, radios, Bren guns, artillery pieces and ammunition. These officers found that the British, while willing to accept the order, could not hold out any hope of a delivery for a considerable time. Col. M. J. Costello and a principal officer of the Department of Finance were then sent to the US to enquire into the availability of warlike stores there and the cost thereof. In the event of purchase in the US, orders placed with the British War Office were to be cancelled and any equipment purchased in America was to be delivered before 31 March 1940. It quickly became evident to Costello that his mission would be a failure. It was illegal for the US war department to supply arms directly, although they were prepared to give the Irish representatives introduction to various armament factories. However, the prohibitive cost of ammunition and the long delay in delivery, among other problems, meant that no equipment, with the exception of 20,000 Springfield rifles, was going to come from the US, although revolvers and gas masks were also on offer. Col. Costello regarded the mission, and especially the response to the purchase of aircraft, as one of the most frustrating and ultimately fruitless tasks of his career. His transfer to Cork some three months later as OC of the southern command may not have been entirely coincidental.

The weapons inventory show the deficiencies in equipment at this time to have been extremely serious. Of a requirement of 298 anti-tank rifles, the defence forces had 4; of a (very minimal) requirement of 32 anti-tank guns, they had none, only the Boys anti-tank rifle; of a requirement of 924 Bren guns, they had 82; and of a requirement of 72 searchlights, they had 4. There were 4 medium and no light or heavy anti-aircraft guns, 4 Bofors guns, 4 searchlights and a few other small items were obtained soon after the outbreak of war. Small-arms ammunition stocks amounted to less than 50% of requirements, while for field artillery, anti-aircraft and mortar rounds, the stocks were only 8% of what was required.

At the outbreak of war in September 1939 the strength of the army as mobilised was substantially below what was required. In a report to the government three weeks later the chief of staff stated that the First and Second Brigades had been organised and mobilised, but were 30% under strength.[19] Five garrison battalions had been mobilised but they were between 270 and 590 under strength. None of the eight rifle battalions had been organised. In summary, nearly all units were under strength and many units provided for had not even been organised. Apart from the deficiencies in equipment, combat efficiency was low: many personnel were only partly trained, and neither of the brigades had any experience of working as a combat team. Total strength, including A and B reservists plus the volunteer force, was little more than 50% of the required 37,500. During the phoney war the army was reduced to 13,000, due again to financial stringencies.

What were the factors which caused the advice and recommendations of the defence forces to have been so totally ignored? During the civil war, military expenditure had soared out of control, making the civil service extremely wary of allowing the army any further say in spending money after the ceasefire of 1923. Thereafter, the relative youth and inexperience of the general staff, their lack of coordination, and at times rivalry to develop the army, weakened the army's ability to convince the civil service of the merits of their arguments. As late as 1938 the Taoiseach referred to the 'contradictory advice he was being given on defence matters'. Another factor weakening the military's influence was that after the Treaty the island's defence was basically in the hands of the Royal Navy, thereby removing the natural evolution of defence policy from the public domain.

Public comments of some of the elected representatives between 1924 and the Emergency did nothing to encourage the military planners. In 1927 Desmond Fitzgerald, the Minister for External Affairs, stated: 'it is practically inconceivable that our army would ever be opposed to the British army'.[20] The same year a TD told the Dáil that we would be much more secure against the attack of a modern army from outside if we had no army at all.[21] A deputy in 1934 suggested reducing the army by half, and contended that we would still have an army adequate for the state's ceremonial requirements and for the support of the police in the event of serious civil disturbance.[22] In 1938 another deputy again recommended complete disarmament as the best defence.[23] While these statements may not be indicative of general thinking amongst members of the Dáil, they do represent quite a prevalent attitude during these years. During the estimates debate of 1940, when the army was finally given money, two former senior army officers who had entered politics made arresting contributions. General Seán MacEoin, a former chief of staff, said: 'I feel the expenditure of such a sum as this on an infantry force is hardly justified. I said only that an airforce and an anti-aircraft gunnery force would be any use for defensive purposes and that this expenditure was a waste of public money.'[24] General Richard Mulcahy, the former commander-in-chief, expressed his conviction 'that this country cannot be invaded and that this country cannot be bombed'.[25] It was from this unpropitious environment that the defence forces emerged to face their greatest challenge since the civil war.

PREPARING LAW FOR AN EMERGENCY, 1938–1939
Seosamh Ó Longaigh

Background

Emergency law was not new to Ireland. The country saw many extraordinary measures during British rule when there existed, at best, ambivalence towards the administration of law among the population. However, achieving independence did not result in a transformation of Ireland's political culture. More importantly, the Irish Republican Army's
opposition to the independent Irish state repeatedly challenged successive governments to ensure the effective administration of law, which
resulted in regular departures from the ordinary law.

In the years after independence, civil servants at the Department of
Justice and senior gardaí regularly complained that Ireland's political
culture militated against the successful prosecution of political cases. At
times, convictions appeared almost impossible when charges were brought
against IRA members. The public was unhelpful to the gardaí and jurors
rarely returned guilty verdicts because of intimidation or sympathy for
the accused. Judges were accused of being lenient towards the IRA. Criticisms extended to other aspects of the system. Writing in 1937, Stephen
Roche, secretary of the Department of Justice, wrote 'the fact that [the
law of evidence] regularly serves to defeat the ends of justice is looked
on as a merit, not a defect in the system'.[1]

Various measures were introduced to deal with the ongoing IRA
problem, including the Treasonable Offences Act in 1925 and internment the following year. These proved ineffectual and the Garda Special
Branch resorted to repeatedly arresting active IRA members in a policy
of sustained harassment. However, the courts deemed these tactics illegal. Indeed, a series of legal successes in the late 1920s and early 1930s
imbued the IRA with great confidence. By April 1931 the Garda Commissioner, Eoin O'Duffy, wrote that the IRA 'feel they have the field to
themselves'. He believed military courts should be established to deal
with the problem.[2] Only after the IRA killed a garda superintendent and

a witness in a trial of IRA members did the Executive Council finally resolve to counter the organisation and its activities.

On 24 August 1931 legislative proposals incorporating the 'necessary powers' to deal with the situation were presented to the Executive Council. The then assistant secretary of the Department of Justice, Stephen Roche, spoke of developing a special tribunal that had the powers of life and death which it was prepared 'to exercise ... freely.' He added it needed 'ample powers to preserve its dignity'. The Department of Justice believed any response to IRA activities should force the 'leaders of disorder' to accept the 'certainty that if they persist in their activities they will suffer death.' A permanent Military Tribunal was established to try members of unlawful organisations. It had no fixed procedure, could accept unsworn testimony and inflict greater punishments than the ordinary law permitted, including death.

Initially the government sought maximum effect in the struggle against subversion and relied on what Stephen Roche called a 'thinly-disguised' court-martial, a 'commission of public safety'.[3] It was to be an effective substitute for the failed jury system and would remove a great deal of the uncertainty involved in trying members of the IRA, and others if the need arose. The government's primary concern was effectiveness, rather than any anticipated adverse political reaction. The constitution was amended by the insertion of Article 2A and became ancillary to the Public Safety Act. Widely criticised, Article 2A was undeniably effective. In operation, it made conviction almost inevitable. As soon as the government applied definite pressure, the IRA quickly retreated. Once those powers were in place and applied, no government would want to lose them. However, once Bunreacht na hÉireann came into force these special powers lapsed.

The 1937 Constitution and the Sudetenland Crisis

In late 1937, new legislation was needed following the enactment of the new constitution. Stephen Roche called for the reestablishment of a special court similar to that created under Article 2A of the old Free State constitution. He believed the basic formula of a constitutional tribunal could be repeated: 'the Military Tribunal was a complete success: it did its work smoothly and efficiently and contributed more than any other single piece of state machinery to the maintenance of law and order in a particularly troubled period.'[4] The establishment of a Special Criminal Court seemed to be straightforward and not necessarily overly controversial. However, Article 2A, for example, also dealt with unlawful organisations, the banning of public meetings, and accorded the gardaí special powers.[5] There was also the Treasonable Offences Act, 1925 to be considered, which dealt with unlawful organisations and offences against the state.

Before the cabinet could properly consider new replacement legislation, the world situation began to deteriorate, potentially endangering the state much more than ongoing IRA activities. Although successive Irish governments had over 15 years' experience of dealing with the anti-state activities of organisations such as the IRA, none had faced a major European or world war, even if Ireland did not become involved militarily. However, the Anglo-Irish Agreement of 1938 had given the government access to the British government's 'war book', essentially its emergency legislative preparations for a second world war. As the Sudetenland crisis unfolded, the Irish government rapidly adapted the 'war book' provisions to Ireland's circumstances.[6]

This legislation was unlike anything an Irish government had ever drafted and was designed to enable the government to deal with any aspect of an emergency that might conceivably threaten the survival of the state. It did not make specific provision for special powers of arrest or the establishment of a military court to deal with subversion. Instead, under section 2(1) of the draft legislation the government could, by means of an emergency powers order, do whatever it deemed necessary to deal with the emergency.[7] However, it was felt the bill should include a comprehensive but general recital of powers which the government was likely to need in section 2(2).[8] These included: the maintenance and regulation of supplies and services; the control of rail, roads, ports and aerodromes; the power to amend statute law; the requisition of any form of property; censorship; the restriction of movement and activities of persons including powers of arrest, detention and search; coast watching; financial and monetary policy, air defence and measures generally to protect the civil population and to maintain public safety and order.

In tandem with the drafting of emergency legislation was the preparation of the Emergency Powers Order to be promulgated on the outbreak of war. It advocated giving specific effect to the emergency legislation. A preliminary draft was prepared by 18 September 1938. Additional orders could be made after the legislation came into force and as circumstances dictated. Once laid before the Oireachtas, TDs could not scrutinise or seek amendments to orders as they would legislation, and unless a majority voted to annul an order it became effective without a vote. Very few were even considered, and none were annulled.

A number of departments, particularly Justice, voiced concern at the breadth of these powers, especially the power to 'suspend the operation of or amend or apply (with or without modification) any enactment (other than this act)',[9] but G. P. Ó hÓgáin of the Department of Finance and manager of the drafting process countered:

> if [that section] is restricted in its scope its value in time of crisis would be greatly reduced. The government must, it is submitted, be relied upon to administer the provision in a due and proper manner, only using the power to amend, etc., when the public safety or the preservation of the state is clearly involved in time of national emergency.[10]

Government inability to take decisive action in an emergency would cause embarrassment. He believed the powers of section 2(1) of the Emergency Powers Act were vital even if the state attempted to remain neutral in some future conflict:

> It is impossible to foresee all the detailed powers which the government might need to exercise in such an emergency, and even if it were possible to recite all such necessary powers there would be the danger that the statutory clauses might not give full effect to the government's intentions to protect them sufficiently against attack in the courts, and, consequently, a general overriding provision is a necessary safeguard.[11]

Political questions aside, with the rapid development of the September 1938 crisis and the absence of a substitute for Article 2A, senior civil servants argued the British model was seriously wanting: '[the British] don't even contemplate that juries will be perverse' wrote one senior advisor to the attorney general.[12] It was proposed the bill contain not only emergency powers orders, but also provision for special courts, treason and treasonable offences, and powers to deal with unlawful organisations.

But such a path created other problems. Under these proposals, special courts would be established under Article 28.3.3 of the constitution (the Emergency Powers Act would derive validity from there). P. P. O'Donoghue, an adviser of the attorney general, argued:

> Article 38(3) recognises as a normal constitutional organisation the establishment of Special Criminal Courts in certain contingencies and, in my opinion, it would be most advisable to utilise the formula contained in Article 38(3) as a preface for the establishment of the Special Courts without any express mention of [Article 28].[13]

Other concerns were raised about including provision for treason and unlawful organisations in a temporary war emergency measure and not as a permanent aspect of law. As the Sudetenland crisis abated, a clear idea of what was appropriate began to emerge. Three separate pieces of legislation would be developed: an Emergency Powers Bill, a Treasonable Offences Bill and a Special Criminal Courts Bill.[14]

Drafting the Emergency Powers Bill and a Constitutional Amendment
Far more worrying for ministers and senior civil servants was that Article 28.3.3 of Bunreacht na hÉireann (although permitting wide-ranging powers if Ireland became involved as a belligerent in a war) made no definite provision for the outbreak of a major war in which Ireland did not participate.[15] A number of preambles to the Emergency Powers Bill had been drawn up, but none resolved the issue. Eventually de Valera requested:

> the question should now be examined further and that a suggestion should be made as to the most appropriate manner in which Article 28.3.3 of the constitution could be amended for the purpose of removing any doubt that, notwithstanding the constitution, the widest possible powers could be taken in the public interest during a war in which this country was not a belligerent but in which the nearness and character of the conflict necessitated emergency measures.[16]

The Parliamentary Draftsman, Arthur Matheson, wrote that the weakest aspect of the phrase 'in time of war' was it necessarily implied Irish involvement, as a belligerent force, in any such conflict.[17] P. P. O'Donoghue and J. J. Hearne added 'Article 28.3.3 cannot be relied upon ... with any degree of confidence to support extra-constitutional legislation, or action based on such legislation, during a national emergency arising out of a war ... in which Ireland is neutral.'[18] Alterations to the article were immediately mooted. It was suggested that the article could be amended by the inclusion of a reference to war in a neighbouring state,[19] but the Parliamentary Draftsman preferred the proposal of the secretary of the Taoiseach's Department, Maurice Moynihan, to simply extend the meaning of 'time of war' to include a war occurring between European powers.[20]

Causing most concern were the proposed sections 2(1) and 2(2) of the draft Emergency Bill permitting the compulsory acquisition of land and property and power to amend statute law, though it was believed the remainder of section 2(2) of the bill could be employed without constitutional difficulties.[21] While the need to rely on those sub-sections and paragraphs could not be gauged until an emergency had arisen, they could not be utilised unless Article 28.3.3 applied.[22] There were other questions – who would determine if a foreign war genuinely threatened the 'vital interests and security' of the state? Matheson argued it was impracticable to leave such a decision to the courts and empowering the government was tantamount to allowing the Executive suspend the constitution. He proposed that the Oireachtas should decide.[23]

When should the constitution be amended was also at issue. Under Article 51, it could be altered by ordinary legislation before 25 June 1941. After that time, an amendment would have to be submitted to the people under Articles 46 and 47. Although an amendment under Article 51 permitted the president to refer the amendment to a referendum,[24] and the Seanad to slow the passage of an amendment for up to 90 days, Ó hÓgáin believed no procrastination would occur if the amendment were introduced after the outbreak of war. If an emergency was likely to occur before June 1941, he urged the constitution be amended by ordinary legislation prior to then because 'a referendum would involve delay'. The rapid passage of an amendment and the enactment of the emergency legislation were vital he believed in legalising the Emergency Powers Order: 'any material time lag would cause embarrassment to the Government. There is particularly the danger of court action during the period between the issue of the order and the passage of covering legislation.'[25] De Valera agreed with Ó hÓgáin's proposals, though he felt the amendment should be introduced before an emergency began, probably during the first six months of 1939.

On 7 December 1938 the attorney general was informed that the Taoiseach wanted the proposed amendment to make 'clear that nothing in the constitution should be invoked to invalidate any law enacted by the oireachtas for the purpose of securing the public safety and the preservation of the state' in time of national emergency arising out of a conflict where Ireland was not a belligerent. The Parliamentary Draftsman took this as the Taoiseach's final view on the subject.[26]

A conference was held on 11 January 1939 to consider the proposed amendment to Article 28, define 'time of war' and determine what constituted a state of emergency.[27] Two possible amendments were drawn up in advance. One, a broad amendment, would permit the declaration of a state of emergency on the outbreak of war (whether or not Ireland was involved) or in the event of a social or economic crisis not related to actual warfare. The other, a narrow amendment, would permit the declaration of a state of emergency only when war was being waged (whether

or not Ireland was involved) in Europe, though the geographical limitation might be removed. The conference was generally opposed to the
broad amendment, particularly in light of the democratic nature of the
constitution. It did, in administrative terms, however, have genuine
merits.[28] Further, only Hearne continued to support the retention of the
geographic qualification.[29] No progress was immediately possible on these
issues, though decisions were made on other important points.

The conference favoured Dáil Éireann deciding whether or not a
crisis threatened the vital interests of the state. It was further suggested
that 'armed conflict' be substituted for 'war' and 'participant' for 'belligerent',[30] as those were in line with internationally recognised usage, and
would allow the government to deal with the effects of unrest in Britain.
In the interests of conferring a state of emergency with 'greater solem-
nity' the officials suggested that the declaration of an emergency could
be preceded by a message from the president. Finally, the officials recommended that bills to amend the constitution should be given distinctive short titles, in this case 'The First Amendment of the Constitution'. The proposed broad[31] and narrow[32] amendments were redrafted.

The principal outstanding issue was the definition of an emergency
and hence in what manner Article 28 should be amended. Three alternative amendments were drafted over the next fortnight and considered
by the government on 24 January 1939. It provisionally accepted that
the amendment should allow for emergency powers to be taken when
the vital interests of the state were threatened by an armed conflict in
which the state was not a participant. It also agreed if such an emergency
was to be declared, both Houses of the Oireachtas should pass a resolution in favour of calling the emergency, following a message from the
President.[33]

Further redrafting was undertaken by Ó hÓgáin, Hearne and Moynihan between 31 January and 2 February 1939, and two alternative drafts
('A'[34] and 'B'[35]) were prepared on 3 February 1939. The main decision
reached was that any amendment should be inserted in Article 28.3.3
(there would be no paragraph 28.3.4) and consideration was to be given
(as is seen in draft 'B') to whether the provision for a message from the
president should be removed. Both those points, it was hoped, would
strengthen the argument that the amendment was a minor one, thus
justifying an amendment under Article 51 as opposed to Article 46
(Article 51 was a temporary article designed to permit minor, verbal
changes to the constitution for three years after it came into force). The
Parliamentary Draftsman admitted the latest drafts might still be un-

satisfactory, though by drawing on both alternatives an acceptable draft could now be arrived at.[36] Debate continued as to how, from the technical point of view, the amendment should be made and how much reliance should be placed on either Article 46 or Article 51.[37]

But Ó hÓgáin argued that the terms of Article 46 of the constitution should be ignored. He argued that this particular amendment should be made under Article 51 alone and by means of ordinary legislation to reinforce the contention that the amendment was a minor one. He made this point in view of what de Valera told the Dáil in 1937 regarding minor amendments (i.e. amendments to remove doubts or minor oversights) and major amendments (ones of principle) which should be dealt with under Article 46.[38] As regards the courts, Ó hÓgáin wrote:

> The amount of risk that exists in relation to an adverse court decision on the question of national emergency arising from a war in which we are neutral is a matter of speculation. I doubt very much whether any court would hold that a European war in which Great Britain was engaged did not in fact create a national emergency for this country, whether or not we are participants.[39]

The Parliamentary Draftsman disgreed, believing that Article 51 could not stand on its own, rather that until June 1941 Article 46 was qualified by Article 51. As a result, the amendment was prepared in a way that would make it suitable for submission to a referendum, as directed by Article 46, but the Oireachtas would pass the amendment. Previous discussions on the form the bill should take were reappraised in view of three final questions to be settled by de Valera, namely: would the message from the President be retained or deleted?; secondly, would the message from the Dáil and the Seanad be retained or deleted?; and, finally, would 'armed conflict' be qualified by 'in Europe'?[40] A further and final draft was now prepared. The wording of the 6 April 1939 draft differed somewhat from previous drafts but it was deemed to include all matters agreed to.[41] The government finally felt that the work had almost reached a conclusion and asked that Ó hÓgáin's draft of 6 April 1939 be circulated for final consideration. The Taoiseach approved the proposed amendment, though he requested that the term 'war' be replaced by 'time of war' and that its definition be further clarified by the addition of the words 'a time when there is taking place' an armed conflict: 'In this sub-section "time of war" includes a time when there is taking place an armed conflict in which the State is not a participant but in respect of which each House of the Oireachtas shall have resolved that, arising out of such armed conflict, a national emergency exists affecting the vital interests of the State.' Final approval of the draft bill was given on 10 May 1939, and the amendment was filed away until an emergency arose.

The Offences Against the State Act, 1939
As the government and its advisers developed powers to deal with the effects of a world war, work continued on legislation to counter subversion. Against the background of IRA preparations for a bombing campaign in England,[42] draft legislation covering a special criminal court, treasonable offences and unlawful organisations, was completed in November 1938. Roche argued that the atmosphere of fear generated by Article 2A had declined since the 1922 constitution was repealed. The situation in late 1938 was very dangerous:

> a small country cannot afford to invite attacks from without by a seeming inability to keep order within its own territory. The danger in this case becomes acute when the unlawful organisations extend their activities into other states, while using this country as a base.[43]

A critical need for new legislation existed and the Department of Justice advised:

> if this kind of legislation is to be undertaken at all it should be sufficiently wide in its scope to cover all the matters which have been found by experience to be a source of embarrassment to the authorities in periods when political crime is common.

The Department of Justice demanded that the essence of pre-1937 public safety legislation, namely the Treasonable Offences Act, 1925 and Article 2A, should be re-enacted (though some departures from those earlier measures were envisaged).

Political and legal reasons dictated that the draft legislation differed from its predecessors. The Special Criminal Court would be employed only for the trial of offences. Vesting it with greater powers would be constitutionally difficult, though Roche clearly had given some thought to the idea.[44] There was no provision for internment.[45] Roche admitted it had certain benefits but continued:

> It is a very arbitrary power and apart from the question of principle there are practical difficulties in interning any large number of people without undue hardship to the individuals and at the same time without giving them opportunities as good as, or better than, they would have outside to make

their plans for the future. Despite its advantages, internment has never been looked upon with favour by this Department and it is not now proposed, although the Government may be forced to use it at a later stage if events take an unfavourable course.[46]

Instead of internment, it was proposed that once arrested, a person could be held for a month (without recourse to legal assistance) 'quite frankly, for the purpose of making things unpleasant for members of such organisations and as some partial substitute for internment' until a summary of evidence was prepared. On the attorney general's direction, the accused could be remanded by the Special Criminal Court for trial.

Also omitted were special powers of interrogation. Roche explained that under Article 2A such powers had been regularly employed to detain and prosecute suspects from whom no information or co-operation could ever be expected and they could thus check the activities of important activists at critical times. Doubtless, strong arguments in favour of retaining such powers could be made. While safeguards should be drawn up to protect those divulging information, Roche concluded:[47]

> No such assurance can, however, be wholly satisfactory: the admission made by the person under interrogation may not be used, as such, against him in subsequent criminal proceedings, but the State knows the facts so admitted and that knowledge may, and very probably will, be brought to bear against the witness in some indirect manner.[48]

Other issues arose. For instance, how should the legislation deal with unlawful organisations?[49] Writing some months later, Roche noted that one of the faults with the legislation prohibiting organisations was that an organisation was 'not unlawful for practical purposes until it has been specifically "suppressed"'.[50] Formal suppression should be no more than an 'ancillary affair'. To this end he wanted the bill to outlaw organisations simply on the basis of their stated objectives or activities.

Further, because of the difficulty involved in establishing unlawful organisations' ownership of property, the Constitution Tribunal (which operated under Article 2A of the Free State constitution) simply ordered the 'closure' of buildings. The department saw this as a useful tool. Premises were not confiscated; a few uniformed gardaí simply blocked the entrance and prevented their use.[51] A solution to possible difficulties that might be experienced by the Special Criminal Court as a result of Bunreacht na hÉireann could be to make the provision of premises for use by unlawful associations an offence; punishment would include the closing of the building.[52]

While the 1937 constitution limited the Special Criminal Court to trying offences, its wider character was yet to be determined. Roche was resolute that it should be a court with 'a high status and extensive powers', which 'should be respected and even feared'.[53] He argued the accused had to believe his 'fate is entirely in the hands of the Court'. The issue of appeals was to remain as it did in 1931:

> It was felt then as is felt now that to ask the Special Court to do its work effectively and at the same time to do it with the same attention to forms of procedure and the law of evidence as is required of an ordinary court is to ask an impossibility.

Essentially, the Constitution Tribunal was established in 1931 because the ordinary courts were unable to deal with the IRA, and therefore the state handed matters over to 'a commission chosen not as lawyers but as men of known courage, patriotism, and ability, who were not fettered by any legal rules, and who constituted in reality, not a court but a commission of Public Safety'. Any attempt to regulate such a court by reference to ordinary procedural rules or evidence would 'lessen its effectiveness'.

A different view was taken by the attorney general's office. It believed creating public respect for the Special Criminal Court was more important than over-awing those brought before it. Giving it absolute discretion would generate unfavourable criticism and could lead to public sympathy for those being tried: provision for appeal would inspire greater confidence in the court. It argued the Court of Criminal Appeal would have overturned very few, if any, of the Constitution Tribunal's decisions. It feared the more drastic the Special Criminal Court's powers the greater the likelihood of the higher courts looking unfavourably on them from some constitutional point of view:

> The danger must never be lost sight of that the Supreme Court might be tempted to invoke principles of natural justice, as they would be called, as animating the judicial provisions in the constitution. The Special Court would be better, therefore, if it were grafted on to the judicial system in the constitution, though not necessarily an ordinary Court.[54]

On this point, the legislation reflected the views of the attorney general's office. Indeed, it would permit internment and special garda powers (though not as extreme as those under Article 2A of the Free State constitution). Initially though, the government opposed provision for appeal and only changed its position when challenged by John A. Costello in the Dáil.

The Department of Justice repeatedly called for the Special Criminal Court to be introduced by means of a separate bill, primarily because it wanted the new court to be separate from the emergency legislation, but was overruled. The Taoiseach's Department favoured combining as much controversial material as possible into one statute.[55] The Treasonable Offences Act, 1925 would be repealed, the sections on treason brought in line with the constitution, and the remainder appropriately re-enacted. Turning next to the Special Criminal Court, Moynihan noted certain provisions diverged from those of the proposed Defence of the State (Emergency Power) Bill, and enquired why differences had emerged.[56] Moynihan also stated that provision for detention for one month was too long; he wanted it reduced to seven days. Roche responded: 'I consider the month's detention the most useful thing in the bill. Weekly remand by a Peace [Commissioner] or a [District Justice] would only be asking for trouble.' It was eventually reduced to a maximum of 48 hours.[57] When the cabinet met to consider the draft legislation between 1 and 10 February 1939 a list of technical changes were approved and the majority of the outstanding issues resolved.[58] The bill was finally ready for distribution to TDs.

Speaking on 2 March 1939, the Minister for Justice, Patrick Ruttledge, told the Dáil the sole object of the bill was 'the prevention of the display, the use, or the advocacy of force as a method to achieve political or social aims.'[59] Making reference to the IRA proclamation of 8 December 1938[60] and to the notices posted around the country,[61] he warned that claims by a particular group to be the real government of the country should not be dismissed as lightly as some deputies had suggested.[62] There was also criticism from the Labour Party, but Fine Gael would not oppose the government on matters of security. Its position was expressed simply when William Cosgrave explained: 'If the situation be as serious as the minister has described it, it is all the more necessary that there should be as widespread support for such steps as the legislature considers necessary as is possible throughout the country.'[63] He expressed unease though, because most of this legislation, except parts covering the Special Criminal Court and internment, would be permanent. The Offences Against the State Act, 1939 became law in May.

REACTING TO WAR:
FINANCE AND THE ECONOMY, 1938–1940
Andrew McCarthy

In February 1938, the secretary of the Department of Finance, J. J. Mc-
Elligott, subjected the defence budget to normal rigorous Finance scrutiny, questioning the basis of the estimate. In advising the cabinet against
additional provision for rearmament and defence, he suggested that 'the
difficulty of precise estimation becomes greater in the absence of any
clear indication of Defence policy, domestic or external'.[1] This set the
combative tone for Finance's general approach to probable conflict and
signifies the start of Finance's own response. As events transpired, Finance would exercise the greatest influence on policy in the pre-war
period and indeed after hostilities commenced. It did so largely by de-
fault in the seeming vacuum in policy formation in the period 1938–40.
    In March 1938, Finance minister, Seán MacEntee, requested the
currency commission chairman, Joseph Brennan, to consider future policy
as the international situation deteriorated.[2] Also, with de Valera's approval, he requested Per Jacobsson, external consultant to the second
banking commission, to advise on appropriate wartime measures.[3] Jacobsson alerted MacEntee to the danger of over exposure to sterling: the
options were to spread investments over gold bullion and dollar securities. But two problems were foreseen: gold might be as unpredictable as
sterling, while the trend in US government finance did not inspire confidence in the more secure, or gilt-edge, market.[4] Jacobsson also advised
stockpiling of import supplies, as later ordering from outside Ireland might
not be possible. MacEntee had already anticipated uncertainties in British policy on exchanges and general financial matters, as in the sterling
devaluation crisis of September 1931. Currently, exchange operations with
countries outside Ireland were yielding large profits, which was helping
to ensure liquidity and enabling the banking systems to discharge their
functions. But in the event of war, foreign assets might suddenly be froz-
en, leading to panic among depositors fearful of losing their investments.[5]

By October, Jacobsson, while more impressed with American conditions, visualised difficulties restraining costs and keeping down prices, considering US wage increases in early 1937. The implications for European states varied but he suggested that the Netherlands, Sweden and Switzerland would not introduce exchange controls since they possessed sufficient reserves to cover themselves in emergencies.[6] He felt Britain would fix the convertibility rate of sterling, while most countries would watch US dollar movements before deciding, but he did not expect any largescale export of capital from the aforementioned three countries. Nevertheless, if investors sought a safe haven, then it would probably be in US dollars. Yet this might have serious consequences: Jacobsson expected the US would continue paying $35 per ounce for all gold sent there during a European war. However, if gold suffered as an international means of payment, then the US, since it had about 55% of the world's gold stock, would be the biggest sufferer. Jacobsson also expected that if war broke out it would be a long one. Unlike 1914–18, higher taxation would be imposed almost immediately. It would have been better if the cost of living and wages had risen less in that war, but at least this time, efforts would be made to prevent them rising at the same level. In this context, any amount of state borrowing to meet a budget deficit would depend on the level of wages and prices. So since it was preferable that state borrowing should be limited as far as possible, any excessive rise in prices and wages should be prevented.[7]

Finance drew lessons from the August crisis of 1914. Among its options was, as then, the proclamation of a bank holiday, to enable liquidity levels to increase and prevent a run on the banks. It also felt that a moratorium on major debt repayments should not be recommended.[8] MacEntee elaborated with a well-received paper on 'War Finance' at Queen's University in October 1938.[9] He said he felt that the general monetary organisation would be better than in 1914. The government 'should be able, therefore, to employ more effectively the full power of the state in defence of the national economy; and what is perhaps even more important, we should have no hesitation in using that power'.[10] This power might become all the more necessary since 'in one way or another a small neutral country may be forced to devote an emergency organisation in the financial, banking and currency spheres, exactly as if it were at war'. Anticipating public reaction, MacEntee desired an increased volume of circulating notes and coin. More money would increase public confidence and provide security against contingencies. This, however, should be achieved by increasing government expenditure. To facilitate this, he pointed to the precedent of 1914, when the bank holiday was extended from 3 to 6 August to allow banks sufficient time to increase reserves of currency. Public demand for additional currency should be met freely to obviate a run on the banks. Although it should be kept in mind that if circulating money increased and the supply of goods contracted there could be a rise in inflation.

However much these measures might allay fears internally, confidence in the currency would ultimately be decided by external factors and MacEntee acknowledged Ireland's inability to influence exchanges. Exchange rates would in effect be determined by British policy. The importation of all unnecessary commodities would be prohibited. Even so, Ireland still might have to increase imports, which could lead to a trade gap, requiring gold transfers to balance it. If gold were exported, then Irish subscriptions to foreign loans or securities would be prohibited. Indeed, in order to protect the exchange rate, Ireland might have to borrow in countries from which it drew imports or even liquidate foreign investments.

MacEntee outlined the steps necessary to maintain the value of a currency: prohibition of foreign loan issues at home and the purchase of foreign securities by its nationals; the release of gold for export; and the pledging and ultimate sale of its existing holdings of foreign securities. The consequences, MacEntee conceded, could be serious: 'such measures will alter materially and detrimentally the economic trend of the country which to any great extent is compelled to resort to them but such is the cost of war'.[11]

He maintained, Germany had dissipated those economic reserves that were 'so vital an element in military power'.[12] Such reserves had been accumulated 'on the sound foundation of prudent finance', which enlarged the free funds and resources available to the state for war emergencies. In addition, by keeping down the pre-war burden of debt and taxation, greater scope had existed for increases in both during war. This would apply to Ireland also. Increases in income tax and other direct taxes would be slow to yield revenue though, perhaps lagging six months or more after their introduction, and taxation would not, in the long run, cover the whole cost of a modern war. In the 1914–18 war, revenue only accounted for about 35% of expenditure. Because of this point, Jacobsson's advice – the prospect of enduring budget deficits, albeit at the lowest level through controlling wages and prices[13] – was diluted. Instead, MacEntee invoked more traditional Finance approaches: 'increased taxation, therefore, must be accompanied by a drastic curtailment or suspension of all expenditure not essential to the war effort of a nation'. Excluded from cutbacks were areas such as the ordinary machinery of government, defence and debt and some social services such as for the old, blind and sick. MacEntee displayed little sympathy for the unemployed, unlike de Valera who grappled with the political implications. In 1940, for example, the decision to approach the banks for credit accommodation was partially influenced by this concern, and he used the potential threat from unemployment as leverage against the banks.[14] MacEntee, however, had deeper convictions on display in Belfast. He argued the war effort 'must ... call immediate halt to long-term schemes of social and economic amelioration', as the British had done in the 1914–18 war.[15] The British, he argued, effectively suspended completely land purchase operations and discontinued proto-public works programmes.[16]

Nevertheless, MacEntee was confident that the economy could be stabilised with an adequate check on inflationary tendencies. He felt that as the availability of luxury goods would be restricted, individuals' purchases would be limited to essential goods. Any surplus money could therefore only be used for the purchase of such limited goods as food and housing. An unstable supply of goods would tend to drive up prices but increased taxation, eliminating non-essential state expenditure and the issue of loans might offset this.[17] He ruled out recourse to pure credit creation as a matter of deliberate government policy. He conceded that as a matter of expediency in the Great War all participants resorted, in some degree, to inflationary credit creation since 'no state is going to be deterred in the last extremity from using the printing press'. But it was never deliberate policy, he maintained, except in Russia after the revolution. In conclusion, he argued that even if inflation caused by credit creation resulted in a reduction of the real burden of existing debt, it could not be achieved without real hardship and injustice to past investors in the state. It would, however, increase more than proportionately the burden of future debts without affecting the real cost of vital imports from abroad during war.

Apart possibly from de Valera's neutrality stance, this was one of the clearest expressions to the public of probable government policy in advance of war. Finance moved quickly to give effect to MacEntee's 'drastic curtailment or suspension of all expenditure not essential to the war effort' with the foundation of the wartime Economy Committee. The genesis of this 1939 committee can be traced to the cabinet decision of 27 September 1938. Government then agreed that each minister would

'consult with the Secretary of his Department with a view to determin-
ing what normal activities could be suspended or restricted' in order to
release staff for emergency work.[18] McElligott undertook an investigation, culminating in January 1939 in a raft of proposed cutbacks.[19] As he
broached the question of setting up 'special services on a large scale', he
recommended that such trained personnel be recruited from the existing
services. This would lead to a curtailment of peacetime establishments,
and decisions on what could be 'dispensed with or cut down, and in what
order'.

Although a matter for the government, McElligott suggested the
three assistant secretaries in Finance undertake the work.[20] He then proposed wide-ranging cuts across the supply services to achieve a curtailment of peacetime activities.[21] McElligott proposed cutting government
expenditure by over £8.25m – out of total government expenditure of
about £28.0m in 1939.[22] And that was only after letting the axe fall on
42 of 69 votes for services under consideration. The biggest losers would
be local loans (£2.5m), housing grants loans (£1.25m), unemployment
payments (£1.16m), employment schemes (£1.15m), and a possible re-
version to the 1925 level of the agricultural grant, saving about £1.3m.
Less serious were cuts in the road fund of £0.5m, restrictions of £0.3m in
the budget of the Office of Public Works (OPW) and a reduction of
£160,000 in the agriculture vote. Some of the 'minor' reductions would,
for many, cut closer to the bone: 'Such social services as the Free Milk
Grant, £90,000 and medical treatment of school children, £33,500
could be completely suspended.'[23]

On the basis of departmental responses to the cabinet decision of 27
September, McElligott estimated that about 2,000 public servants including 16 from his department could be spared for emergency work.[24] While
these numbers were potentially significant, they were nevertheless con-
tingent on government approval. De Valera, always aware of the political ramifications of such decisions,[25] proved hesitant. When the Committee on Emergency Measures, chaired by him, reviewed McElligott's
memorandum on 13 April, de Valera was less than enthusiastic. However, with typical ambivalence, he held that while it would be difficult
to secure curtailments at the outset of the emergency, it would nevertheless be useful to have accurate statements of the options.[26] This reluctance to confront numbers was reflected in the cabinet's eventual decision
on 4 July. It decided that all departments should consider what services,
apart from considerations of economy or release of staff, could be dispensed with in time of war.[27] McElligott, however, persisted in seeking num-

bers, and on 24 July he asked that the earlier decision be rescinded. Instead, all departments should state what changes and staff requirements
a war would bring, and inform Finance of the numbers and grades of officers possibly freed by the changes.[28] The cabinet finally approved these
measures on 1 August.[29] Finance was careful to moderate its language
here, not suggesting that it anticipated reductions in all departments. Finance's establishment officer, Seán Moynihan, having earlier requested
the reductions expected in the Taoiseach's Department,[30] received a suitably indignant response. His brother, Maurice, replying to a 'semi-official'
letter of 16 July, advised him that 'we see no prospect of being able to
release staff – on the contrary it is extremely probable that our establishment here would have to be strengthened'.[31]

The cabinet acceded to further Finance demands the following
month. On 5 September, it decided that, as far as possible, staff for the
emergency should be drawn from within the service. More significantly,
it held that in the event of conflicting views, the final say would go to the
assistant secretary in charge of the Establishment Division in Finance.[32]
This victory for Finance contained a sting, however, as the cabinet also
decided that Finance should conduct 'a systematic investigation with a
view to the reduction of the numbers employed in the lower grades of
the civil service'. The cabinet's concern with numbers may at this stage,
since the war had already broken out, have given way to the realisation
that such numbers would still have to be paid from at best stagnant, or
decreasing, revenues. Finance, with responsibility for the overall civil
service, was, however, not in the business of cutting its own numbers –
either previously or presently. Seán Moynihan privately balked at the
suggestion, but, in response, bemoaned the work burden of the emergency
services for preventing his like desire.[33] Patrick Kennedy, a future secretary at Health, informed McElligott that 'the proposed investigation
should be postponed to a more favourable time'.[34]

These considerations aside, September 1939 was an appropriate time
for McElligott to resurrect his January proposals rejected by the government. Now, however, since the establishment officer was made arbiter of
last resort by the cabinet on 5 September, it was no longer necessary for
him to insist that the 'most effective method' would be a committee of
Finance's three assistant secretaries. Instead, he recommended that an
'Inter-Departmental Committee be set up forthwith under the Chairmanship of Mr Hugo Flinn', parliamentary secretary to the Minister for
Finance since 1932. Finance did, however, set out the general guidelines
on which the committee should proceed, though these did not contain

the specific proposals of the previous January.[35] These guidelines were relatively simple but potentially controversial. There would be some distinctions in respect of unemployment schemes and assistance. In so far as 'rural areas may be affected the interests of the Exchequer must be of primary concern, in view of the special measures which will be taken to stimulate agricultural production'. However, 'in urban areas those State services which provide in one way or another for the unemployed should not be unduly restricted'.[36] In addition to nominating the remaining six members of the committee,[37] Finance enhanced its control when Arthur Codling, assistant secretary in charge of the Finance division, suggested they hear evidence from senior Finance officials first. And so at the second meeting on 19 September, McElligott and Seán Moynihan gave evidence.

McElligott rejected either tax increases or borrowing to meet an anticipated budget deficit and left no doubt as to the necessity for economy. He argued that further borrowing would undermine both government credit and the currency itself, even if it proved possible to float a loan, which he doubted, on the precarious Dublin and London markets. Economy was the only alternative. Having suggesting modifications in the operation of the Military Service Pensions Board, the civil service and the gardaí, he broached unemployment. He recommended that unemployment assistance payments be suspended immediately in rural areas in the national interest since it was now necessary to entice about 50,000 persons back into agricultural labour for a tillage campaign as their jobs in protected industries could not now be sustained.[38] He may have been encouraged by the simultaneous expression of such sentiments by Fine Gael. A memorandum submitted to the Economic Committee[39] on the same day concluded that war would possibly lead to more expenditure, necessitating increased taxation and/or further debt.[40] However, Fine Gael viewed 'with the gravest apprehension any addition to the present high level of taxation and further addition to the National Debt to balance budgets – a still more dangerous policy'.[41] Their solution lay in increased agricultural production. Having catered for Ireland's own needs, it would be desirable to develop those areas most suited to rapid expansion, such as pigs and poultry, in order to increase the national income by export trade. Such measures would better prepare Ireland for problems of post-war trade. Some basic security requirements would defer to this agricultural focus as Fine Gael's criticism of government measures illustrated: 'The mobilisation which they [Fianna Fáil] have ordered makes the financial position much more difficult and is given importance in comparison with agricultural production which there is no evidence forthcoming that it merits'.[42]

Meanwhile, in its first interim report on 12 October 1939,[43] the Economy Committee recommended slowing down the resale of estates by the Land Commission, which would free agricultural officials.[44] This would result in savings without harmful effects since, it was argued, the beneficiaries were not really unemployed – being merely allotees or relatives – so it would not restrict employment unduly as the nature of this work was something of a windfall.[45] The anticipated saving of £97,500 was placed in firm perspective by McElligott the following day when he warned that total additional demands on the exchequer ran to £3.14m.[46]

Its second interim report on 2 November considered unemployment assistance and schemes. These programmes were designed to relieve hardship arising out of 'unemployment or under-employment among able-bodied persons'.[47] Most enticing for Finance was their price tag: it approximated towards the anticipated £3.14m overrun in recurrent budget expenditure. The potential here was enormous, particularly when viewed against chairman Flinn's guideline: that the committee was 'not required to take political consequences into account – that was a matter for the Government'.[48] This was perfectly consistent with de Valera's stance the previous April on the utility of having a full range of options.[49] The committee showed restraint though and as the schemes paid roughly only £10 more than assistance, they felt a 'moral commitment' to retain them.[50]

There were, however, possible benefits from tampering with unemployment assistance. There was a distinction between the unemployment 'black areas' – the congested districts and the western seaboard generally – and 'yellow areas' – most of the remainder of the country. In 'black areas', the problem was 'mainly one of endemic poverty due to the underemployment of large numbers of small holders'. Applications for unemployment assistance were therefore much greater here than in the 'yellow areas'. Payment of this assistance was a useful barometer that would provide the guidelines for indirect social engineering, which was the ultimate thrust of the report. While noting the payments indicated 'how far the productive capacity of each area fails to meet the necessities of its population', the committee felt withdrawing payments might be 'an assisting factor' in encouraging migration from west to east Galway and west to the east generally.[51] This was desirable in Galway since it was unlikely that increased tillage would make 'any noteworthy contribution to the relief of poverty' while, to a limited extent, schemes had taken men away from the land in the spring months.[52] In view of the possible moral – not to mention electoral – repercussions associated with so sensitive a subject, it was little surprise that the cabinet decided that the reports should not be published![53]

Due cognisance of the 'political consequences' was taken by the government. The essence of the committee's Second Interim Report was that some 20,000 people would have their seven-month entitlement to unemployment assistance reduced by three months. As this threatened perceived Fianna Fáil support in the Congested Districts (the main beneficiaries), the government diluted the proposals, providing 'that the position in the "Black Areas" will be given further special consideration'.[54]

Equally sensitive was the issue of unemployment schemes, as the government also rejected the committee's proposal to reduce its funding in the current year by £200,000, while deferring a decision on proposals to introduce restrictions the following year.[55] Likewise, the government diluted recommendations concerning the winding down of housing grants and restrictions on the provision of monies from the Local Loans Fund for allocation to local authorities for housing grants.[56] The government developed a distinct distaste for the further statements of the options that de Valera invoked in April. Government reaction to the Final Report of the committee demonstrated that even in a serious economy drive, retrenchment would have to defer to political considerations. Completed on 23 November 1939,[57] the report was largely ignored the following February when the government reviewed it.[58] Government dismissed recommendations that expenditure on the agricultural grant, buildings and telecommunications should not be incurred. Individual items were thus referred back to departments, leaving a range of proposals that the government lacked the will to implement.

If Finance's approach of economising appeared to run into the sands, then what were the alternatives? Shortly after the outbreak of war, Professor Timothy Smiddy, sometime advisor to Cosgrave and de Valera, outlined the war's probable effects on the economy.[59] It made for grim reading, exposing serious limitations in the industrialisation drive when viewed in a wider context. Using 1936 estimates, Smiddy argued that a curtailment of imports and exports would have very serious consequences. In 1936, imports of raw materials constituted almost a quarter of the £105.2m total output of agricultural and industrial goods. Consumption of all goods, agricultural and industrial, was valued at about £100m, of which imports ready for use amounted to £16m, while exports were about 20%. However, impressive as these figures might appear, they did not reflect the full extent of the seriousness of a curtailment of trade. There was a major caveat: 'to a very considerable extent our raw material imports consist of goods which under normal conditions would not economically be manufactured here and the same observation applies to much of our imports of goods ready for use'.[60] Irish manufacturers would have to substitute Irish materials for imports, leading to price increases or poorer finished goods, or both. Because of the dependence on imports, unless supplies could be maintained, production would decline and unemployment result. Furthermore, increased home production only resulted in further importation of raw or semi-manufactured goods, with only a 'minor degree' of increased industrialisation based on native materials. Except for hides, woollen and cereal industries, Ireland lacked 'some of the most vital raw materials'.[61] Even if imports could be obtained, increased charges, competition and other factors would inflate their price. To meet the price increase it would be necessary to export to a corresponding value, effectively necessitating an increase in exports since these prices might not rise commensurate with imports.[62] This would be extremely difficult in view of the actual performance of, compared to general effects on, the agricultural sector during the last war:

> between 1913 and 1918, while exports from all Ireland increased from £74 millions to £153 millions, prices increased by nearly 150% but volume actually declined by 16%; the decline in the volume of exports of farm produce was no less than 21% between 1913 and 1918. It seems likely that total agricultural output also declined in volume. Irish agriculturists cannot hope for such easy profits in the present war and they should make strenuous efforts at once to increase their output.[63]

This was predicated on the certainty that the British would make 'strenuous efforts to control the price of foodstuffs', through price control and rationing, making it imperative that the volume of exports, especially agricultural exports, be increased. The urgency could be gauged from the fact that by September 1939 substantial increases had already been noted in wholesale prices, especially imported commodities such as iron and steel, furniture, paper and chemicals.[64]

Shortages of materials would have serious direct employment consequences on particular industries, and indirectly on related services. In the motor industry, for example, the supply of petrol, normally about 41 million gallons valued at £700,000, could become a bottleneck with knock-on effects for the 25,000 people directly employed in the industry. Similarly, it would be crucial to maintain supplies to the building industry, which employed 40,000 people and ranked second only to agriculture in importance to the economy. The less conspicuous but vital – accounting for more than half of current exports – 'invisible' exports would also come under pressure. While most foreign investments in British government securities were unlikely to show a marked decline, a decrease in their capital value was expected due to the increase in the bank rate. Emigrants' remittances (money sent back to families in Ireland to 'help out') would most likely decrease, while the future of the Hospital Sweepstakes was 'most precarious'. An almost certain cessation of inward tourist traffic might, however, be offset by a decline in outward tourists and the possibility of some British people opting to live in Ireland.[65] While these were possible consequences, unemployment was a certain danger. Having risen by an unprecedented 5,000 since the start of the war, Smiddy expected further increases as this rise had resulted from a loss of public confidence rather than an immediate shortage of materials.[66] Circumstances were very different from the last war. Between 1914–18, British Ministry of Munitions orders in southern Ireland were valued at £2.5m, employing 2,000 people, while War Office contracts were worth £25m, though these were mainly placed in the North. Also, Allied servicemen then quartered in Ireland provided considerable external revenue which, like the 1,000 jobs in naval repairs at Haulbowline, would not arise this time.[67]

Smiddy left few illusions as to the nature of the economic challenge. He recommended agencies and committees to plan and regulate measures affecting the economy. In relation to coal, for instance, he felt the volume of existing imports was unnecessary. Apart from industrial requirements, its domestic usage should be rationed, with price controls enforced. Likewise, in the building industry, substitution and improvisation was essential; relevant experts should be empowered to investigate possibilities. As this industry employed 40,000 people, 'the social consequences' of contractions 'would be most serious'.

Similarly, the proposed petrol rationing would impact on the motor industry, possibly resulting in the immediate unemployment 'of not less than 6,000 men'. Further rural unemployment would result from a decreased grant from the motor engine tax to road repairing and construction. Therefore, even at increased cost, arrangements should be made to charter neutral petrol tankers, with preparations put in hand to construct large storage facilities. Road repairs, which employed an average of 16,000 men per month, might also be affected by the unavailability of bitumen for re-surfacing. While tar could be substituted, and was available, only 20% of needs could be produced at home. The problem was not so much importing it as providing the requisite steel containers for holding it, though Irish Steel might be able to produce them.

The clothing industries would have to tailor their cloth to the country's basic needs: there was 'no place for luxurious standards of taste in a crisis'. The expected price increases here were not as definite as those anticipated in the tanning industries. Even after improvisation, 'leather of all kinds' would have to be imported to the value of £250,000 at current prices.[68]

Seán Lemass, formerly Industry and Commerce minister and newly appointed Minister for Supplies, contemplated planning the economy for war shortly after its outbreak, warning de Valera in November that the government 'has not yet attempted to consider the economic position as a whole or to formulate a programme to see us through the war with the least possible damage'.[69] He immediately focused on unemployment, suggesting that its reduction should be the 'central aim'. His means were far from clear, however, as he mixed 'sound' traditional finance with expansionist tendencies. He argued that 'we must endeavour to deal with unemployment without increasing taxation', which was at or near its limit. Direct subsidisation of employment-giving activities could not be undertaken. If tax yields declined, expenditure should also. But he followed that orthodox line with an intriguing suggestion: 'We can however utilise our capital resources. If our borrowings do not exceed the bona-fide savings of the people there are no inflationary consequences to be feared. It would be necessary to ensure that these savings are utilised fully for the most important purposes under machinery to be devised by the Minister for Finance.'[70]

Lemass either underestimated Finance's traditional orthodoxy or overestimated its appetite for innovation. By vesting control in Finance he effectively invited no response. Furthermore, his tentative proposals for four sectors of the economy – the building industry, industrial finance, agriculture and transport – were hardly inspired. With regard to the building industry, which consisted of 40% public building and the rest private, he suggested that 'public building should not be reduced and although costs will be higher, should be increased'.[71] Money would not be a problem for 'if the provision of capital is a main difficulty we can get over it by control of investments by the public'. That assertion would immediately arouse suspicion, even if shortages of materials and labour – susceptible to wage rates in Britain – and difficulties attracting private investors could be overcome. Equally dubious was Lemass' proposal for industrial finance. He felt that war difficulties had 'increased the capital needs of many concerns': in fact, he meant credit or working capital. As for investment capital, he felt that 'the possibility of financing new industrial enterprises by public issues of shares is non-existent'. Therefore, the Irish Credit Corporation (ICC) 'should be authorised to make known publicly that it is prepared to finance approved industrial projects on the basis of postponing until after the war the sale of shares to the public'.[72] Any sceptical official would have little difficulty in undermining this approach. Since Lemass had earlier conceded that the money required would be raised by internal borrowing, the proposal was, in essence, that the public's money should be used to start enterprises which would later – however later that might be – be offered for sale back to the public. Yet, might not the discerning public, while still entitled to repayment of its initial loan, snap up the successful ones, and leave the government with control of a herd of home-grown white elephants? As an emergency measure it might work, but what would be the price in short run money terms and long run impact on entrepreneurial capacity? Lemass said little about these. Lemass also said little about agriculture, merely assuming 'agricultural production will expand, and economic conditions in rural areas improve'.[73] Again, he assumed that the Department of Agriculture had schemes in hand to 'cover all the credit needs of farmers'. On transport, he argued that increased capital expenditure was 'long overdue'. However, beyond asserting that 'the state should provide the capital required', his argument was not convincing. If anything, it was alarmist since he rather carelessly suggested that the 'State can protect itself against ultimate loss, at the expense of the shareholders in these concerns, if it is considered good policy so to do'.

Lemass also underestimated the extent to which de Valera or his officials had already considered the consequences of war. Even before MacEntee unveiled the Finance plan in Belfast, Moynihan outlined twelve measures requiring 'immediate attention'. The first items on the list were food supplies, essential commodities and regulation of external trade. Censorship, counter-espionage and control of communications and publicity came next. Coast-watching assumed third priority, while monetary affairs came in fourth place. Transport and military measures occupied the next two places, while the remaining six were merely precautionary measures to be put in place. The significance of their ordering may be gauged from the assertion that the first three were of the 'greatest urgency'.[74] But it would remain to be seen how effectively Moynihan's further recommendations would be acted upon, for he also advocated a cabinet committee of three or four members to consider emergency measures; although, to avoid 'extra cogs', he conceded that a full committee of the cabinet might be more effective. In addition, irrespective of whether this body materialised, he also recommended a committee of heads of departments, consisting of Agriculture, Defence, External Affairs, Finance, Industry and Commerce and the Taoiseach. Their duties would be to prepare proposals, prioritise them, prepare an Emergency Book of Instructions, and supervise the operation of approved policies. It would be engaged in 'planning, co-ordinating and supervising', but would 'not have executive functions'. The following day, the cabinet approved the formation of this committee, with the inclusion of the head of the Department of Justice.[75]

Moynihan had also drawn lessons from the Great War. He recognised that, unlike then, maintenance of supplies and services would now rest with the Irish government. In that war, some evil effects were mitigated because of the increase in agricultural prices, and increased industrial production and employment. Also, the enlistment of about 250,000 men in the forces prevented large-scale unemployment. Now, however, the maintenance of Ireland's position would depend on the goodwill of the British – while they had the seas – though they would still require Irish agricultural output. More alarmingly, the Irish government could now anticipate, for whatever reasons, the return of 'perhaps hundreds of thousands' of Irish from Britain. These would add to those already unemployed, and increase the non-productive numbers such as the young, old and invalid. To compound matters, the agricultural bonanza of 1914–20 could not be expected due to anticipated regulatory measures by the British, while restrictions on essential raw materials would increase unemployment even more. There would also be knock-on effects from a contraction in production of import-dependent industries, leading to a further contraction of spending. Against this, increased agricultural production might materialise, but it could not be expected to 'absorb much, or, indeed, any additional labour'.[76]

Thus, whether as a neutral, active or non-active belligerent, the prospect of war was already a nightmare scenario for the government. Ireland was of course fortunate merely to endure the nightmare of the neutral. The more so since the number and range of possible responses in the period 1938–40 was hardly inspiring, making it relatively simpler for Finance to seize the initiative and hold the reins. That may seem an oversimplification with the benefit of hindsight, but a timeless adage warns that those who neglect to do any thinking for themselves are usually forced to live with other peoples' ideas. And what of Finance's policy response of curtailing non-essential expenditure, ruthlessly undertaken through the aegis of an 'Economy Committee', largely directed by Merrion Street? It envisaged a selective agenda – one which challenged many established features of social expenditure – for Ireland in the war years and probably after. Many of Finance's proposals touched on matters of general policy – matters to be determined by government. In the absence of any alternatives – and there were few feasible alternatives postulated in the pre-war period – Finance's approach was logical to the point of attractive, if for no other reason than it involved fewer commitments and nothing new. That its policy was undermined in execution simply reflects the routine hazards facing any policy. That it was undermined piecemeal without alternatives probably bears adequate testimony to the nature of the Irish response to the war.

EMERGENCY LAW IN ACTION, 1939–1945
Seosamh Ó Longaigh

Days after the commencement of hostilities in Europe in September 1939, Ireland witnessed the first amendment to the constitution and the enactment of the Emergency Powers Act, 1939. This granted the government the widest possible powers to deal with the unprecedented emergency then beginning, and this followed the enactment of the Offences Against the State Act, May 1939, which was introduced to deal with a different type of emergency – that of the ongoing anti-state activities of the IRA.

Enacting the Emergency Powers Order
Germany invaded Poland on 1 September 1939. The following day the Taoiseach, Éamon de Valera, addressed the Dáil, explaining how he envisaged dealing with the emerging crisis. He admitted to the Dáil that the order paper for 2 September 1939 looked suspiciously like a list of guillotine motions, but assured the Dáil that that was not the government's intention.[1] The purpose of the constitutional amendment was one of 'extending "time of war" or, if not extending it, we are making it clear that "time of war" should mean a crisis such as the present, when there are hostilities and conflict about us.'[2]

William Cosgrave asked why the government had waited until now to introduce the amendment. Labour's William Norton sought assurances that the emergency powers would not be abused. De Valera found himself unable to give a satisfactory guarantee, replying:

> the trouble is this, that when this amendment is passed if you get an unscrupulous majority, both in the Dáil and in the Seanad, it could by pretending to have an emergency and by pretending to submit to the rules of law and the constitution, do that.[3]

It was quickly enacted, and the Emergency Powers Bill was introduced immediately. A number of amendments to the bill were tabled.[4] Concern was expressed in respect of compensation for property compulsorily acquired,[5] military and industrial conscription, and the trial of civilians by courts martial.[6] Fine Gael's Dr T. F. O'Higgins, who expressed disappointment at the case made for the bill, explained he would support it unenthusiastically and uneasily. Nonetheless he added: 'I would stand at all times for giving any Irish Government any powers whatsoever that they asked for on any occasion when they were demanded and the Government itself said that those powers were necessary.'[7] However, a fellow Fine Gael TD, John A. Costello, criticised the delegation of powers to the executive, saying 'we are asked not merely to give a blank cheque, but, to give an uncrossed cheque to the Government.'[8]

The bill was quickly enacted, and the Emergency Powers Order was immediately promulgated; for example, garda powers of arrest and search were extended. It also provide for the compulsory cultivation of land, curfews, and the creation of temporary police forces. During the Emergency, supplemental orders dealt with matters as diverse as the establishment of an auxiliary police force, the wearing of military uniforms by non-military personnel, official secrets,[9] transport restrictions,[10] and compulsory queuing for buses.[11] There were major changes in the functioning of the courts, particularly juries. In total, 7,864 Emergency Powers orders were made,[12] not including orders made by local authorities acquiring land compulsorily. 522 orders were made by the government, while 7,303 orders, 22 regulations, 3 rules and 14 schemes were made in exercise of powers conferred by a Government Order. Of the 7,303 subsidiary orders, 5,330 were made under the Wages Standstill Orders.[13]

Dealing with the IRA

But it was, however, the Offences Against the State Act and dealing with the IRA, particularly in the context of war in Europe, that was of immediate government concern. Gerald Boland was appointed Minister for Justice on 9 September and immediately the gardaí arrested those believed to be the most active and important members of the IRA. Internments were ordered and several persons were charged before the Special Criminal Court. By December 1939, 30 IRA members had been tried by the court, and 76 interned.[14] Even at this early stage, these powers were not used solely to deal with the IRA. Members of the Milk Producers' Association of Dublin were tried before the Special Criminal Court when disturbances followed a short-lived campaign of withholding milk supplies from the city as a protest against cost increases caused by the war.[15]

As happened in the past, the focus of IRA activities shifted to the prisons and several members began refusing food, eventually forcing their release. Other avenues were also pursued and the internment provisions of the new legislation were quickly challenged. The first challenge was made in December 1939 when the brother of one of the internees sought an order of *habeas corpus*. To the government's surprise, Mr Justice George Gavan Duffy ruled in the High Court that internment did not respect the individual's right to liberty and that the minister was acting judicially when he ordered an internment. He directed the internee, Burke, be freed. The government's appeal was not considered. The Supreme Court, relying on an English precedent from 1890, ruled there was no appeal to Gavan Duffy's ruling. All internees had to be released.

Despite this unexpected setback, Stephen Roche, the secretary of the Department of Justice, took an opportunity to severely criticise the Irish judicial system. Writing in early December 1939, he argued that provisions for internment and the Special Criminal Court in the Offences Against the State Act did not embody the 'best effort that the Government and its advisers' could make 'towards the solution of one of the most important problems with which this country is faced, *viz.*, the weakness of our judicial system in the face of outbursts of violence and disorder … prompted by organisations such as the so-called IRA.'[16] He continued:

> The fact is that trial by jury has no real roots in this country and is quite unsuited for dealing with our most serious form of crime, *viz.*, political crime. Instead of recognising that fact frankly, we have put up the pretext that occasionally – once in ten years or so – we may find to our surprise that juries will not convict in political cases, whereupon the Government makes proclamations under the Offences Against the State Act.

The simple reality he argued was: 'we are living in a permanent state of emergency as regards the administration of justice.' He characterised members of the High Court as unable to deal with criminal cases 'in a sensible way', and claimed they strained 'the law beyond all reason in favour of the accused'. Roche argued that a High Court judge was not usually selected for his capacity as an administrator or a criminal lawyer. Moreover, a senior judge was often 'only too willing to direct his mind, as he is invited to do by the appellant's counsel, from the realities of the case into a discussion on forms, precedents and theories.' What was needed therefore, was a 'more rational and much firmer administration of the criminal law, not as an emergency measure but as a permanent necessity'. He envisaged repealing the internment and Special Court provisions of the Offences Against the State Act, and creating a special permanent jury-less High Court to deal with all criminal cases (irrespective of political motivation), equivalent in status to the existing High Court which would thereafter deal solely with civil cases. The High Court for criminal offences would consist of a president and four ordinary members, and would replace the Central Criminal Court, 'to the great relief of the Dublin jurors'. It could also order internments. He concluded: 'we need a High Court for criminal cases which will be a respectable and permanent feature of our judicial system and not a temporary expedient, a Court Martial thinly disguised which functions in a half-apologetic way under the jealous scrutiny of the "ordinary" Courts.' The secretary's recommendations rested there.

When members of the IRA broke into the Magazine Fort in Phoenix Park on 23 December 1939, taking over a million rounds of the army's ammunition, Roche's initial arguments suddenly became academic and he wrote: 'the *urgent* thing (as we must admit if the point is put to us) is to have the power *now* [emphasis in the original].'[17] The Department of Justice was mindful, however, that any haste in resolving these legal problems could be dangerous.

Inevitably, the government took steps to intern persons under the Emergency Powers Act, as it was not open to judicial scrutiny. It was quickly amended to reverse the prohibition on interning natural-born Irish citizens added in September. But the government was not content to leave the issues raised by George Gavan Duffy unresolved. There were weighty reasons for the enactment of the Offences Against the State (Amendment) Act, 1940, though it differed only slightly from the original. The language of the amendment indicated that, contrary to the original, the minister would no longer be 'satisfied' that a person was 'engaged in activities calculated to prejudice the preservation of the peace, order, or security of the State' but would have formed that 'opinion' when ordering an internment.[18] Most important was the government's desire to definitely settle whether or not it had the right to intern persons at times other than wartime.

On 6 January 1940, the president submitted the amended Offences Bill to the Supreme Court where its constitutionality was examined before being signed into law. Without specific reference to the Burke Case, the Supreme Court held that internment was not punishment but preventative justice, and did not take away the right of *habeas corpus*. Relying on the 1917 British case *R(Zadig) v. Halliday*,[19] Chief Justice Sullivan declared: 'the only essential preliminary to the exercise by the Minister of the powers [of internment] is that he should have formed opinions on the matters specifically mentioned in the [act]. The validity of such opinions cannot be questioned in any court.' Noting the constitution did not specifically prohibit internment without trial, and with reference to its preamble, he said:

> It seems to us difficult to understand how the dignity and freedom of the individual member of the State can be attained unless social order is maintained in that State. There is nothing in this ... which could be invoked to necessitate the sacrifice of the common good in the interests of the individual.[20]

Increasing numbers of the IRA were arrested in early 1940. Serious charges were brought in several cases, though initially there were few internments. Again the IRA resorted to the hunger strike to demand political treatment.[21] However, unlike six months earlier, government policy had unmistakably stiffened. If de Valera was 'indecisive' at times in his dealings with the IRA, Gerald Boland would not shirk his responsibilities.[22] Within a year of being appointed Minister for Justice, he claimed: 'Mr de Valera would not try to force me to do anything.'[23] Given the prevailing circumstances and the embarrassment caused by recent IRA tactics, there could be no retreat by the government. Two of the hunger strikers died, Tony D'Arcy died on 17 April and Jack McNeela two days later.[24]

The situation deteriorated in May 1940. After two gardaí carrying diplomatic mail were shot on 7 May 1940, de Valera warned:

> The policy of patience has failed and is over ... I warn those now planning new crimes against the nation that they will not be allowed to continue their policy of sabotage. They have set the law at defiance. The law will be enforced against them. If the present law is not sufficient it will be strengthened; and in the last resort, if no other law will suffice, then the Government will invoke the ultimate law – the safety of the people.[25]

On 23 May, days after the German invasion of Belgium, Luxembourg and the Netherlands, gardaí discovered the safe house of the German spy, Hermann Görtz, in Dublin.[26] The further unearthing of plans for a German invasion of Northern Ireland, assisted by the IRA, added to the alarm.[27] In de Valera's words, the IRA was 'meditating treason', and in light of the German–IRA link there 'was no time for nonsense'.[28] Drastic steps would now be considered to deal with the IRA.

An all-party 'Defence Conference' was established on 28 May 1940 to assist with the Emergency and to keep the opposition parties informed of developments.[29] The conference was composed of: the ministers for Justice, Defence and the Co-ordination of Defensive Measures; Richard Mulcahy, James Dillon and Dr O'Higgins of Fine Gael; and William Norton and William Davin of the Labour Party.[30] It first met on 30 May 1940 and revealed a compromise among the opposition parties in favour of internment.[31] Gerald Boland consulted with garda headquarters to ascertain who might be regarded as a danger to the state.[32] Arrests began almost immediately. Over 400 were interned during the month of June. By war's end, over 1130 were interned. By 1946, the Special Criminal Court had prosecuted 1013, convicting 914.

Military Courts

There was another immediate reaction to the discoveries of 23 May 1940. The Department for the Co-ordination of Defensive Measures and the Parliamentary Draftsman's Office quickly drew up a proclamation under Article 28.3.2[33] of the constitution and drafted an order equivalent to a declaration of martial law to be made in case of invasion.[34] The Department of Justice also suggested it would be 'a salutary gesture to make provision for the imposition of the death penalty under the [Explosive Substances Act, 1883] in certain circumstances'.[35] Three days later the Department of Justice wrote that the purpose of its proposal was:

> to impress and terrify possible offenders and in considering this aspect of the matter the speed and certainty of the punishment are most important factors ... if death is threatened at all, immediate and certain death should be threatened subject only to the possibility of the exercise of the prerogative of mercy.[36]

It added the death penalty should be extended to: the possession of firearms with intent to endanger life; undertaking sabotage; conducting espionage; and active membership of an unlawful organisation. The Department of Justice also sought provisions allowing suspects to be held for eight days.[37] Most importantly, it proposed the creation of a new special military court with full control over its procedures to prevent all but the most unavoidable of delays. If the military court found a suspect guilty, it could only impose the death sentence and there would be no appeal. The government would confirm its sentences and those found guilty would, if no reprieve were forthcoming, be executed within 24 hours. The cabinet immediately approved these proposals.[38]

A draft Emergency Powers (Amendment)(No. 2) Bill, 1940 was prepared by the Parliamentary Draftsman by 28 May 1940[39] and was, after
amendments, approved by the cabinet.[40] The special court proposal was
then considered by the 'Defence Conference' and introduced into the
Dáil on 5 June 1940.[41] The bill passed the Seanad on 26 June 1940,
where Boland told senators:

> The Government has decided to ask for these powers because they felt that
> they are absolutely necessary … this Bill is intended for a state of affairs
> such as existed in the immediate past. For some time past there has been no
> shooting or blowing up of public buildings, but if a state of war should come
> there will be a more drastic order … nothing short of drum-head Court
> Martial.[42]

The first military court envisaged by the Emergency Powers (Amendment)(No. 2) Act, 1940 was finally established, with a relatively small
number of scheduled but serious offences, on the proviso that the death
penalty would not be enforced unless the government had an opportunity of first commuting it to penal servitude or imprisonment. The secretary of the Department of the Taoiseach, Maurice Moynihan, later
recalled:

> that they were discussed as a disagreeable necessity. Everyone had their say.
> No one appears to have dissented. And everyone at the Cabinet table seems
> to have had a shared concern that the failure to execute members of an
> organisation who had killed policemen would have had repercussions in
> the gardaí.[43]

Some years later Boland informed the Dáil:

> This court has been described outside as a terror court. I have no objection
> to its so being described. That is exactly what it was. It was a terror court –
> a court set up to meet terror in a drastic and summary manner in order to
> save this nation from perils which threatened it at the time.[44]

The military court, staffed by the members of the Special Criminal
Court, first operated in August 1940.

The gardaí, frequently supported by soldiers, quickly arrested a large
number of active members of the IRA. The state pursued the organisation more aggressively than at any time since the civil war.[45] In addition to a stricter policy regarding arrest, trial and imprisonment, the
Special Criminal Court sentenced at least three IRA members to be

flogged.[46] Although there had been a great deal of confrontation between the IRA and the gardaí prior to the summer of 1940, events after May 1940 escalated into what J. Bowyer Bell described as a pattern of 'provocation, retaliation and revenge'.[47] There were 26 incidents between May and August 1940 involving the IRA and the Special Branch, and many afterwards.[48] Inevitably, IRA–gardaí encounters ended in tragedy.

A further indication of the seriousness with which the government now regarded the situation was its desire to see Tomás MacCurtain, son of the former lord mayor of Cork, executed. MacCurtain was convicted by the Special Criminal Court for the murder of Garda John Roche in Cork on 2 January 1940 and sentenced to death. However, not all ministers believed he should die and Seán T. O'Kelly intervened. Speaking of the assistance O'Kelly gave, Seán MacBride, MacCurtain's counsel, recalled:

> [O'Kelly] advised me to take any sort of delaying action I could in the courts, which I did. I planned the moves very carefully. I went seeking a conditional *habeas corpus* at 3.30 in the afternoon, the courts then rising at 4 pm. I knew that I would be thrown out. At 3.55 Gavan Duffy refused the order. I lodged my appeal just before the office closed. MacCurtain was due to be hanged in Mountjoy the next day, so it was a very close shave. They tried to bring the Supreme Court together that evening, but they were unable because [Mr Justice] Murnaghan ... was out, diplomatically maybe, walking with his dog ... Straight away they had to postpone the execution for a couple of days.[49]

While MacBride saw little prospect of success, the conviction had, nonetheless, to be challenged. His various and tenacious legal argumentation, though repeatedly rejected, served the purpose of delaying the execution and placing pressure on the government.[50] The death sentence, which was passed on 13 June 1940, was to be carried out on 5 July. An appeal was lodged in the High Court on 4 July, and the Supreme Court forced a suspension of the execution until 13 July. On 10 July, the government announced the sentence was commuted.

Following MacCurtain's reprieve, the government began to transfer IRA members convicted of the most serious offences to Portlaoise prison, subjecting them to a harsh prison régime. It was clear that if other IRA members were found guilty of murder they would certainly die. On 16 August 1940, Garda Special Branch raided a house in Dublin seeking to arrest IRA members Patrick McGrath and Francis Harte. In the ensuing gun-battle, two gardaí were killed, and Harte and McGrath arrested.[51] Later that day the military court was established. Tried three days later, they were sentenced to death and shot by firing squad on 6 September 1940.

Before their execution, they sought relief before the High Court.[52] The death sentence was temporarily suspended while the appeals were heard. Their counsel contested the validity of the emergency legislation and orders, the trial by the military tribunal, and the prisoners' convictions, on several technical grounds.[53] All arguments were dismissed. For instance, the insistence that the order of the tribunal was that of an inferior court was dismissed by the Supreme Court, where Chief Justice Sullivan explained, 'the Orders in question ... are Orders made by the Government in express exercise of the powers conferred upon them by the [Emergency Powers] Acts'.[54] As regards the alleged absence of provisions regulating the tribunal's make-up, the selection of members, its procedure and the bringing of an accused before it, the Supreme Court stated:

> In our opinion no such provisions were necessary. Any three persons having the qualifications specified in clause 3 of the Order would, in our opinion, constitute such a court, and would have jurisdiction to try an accused person charged with a specified offence and brought before them for trial.[55]

The retrospective nature of the order was also held to be valid.[56]

In total, eight trials were held before the military court under the Emergency Powers (No. 41) Order, 1940, with five persons executed. In June 1940, Gerald Boland promised if the special military court proved inadequate[57] 'if a state of war should come',[58] 'drum-head courts martial' would be established. The drafting of such a court system occurred in parallel to work on Order 41. Although the attorney general believed the constitution prohibited martial law, in the event of an invasion, Article 28 permitted the government to confer both specific and general powers on the army to deal with the consequences of the invasion.[59] Initially, in May 1940, it was proposed that a proclamation and order would be made under Article 28.3.2 of the constitution, and the government and army could take whatever actions were necessary. However, the drafting and issuing of an Army Emergency Powers Order (eventually Order 65) and Instructions (as might be revised) would render any action under Article 28.3.2 unnecessary.[60]

This second draft Emergency Powers Order would permit a more decentralised administration of justice by military tribunals and would deal with a wider range of offences. It was finally considered by the government on 29 November 1940. Redrafting – with amendments suggested by the government, the army and the attorney general – was completed by 27 December 1940. The order was secretly printed in case of imme-diate crisis. It would come into force once the country had been invaded, the presumption being that the necessary administrative arrangements had been made beforehand.[61] On 2 May 1941 the government approved the instructions prepared by the Department of Defence regarding the powers of the military in relation to the civilian population in the event of an invasion.[62] No further action on the part of the government would be necessary. Philip P. O'Donoghue of the attorney general's office explained:

> If, in the event of an invasion, the powers were exercised by the military, such exercise could and would be related back to the approval already given by the Government and no additional direction given by the Government in the event of an invasion could add anything to the approval already ac-corded. Furthermore, the fact that the approval had been given before in-vasion would not in any way clash with the provisions of Article 28.3.2. The Dáil would, of course, have to be informed when it met, of the fact that the Government had approved of the exercise of the powers.

Although the government prepared for the worst eventualities, its hand-ling of the IRA had been highly effective. Indeed the FBI noted that IRA setbacks between 1939 and 1941 had:

> resulted in a marked deterioration in the quality and quantity of IRA per-sonnel. As a result of this, allegedly considerable dissatisfaction developed, particularly among the northern members of the Irish Republican Army ... [Stephen] Hayes [IRA chief-of-staff] was successful in avoiding arrest dur-ing this entire period and according to some reports, some suspicion arose concerning him.[63]

By the summer of 1941 senior northern members of the IRA concluded that Stephen Hayes was, in fact, a garda agent. This perception resulted in the IRA inflicting irreparable damage upon itself. Seán McCaughey and others abducted Hayes on 30 June 1941 and proceeded to question him over a period of weeks.[64] Eventually, a detailed 'confession' was ex-tracted claiming that all the events in which the IRA was involved since 1935, including the bombing campaign in England, the Magazine Fort raid, etc., were elements of an elaborate conspiracy designed by the Dub-lin government to discredit and destroy the organisation. Before Hayes could be killed, McCaughey was arrested.[65] The veracity or otherwise of Hayes' 'confession' has never been satisfactorily established. But soon after McCaughey's arrest, Hayes escaped from his remaining IRA captors and surrendered to the gardaí. The IRA continued to fare badly after this,[66] with the gardaí finding large amounts of IRA arms.[67]

Coincidentally, the Hayes affair also resulted in gardaí tracking down the body of Michael Devereux, who had been shot by the IRA on suspicion of being an informer. Four were charged with his murder and brought before the Special Criminal Court. Michael Walsh and Patrick Davern, apparent accomplices in the killing, turned state's evidence, but then refused to testify, claiming they had been coerced into making statements. The case before the Special Criminal Court collapsed. However, the matter did not rest there. The case was transferred to the military tribunal and the government issued Emergency Powers Order 139 which facilitated the use of Walsh's and Davern's retracted statements. These were read to the tribunal by a member of the gardaí, and accepted into evidence. Three of the four were found guilty.[68] They sought relief from the military tribunal's conviction in the High Court and then the Supreme Court.[69]

Their counsel argued that Order No. 139 made such inroads into the normal laws of evidence as to constitute a fundamental change in the law which robbed the military court of the attributes of a judicial tribunal, and prevented a trial as contemplated by the Emergency Powers (Amendment) (No. 2) Act, 1940. Counsel also attempted to limit the scope of Article 28.3.3, arguing that the phrase 'nothing in this Constitution' had to be given a limited and defined meaning, for example, to apply it to the institutions established under the constitution was an 'absurdity'. Essentially, it was contended that Article 28.3.3 left intact rights 'over and above those conferred by the Constitution'; for example, *habeas corpus* was affirmed and not created by the constitution.[70] All arguments were dismissed. Mr Justice Gavan Duffy explained that the High Court was not in a position to intervene:

> the applicants have come for relief to a court which has no power to give them relief. Their right to escort to the High Court springs from constitutional guarantees, entrusted to the protection of the High Court, and that right is suspended. The right to *habeas corpus* in this State is now very carefully defined by the constitution, and the right to a trial in due course of law is enshrined in the constitution ... so long as the jurisdiction of this Court to enforce those constitutional rights remains in abeyance in pursuance of an Article of the constitution, persons in the position of the applicants cannot justify an application to this Court by reference to the guarantees in the constitution.[71]

The Supreme Court refused to accept that the changes in the rules of evidence denied the military court its jurisdiction.[72] Regarding arguments that the Emergency Powers Orders were 'manifestly oppressive and unjust' to the accused, Chief Justice Sullivan explained:

> In our opinion this contention is based upon a misconception of the duties and the functions of the Court. This emergency legislation is of a temporary character, passed for the purpose of securing the public safety and the preservation of the State during a time of national emergency. During such period the duty of determining what provisions are necessary for securing that object is vested in the Government, but every such provision must be laid before each House of the Oireachtas and may be annulled by a resolution passed by either House. Many of the arguments addressed to us would be more fittingly addressed to either House of the Oireachtas when considering the propriety of, and necessity for, the Order in question. They are not matters which can properly be relied upon in a Court of law.[73]

The convictions were upheld, though only one of the three death sentences imposed was executed.

As expected, there was some condemnation of the order in the Dáil.[74] Deputy J. A. Costello, attorney general when Article 2A was drafted, declared: 'It is ... no exaggeration to say that the provisions of the order we are discussing have shocked both lawyer and layman.'[75] His objections were not entertained. Gerald Boland replied:

> I think that if there is one charge that can be made against the Government – and it has been made often – it is that we have been too lenient and have allowed things to go on with which we should, perhaps, have dealt far more seriously ... The order, as I say, is absolutely necessary if we are to put down organised crime and, particularly organised murder ... I say it is far more important for us to see that organised murder does not exist in this country than that we should have these laws of evidence as they have come down to us from Britain.[76]

Unquestionably, the IRA had by then been neutralised as an effective force in Ireland. Bowyer Bell writes:

> In the autumn of 1941, the IRA no longer seemed a clear and present danger to the men of Leinster House ... [the Government] felt the worst was over, but the pressure was kept up to finish what the Hayes affair had begun – the elimination of the IRA from Irish politics ... the unrelenting process of arrests continued unabated.[77]

Regulating Supplies

Although government and garda actions effectively contained subversive activities, the continuing world war began to take its toll on Ireland and the general population. This was especially evident during 1941 when more basic difficulties, such as the procurement and control of essential supplies, became highly problematic. This had been anticipated when contingency planning began in earnest in 1938 and, at the outbreak of war, two new government departments, Supplies and Co-ordination of Defensive Measures, were established. The Department of Supplies had a very wide remit, and as the war began to adversely affect the Irish economy, it instigated a number of extraordinary steps to ensure the government maintained control of the economy, and that there was enough to eat.[78]

The supplies situation deteriorated rapidly after December 1940 when the British imposed strict trade restrictions following Ireland's refusal to enter the war. By then severe petrol restrictions were in operation. Coal imports dried up by the end of 1941, and acute shortages of tea, sugar, tobacco, bread, fruit, feeding-stuffs and fertilisers also occurred. Prices rose rapidly, while wages were kept low by wages standstill orders, and trade union activities were restricted by the Trade Unions Act, 1941. Black-marketeering and overcharging became rampant though general rationing was not introduced until the summer of 1942.[79] In order to enforce general rationing, the government introduced the Emergency Powers (Amendment and Continuance) Act, 1942 in July 1942.[80] Amongst other things, it provided for increased punishments for offences against Emergency Powers Orders, punishments for non-compliance with orders and a system of minimum penalties.[81]

Although normally silent on matters of state security and emergency legislation, the Opposition expressed dissatisfaction at the use of Emergency Powers legislation in a number of areas when it was being renewed the following summer. It was argued that more than half the Emergency Powers Orders promulgated could have been introduced by means of ordinary legislation. William Cosgrave pointed specifically to the wages freeze, arguing that the government should justify particularly contentious and controversial orders to the Dáil, noting that while wages had been kept constant, prices had risen by 50% or 60% since the war began.[82] Cosgrave further complained that the Emergency Powers (Amendment and Continuance) Act, 1942 enabled the government to impose penalties in addition to those levied by the courts and criticised the revoking of traders' licences.[83] The Fine Gael leader concluded: 'The

Government knows well that we are going to support the principle of having a measure of this sort. The Government has been told that we object to its abuse.'[84]

In his response the Minister for Supplies, Seán Lemass, explained the licensing of traders of certain goods was essential to the efficiency of the rationing system. Rationing applied to a very large number of goods, which enabled the government to control supply by ensuring (or attempting to ensure) conformity in their sale.[85] For example, in July 1943 there were 41,727 traders licensed to sell tea and sugar. Of those, 1,290 had been prosecuted under price control and rationing orders. Licences were withdrawn in 31 cases. Notice of withdrawal had been given to others but not enforced because it was felt that several traders did not appreciate the seriousness of their activities. Despite some initial leniency, he warned that henceforth any trader contravening emergency orders – i.e. failure to keep records, false records, absence of price tags, overcharging, etc. – would lose their licence. He explained the government could not rely on the courts to determine whether or not a trader's licence should be revoked.[86] Lemass defended the government's powers, saying 'it would be impossible for any Minister for Supplies to carry on the rationing scheme in operation and exercise proper supervision over the sale of goods, unless he had the power to require traders to have licences and also the power to withdraw them, if his regulations were not upheld.'[87]

As the war progressed, the Special Criminal Court tried fewer and fewer members of the IRA and focused more on black-marketeering and rationing offences.[88] Fine Gael TD John A. Costello objected to this. He questioned the use of the Special Criminal Court in matters other than those concerned with public safety, believing the ordinary courts sitting with juries should have disposed of such cases. He queried the practice of offering persons suspected of involvement in Emergency Powers offences immunity and anonymity in return for evidence against accomplices. Costello's objections were dismissed. It was explained that while most cases of offences against Emergency Powers orders were disposed of by the ordinary courts, some were tried by the Special Criminal Court, reflecting the seriousness of the offences.[89] Between 1939 and 1946 there were 123 Special Criminal Court convictions for black-marketeering, 15 for overcharging, and 7 for wholesaling offences. Other non-political offences were tried, including a number of agrarian offences.[90] Indeed, by mid-1943, the *Irish Times* claimed that there was a 'mounting crime wave in Ireland'.[91]

After several years of life under emergency law, rumblings of discontent were finally noted in the press.[92] The *Irish Independent* accepted that few could have questioned the necessity of vesting such extraordinary powers in the executive at the beginning of the war, and that powers were generally used for the 'good of the community as a whole'.[93] However, it stated: 'it cannot be denied that there have been many instances in which the emergency powers have been used harshly or excessively, or in spheres in which even the emergency conditions did not justify their application'.[94] It recommended formulating a new system to give the Dáil a voice in the development and use of emergency powers. It continued:

> We fear, too, that the inevitable tendency of officials is to gather more and more power into their own grasp. There is to be said for officials: they cannot hit back when attacked. And hence they naturally seek to make themselves immune from attack by presenting the public with orders which have immediate force of law. That is one of the dangers of office made law rather than Parliament made law. Hence too, the menacing growth in the tendency of officials to have their acts and deeds placed above the reach of the Courts of Justice, to make the officials their own final court of appeal.[95]

Peacetime

When the war in Europe ended on 8 May 1945 the government faced ongoing supply difficulties. Although Article 28.3.3 was amended a second time on 30 May 1941, allowing the Oireachtas to maintain the state of emergency until it 'resolved that the national emergency occasioned by such war, armed conflict or armed rebellion has ceased to exist', its continued reliance on emergency powers (notwithstanding persistent supply problems), would have been difficult to justify.

By May 1945, 78 persons were still interned,[96] and the Department of Justice had to decide what was to become of them.[97] Of the 72 Irish internees, the department felt it safe to release 58, but added that the minister had 'doubts about whether it would be wise to release the remaining 14 at the present time'. De Valera told the Dáil:

> the feeling was that even when the war was over it would be necessary in the interests of public safety to keep a number of these internees, the hard core of the organisation, in custody indefinitely until such time as the Government was satisfied that it could, with safety to the community, release them.[98]

However, the government ordered everybody released in June 1945.

Efforts to revive the IRA began immediately and within a fortnight the gardaí were anxious to reintern at least one individual.[99] The provisions of the Offences Against the State (Amendment) Act, 1940 came into force with a proclamation issued on 24 July 1945.[100] Despite the IRA's efforts to reorganise, by 15 July 1947 the Department of Justice reported: 'the situation has materially altered since the making of the proclamation. The IRA has disintegrated and the gardaí reported that it can no longer be regarded as a serious menace to peace and good order.'[101] It would be nine years before the IRA again made a noticeable impact on Irish politics and society.

Initially, the Minister for Justice wanted to repeal the internment provisions of the Emergency Powers Act and simultaneously bring those of the Offences Against the State (Amendment) Act, 1940 into operation.[102] But the Offences Act alone would have made no provision for the continued detention of the six aliens. As Roche explained it, the act:

> authorises a Minister to order a detention only when he is of the opinion that the person to be detained *is engaged* in activities prejudicial to the preservation of public peace and order or to the security of the State. As all these men have been in custody for several years, it would be impossible for the Minister to say that they are at present engaged in such activities.[103]

Therefore it was deemed necessary for the Emergency Powers Act to revert to its September 1939 format to permit the continued internment of non-natural born Irish citizens and aliens.

Although the issue of internment was, more or less, satisfactorily resolved by July 1945, the problem of essential supplies did not disappear immediately. While several portions of the Emergency Powers Acts, 1939–1946 could be abandoned in mid-1945, and a large number of Emergency Powers Orders rescinded, emergency powers would remain necessary in the areas of production, rationing and price control for some time.[104]

An initial step in the process of revoking several hundred emergency orders[105] was considered by the cabinet on 5 June 1945.[106] It decided to discontinue the Emergency Powers (Amendment)(No. 2) Act, 1940, and the Emergency Powers (Continuance and Amendment) Act, 1942. All departments were asked to identify the emergency powers (i.e. sections of acts and actual orders) which could be dispensed with and those which remained essential would be incorporated into the ordinary law.

The Department for the Co-ordination of Defensive Measures re-commended deleting the censorship provisions of the act and permitting the Air Raid Precautions (ARP) to operate in peacetime.[107] The De-partment of Agriculture believed only section 7, relating to the hearing of court proceedings in camera could be discontinued after September 1945.[108] The government made about 60 Emergency Powers Orders on behalf of this department,[109] which were classed under three groupings.[110] Proposed legislation would, in certain instances, require only amend-ments to existing statutes, but in other cases, entirely new bills would have to be introduced. Given the volume of work, the department felt that the emergency legislation should remain on the statute book for more than six months.

The Department of Justice believed that special powers of arrest, controlling movement and internment could be dropped from the Emer-gency Powers Act.[111] The department also identified articles of the Emergency Powers Order, 1939 and other emergency orders that could be revoked, those it considered non-essential, and those covering sup-plies and services. The Minister for Justice was expected to submit plans to incorporate various other orders.

The Department of Local Government and Public Health's primary concern was the threat of infection and continuing Order 46.[112] It be-lieved that this would remain vital because of the freedom of movement afforded by the end of hostilities. It hoped to include it in the proposed Public Health Bill but that legislation was not likely to be ready until 1946.[113]

J. P. Walshe, secretary of the Department of External Affairs ex-pressed a somewhat different view:

> Although hostilities in Europe have ceased, people in Great Britain and the United States do not regard the war as being over. The war psychosis re-mains and it is a question for consideration whether, as long as this is the case, the Government can safely divest itself of the powers necessary to en-able it to deal with a certain type of activity here (public demonstrations, propaganda, Fascist or other subversive organisation, etc.) capable, if it takes certain forms or is pursued to provocative lengths, of creating tension in our relations with other countries and, even, of exposing the State to danger.[114]

This related specifically to the powers the Department of Justice believed could be dropped. If legislation were enacted adapting Emergency Powers Orders the Department of External Affairs felt that it should be specifically declared that these enactments would not in any way prejudice the exercise or continuance of emergency legislation.

The Emergency Powers (Amendment) Act, 1940 would be repeal-
ed. It was decided that the parent act should be kept in force for a further
12 months given the variety and volume of legislation which would
have to be drafted.[115] However, provisions relating to censorship were
repealed. Emergency Powers (Amendment)(No. 2) Act, 1940 was also
repealed, and the provisions regarding minimum fines in Emergency
Powers (Continuance and Amendment) Act, 1942 dropped.

The news that the Emergency Powers Act was being continued for
one more year was greeted with dismay by the Dáil. While a number of
acts were repealed and the government continued the process of divest-
ing itself of Emergency Powers Orders, de Valera's assurance that 'it was
not the desire of the Government to retain the Emergency Powers Acts
in operation for a moment longer than the public interest required,' left
TDs unimpressed.[116] Deputy Michael Donnellan believed 'it was a mistake ever to give such powers to the government. No government,
whether Fianna Fáil, Fine Gael, or any other should have such powers.'
Éamon Coogan (Fine Gael) criticised the government's use of the IRA
as a 'bogey' and 'excuse' for continuing the legislation, while Dr Thomas
Francis O'Higgins now described the legislation as undemocratic, and
claimed there was discrimination and abuse involved in the application
of the emergency powers. The powers would continue until 1946, and
then lapse. However, planning for future emergencies, which had begun
in 1944, would continue for several years to come.

NAZI GERMANY, SPIES AND INTERNEES

A TALE OF GERMAN ESPIONAGE IN WARTIME IRELAND
Mark M. Hull

The much-vaunted German intelligence service, the Abwehr, was interested in Ireland for a variety of purposes: to liaise with the IRA as an adjunct to its larger effort against England; to operate as a weather reporting station; and to exploit the island as a transit point to Great Britain. Public pronouncements fuelled the optimistic German hope that Ireland could be regarded as a 'friendly neutral' whose national policy mandated an even-handed approach to Allies and Axis alike. Thus encouraged, Germany sent several covert missions to Ireland. Their clandestine agents required support networks to operate undetected, and the Abwehr believed that in-place assets – German nationals – might make up for any lack of enthusiasm on the part of the German legation in Dublin.

Part of the difficulty as it applied to local support was that soon after the war started, the bulk of German resources in Ireland were returning to the Fatherland. In an arrangement brokered by the Irish government, British authorities allowed some 50 German nationals, many of whom had ties to the pre-war NSDAP (the Nazi Party) overseas affiliate (the Auslandsorganisation), to leave Ireland on the *Cambria* and, after a brief stop in England, were permitted to continue their journey to Rotterdam, and then home to Germany.[1] While arguably fortunate from the point of view of those passengers, it proved a less than ideal circumstance for German intelligence. In one act, those German nationals most likely to assist covert intelligence missions were removed from play. The few remaining Germans were either ideologically disinterested, unsuitable for one reason or another, or hopelessly out of contact. There were, however, two exceptions.

Johannes 'Juan' Ernstberger
Günther Schütz's landing in March 1941 exposed Irish Military Intelligence (G2) to this degraded network, and the potential for danger if it were allowed to go unchecked. Landing by parachute in Co. Wexford –

quite some distance from his intended drop zone near Naas – Schütz (alias Hans Marschner) set off to meet his local contacts. His mission was of unlimited duration and Schütz was well provided for financially: he had been given £1,000 sterling and $3,200. Unknown to Schütz the English £5 notes were counterfeit, but the £1 notes and the US dollars were genuine. As part of his task, he was to give £300 to Werner Unland in Dublin and £100 to Cork resident 'Juan' Ernstberger, both German nationals who entered Ireland in the pre-war period. Before he could meet either contact, Schütz was arrested by members of the gardaí, a mere 10 hours after his arrival. Throughout his interrogation and subsequent incarceration he maintained he was Hans Marschner from German South West Africa. While examining his possessions, Irish intelligence officials discovered a microphotographic (microdot) list with the names and addresses of Ernstberger and Unland.

Juan – or more accurately, Johannes Paul – Ernstberger was an unusual element in the story. Schütz was supposed to make a payment to him, suggesting that he, like Unland, had a continuing relationship with Abwehr I, the branch of German intelligence responsible for information collection. However, Ernstberger had not been in regular contact for some time, a clear indication that the Abwehr was scraping the bottom of the agent resource barrel.

Born in Freiburg in 1900, Ernstberger emigrated from England to Ireland in 1939, followed by his wife, Hedwiga, on 5 July. He found work at the Sunbeam Wolsey plant in Cork and moved into an apartment at 30 Wellington Road, the contact address provided to Schütz. If Ernstberger sent a change-of-address card to the Abwehr, they did not receive it; in June 1940 – well before Schütz's arrival – he moved to a different address in Cork, before finally relocating to Dublin in 1944. G2 was unaware of Ernstberger's ties to the Abwehr until Schütz was apprehended and his microdot list examined. Consequently, they had not targeted him for ongoing mail or telephone surveillance. The only revealing letter subsequently intercepted was written by Hedwiga Ernstberger in December 1945, well after the end of the war in Europe. Frau Ernstberger reviewed their dismal situation: 'our people in the dock, our Hitler dead ... and the jews [sic] on top again'. Had surveillance been initiated at an earlier point, it might well have revealed something more interesting.[2] After the war, Ernstberger went to work for the Balbriggan Hosiery Company, with no obvious ill-effects from his brush with the German intelligence service. This despite the fact that Col. Dan Bryan (the Irish G2 chief) correctly classified Ernstberger as an '"A-Category" Nazi sympathiser.'[3]

Though Ernstberger's exact role is unknown, in 1941 he clearly had some use to the Abwehr, whether practical or theoretical. The Abwehr anticipated further communication between Ernstberger and Germany, and Schütz was supposed to deliver a new set of coded letter phrases to Ernstberger: 'My dear friend John'; 'How are you?'; 'How is Hedwiga?'; 'Mrs Ottilla is well'; 'The bearer of this letter is a friend'; and 'Compliments of Mother Emma'. Since the two had never met, Schütz was to use a series of agreed-upon recognition phrases on arrival:

> Schütz: 'Kind regards from Charlotte.'
> Ernstberger: 'Is she still in Manchester?'
> Schütz: 'No, she has gone home.'[4]

However, Schütz's interrupted rendezvous with Ernstberger was only half of the story. G2 interrogators asked Schütz about IRA contacts, and told him about both Wilhelm Preetz and Walter Simon, who had also carried transmitters similar to his. This was the first that Schütz had heard of either one of these two earlier agents, an indication of his lack of mission preparation.[5] Having reviewed his personal effects, the officers questioned Schütz about the photograph he held in his wallet. He replied that it was a picture of his Abwehr supervisor at Hamburg, Dr Lorenz (an alias of Hauptmann Schauenburg at Abwehr I). It was, in fact, a passport photograph of Werner Unland, with whom the G2 officers were already acquainted. Further confirmation of the relationship between 'Marschner' (Schütz) and Unland came to light when Dan Bryan noticed that Schütz carried a piece of paper with a lipstick impressed kiss – the same distinctive type that Unland had used in his covert messages to Barcelona. The obvious conclusion was that this was to serve as a recognition sign between the two spies. It was also the first indication that 'Marschner' was an alias for Unland's Barcelona pen-pal, Günther Schütz.[6] Ironically, one reason that Schütz continued to maintain the fiction of being Marschner was to avoid implicating Unland. It did not work; Unland was arrested very soon afterward.

Werner Unland: The Abwehr's Man in Dublin

Werner Unland certainly owed his arrest to Schütz's arrest, but he had attracted the attention of the Irish and English authorities much earlier. In a world infatuated with the idea of the 'master spy' Unland remains very much a humbug, his sole contribution to the German intelligence war being the scale of his fraud. His negligible contribution to the secret war is his only legacy.

Very little is known of Unland's background. He was born in Hamburg on 6 August 1892, and is believed to have served in an Uhlan (German lancers) regiment during the First World War.[7] He arrived in Britain in 1929 and promptly applied for an alien registration certificate; apparently he was there to stay. Prior to his arrival in England, Unland had met an Englishwoman named Muriel Dugarde, and they married in September 1930. Mrs Unland had relatives in Hendon and it was suspected that Unland returned to England to take advantage of this family connection. Mrs Muriel Unland did not work, but had briefly been a child actress at the age of ten, from which position she had acquired skills that would later prove useful.[8] Her husband became a commercial agent for German textile firms and a trader in hardware, ribbon and cotton twine.

He soon became an agent of an altogether different sort. While on a visit to Germany, Hauptmann Dierks of Hamburg Ast section I-M (naval intelligence branch of the Abwehr) recruited Unland for low-grade intelligence work and he was eventually passed over to his controller, Dr Praetorius of section Abwehr I/Wi (economic intelligence). Unland was to report items of interest on industrial or technical matters in exchange for a monthly payment of £25.[9] On his return to England, Unland became the notional manager of an equally notional company by the name of Ferrum Stock Services Ltd, which was registered with British authorities in 1938.[10]

Later investigation established that Ferrum Ltd was a front, and never engaged in commerce of any kind. The physical address of the business was 14 Curistor Street, London, in a room rented from the General Office Agency. Mr E. C. Wheatley, manager of the General Office Agency, remembered Unland well when he was later questioned by the police. Unland insisted that he was of Swedish nationality; Wheatley simply did not believe him. Furthermore, Wheatley remarked upon the lack of business activity from the rented office. In January 1939, Unland visited Hamburg, and eventually received a first payment of £40 from Kol & Co, on the orders of a Mr P. Straaten – identical in both respects to the earlier Abwehr payments made to fellow agent Walter Simon in 1938.

For reasons that are not entirely clear, the Unlands left London suddenly, to arrive in Dublin on 29 August 1939, leaving behind a total of £96.18s.6d in various debts and one step ahead of a worthless cheque charge.[11] Unland had visited Ireland in July, when he opened an account at the Northern Bank, Grafton Street. Returning briefly to England,

Unland told Mr Wheatley that he would be out of town for a short time and asked that any mail for him be forwarded to his home in Hendon. In actuality, this was his mother-in-law's address, and it was soon apparent that the Unlands would not be returning to England voluntarily.

Upon arrival in Dublin, the couple checked into the Royal Marine Hotel, Dun Laoghaire, soon relocating to the Gresham Hotel.[12] The Unlands went to extraordinary lengths to keep their affairs private.[13] While staying at the Gresham, Unland and his wife went house-shopping, approaching Mr Charles Archer about renting a house at 22 Ely Place, Dublin and giving the address of Ferrum Stock Services Ltd as a reference, presuming that Mr Archer would not go to the trouble of checking. He did. When Mr Wheatley in London received the letter addressed to Ferrum Ltd, he opened it; he had not heard from Unland for quite a while and there was back rent outstanding. Wheatley promptly notified the police.

Unland was registered as a German national and his unexplained disappearance at the outbreak of war worried British security officials. Detective Constable Walton arrived at Unland's last known address and happened upon an elderly lady packing boxes. DC Walton learned that he was talking to Mrs Dugarde (Muriel Unland's mother) and that the Unlands had gone away, but their location was unknown. This was ridiculous, since she was obviously packing the Unlands' possessions and had already admitted that she had forwarded mail to them. Mrs Dugarde admitted that she had several letters for their attention yet to post, but these were at her home. She reluctantly agreed to allow DC Walton to see the letters and get the address, but angrily urged that this would be impossible until 5 October. When Walton arrived at Mrs Dugarde's home as arranged, she showed him some mail that had arrived on 4 October, but denied having any other letters. According to DC Walton's report, Mrs Dugarde was 'obviously comfortable about lying to the police'.[14]

With a working address for Unland at the Gresham Hotel, the Metropolitan Police passed the investigation over to the Irish authorities, and the Garda Detective Branch (Special Section) took over the surveillance of Werner and Muriel Unland. The highly effective Detective Sergeant Michael J. Wymes, who was later to become Garda Commissioner, led this division of the Irish police. Wymes' reports, which were both thorough and occasionally humorous, provide a day-by-day record of Unland's activities before his eventual arrest.

Though Unland looked to be every bit the stereotypical rotund, balding civil-servant, his romantic life (in no way confined to his wife) would be the envy of many more physically attractive men. In addition to using the premises of the Northern Bank for his routine monetary transactions, Unland also received personal mail at this address. While much of it consisted of material nominally related to espionage, he also maintained an active correspondence with a number of women overseas. In a letter received during December 1939 at the Northern Bank, a Mrs Anna Hart of the Hague wrote to Unland that 'What I am missing is my big comfortable bed. I am longing for it and other things too. I hope you do the same.'[15] Not put off by the incidental fact that Unland was married – if she knew it – Mrs Hart later added, 'I am only living for the time when we can be together again.'[16] Unland also maintained an equally passionate long-distance relationship with a Fräulein Hildegarde Schlattau.[17]

In April 1940, the Unlands finally moved from the Gresham to a first floor apartment at 46 Merrion Square.[18] The gardaí searched this address in May, but discovered nothing of interest. Following the outbreak of war and the departure of most of Ireland's German community on the Cambria, German agents still in the field went unsupervised, thus no one in authority could properly investigate whether their reports were accurate. Unland used this fact to his short-term advantage. In a real way, he was the German version of Graham Greene's character Jim Wormold in Our Man in Havana and he succeeded in convincing the remote German Intelligence headquarters that he had a fully functional network established in Ireland. Unland's 'network' was fictional and his skill in deception worked not against Germany's enemies, but rather their own war effort. In a broad sense, Unland's messages can be classified into several different categories: whining requests for payment, fictional descriptions of his intelligence contacts and serious efforts to dissuade the Germans from sending more agents to Ireland who would expose his tissue of deception.

Unland's Messages

Beginning in November 1939, Unland was addressing mail to the Dansk Import and Export Co. in Copenhagen, Denmark. This was actually an Abwehr LLD (Live Letter Drop) under the guise of a legitimate business. Unknown to Unland, who took only minimal precautions with security, his correspondence was regularly intercepted, copied by the gardaí and forwarded to Irish Military Intelligence. His first message read: 'Mr Ryan, the buyer from Harland and Wolff, requires your present prices for a re-

peat order of the machine tools delivered earlier this year.' In the language of spycraft, Unland used what is known as a 'jargon code', and this
is somewhat difficult to decipher. The most likely meaning suggests that
someone in Northern Ireland had received a shipment of arms from Germany, but this is not conclusive.[19] In late November, Unland sent a
number of letters to his Danish drop discussing a contract proposal for
Lux and Palmolive toilet soap. He repeatedly used the word 'tablets',
leading Irish Intelligence to suspect that he was actually referring to ammunition. A December letter to the same address, speaking of orders for
'bacon and butter' is equally ambiguous: 'If there are any orders to fill for
your Belgian clients, please let me have the details, as this could be very
well attended to from here.' This too could refer to orders for weapons.
In his letters to Abwehr, Unland repeatedly mentions his 'contacts' in
Northern Ireland and stated that he would be out for several days on
'buying trips' and meeting 'clients'. This no doubt pleased those at headquarters, but they had no idea that during the time in question their agent
never left his apartment at 46 Merrion Square. In an early assessment of
Unland prepared for G2, the gardaí concluded that:

> It would appear that Unland is an elderly pagan, extremely fond of himself,
> who adventured in younger days, but came to live in Ireland mainly to save
> his own skin … He speaks of 'trips' when it is known from Garda reports
> that he has not left his rooms, and 'friends' when from the same source it
> appears that he had no acquaintances whatsoever. He has all the average
> German's contempt for and impatience with Ireland.[20]

Unland continually reminded his masters at Abwehr to forward his
cheques. In the era before direct bank deposits, Unland depended on
these cheques, drawn at a number of banks in different countries, as his
only source of income. His usual monthly 'salary' from Abwehr was
£24.15.10 (posted from both London and Sweden) and on at least one
further occasion, a £40 payment from a Kol & Company in Amsterdam.
In his letter to 'Dansk' in January 1940, Unland mentions that the
'Technical director, of whose arrival I had been advised with your letter
of December 9th, 1939, has not turned up so far'. This could conceivably
be a reference to Ernst Weber-Drohl, who landed in Ireland in February
1940.[21] Unland continues in this same letter to ask that more attention
should be paid to 'remitting my commissions regularly'. Though he complained vociferously, Unland continued to string the Abwehr along with
tales of espionage success: 'Our clients in Northern Ireland are clamour-
ing for the prices for the repeats for the machine tools … I really expect

very good and numerous orders as well as important new business.'[22]

G2 and garda officers were puzzled on a few occasions when Unland made bank deposits in cash seemingly without receiving cheques from abroad. It was suspected, but never established, that he may have been paid by a local source, the German legation at Northumberland Road. Despite their later claims of innocence and a claim Éamon de Valera would support, the German legation was actively involved in supporting espionage operations in Ireland. While German minister, Dr Edouard Hempel, carried this out with very little enthusiasm or competence, he acted as a clearing-house for information passed to Germany, and transmitted Abwehr messages to the agents through his Foreign Ministry communication channels.

Beginning in October 1940, Unland's reports began to refer to the US Head Office. For example, in the letter dated 7 October, he asked: 'Could you please very kindly arrange for our (U.S.) Head Office to accept my bill for November till January 1941?' In another instance he wrote, 'Will you please see to this [payment] for us and cable the (U.S.) Head Office?' Similarly, 'I can always send copies of my letters to the (U.S.) Head Office.' G2 was convinced that 'U.S. Head Office' referred to the German legation in Dublin, 'our friends at H. Office' was the Abwehr Stelle in Hamburg, 'my family' meant the British, and 'contracts' was his jargon code for reports. As an example, Unland wrote on 12 February 1941, that 'Contracts have been sent direct to the H.Q. (in the US) as arranged.' In addition to showing that Unland was very unimaginative in matters of communications security, it points to the participation of the German legation in his activities.

Unland became concerned when in February and March 1940 he began to receive correspondence from his new 'handler', Anderson. Anderson repeatedly invited Unland to a meeting on the continent or, alternatively, suggested sending a representative to Ireland. Unland, no doubt in a panic, responded, 'Owing to local conditions, I do not feel justified to ask for a further increase in the staff, as suggested by you during January/February and early March.' He signed this letter 'Walsh'. In a subsequent exchange of letters, Unland did his best to prevent another agent being sent to examine his operation. However, the Abwehr did send 'a representative from the firm' to see him; the same 'representative', Walter Simon, was arrested before he could make contact.[23]

In June 1940, Unland received a message instructing him to send any future correspondence to Günther Schütz via Barcelona. This relationship was to have unfortunate, unintended consequences for both

Unland and his new Abwehr controller, Schütz.

Unland's movements were closely watched, as were his banking transactions, telephone calls, mail and purchases at local shops. The gardaí were puzzled when the Unlands (both Werner and Muriel) began buying large amounts of nail varnish. A theory since put forward that, as this product contained acetone, it might be used for some kind of secret writing, has never been proven.[24] Unland usually left his apartment only to visit the bank or on shopping trips. He visited the Ulster Bank on O'Connell Street, in particular the floor which contained the offices of M. Devlin and Co. Ltd, and also the Dublin agent for the Leipzig Fair, but no illicit connection to either was ever positively established. Like the senior German agent Hermann Görtz, Unland apparently could not resist the patriotic appeal and took his dirty clothes to the Swastika Laundry.[25] That both Unlands were involved in pseudo-espionage was beyond doubt; they sent letters to themselves on several occasions to discover whether their mail was under surveillance.[26]

Unland's fate was sealed on 13 March 1941 when Günther Schütz arrived by parachute in Ireland. The evidence against Werner Unland was overwhelming: the microdot instructions Schütz carried contained Unland's name and address; Schütz had a sample of the distinctive paper he used in correspondence with Unland in the Barcelona messages; and he carried Unland's passport photograph in his wallet. According to the microdot instructions, Schütz was supposed to give Unland $300 in six monthly instalments, as well as a new recognition code. It is assumed that Schütz was sent on the mission to Ireland specifically because of his earlier contact with Unland. This indicates that the Abwehr mistakenly (and foolishly) trusted Unland's fiction regarding the Irish spy network.

Unland was arrested on 21 April 1941 in Clare Street, Dublin while walking with his wife. She returned to the apartment with two detectives, who executed a search warrant. They seized a briefcase with miscellaneous correspondence, a portable typewriter, papers relating to the Northern Bank account, as well as the book *Secrets of German Espionage* by Bernard Newman, which dealt with codes, ciphers and communications.[27] Detective Sergeant Wymes interrogated Mrs Unland, but she revealed very little. She was described as 'a shrewd type of person who was evidently prepared for questioning, and she was none too candid in her replies to questions'. Muriel said her husband was an agent for textile goods or firms (this conflicted with his own account to the detectives of being a shoe importer), and admitted sending letters to her husband addressed to 'Unland c/o National Tourist Bureau'. Mrs Unland's purse was searched, revealing a receipt for £170 in jewellery from Messrs West and Co., Grafton Street and cash to the amount of £60 in English £5 notes and two Irish £5 notes. Several of the Bank of England bills had sequential serial numbers.[28]

Unland himself was circumspect when questioned by the gardaí. He admitted writing the Dansk letters and those to Schütz – a minor confession since a forensic analysis of the typewriter had already matched his machine to the notes. When questioned about his curious financial transactions, he would only reply that both he and his wife brought money from England, but that neither had any idea how much the other had. Unland's responses to any other questions consisted of only three answers: 'It's a rather sad story for me'; 'I wouldn't be surprised'; 'Everybody has his duty to do'. He maintained that the letters to Schütz were an attempt to get orders to and from the Dana Shoe Company of Copenhagen (which, he said, also had an office in New York), apparently unaware that the Irish had previously checked and discovered that there was no Dana Shoe Company of Copenhagen.[29] Unland's cover story was unravelling.

He was eventually transferred to Arbour Hill prison and then to Athlone. Irish authorities decided not to intern Mrs Unland, though evidence strongly indicated that she had aided and abetted her husband's espionage activities. When Mrs Unland was allowed to visit her husband at Arbour Hill, it was almost as if the two had rehearsed the scene. She seemed bewildered by his arrest, and he explained that another person had entered Ireland illegally, coincidentally possessing Unland's passport photograph. Unland told his wife that he had no idea how this situation had occurred and asked Muriel to contact the German legation, which she did.[30]

Interned along with other equally unsuccessful German agents, Unland became the spokesman for the other prisoners. This is thought to be due to his service in the First World War, which made him the only prisoner with prior commissioned military experience before Hermann Görtz's capture in November 1941. Mrs Unland frequently complained to the German legation, demanding a £30 monthly allowance while her husband was interned. Having sought approval from the Foreign Ministry, Dr Hempel agreed.[31] Unland caused no trouble in captivity, and sat out the war with patience. At war's end, he was paroled along with the other prisoners, most awaiting deportation.

The publication of an article in the *Daily Mail* on 15 April 1947 caused Unland (who was still on parole) to emerge from his cocoon.

Under the headline 'Deportation by Air Order – De Valera Rounds Up German Spies – Court Writs Due Today', the paper told the story of the remaining German agents being prepared for transfer back to Germany. Both Görtz and Unland, jointly represented by Counsel John A. Costello, filed suit against the Daily Mail and its correspondent John Murdoch, claiming libel.[32] Their objection was to the word 'spy' in the headline and the suggestion that they were Nazis. In his complaint, which was immediately reported by the press, Unland lied: 'I have never at any time directly or indirectly associated with espionage. I have never been associated with any Nazi organisation either in this country or else-where.'[33]

Though G2 could certainly prove otherwise, it was difficult for the Daily Mail to obtain the hard evidence showing that Unland was an active enemy agent, if indeed the adjective 'active' could be applied to Unland in any sense. Görtz returned to his usual refrain that he was not a spy, but rather a military officer on a legitimate mission – despite the fact that he had operated in a neutral country without the benefit of his uniform. He committed suicide in 1947. Unland's claim was eventually settled out of court for an unspecified amount of damages. In its story covering the settlement, the Evening Herald mentioned that Unland was in a commercial partnership with a former Irish army officer from Internment Camp No. 3, Captain J. Kirby.[34] This was said to be an import/export business based in Dublin and one story had them selling women's scarves, among other things.[35] Bygones apparently were bygones. Werner Unland died in Dublin on 20 August 1962 from a heart attack, at the age of 70.[36]

The Ernstberger and Unland episodes permit a glimpse into the unofficial support network of German nationals available to Abwehr agents operating in Ireland. The available material on Ernstberger is too sketchy to draw any conclusions on his activities prior to 1941; he may or may not have been of previous service to the Abwehr. Unland's case is strikingly different and he exemplifies the old adage that a friend can sometimes be the worst enemy. The damage he did was purely against his own side, not from any ideological motive, but rather from his venal ability to perpetuate a fraud for personal gain.

The Abwehr's lack of information about their local assets is telling, and indicative of a larger problem in the organisation itself. Ireland is geographically close enough to Germany that they should have, at the very least, known the status of their own personnel, particularly in the pre-war period when travel was relatively easy and before G2 was able to muster the considerable powers of surveillance available to them once war began. This type of positive check is basic to any intelligence service, yet seems to have been woefully neglected by both the pre-war and wartime Abwehr. The results were predictable: espionage operations were doomed to failure because the Germans failed to take even elementary steps to ensure a minimum level of success. This effectively threw the agents to the winds of chance, a dangerous prospect, considering the low quality of personnel deployed on the missions. The combination of poor agent selection, lack of local knowledge and a non-functioning support system made attainment of even minimal goals impossible. By contrast, Britain and Ireland's highly efficient counter-espionage organisations helped make this into one of the greatest mismatches in espionage history – a happy result in the larger war against Hitler's Germany.

BERLIN'S IRISH RADIO WAR
David O'Donoghue

From December 1939 to May 1945, Nazi Germany's external radio services adopted a 'friendly neighbour' approach to listeners in neutral Ireland. The public broadcasts, however, managed to conceal the harsher
reality of the régime's attitude, which included dropping agents on Irish
soil, attempting to use IRA leaders to foment rebellion and drawing up
a plan to invade Ireland.

In December 1939, some three months after the outbreak of the
Second World War, Irish army officers at McKee Barracks in Dublin were
puzzled when their monitors tuned into a fluent Irish speaker on Radio
Berlin. At first they thought it was a pirate broadcast by the IRA some-
where in the Dublin area, or perhaps a practical joke. At that time, the
only broadcasts being made in Irish were by the state broadcaster Radio
Éireann, an illegal IRA transmitter and the BBC's Scottish service which
made a few short broadcasts every week in Scots Gaelic.

Despite their puzzlement, it did not take too long for the army to
identify the mystery speaker. At the outbreak of the emergency in Ireland, the army had taken the precaution of drafting in a number of lin-
guistic experts to help monitor foreign broadcasts, translate foreign propaganda material and even – later in the war – to assist in interrogating
German spies in Athlone Barracks and stranded Luftwaffe and Kriegs-
marine personnel in the Curragh camp. Among the foreign language experts was a young University College Cork (UCC) teacher from Cobh
called Joe Healy. Listening to the 10 December broadcast (made from a
studio in Berlin but via the Hamburg and Bremen transmitters), Healy
immediately recognised the voice as that of Professor Ludwig Mühlhaus-
en who was professor of Celtic Studies at Hamburg University. Both
men knew each other well as Mühlhausen had stayed with Healy's parents in Cobh in the late-1920s on his way to study Irish on the Blasket
Islands off Kerry. Healy had, in turn, stayed with the Mühlhausen family
in Hamburg when studying German there. Healy must have been taken

aback to hear the distinguished German scholar broadcasting Nazi propaganda in Irish, particularly as the Cork man had been instrumental in helping him to learn the language. Healy wrote the following report for his army employers:

> In good Irish, a mixture of Kerry and Western dialects, Mühlhausen said it was a pleasure to talk over the air to his Irish friends, imagining himself seated 'cois na tine agus boladh na móna im' shrón' [by the fire and the smell of the turf in my nose]. He characterised as lies, statements about the persecution by the Germans of Czechoslovakian and Polish Catholics, and reminded his listeners of the atrocities committed in Ireland by the Black and Tans and the Auxiliaries – 'Is cuimhin libh fiche bliain ó shin na Black and Tans' [You remember the Black and Tans 20 years ago].[1]

From the end of 1939 to mid-1940, the total of Berlin Radio's output to neutral Ireland was a 15-minute talk each Sunday night by Professor Mühlhausen. In 1940, the German professor was joined on air by his 29-year-old protégé, Dr Hans Hartmann, who also broadcast a 15-minute talk, but on Wednesday nights. Before the war, both men had studied Irish in the Gaeltacht regions. Mühlhausen, as we have seen, began his studies in 1927 in Kerry, and also visited Connemara in 1934, as well as spending six weeks in Teelin, south-west Donegal in the autumn of 1937. Hartmann came to Ireland as an exchange student in 1937 and worked for a while at the National Museum in Dublin before switching to the Folklore Department in University College Dublin's (UCD) Earlsfort Terrace campus. Hartmann studied Irish mainly in Connemara but also briefly studied the Donegal dialect in Bunbeg.

It is perhaps pertinent to ask why the German Radio service bothered to use its scarce resources in the midst of a war economy on broadcasting Irish language talks. The answer would appear to be that it was the result of German thoroughness rather than a specific intent to target Ireland *per se*. Hitler's propaganda minister, Joseph Goebbels, considered radio to be the most useful means of spreading the Nazi doctrine to mass audiences both domestically and abroad. Newspapers and cinema newsreels were the poor relations of radio, according to Goebbels, who had suspended closed-circuit television transmissions after the 1936 Berlin Olympics (the British also ceased transmitting television programmes during the war). Radio was used to maximum effect and programme output was tailored for specific audiences. Thus, the Deutschlandsender (Germany's domestic radio service) carried more anti-Semitic material than German Radio's foreign services. American listeners to German shortwave radio transmissions could sing along with Charlie's jazz band while jazz was strictly *verboten* [prohibited] on German Radio. Later in the war, listeners to German Radio's Irish service were regaled by traditional jigs and reels, as well as classic recordings by Count John McCormack, while McCormack himself was performing live concerts for Allied troops.

In the course of the war, Radio Berlin broadcast in no less than 54 languages, 9 more than the BBC could manage.[2] It was not so much that Nazi Germany was wooing Ireland – Hitler wanted Éire to remain neutral, as it meant one less battlefield to worry about – but, in fact, German Radio's overseas services broadcast in almost every language, ranging from Irish and Icelandic, through to Hindustani and Latvian. The Germans were very keen to support discontented groups within nation states, such as the Flemish in Belgium, and Scottish and Welsh nationalists in Britain. They also lent support to other nationalists fighting for independence from Britain, such as the Indians and South African Boers. In this respect, the IRA was a natural ally of Nazi Germany and, thus, IRA actions against the security forces in Northern Ireland were praised on Berlin radio. The execution of IRA prisoners in Northern Ireland was always criticised on German Radio, yet the Berlin broadcasters maintained a guarded silence whenever IRA men were executed in Éire. This seemingly contradictory position reflected Nazi Germany's deliberate policy of not publicly interfering in Ireland's domestic political affairs. (As we will see later, the German Radio service did attempt to interfere in the 1943 Irish general election, although not without provoking a formal diplomatic protest.)

In neutral Ireland's case, the Germans were pitching their message, *as Gaeilge*, to what they perceived to be a strongly nationalistic – and thus, anti British – audience. The staple radio diet was praise for Hitler and the achievements of Nazi Germany, triumphant military dispatches, anti-British invective and praise, too, for Ireland's historic struggle against England. The implication was that Irish unity could result from a German victory. In targeting Irish speakers, however, German Radio used valuable broadcasting resources to reach a negligible audience. The weakness of this policy can be seen from the fact that there were fewer radio sets in the Gaeltacht than anywhere else in the country. There were approximately 180,000 licensed radio sets in wartime Ireland (the number of unlicensed sets is unknown) but only one in every 32 people in Kerry, for example, had a set. The figures for Galway were one in 30, and Donegal, one in 26. This compared poorly to Dublin where one in 9 people had a radio.[3]

It would therefore appear that during the 1939–41 period Nazi radio propaganda was not reaching a mass audience in Ireland. Nevertheless, German Radio's Irish service had the ear of government ministers, including Éamon de Valera, who were circulated with transcripts of the more important broadcasts by the Irish army's monitoring section. The BBC also had a monitoring service whose transcripts of Irish interest were sent to the Northern Ireland cabinet office at Stormont.

By 1941, Goebbels realised his message was not getting through in Irish. By then, however, it was almost too late for the propaganda minister to improve the situation as his arch-rival in the Nazi hierarchy, foreign minister, Joachim von Ribbentrop, wanted to take over the service himself. By the end of 1941, Ribbentrop's Irish expert, Adolf Mahr (an Austrian Nazi who had worked in Dublin before the war as director of the National Museum in Kildare Street) had sacked Professor Mühlhausen and installed Dr Hans Hartmann as head of a new, revamped nightly English-language radio service for Irish listeners. From then until the end of the war, the role of Irish on the radio service was scaled down, with Hartmann alone providing talks, news bulletins and extracts from Wolfe Tone's diaries in Irish, while the rest of his staff spoke only in English.

Although broadcast nightly from late 1941 to the spring of 1945, it is doubtful if Hartmann's programmes had any great effect in Ireland; as the war progressed, listeners were tuning to the BBC and Radio Éireann in greater numbers as it became clear that the Allies would win. A flaw in Hartmann's service was its excessive reliance on historical themes such as British atrocities in the Irish War of Independence. The overall, and unavoidable, impression was of a radio service whose historical perspective was frozen in a time warp. It was as if Ireland had never successfully negotiated independence from Britain in 1921, as if the Civil War of 1922–23 had never happened, and as if de Valera had never led the majority of anti-Treaty men into mainstream politics in 1926. As far as German Radio's Irish service was concerned, Ireland was still engaged in a life-or-death struggle against British imperialism and plutocracy. Ireland's saviour in this fiction was, of course, Hitler's Germany.

Nonetheless, the German Radio bosses continued to broadcast to Ireland in the hope of reaching the hearts and minds of a people they considered anti-British and who, therefore, could be attracted to the idea of a German military victory. While much of what German Radio broadcast to neutral Ireland during the Second World War broadly followed the general thrust of Nazi propaganda for other neutral states, in

some respects the Irish style was subtly different, adopting a more per-
sonalised, and less warlike approach to radio listeners in the 26-counties.
For example, Ludwig Mühlhausen had a habit of sending greetings over
the airwaves to his friends in Ireland and on one occasion read out the
exam results of one of his Irish students at Hamburg University; Séamus
'Kruger' Kavanagh had returned home to Kerry just in time to avoid the
outbreak of war in 1939. In the run up to Christmas 1939, Mühlhausen
broadcast seasonal greetings to a Donegal teacher, Seán Ó hEochaidh,
who had helped the German professor to learn the south-west Donegal
Irish dialect on a visit to Teelin in 1937. The morning after the broadcast, Garda Special Branch officers swooped on Ó hEochaidh's bedroom,
demanding to know the nature of his relationship with the German.
The Donegal man recalled years later: 'When Mühlhausen named me
on the radio the gardaí thought I was some sort of fifth columnist, which
I was not.'[4]

During 1940, Mühlhausen rejoiced in Luftwaffe raids on English
factories and other enemy targets, assuring his Irish listeners that England would soon surrender. But the Nazi bosses at the Rundfunkhaus
(radio centre) in Berlin were – no less than Dr Goebbels – tiring of Mühlhausen's ranting in Irish. They guessed, rightly, that his talks were having a negative effect in Ireland. In fact, students at University College
Galway pilloried the German professor. One such student, Seán Mac
Reamoinn (who became head of RTÉ radio in the 1960s) recalled sending up the German professor during UCG's annual rag week, nicknam-
ing him 'Dr Fool-hausen'. The only reason the students heard the German at all was that his talks piggybacked onto the end of Sunday night
'Views on the News' broadcast by William Joyce (Lord Haw Haw), which
was very popular among west of Ireland listeners. Joyce had spent most
of his youth in Galway and studied under the Jesuits at St Ignatius College. According to a 1940 BBC survey, Joyce's talks were attracting
15.7% of English listeners, and a similar figure in Ireland (this would
amount to an Irish audience of approximately 60,000).[5]

Mühlhausen's talks failed to enjoy popularity elsewhere in the country. The historian and biographer, Seán Ó Lúing, remembered:

> hearing one of the first Mühlhausen broadcasts at the end of 1939 while in
> the house of a neighbour, Pádraig Búlaeir, at Gortmore, Ballyferriter in the
> Kerry Gaeltacht. The young people of the parish held card sessions there.
> The radio was turned on in anticipation, and the young people, all locals
> who would enjoy the English-language broadcasts of Lord Haw Haw, ex-
> pected something in the same style. We were all disappointed. Mühlhausen

was anything but an effective speaker. He was laborious, ineffective, with a slow and poor delivery of words, giving out official German propaganda. He was dreary. After a few minutes, interest vanished and someone said, 'Sea, roinn amach na cártaí' [Right, deal out the cards].[6]

Unfortunately for Professor Mühlhausen, his paymasters in Berlin were even less enamoured of his radio talks than were the listeners in Galway and Kerry. Plans were afoot to revamp the programmes to Ireland and the professor – who had ruthlessly used his membership of the Nazi party to further his academic career – was packed off to join an SS unit working with Breton nationalists in occupied France. His assistant, Hans Hartmann, took over as head of a new nightly service at the end of 1941. The test transmissions for the new service had begun some months earlier, on 26 August 1941, using the powerful Zeesen transmitter in Berlin.[7]

The radio audience in Ireland was unaware of a major internal feud going on between Dr Goebbels' propaganda ministry and Joachim von Ribbentrop's Foreign Office, for control of the Irish service, or Irland-Redaktion as it was known in German. Both men wanted the Irish service as part of their respective media empires. To complicate the power struggle, the head of German Radio's foreign services, Dr Toni Winkelnkemper, was an SS officer. He presided over the daily radio managers' conferences (at which Goebbels' broadcasting directives were handed down), dressed in full SS uniform, while his employees, subordinates such as Dr Hartmann, wore civilian attire.

For a brief period of five months, from June to October 1941, Goebbels had the upper hand and appointed his nominee, Wolfgang Dignowity – a 28-year-old journalism graduate from Chemnitz – as head of the Irish service. The only drawback was that Dignowity had never been to Ireland and knew little or nothing about the country. In fact, Dignowity recruited his 'Irish' team in Paris. They included: a Breton aristocrat, Count Alain Keroer; another Frenchman, Jacques Piche, who had worked as a journalist in America; a Russian woman, Sonja Kowanka, whose family had fled the 1917 Bolshevik revolution; and a Scotsman, James Blair (whose mother was Irish) who had been working as a Paris-based stringer for some American newspapers.

The only genuine Irishman on Dignowity's team was John O'Reilly who joined the radio service in September 1941. Born in Kerry in 1916, O'Reilly grew up in Kilkee, Co. Clare. He arrived in Berlin having been recruited by the Germans when they invaded the Channel Islands. Before joining the radio service, O'Reilly had managed to recruit over 70 Irish navvies on the Channel Islands to work at a German armaments factory in Watenstedt. Jack O'Reilly, later described as a 'wild boy' by Irish military intelligence (G2), was something of an enigma in wartime Germany. His prime motivation for aiding the Germans appears to have been financial. There was an delicious irony in the fact that his Royal Irish Constabulary (RIC) sergeant father, Bernard, had arrested Sir Roger Casement in Kerry just days before the 1916 Easter Rising. Thus, what the father had achieved in thwarting German plans to assist Ireland at that crucial juncture in its history, the son would attempt to counteract, aboard a Luftwaffe bomber over neutral Co. Clare some 27 years later.

Wolfgang Dignowity's non-Irish team was not destined to last very long at the Berlin radio centre. Ribbentrop had his eye on the Irish service and sent one of his top Irish experts, Dr Adolf Mahr, to unseat Dignowity. Mahr, an Austrian Nazi, was on leave of absence from his job as director of the National Museum in Dublin, and was acquainted with Ribbentrop whom he had met on a number of occasions when the latter was German ambassador to London from 1936 to 1938. On 12 May 1936, Mahr had accompanied Ribbentrop to the coronation of King George VI in London, where the Austrian represented the Ortsgruppe or Irish branch of the Nationalsozialistische Deutsche Arbeiterpartei or National Socialist German Worker's party (NSDAP). Mahr left Dublin in July 1939 with his wife and four children to holiday in the Austrian Tyrol.[8] In August 1939 he went to Berlin as the official Irish delegate to the sixth international congress of archaeology. The congress ended a week before the outbreak of war, but Mahr remained on because he was scheduled to attend the annual Nazi party rally at Nuremberg in September (the rally never took place, being cancelled on the outbreak of war).

In wartime Berlin, Mahr drew up a damning report on the ineffectiveness of the Irish service, on foot of which Dignowity and the two French men, Piche and Keroer, were sacked. Mahr also produced a 15-page blueprint to revamp the Irish radio unit, turning it into a nightly bilingual service in Irish and English (at its height, from 1942 to 1943, the Irland-Redaktion was on air for three 20-minute segments every night of the week). The use of Irish was reduced on Mahr's radio service from 1942 to 1945. In his report for Ribbentrop, Mahr noted that:

> approximately 5% of the population of Éire speaks Irish (Gaelic) as their native tongue. They like to listen to the Gaelic language programmes from Germany (it flatters their linguistic identity), but as an important language in the political sense Gaelic is not relevant. The only native Irish speakers

live in the West and are mostly small farmers. Gaelic broadcasts from the
Continent [i.e. Germany] can hardly be received by them.

The only reason for carrying Irish-language radio material at all, according to Mahr, was to reach

> a politically much more important element, namely language enthusiasts
> amongst the educated sections of society throughout the whole country,
> who initially had to learn the Gaelic language. In Gaelic language policy,
> which they defend with all their might, they see a nationalist political fac-
> tor of the first order, and the Gaelic broadcasts from Germany naturally
> have a very positive effect on them. These must therefore be maintained.

While grudgingly accepting that some Irish-language material would
have to be carried on the revamped radio service to Ireland, Mahr was
adamant that a strong English-language content was required, too, in
order to target a wider audience, including 'the older generation of nationalists who were unable to learn Gaelic', 'nationalists in Northern
Ireland', 'emigrants' and the 'approximately 10 million people with an
Irish ethnic identity, of whom 99% speak English as their mother tongue
and who play an important, often highly important, part in all Anglo-
Saxon countries'.[9] Mahr's report was accepted in full by Ribbentrop at a
top level Foreign Office meeting in Berlin on 22 May 1941. It concluded
that 'the overthrow of British imperialism ... will bring with it Ireland's
reunification'. Mahr's rhetoric appealed to Ribbentrop who at the same
time, but through diplomatic channels, was trying to impress upon the
Dublin government that post-war Irish unification was likely in the event
of a German victory.[10] With German Foreign Office backing, Mahr then
set about establishing his Irish radio service in Berlin. He appointed
Hans Hartmann as the new head of the service, while Kowanka, Blair
and O'Reilly were kept on. Mahr also transferred his Foreign Office
assistant, Hilde Spickernagel, to the radio centre where she worked as a
secretary-typist and occasionally read out news bulletins.

Hartmann was intent on presenting a friendly German face to neutral Ireland, and his programmes were interspersed with Irish traditional
music and songs by John McCormack. After the German invasion of
Russia, on 22 June 1941, Hartmann's team began broadcasting anti-
Soviet propaganda emphasising the communist threat to Ireland's Catholic way of life. Hartmann himself exhorted his listeners to *Coinnígí
bhur neodracht* (Keep your neutrality) and kept stressing the importance
of Ireland remaining out of the war. In later years, he explained his radio

talks were based on the fact that Irish neutrality 'was a part of the [German] war aims'. He added:

> One can start from the assumption that Hitler did not actually want to attack England. He favoured a solution, or a distribution of the world, leaving the east to him and the seas and the west to England and America. Then, when de Valera declared his neutrality, Hitler said to himself that that was the best thing for him, too. He really wanted to respect Ireland's neutrality if Ireland was not foolish enough to make some move to make that difficult for him; to force him into another attitude. Irish neutrality was really one of the objectives which was in conformity with German policies.[11]

Hartmann's post-war explanation of his pro-neutrality line echoed one of his first wartime broadcasts as head of the Irland-Redaktion. On 28 December 1941, he stated:

> Ireland stands alone in the midst of great nations who are engaged in war to the bitter end and it might appear that she will never be able to maintain her neutrality, especially as the USA, on whom she placed all her hopes, is participating in the war ... [however] the fine edifice of the republic would collapse immediately if the Irish government did not succeed in avoiding war and maintaining neutrality. In addition, it is likely that in such a case the war would be fought on Irish soil despite the long-standing friendship between Germany and Ireland. This means that there is no other course open to the Irish people, if they have sense and do not wish to commit suicide, but to defend their neutrality at any cost.

In a chilling footnote to his broadcast, Dr Hartmann concluded: 'I should not like to see Ireland completely destroyed and to see everything achieved after the last war brought to nothing again. The greatest vigilance is called for. God bless and save Ireland.'[12] The implied threat of German military intervention, in the event of Ireland abandoning its neutral stance, was less than subtle.

Apart from Hartmann's Irish language talks, there was little about the Irland-Redaktion that could be called Irish. As we have seen, the only Irish member of the radio unit at this time was John O'Reilly. Behind the scenes, however, O'Reilly was enjoying less than cordial relations with his employer, Dr Hartmann. Both men were involved in fierce rows over what should and should not be broadcast to Ireland. Hartmann wanted the Kilkee man to read extracts from Wolfe Tone's diaries but O'Reilly claimed that such material would be of no interest to Irish listeners. O'Reilly was ordered to carry on reading the extracts in English, while Hartmann also read them in Irish. As with most things relating to Irland-Redaktion, however, the real reasons lay deeper.[13]

After a year working at the Rundfunkhaus, O'Reilly decided to leave because he was frustrated. Initially, Hartmann tried to prevent him leaving, but later relented on condition that O'Reilly find a suitable Irish replacement for the broadcasting work. O'Reilly chose his friend, Liam Mullally, who had been teaching English in a Berlitz language school in Berlin. By September 1942, he could see that Hitler's Russian campaign was no blitzkrieg, as the 1940 invasion of the Netherlands, Belgium, Luxembourg and France had been, and so he duped the Germans into sending him home to Ireland on a spying mission. According to his post-war memoirs, O'Reilly had to make two attempts to convince the Germans to send him home.[14] On 17 September 1942, he began training in Bremen with German naval intelligence for a spying mission to Ireland (the plan was to drop O'Reilly by U-boat off the Clare coast) but the plan was dropped in January 1943. O'Reilly later claimed the mission was cancelled lest it 'jeopardise Ireland's neutrality'. He was finally repatriated on 16 December 1943 as part of another mission sponsored by the SS-controlled Sicherheitdienst (security service) or SD. This mission also included another Irishman recruited by the Germans, Dubliner John Kenny, who landed by parachute three days after O'Reilly. The two Irish parachutists were the last agents to be sent to Ireland by Nazi Germany during the war.[15]

O'Reilly was arrested soon after landing by parachute near Kilkee in December 1943, which suggests that G2 knew in advance of Jack O'Reilly's journey homewards. In fact, G2 had close contacts with the British security service, MI5, whose senior officer Guy Liddell occasionally dined at the Shelbourne Hotel with the head of G2, Col. Dan Bryan. MI5, in turn, was being tipped off from the head of German counterintelligence, Admiral Wilhelm Canaris, who was executed for treason by the Nazis shortly before the end of the war. The spy from west Clare spent the rest of the war in Dublin's Arbour Hill prison, apart from a brief period of freedom in 1944 when he escaped and returned to the family home at St Brendan's Villas in Kilkee. There he was rearrested but Jack's father, Bernard, the shrewd ex-RIC sergeant, claimed the £500 reward money (about €50,000 in today's values) for handing over his son to the authorities.[16]

In Berlin, Hartmann was having more success with the Irish writer and republican activist, Francis Stuart. In 1942, both men were working as lecturers at Berlin University and the German had little trouble in persuading his colleague to contribute a weekly talk to Ireland, entitled

'Through Irish Eyes'. At around the same time, Hartmann also hired an Indian-born Briton, Mrs Susan Hilton, who broadcast under her maiden name of Sweney. Her brother Edward Sweney, who lived at Oldcastle, Co. Meath, was convinced that she had been coerced into doing propaganda work as the alternative was incarceration in a camp. In fact, Edward Sweney's assumption was correct. Susan Hilton had originally arrived in occupied France in 1940 as a prisoner of the Germans (she had been taken prisoner in the Indian Ocean after her passenger ship, *Kemmendine*, bound for Rangoon from Glasgow, was captured by the German raider *Atlantis*). After a period of incarceration in the occupied French port of Royan, Hilton was offered her freedom on condition she engaged in propaganda work for the Germans in Paris. In the course of the war she wrote a book on her maritime adventures, as well as writing pamphlets and broadcasting on the Irland-Redaktion. In 1944, however, having tried to escape from the Third Reich while on a trip to Vienna, she was locked up in Liebenau internment camp. Despite suffering from malnutrition, Susan Hilton managed to survive the war but was sentenced to 18 months in Holloway Prison in London in 1946, on charges of assisting the enemy. The court was not told that she had been found in a German camp at the end of the war. Mrs Hilton was considered an enemy agent both by Nazi Germany and Britain, which – for someone who had arrived on the continent as a prisoner of the Germans – was a rare, if unfortunate, achievement.[17]

Francis Stuart's first talk on German Radio was broadcast to Ireland on St Patrick's Day, 1942. He stuck close to Hartmann's propaganda line, criticising the recent arrival of US troops in Northern Ireland and supporting Irish neutrality: 'What a blessing it is that we are celebrating this day at peace, not having escaped war by dishonourable and cowardly means, but by refusing, as far as lay within our power, to waver from a strict and fearless neutrality.'[18]

In line with the Nazi hierarchy's directives, Stuart supported de Valera's neutrality policy, but he was less inclined to support Dev in the run up to the general election of 22 June 1943. The dissolution of the Dáil sparked a number of election broadcasts by Stuart who advised Irish voters to ignore the mainstream parties and vote for extreme republican candidates. While the Irish leader had maintained silence in the face of the German Radio broadcasts until then (even, at one stage, telling the Dáil that he personally knew nothing of their content), Stuart's advice to Irish voters proved to be more than de Valera could take. He dispatched his *chargé d'affaires* in Berlin, William Warnock, to the German

Foreign Office to lodge a formal protest about this 'unwarrantable inter-ference in our internal affairs'.[19] The Germans took de Valera's point (that the broadcasts were compromising his neutral position), and the formal complaint put an end to Stuart's election broadcasts. In any case, de Valera won the election.

It is worth noting that Stuart occasionally consulted his friend Frank Ryan on the content of his talks. The two men met socially for lunch in wartime Berlin – Ryan was accorded generous food coupons in line with his status as a special guest of the Nazi State – and even attended nightclubs with senior Nazi Party figures.[20] Both men agreed that the broadcasts should support Irish neutrality and should not be critical of the Soviet Union. Ryan, a senior IRA figure, lived in Nazi Germany – under the cover name of Frank Richards – from the time he was released from Burgos prison in Northern Spain in the summer of 1940 (where he had been incarcerated having fought for the Interna-tional Brigade in the Spanish Civil War), until his death from tuber-culosis in a Dresden sanatorium on 10 June 1944. The Germans had tried to land Ryan and IRA leader Seán Russell from a U-boat on the Dingle peninsula in Kerry in August 1940, but the plan was dropped when Russell died of a perforated ulcer aboard the vessel, and Ryan re-turned to Berlin.

Francis Stuart had an unfortunate, albeit deliberate, ability to pro-voke controversy on the airwaves. For example, on 15 May 1943 he urged Northern-Irish-born members of the British army to mutiny and join the German or Italian forces. Stuart commented:

> If the worst should come to the worst and any of you be conscripted and be sent to one of the battlefields, you have only to wait for a suitable opportu-nity and go over to the Germans. That has been proved to be not a very difficult thing to do in the latest form of warfare where there are no very determined lines and where there is rapid movement. As I say, you have simply to submit to the training and all the rest and wait patiently until you are actually at the front and then – having arranged a suitable plan among your fellows, even if you happen to be only two or three who will probably be split up among different regiments – you can go over to the Germans or to the Italians as the case may be, and I can promise you that you will be received as friends and well treated as soon as you've explained who you are. For the case of the Six Counties is well known here in Germany.[21]

Apart from its deliberately naïve advice which could have cost lives, this broadcast was also fraught with danger for Stuart himself since he could have been hanged for treason for it after the war on the basis of his Australian birth, Northern Irish parentage and Co. Antrim upbringing. Luckily for him, however, while the BBC monitored the 'mutiny' talk they did not identify Stuart as the speaker (although the Irish army monitors did). Long after the war, Stuart admitted to me that he had taken a major risk in making the 'mutiny' broadcast. But he had also made sure that at the end of the war he would be eventually captured in an occupied zone of southern Germany, close to the Swiss frontier, that was controlled by French troops, not British ones, to avoid the possibility of lengthy imprisonment or execution. In the event, the British did come looking for a traitor at the Dornbirn internment camp, but Stuart was not their quarry. They were seeking another enemy broadcaster, Norman Baillie-Stewart, who was later imprisoned for treason.

With the tide of war going against Nazi Germany, time was now running out for Hartmann's beleaguered radio team. As the Allies increased their bombing raids on Berlin, it was decided to move staff from the Rundfunkhaus to the more secure surroundings of the Radio Luxembourg studios in August 1943. In January 1944, Stuart left the radio team in protest at increasing pressure to broadcast anti-Soviet propaganda (he secretly admired Stalin and at one stage, prior to Operation Barbarossa on 22 June 1941, had tried to get a teaching job in Moscow). After the war, Stuart made it clear that he had refused to take an anti-Soviet position on German Radio:

> because of all countries waging war … the only one which was waging what one might call a really honourable war were the Russians. They had been attacked in an extremely vicious and underhand way. They were protecting their country. They weren't carrying out devastating bombing on civilians such as the Germans and the Allies were.[22]

Stuart's remarks in this context could well be regarded as disingenuous because, by this stage of the war, he had willingly worked with Irland-Redaktion for almost two years, and at a time when Germany and the Soviet Union were at war. A year earlier, he had had even praised the German army's 'triumph of flesh and blood' at Stalingrad. Thus, along with his other radio colleagues, Stuart had obeyed Goebbels' media directive to depict one of the greatest military defeats in history as a success.

In a number of post-war interviews, Stuart defended his sojourn activities in wartime Berlin as enabling him to develop as a writer, but it was an argument his critics refused to accept. However, in at least one interview Stuart recognised that in some respects he had erred in working for the Nazi régime:

I felt I was too closely involved with a brutal and barbarian [sic] regime for
my own good or for my own liking ... I went to Germany under a misappre-
hension of course ... I thought Hitler would have been some sort of international revolutionary destroying the whole system, which I soon found he
was far from.[23]

The D-Day landings, on 6 June 1944, heralded major Allied advances
on mainland Europe. In September that year, Hartmann's radio staff
were forced to move to the small town of Apen in north-west Germany.
From Bremer's Hotel they continued to put out programmes to Ireland,
with Hartmann even managing a special St Patrick's Day programme on
17 March 1945. By the end of April, American troops were patrolling
the countryside around Apen, yet Hartmann still managed to continue
broadcasting programmes to Ireland against all the odds. His last broadcast (before fleeing on a bicycle to a relative's farm at nearby Wester-
stede) went out on 2 May 1945 and included a news bulletin in Irish.
After that, there was only time for one more recording – John McCormack singing 'Come Back to Erin'. It was the swansong for a very unusual radio service.[24]

GUESTS OF THE STATE
T. Ryle Dwyer

Within minutes of Britain's declaration of war on 3 September 1939, the Irish were faced with the thorny problem of how to treat belligerent servicemen when two Royal Air Force (RAF) seaplanes set down in Irish waters. They had been flying from Pembroke to Stranraer when they became separated. One of them set down in Dun Laoghaire harbour at about 11.30 a.m., while the other landed north of the city off the seaside village of Skerries. The pilot of the second aircraft, Squadron Leader M. C. Collins, went ashore and made some telephone calls from the garda station at Skerries. The aircraft at Dun Laoghaire then took off and set down beside the other one in Skerries.

Numerous people went out in small boats to the two aircraft and were given guided tours while Squadron Leader Collins waited on shore as the Irish authorities pondered their next move. It had never occurred to Collins that he and his crew might be interned. They had taken off before Prime Minister Neville Chamberlain's radio broadcast announcing that Britain was at war with Germany. Having consulted de Valera, Minister for Defence Oscar Traynor ordered that the airmen be treated as distressed mariners and allowed to leave. Collins was returned to his aircraft and the two planes then took off at about five o'clock.

Even though the censor prohibited any mention of the two planes in the press the whole affair was the subject of much public comment. On 14 September the Taoiseach, Éamon de Valera emphasised his sympathy with the British, when he met Sir John Maffey, who was shortly to take up residence in Dublin as British representative to Ireland. 'England has a moral position today,' he said. 'Hitler might have his early successes, but the moral position would [sic] tell.'[1] The Taoiseach knew the British could not tolerate German submarines or aircraft sheltering in Ireland, but he could not deny the Germans access and at the same time allow British military planes or warships to use Irish facilities. 'His intention was to be helpful,' Maffey reported. 'He wanted to oblige us by having strict rules about submarines. He understood that suited us.'[2] He felt it necessary to intern British airmen who landed in Ireland, if he were to justify taking action against German submarines or aircraft. At one point the Taoiseach's telephone rang, and after a brief conversation, he hung up, turned to Maffey and said, 'There you are! One of your planes is down in Ventry Bay. What am I to do?'[3]

An RAF seaplane with 12 men on board had set down in Ventry harbour, in Co. Kerry, at nine o'clock that morning. The pilot and a mechanic had come ashore with a broken fuel pipe, and a passing motorist took them to Dingle, where the pipe was repaired at a garage. De Valera said he would have to intern the crew. 'It was quite obvious he found this course most unpalatable,' Maffey noted. 'I said that in view of the Skerries precedent he should warn the British government before introducing internment in any such cases. The men concerned had probably had no warning of any such possibility.'[4] While they were discussing this, the telephone rang again and de Valera told Maffey that the aircraft had taken off again.

'On the subject of the neutrality of Éire,' Maffey wrote, 'Mr de Valera said that two-thirds of his people were pro-British, or at any rate anti-German, at the moment. But there was a very active minority. Personally he had great sympathy with England today.' In fact, he wished to help Britain 'within the limits of that neutrality to the full extent possible'. When the Irish coast-watching service observed any belligerent aircraft, ships or submarines, they would broadcast the information at once. 'Not to you especially,' the Taoiseach said. 'Your admiralty must pick it up. We shall wireless it to the world. I will tell the German minister of our intention to do this.'[5]

Both the British and Germans would be free to listen into such messages, which would have the effect of reporting the sightings to both sides. Germany was too far away to make use of reports about Allied flights, whereas British forces were near enough to react to sightings of German aircraft and submarines. The messages were to be broadcast on a radio frequency agreed with the British, so this would have the effect of informing Allied planes of their position, if they were lost over Ireland.

Little over a fortnight later there was a further incident in Ventry harbour. Early on the evening of 4 October 1939, the German submarine, U-35, sailed into harbour and left off 28 sailors from an Allied ship that it had sunk. The men had little chance of survival in the rough seas, so the U-35 rescued them. Little over a week later *Life* magazine highlighted the incident as its cover story.

Almost a year later during the Battle of Britain, the first German aircraft came down in Ireland on the slopes of Mount Brandon, on 20 August 1940. The whole area was shrouded in a thick fog and the crew of the Focke Wulf Condor had thought they were over the ocean. The pilot, Stabfeldwebel Robert Beumer, only saw the mountain at the last moment. He instinctively raised the nose of the plane, but as he did, a large rock tore off the under turret. Had Beumer planned it, he could hardly have done any better. The rock slowed them drastically and by sheer luck the aircraft with its nose up was moving virtually parallel to the mountain slope as it proceeded to make a belly-landing going up the slope.

Only two of the six-man crew were injured. Oberleutnant Kurt Mollenhauer fractured his right ankle and Beumer suffered a painful back injury. They were taken to the county hospital in Tralee, while the other four members of the crew were transferred to Collins Barracks, Cork, where they were detained for ten days. From there they wrote letters home commenting on the friendliness of the Irish people. 'You need have no anxiety about me, since we are here removed from the vicissitude of the war,' the 25-year-old meteorologist Eric Kruger assured his mother. 'I have here a lazy life, and perhaps the abundance of sleep and good food will have a good affect even on me.'[6] 20-year-old Gefreiter (Corporal) Kurt Kyck from Allenstein, also noted that 'the people are very friendly and put everything at our disposal that we need, the food even first-rate, only we are interned and must put up with it. When the war is over I shall probably come home again. I hope it won't be long now.'[7] It was to be a 5-year stay. Mollenhauer and Kyck would meet their future wives in Ireland. In fact, Kyck got married while he was interned and eventually settled in Ireland.

On 31 August 1940, Mollenhauer and Beumer were transferred from Tralee to the Curragh Military Hospital, and the four others were moved from Cork to 'K Lines', or the No. 2 Internment Camp, as it was officially called. It was a newly constructed barbed wire compound at the Curragh, about a mile from Tintown, the No. 1 Internment Camp, in which members of the IRA were being held.

The Curragh itself was a 12-square-mile plain about 30 miles southwest of Dublin. During the Crimean War the British had built a small instruction camp at the Curragh to serve the military in the nearby garrison towns of Kildare and Newbridge, each of which was about 3 miles away. The new camp expanded rapidly and the Curragh became one of the first examples of a complete military town. After independence, the

Irish army took over the Curragh and its 7 red-brick barracks, which housed 227 officers and 5,340 men, with married quarters for 86 families. By Irish standards the Curragh camp was a town, with various conveniences. Being a military camp it had the advantage of having some of the country's most advanced sporting facilities, with a gymnasium, indoor swimming pool and courts for squash, handball and tennis, as well as a golf course and playing fields for various outdoor sports.

At the outset there was a certain amount of tension between the internees and their guards, who were not as easy-going or as friendly as the soldiers had been in Cork. The guards at the Curragh initially performed interchangeable duty between K Lines and Tintown, and this had an unfortunate influence, because relations between the guards and the IRA internees were very strained. It was inevitable that the tension in Tintown would affect the attitude of the guards towards the internees in K Lines.

When the German minister, Edouard Hempel, visited K Lines on 2 September he found the German airmen uneasy about the tight security. They complained of being treated like prisoners-of-war. In a strict sense they were not prisoners, but guests of the Irish state, which was merely obligated to ensure that they took no further part in the war. However, Col. Thomas McNally, the officer in charge of the Curragh command, considered them prisoners. 'These prisoners in my opinion are the type, who consider it a duty to affect escape at the first available opportunity,' he wrote. 'As a race they are very tough and methodical and I feel will avail themselves of any laxity in the regulations which govern their internment.'[8]

Comdt James Guiney was responsible for both internment camps, but, as he was preoccupied with Tintown, he left the day-to-day running of K Lines to Lt. James A. Kelly, who was selected because he had attended a Jesuit secondary school in Germany and was able to speak fluent German. Of course, he had to feel his own way in running the camp, which he did rather cautiously.

While in Cork the men were permitted to drink alcohol, read Irish newspapers and even listen to the radio. Now these facilities were being denied for no good reason. The Germans were not even allowed to have garden implements with which they might have relieved their boredom. At the Curragh Military Hospital, where they remained for 12 days, Mollenhauer complained that he and Beumer were not able to get enough fresh air, because large nails had been driven into the window frames to prevent the windows being opened more than a few inches for fear he or

Beumer might try to escape. There was already an iron grill outside the window, and the two men were obviously incapacitated – Mollenhauer had his leg in plaster and his colleague was still recovering from the painful back injury.

Given the stifling atmosphere of the military hospital, they welcomed their transfer to the barbed-wire compound in K Lines, where they were able to get all the fresh air they wanted. But now they had the added nuisance of being awakened at regular intervals throughout the night by noisy guards checking their rooms and shining flash-lights in their faces.

The six internees were housed in two separate wooden bungalows – officers in one and NCOs in the other. However, all ate together in the same mess, at their own request. Mollenhauer and Beumer were still recuperating, so they made regular visits to the military hospital, and they were allowed to exercise outside their compound under guard. Mollenhauer asked Hempel to secure the same exercise privileges for the other men. Hempel called for a relaxation of the prison-like procedures at K Lines, but the wheels of bureaucracy moved slowly until his request was given a new urgency with the internment of the first British airman on 29 September 1940. This added a whole new dimension to the internment question, especially as Pilot Officer (PO) Paul Mayhew was the son of a prominent British businessman. Mayhew had shot down a German bomber, but lost his bearings and landed in a field in Co. Wexford with only five minutes' fuel left. At the time he thought he was over southern Wales.

The British did not protest against his internment, because they believed that 'unconditional internment' would operate in their favour, according to Maffey. Unless the Irish government adopted stringent rules of internment, the British feared that German aircraft would be able to exploit the international law applicable to combatant ships needing repairs. The planes would 'alight on Irish soil under the pretense of needing repairs, obtain fuel, and then continue on their combatant patrols, having had the benefit of Southern Ireland as a fuelling station'.[9] To prevent this the British accepted the internment of their own airmen.

Mayhew was initially held at the Curragh under armed guard in Ceannt Barracks, while a new barbed wire compound was built as an extension to K Lines. He was allowed a certain amount of freedom, such as the use of the billiard room and had access to all reading material in the officers' mess. His food was the same as that served to Irish officers.

He was permitted to have visitors and take whatever walking exercise he desired. At all times, however, even when going to the toilet, he was accompanied by an armed guard, who was under secret instructions not to use his gun. He was to let the pilot go rather than shoot him in the event of an escape attempt.

Frederick H. Boland, the assistant secretary at the Department of External Affairs, warned Military Intelligence (G2) that the internment of the British airmen was going to 'give rise to questions in some ways more difficult than we have to face with the present six men'.[10] The guards would be obliged not to show favouritism, so he thought it advisable to anticipate and make concessions to the Germans immediately rather than be compelled to make them later under British pressure. 'What we must be sure of,' Boland wrote, 'is that we do not withhold reasonable and usual amenities which it might later be deemed to be expedient to grant to military internees of another nationality to obviate, for example, attacks in the British press.'[11]

A conference between representatives of the Department of Defence, the army, and the Department of External Affairs was convened on 2 October 1940. Those in attendance included Col. Liam Archer, the head of G2, Boland from External Affairs and his counterpart at the Department of Defence, General Peter MacMahon, as well as Col. McNally. Boland argued that the internees should be as content as possible with their lot in order 'to minimise their anxiety and quite natural desire to escape from our custody.'[12] He believed the German requests were reasonable, as he saw no grounds for denying the men a radio, newspapers, or magazines. 'None of the points are very serious,' he explained. Hempel, whom he described as 'a difficult character', had put forward the suggestions 'in a reasonable conciliatory way.'[13] Boland summarised the views of the Department of External Affairs in this way:

> We are under international obligation to keep these men in this country and to ensure that they do not escape and return to Germany. Any failure on our part to carry out this obligation would land us in a diplomatic incident. Within the limits of this general obligation to ensure the safe custody of the men, however, our view is that once their safe custody is assured the men should be granted every facility and amenity calculated to soften their captivity and relieve their monotony. There is no point whatever in our view in refusing them any amenity that does not detract from the measures taken for their safe custody. On the contrary, the task of everybody and particularly the officer immediately responsible would be lightened by a policy directed towards making the men as satisfied as circumstances of their internment allows. I am satisfied that this is not the only course dictated by the general practice of neutrals in the treatment of military in-

ternees, but the best in our particular circumstances. It is the wisest policy to pursue.[14]

Henning Thomsen, the Counsellor of the German legation, presented the internees with a radio and the Irish army erected an aerial. The nightly inspections were discontinued and the officers were given an allowance of £3 per week and the others £2 per week as well as £5 each to purchase civilian clothes. This money, along with the cost of their food and medical expenses, was to be recouped from the German government. The internees were also given gardening tools and they quickly set about cultivating a vegetable garden, because they were unhappy with the quality of the vegetables being served by their Irish cook. The Germans found it difficult adjusting to their diet. They complained of getting too much meat and not enough vegetables.

On 17 October 1940 Mayhew was transferred to K Lines, where he was to remain the lone British internee for almost two months. Physically, the camp was not unlike many of the other internment camps scattered throughout Europe. It was rectangular in shape with a double fence made of barbed wire stranded on large wooden poles, with a large double gate made of barbed wire on strong wooden frames at the outer entrance. Between the two fences there was a grass corridor connecting four gun posts at each corner. Camp guards patrolled within the corridor, and there was a residence hut inside the main gate for extra guards on call in the event of trouble. The area within the double fence was divided into two separate compounds by a corrugated iron fence, topped with barbed wire. There were separate entrances consisting of two smaller barbed wire gates on wooden frames. Just inside those gates, the guards had an administrative hut on the dividing line with a door and a window into each compound. The Germans were interned in what was known as G Camp, and Mayhew in B Camp.

Mayhew was paid directly by Maffey's office. The Irish wanted his salary restricted to £3 a week, because they feared he would be able to bribe the guards, most of whom were paid less than £1 a week, but the British refused to comply. He was therefore given his full salary and was provided with an army cook free of charge, but he had to pay for his food. The 21-year-old Mayhew found life boring. He availed of parole most afternoons to play golf. He usually played with retired officers who had served in the British army, or with serving Irish officers. 'I expect to be British Amateur golf champion in 1944,' he remarked facetiously in a letter to his father.[15]

Dublin asked the German government to give the men permission to sign parole. Under Article 11 of the Hague Convention (1907) the Irish government could 'decide whether officers can be left at liberty on giving their parole not to leave the neutral territory without permission.'[16] As far as de Valera was concerned, the internees could be permitted to move about relatively freely, if they would promise on their honour not to try to escape or take part in any activities relating to the war effort. As things stood, however, the men were under an obligation to try to rejoin their units and Hempel was unwilling to authorise parole without permission from Berlin. When Berlin authorised the internees to sign a limited parole, a system was introduced allowing them out of the camp each day. They would give their word of honour to return to the camp. Initially the freedom granted was quite modest, but it gradually expanded.

Before the end of the year, five more Germans and five more British airmen were interned. 1941 was to be the busiest year of the war for the internment of airmen. A total of 25 more Germans were interned at K Lines, along with 34 further Allied airmen. The Allied men included 9 Canadians, 2 Poles, a Free French pilot, a New Zealander and an American serving with the Eagle Squadron of the Royal Air Force.

The system of parole was further eased during 1941. The two sets of internees were allowed out on parole to go to the cinema two nights a week, but the Germans resented being escorted by Irish troops. They contended that this implied a questioning of their honour, whereas the camp authorities feared that they might be attacked because there were still many people with strong British sympathies in the area, as it was less than 20 years since the British army were camped at the Curragh. Mollenhauer, the senior German internee, tended to represent the interests of his men with the zeal of a trade union official, and this irritated some of the Irish officers, who resented his complaints about heating and food at the camp and felt their honour was being questioned. He saw no grounds for any restrictions within the camp other than those to ensure that nobody escaped. 'At the root of all our difficulties about military internment at the Curragh lies the tendency of the Minister for Defence to think of them as being in the same category as prisoners-of-war or persons interned under the Offences Against the State Act,' F. H. Boland complained. 'This is a fundamental misconception.'[17]

The British internees initially seemed to settle in better, but most of them never really accepted internment. While the Germans realised that there was little chance of escaping and returning to Germany, their

Allied counterparts were preoccupied with plans to escape to Northern Ireland. They tried all methods from mass break-outs to tunnelling, to pretending to go mad, to faking suicide, and some even tried to enlist the help of the IRA. Eleven of the Allied internees managed to escape and make it to Northern Ireland, but one of them had to return because of questions about the way he had exploited parole to escape. The Germans tended to make the best of their internment, by organising language and other classes and cultivating gardens within their compound. The Allied compound was a mess, as the men wished to emphasise that they resented internment and could not wait to get back into the war. Only one German internee, Leutnant Konrad Neymeyr, escaped during the war. He then stowed away on a boat bound for Portugal, but he was caught when the ship put into Bristol and he spent the remainder of the war in a British POW camp. Conditions there contrasted greatly with conditions at the Curragh, but then K Lines was a most unusual camp.

When PO William Proctor's wife visited him in March, he was given three nights parole to stay with her at the Central Hotel in Newbridge. Sergeant Sydney Hobbs was visited by his English girlfriend and they actually got married at Ballysax Church on 7 June 1941. He was the first of eleven internees – seven Allied and four German – to marry while interned. As he was not an officer, he was only given extended parole for two nights a week. He had to be back at the camp by midnight on the other nights.

There were three types of parole. Camp Parole, in accordance with which the men were allowed out in military uniform, but had to remain within the precincts of the Curragh Camp. On Local Parole they could go outside the camp area but only when dressed in civilian clothes and then they had to remain within the triangular area bordered by the three towns of Newbridge, Killcullen and Kildare; this area was soon extended to a ten-mile radius from the camp to include the town of Naas. Special Parole was accorded in specific circumstances, which were gradually expanded. At first the internees were allowed a quarterly visit to Dublin, but those became monthly visits in 1941 and weekly visits in early 1943.

In July 1941 parole was extended so that the internees only had to report at the camp by 8 a.m. All the men, therefore, essentially enjoyed the right to sleep where they wished within the parole area. This was extended to noon for the married officers, Ward and Midgely, while their wives were visiting the Curragh area. Later in June 1943 Ward was given special parole for two weeks to visit his wife, who was sick in England.

The German internees were entitled to the same hours, but Mollen-

hauer insisted on the implementation of a differential system in accordance with which his permission was needed for officers to stay out later
than four in the morning, two o'clock for senior NCOs, one o'clock for
other NCOs, or after 11.30 on weeknights and 1 a.m. on weekends for
other ranks.

Despite their Irish army orderlies and their segregated dining and
recreation rooms, the Allied officers did not have many privileges over
their colleagues. The Allies and the Germans had their own bars within
the camp in which beer and spirits were served by an Irish army bartend-
er at duty free prices. A glass of beer or spirits cost only 5d per glass. The
bar was always well stocked and well utilised. Sgt Charles Brady of
Toronto learned after some weeks at the Curragh that he had received a
commission, but he noted that his promotion made little difference
other than opening 'a few more doors to the Gentry of Ireland'.[18] Once
they were accorded the right to visit private homes in June 1941, the
Allied officers were in particular demand with what remained of the
ascendancy element as well as some wealthy people involved in the
horse-racing scene. They were invited to meals at Ballymore Eustace
House, Bennettstown House, Brownstown House, Castletown House
and the homes of retired British officers like Captain Darby Rodgers at
Ifield Lodge or Captain Jack Daley at Rushmore, Co. Wicklow. These
invitations were usually for the officers only, but the others had the
benefit of the extra food at the camp. 'Because of so many eating out at
friends,' Sgt Fred Tisdall explained, 'the supply was good for those eating
at the camp'.[19]

The internees were frequently invited to dances, but Ward and Mollenhauer were anxious that their men should not attend the same functions. They were afraid of loose talk about fraternisation between the
enemy internees. They had been embarrassed by rumours that the English internees had helped the Germans overcome language difficulties
while shopping in Dublin. Of necessity they frequently had to travel on
the same bus to Dublin, but there was no truth about them fraternising.
What had happened was the English internees helped out the two Poles
and some bystanders mistook them for Germans. Visitors to the camp's
cinemas were often surprised when the lights came on after a show to
find a row of grey-uniformed Luftwaffe airmen on one side of the hall
with a row of blue uniformed members of the RAF in the row across the
aisle from them. On a couple of occasions internees from each side
turned up at Protestant services and word got out that they sat next to
each other, but the idea of sitting next to Germans even in church was

too much for the Allied internees.

For a while a system was devised by which the first side to apply for permission to attend any function would be granted the sole right to attend it. Later the system fell into disuse as the various internees became accustomed to ignoring one another. All the men were free to join local clubs. Several of the Germans joined the Newbridge Tennis Club, as did four of the Allied internees. Other Allied airmen joined the golf club, or the Newbridge Rugby Club, where three played on the first fifteen. Three others played on a local soccer team and others enjoyed riding at some of the nearby stables, where they were allowed to exercise the horses. One of the English sergeants had his own hunter, which he rode in some point-to-point meetings, and three of the Allied internees hunted with the Naas Harriers. PO Wolfe, the camp's lone American, used to turn up in western attire. A native of Ceresco, Nebraska, he raised many eyebrows in those staid circles as he charged ahead of the field in his cowboy hat, riding with a one-handed style that shocked members of the hunt.

At the camp the internees formed teams of their own. The Allies had their own tennis, cricket, soccer and table tennis teams, and these played Irish army or local community teams, as did similar German teams. But the German and Allied teams never played each other. On a few occasions some German and Allied internees did meet in individual competition and then the rivalry was intense. The Allied table tennis team accepted a challenge to play a Newbridge club team not knowing that two of the Germans were playing with the local club. 'I drew one of them as my opponent,' Ros Tees recalled. 'Although I am usually a good loser, I was thoroughly chagrined when I lost to him. It was like losing the war!'[20]

'Sport was perhaps the only outlet for those deep periods of mental depression that used to come on from time to time and we took every opportunity for exercise,' the New Zealander Fl. Lt. Bruce Girdlestone wrote. 'Fortunately facilities were excellent and the Irish army gave us access to most of their fields and sports clubs. From their point of view it aided our security by contenting us physically and mentally thereby lessening our desire to escape. That, we termed psychological security and on some of the internees it had the desired effect.'[21]

John D. Kearney, the Canadian High Commissioner, presented the men with a table tennis table and equipment. He also sent Canadian newspapers and magazines to the camp. When the Canadians visited Dublin, he organised free passes for them to certain cinemas, but the

High Commissioner still kept a certain diplomatic distance from the men. Unlike the British representative, Kearney was slow to visit the camp personally and did not report on conditions there until specifically instructed to do so by his government. Yet, because of his hospitality in Dublin, the Canadian internees were convinced he was more concerned about their welfare than Maffey was about their British colleagues. 'There is no question that John D. Kearney did all he could to make life better for the Canadians,' Brady recalled. 'I think it fair to say we Canadians felt that at least our representative in Éire was concerned for us and, without placing his position in jeopardy, did all he could for us.'[22]

Despite the recreational facilities most of the Allied internees were preoccupied with thoughts of escape. On the night of the Irish Derby at the Curragh racecourse, 26 June 1941, the Allied internees made a major break. As the last two men were coming off parole, they pretended to be extremely drunk and distracted the guards while the other internees rushed the gate and nine escaped. Three of the men were quickly recaptured, but the other six went into hiding with friends on the outside and eventually, with the help of MI 9 (the British escape organisation), which provided disguises, they made it across the border to Northern Ireland. Mayhew was among those who escaped; he was killed in action the following year.

The army complained that the involvement of the internees returning from parole had been a parole violation, and asked the government to demand the return of the six escapees, but Maffey warned that such a request would likely lead to diplomatic complications. Consequently, de Valera did not pursue the matter. There was an unsuccessful mass breakout attempt on 9 February 1942 which led to a running battle with the guards, and a further attempt on 17 August 1942 when nine men escaped over the wire. Six were later caught but two Canadian officers and an English sergeant managed to reach Northern Ireland.

PO Wolfe, who had been serving in the Eagle Squadron of the RAF, was the only American interned in Ireland during the Second World War. His distinction was all the greater when one realises that at least 260 other American airmen came down in Ireland during the next three and a half years, but all of them were quietly let go. During the nine months following the arrival of the American troops in Northern Ireland, all Allied survivors from forced landings in Ireland were promptly released with one temporary exception. On the evening of 24 April 1942, PO Donald Kennedy arrived at K Lines. But that night Wing Commander Malcolm Begg, the British Air Attaché, collected him at K

Lines and took him to Northern Ireland. Begg advised the RAF to in-
struct all aircrews not on training flights to pretend they were on rescue
missions if they had to land in Ireland. They should say that they were
'engaged in air-sea rescue operations in response to an SOS from an unidentified aircraft believed to be German,' he suggested.[23]

Irish authorities were prepared to release any Allied airmen in circumstances where publicity could be avoided, or where it could be shown
that the planes had not been on combat missions. Many of the aircraft
which landed in Ireland were simply being delivered from the United
States, while trainee pilots were flying others without armaments. David
Gray, the American representative, sought to get the Department of External Affairs to formalise the non-operation procedure on 30 November 1942. 'I asked Mr Walshe if his government was prepared to recognise, in principle, the distinction between such non-combatant transport
or training flights and flights which were manifestly combatant,' Gray
reported.[24] Having discussed the matter with the Taoiseach, Walshe
wrote to Gray:

> In practice our attitude of friendly neutrality towards the United Nations
> results normally – in so far as aircraft and their crews are concerned – in
> internment of only such crews as are on operational flights. After full con-
> sideration of the matter, I am inclined to think that the existing relatively
> satisfactory situation should be left as it is. New and formal regulations or
> agreement are more likely to create difficulties than lessen them.[25]

In short, the Dublin government was pursuing the policy desired by the
Americans but wished to keep the whole thing on an informal basis.

Although Allied airmen were supposed to be instructed to say that
they were on 'non-operational flights', the pilots of five of the next six
American planes which came down in Ireland failed to do so, but all 40
of those on board were released anyway. One of the planes was carrying
four generals: Lt. General Jacob Devers, the American commander of
the European Theatre of Operations, Major General Edward H. Brooks,
and Brigadier Generals J. M. Barnes and C. D. Palmer. Their Flying
Fortress crash landed near Athenry, Co. Galway, on 15 January 1943.
They had lost their way *en route* from North Africa to a conference in
London. Running dangerously low on fuel, the pilot put the plane down
in a field near the Agricultural College in Athenry. They were promptly
driven to the border. Hempel soon learned of the release of the Americans and demanded an explanation from the Department of External
Affairs. It was probably in view of Hempel's uneasiness over the whole

affair that the five-man crew of an RAF Wellington bomber were interned a few weeks later. But the crews of all of the other 77 Allied aircraft
that landed in Ireland from then until the end of the war were quietly
let go without delay. 'Under the circumstances,' the Canadian High
Commissioner wrote, 'the meaning of the words "non-operational fight"
has, sometimes been stretched almost beyond recognition.'[26] The whole
argument was merely a 'convenient fiction' to allow Ireland to help the
Allies, according to Randolph Churchill.[27]

In his reports Maffey indicated that he had been playing up Britain's
grievance over de Valera's policy. 'These years were years of heavy trial
for England and would leave their mark,' he reportedly warned the
Taoiseach in February 1943. 'In her post-war relationships England
would not forget that while she was fighting for her life Dublin harbour-
ed Axis legations and interned British airmen. Mr de Valera could only
regret that the situation here was too difficult to admit of any other line
of action.'[28]

In the following months Maffey pressed de Valera to apply the non-
operational argument retroactively. He contended that only 13 of the
Allied airmen then interned had been on operational flights. The
Taoiseach indicated that he was prepared to interpret the phrase 'non-
operational flight' in a liberal way. He agreed to release the 18 who were
supposedly on non-operational flights but also two other officers who
had come down while on combat missions – the Canadian Charles
Brady and the Frenchman Maurice Remy, who had shot down a German
bomber over Ireland. Before releasing the men, however, de Valera insisted that it would first be necessary to move the Allied internees from
the Curragh to a new camp at Gormanston, Co. Meath. 'As a matter of
interest to our High Command,' Maffey informed the Dominions Office,
'it might be pointed out to them that operations off Éire may now be
conducted on the assumption that no risk of internment exists.'[29]

The Allied airmen left the Curragh camp for the last time on 18
October 1943. 'There were no tears shed,' Girdlestone wrote.[30] They
travelled to Dublin in a military convoy. The 20 men being released
were in one truck and the other 11 men in a separate truck. The convoy
split up in Phoenix Park, Dublin, with the men being released heading
for Northern Ireland, while the others went on to Gormanston. The
families of the released men were notified that they had been freed but
were given no details, other than a suggestion that they had actually
escaped. 'I have to ask that you will treat this information as confidential and do your utmost to ensure that no mention of his escape appears

in the press,' the New Zealand naval secretary requested of Girdlestone's mother.[31]

The eleven men interned at Gormanston were all sergeants – six English, three Scots, a Welshman and a Canadian. They were what remained of three different crews who had admitted that they were returning from bombing missions when they got lost and overflew Britain. They were accorded a local parole area extending ten miles from the camp and were permitted to visit Dublin once a week. Sgt Eric Ross was given special parole to attend classes at Rathmines Technical College in Dublin two days a week. Ross, George Slater and David Reid joined Drogheda Rugby Club and won places on the club's first fifteen. They played in all the club's home games and were given special parole to travel outside the parole area for a vital cup match with Dundalk.

When de Valera was questioned in the Dáil about the release of the Allied internees, he declined to answer in the interest of national security. The Irish placated Hempel with concessions, including the acquisition of new staff. The Germans had tried to increase the size of their legation by transferring some diplomats from the United States in December 1940, but de Valera insisted that the new people had to arrive by normal commercial means, which would have meant travelling through Britain. Hempel was given permission to employ one of the internees as a replacement for his coding clerk, who was seriously ill with cardiac trouble. Unteroffizer Hans Bell of Dusseldorf took up duties at the legation on 10 November 1943, and he was joined later by a naval NCO, Horst Huse from Danzig, who acted as doorman at the legation.

Mollenhauer's request for a 48-hour parole in Dublin in the run up to Christmas 1943 was granted. 'The fact that we have released so many British and the German minister is aware of the fact,' Freddie Boland argued, 'makes it morally difficult to refuse the present request and its refusal might conceivably exacerbate German feeling over the recent release.'[32] Hempel also managed to get special parole for four of the internee officers to move to Dublin in order to attend University College Dublin, early in the new year. The four, Rudolf Laurer, Eric Kruger, Walter Habich and Arthur Klanke, got a house together in the Mount Merrion area, from where they cycled to the college. Shortly afterwards they were joined by another of the officers, the Berliner, Ernst Müller. In accordance with their parole conditions, they were supposed to avoid the waterfront and remain within a radius of ten miles from the General Post Office on O'Connell Street. They were also supposed to remain indoors at their residence between midnight and seven o'clock in the morning and stay away from bars frequented by visiting Allied service-men, especially the bars in the Gresham, Hibernian and Dolphin Hotels. In addition, they were not to associate with people active in Irish or international politics or 'do anything that has the slightest political flavour.'[33]

It was just as well that these concessions had been made because the authorities were shortly to be confronted with the greatest influx of Germans. In December 1943 the Irish ship *Kerlogue* picked up 166 German sailors in the Bay of Biscay following a naval engagement. Two were found to be dead and were buried at sea. The ship deliberately maintained radio silence until it neared the Irish coast. It was supposed to go to a British port first but decided to go straight for Cobh so that the sailors would not be imprisoned. The captain of the *Kerlogue* argued that some of the men were seriously injured and in need of immediate medical aid. In fact, one died before they made it to Cobh.

Maffey, having failed to get the Irish government to compel the *Kerlogue* to stop at a British port first, was insistent that the sailors should be interned and not allowed to roam about Ireland. While there was a dubious aspect to the application of the non-operational argument, there was none about the status of the rescued German sailors. Under international law they were distressed mariners, rescued on the high seas. They should not have been interned, but Maffey warned de Valera that 'a German in Éire is a menace to England, while an Englishman in Éire is no menace to Germany'.[34]

Even before independence had been achieved de Valera had stressed that Irish territory would never be used against Britain in time of war. A new internment compound was prepared for the German sailors. It adjoined Tintown, which housed some 500 IRA internees. It was opened on 24 January 1944 when a German officer and five NCOs were transferred there from Cork. Kaptaen Leutnant Joachim Quedenfeld and 146 others followed the next day, while the remaining 10 men stayed on in Cork for varying periods of recovery.

Hempel announced that Quedenfeld was taking over as the commanding officer of all of the German internees. K Lines was shut down in March 1944 and Luftwaffe internees were transferred to the naval camp. While in K Lines the Luftwaffe officers had been provided with Irish army orderlies, as there were no German privates to do menial duties, but now those orderlies were withdrawn as there were naval ratings available to undertake such tasks there.

Initially the Luftwaffe internees enjoyed the same parole hours which had developed over the past three and a half years at K Lines. Officers were permitted to stay out until eight o'clock in the morning and NCOs did not have to return until five o'clock. All naval internees, on the other hand, had to be back at the camp by midnight. 'In such circumstances,' Quedenfeld complained, 'I, as a senior officer, get less leave than a Luftwaffe NCO.'[35] The Irish response, however, was not to extend the hours of the sailors, as the German commander wished, but to restrict the airmen to the shorter hours. Henceforth all internees had to be back by midnight, except one night a week when the NCOs had an extra half-hour and the officers had until two o'clock in the morning. This gave rise to an understandable sense of grievance on the part of the interned airmen.

Parole hours were at the discretion of camp authorities, who regularly extended local parole hours for late-night parties when individual internees asked in writing for an extension. What Quedenfeld was really looking for was the right to grant those extensions himself. 'Leave it to me and I will see it is not abused,' he wrote. 'This will give me more scope for the management of the camp.'[36]

The problems concerning parole really needed to be seen against the backdrop of the infamous American note of 21 February 1944, in which the United States had formally demanded the expulsion of the German and Japanese representatives from Ireland on the grounds that they supposedly posed a threat to the lives of Americans preparing for the upcoming invasion of Europe. Following the successful Allied invasion of Normandy on 6 June 1944, Maffey exerted strong pressure on de Valera to release the remaining airmen in Gormanston. Initially the Taoiseach resisted. 'In regard to our interned airmen,' Maffey reported on 10 June, 'he told me in the most explicit manner that he had re-examined the matter with every desire to be helpful – particularly to me personally – but that he found it quite impossible to give way on this point.'[37] But Maffey warned that 'Quite unforeseeable complications would accrue if this question produced no more than an impasse'. The British representative was going to London for consultations and he demanded to know exactly where de Valera stood in the matter. 'Mr de Valera paced about the room uneasily and said that as today was Saturday he would not be able to get in touch with his cabinet before my departure,' Maffey noted. 'I said that we required to have his answer in London at the latest before early on Tuesday morning. I should expect a telephone message in London from Mr Walshe one way or the other on Monday evening. Mr de Valera said he would arrange this.'[38] In effect, the British representative had issued an ultimatum that unless Dublin released the remaining Allied internees, Britain was going to tighten the economic screws.

'He was obviously badly shaken,' Maffey reported. 'It is so much for a neutral to think that supplies are a kind of manna dropping as the gentle dew from Heaven. Fortune has spoiled Mr de Valera by paying him unfailing dividends for his untiring obstinacy.' The British representative noted that it was 'impossible to forecast' the Taoiseach's decision. 'He has the martyr complex and would hunger strike for a principle.[39] But there are one or two hardheaded men in the government and we can only wait and see. At any rate the long chapter of arguments and dialectics on this subject is now closed. It may be necessary to give a turn of the screw.'[40]

De Valera duly relented. On 15 June 1944 the remaining Allied internees were secretly released and driven to Northern Ireland. The parole conditions were further relaxed for the Germans and 20 of the men were permitted to move to Dublin to take third-level courses. Hempel hired a technical instructor to give courses at the Curragh. Wilhelm Masgeik had come to Ireland from Germany in August 1938 as chief engineering adviser to Irish Steel in Cork, but due to the lack of raw material, the company closed down during the war. So the German legation employed Masgeik to hold classes at the camp, but this led to an extraordinary situation when he tried to stay there overnight. Permission was refused. The following night he announced he was staying anyway and he had to be ordered from the camp. As a result he was then barred.[41] He must have been the only person in all of Europe who got himself barred for trying to stay in a internment camp.

Quedenfeld asked that the German orderlies and cooks be paid extra, or else replaced by Irish army personnel, who had done nearly all of this work at K Lines. Internees working within the camp were really being discriminated against, because they were not paid for this work, and could not avail of the opportunity of earning extra money by joining colleagues working for the Irish Turf Board, cutting peat in a nearby bog.

Instead of paying the men for their work at the camp, the Department of Finance in Dublin suggested that the allowances of those working in the bogs should be stopped. Fortunately saner heads at the Department of External Affairs prevailed, but the kind of bureaucratic thinking that inspired the suggestion went some way to explaining why some of the German officers felt so frustrated.[42]

The second biggest influx of German internees occurred in March

1945 when 48 members of a U-boat crew landed in Co. Cork, after their submarine, U-260 went down off the Cork coast on 11 March. Two days earlier the look-out post had reported sighting a U-boat off the coast and about two hours later there were further reports of British aircraft dropping depth charges. The Germans stated that they were sunk about 50 miles off the coast.

After the end of the war in Europe the British asked Dublin to hand over all German internees. De Valera agreed on condition that Britain guaranteed that none of them would be executed, nor forced to return to the Soviet zone of Germany. The US minister complained that de Valera was trying to undermine the wartime alliance by having the British and Americans discriminate against the Soviet ally. He failed to persuade the State Department to put pressure on the British to reject de Valera's conditions.

Comdt James Guiney informed Quedenfeld of the impending repatriation on 30 July 1945 and asked for a breakdown of the zones from which the men had come and the number wishing to return to those zones. In all only 138 desired to return to their homes; this included 43 of the men whose homes were in the Soviet zone. The bulk of the men wished to remain in Ireland, but they were not given that choice. Their only option was to return home or, in the case of those coming from the French or Soviet zones, to choose between their homes and either the British or American zones of occupation in Germany.

Alfred Heinzl and his fiancée, Eitne Rea of Dublin had planned to get married in September, so they brought the date forward to 10 August. He then made representations to be allowed to stay in the country. He was brought to Dublin, where he met with de Valera, who authorised him to stay, along with three other Austrians.

It was shortly after midnight on 13 August when the convoy of ten buses left the Curragh. They were brought to Alexandra Quay, where they boarded the HMS St Andrew. 'We marched on board dressed in civilian suits, carrying tennis racquets, fishing rods and all speaking good English,' Arthur Voight recalled.[43] 'Who the hell are they?' Voight heard one soldier ask. 'Soldiers or bloody tourists?'[44]

IRISH DIPLOMATS
AT HOME AND ABROAD

'A MOST HEAVY AND GRIEVOUS BURDEN':
JOSEPH WALSHE AND THE ESTABLISHMENT OF
SUSTAINABLE NEUTRALITY, 1940
Aengus Nolan

> Of course, I should be only too delighted to help in recalling the events of
> the war years. But you will remember, Sir, how extremely careful you always
> were, and it is doubtful if we have a single note in the Department, beyond
> perhaps something in regard to Gray's pernicious manoeuvres. However,
> when the other side have done all their work of publication, perhaps we
> could do something to fill the gaps, if circumstances and prudence permits.

> – Joseph Walshe to Éamon de Valera, 19 January 1954[1]

Towards the end of 1940, Winston Churchill stated that Irish neutrality
caused Britain 'a most heavy and grievous burden'. In reality, however,
the implementation of this policy was also a burden on Éamon de Valera
and the secretary of the Department of External Affairs, Joseph Walshe,
the protagonists in the formulation and execution of Irish foreign policy.
They shouldered the burden of devising and maintaining neutrality
particularly during 1940, as the 'phoney war' came to an end. With the
recommencement of hostilities on the continent, a period of frenzied
activity occurred in Iveagh House as Joseph Walshe endeavoured to
establish Irish neutrality in the international diplomatic landscape. To
facilitate this, Walshe engaged in detailed discussions with all sides. He
travelled to London on many occasions but the majority of his contacts
were in Dublin with John Maffey (the British 'representative'), David
Gray (the US minister) and Edouard Hempel (the German minister).
Walshe's and de Valera's anxieties not to incur the wrath of the Allies
were reflected in their policy of cooperative neutrality. Notwithstanding
covert assistance to the Allies, the Irish government did not desire to
enter the war against Germany. This formed the basis of the triangle in
which Walshe found himself. Balancing on a neutral tightrope with a

gulf of Axis or Allied belligerency on either side was no small concern when falling one way or the other could have meant certain destruction.

Throughout 1940, Walshe's attitude towards the war underwent substantial adjustment. He initially believed it likely that Germany would be victorious. The fall of France in mid-June, in particular, encouraged Walshe to maintain Ireland's favourable standing with Edouard Hempel. His assessment made covert collaboration with Britain unappealing though it continued nonetheless. From meetings held in London in late April and early May 1940, Walshe reported the appearance of 'a general desire to see the end of Partition' among British officials.[2] This, he believed, was inspired by their pessimistic estimation of their chances in the war. At first Walshe presumed this presented an opportunity and suggested Britain hand over Tyrone and Fermanagh to the Irish government as a 'gesture' of good will.[3] Walshe outlined his hopes to British officials and, therefore, may have deluded the British government into believing de Valera might compromise on neutrality if it meant significant progress on partition.

However, Walshe ultimately rejected any notion that Ireland should trade its neutrality for a deal on partition. From his meetings in London in early May, he gained the impression that Britain was desperate for support from any quarter. He informed de Valera that the British government was 'too soft, too class-prejudiced (they are almost all of the wealthy Tory family type) to be able to win a war against men of steel like Hitler, Stalin and their followers'.[4] He queried Britain's strength at this stage and when it was suggested to him that the war was being fought in the interest of 'all those in the world to whom freedom and democracy were precious' he rejected these ideological supplications.[5] It seems he perceived little reason to support continued Irish covert cooperation with Britain and his views towards Russia are enlightening when in conversation with Anthony Eden, the British Foreign Secretary, he stated:

> the establishment of close relations with Russia (however remote that might be) might make a very real change in the general Irish attitude towards the Allies. The leaders of Germany were indeed anti-Christian but a large section of the German people were good Catholics and good Protestants and might be trusted in the end to re-establish the prestige of Christianity in their own country, but Russia's atheism was aggressive and incurable.[6]

Thus, while Walshe may have shared the same worldview as Britain he was not, perhaps, opposed to all of Germany's wartime objectives. This has contributed to the general consensus that Walshe was pro-German.[7] However, the evidence suggests that for every statement to British officials critical of Britain, Walshe had an equally argumentative message to present to the German side. Walshe's diplomatic memoranda must be read in this light

Soon after Walshe's talks with Eden, de Valera publicly stated the Irish government's stance on the moral implications of the war. On 12 May 1940, he presented a speech to a Fianna Fáil convention in Galway referring to the German invasion of the Netherlands, Belgium and Luxembourg. He stated: 'Today these two small nations are fighting for their lives, and I think it would be unworthy of this small nation if, on an occasion like this, I did not utter our protest against the cruel wrong which has been done to them.' De Valera also identified a close convergence of interests between Britain and Ireland:

> My one regret at a time like the present is that there is still a cause of difference between the two countries. I believe ... that the destiny of the people of these two islands off the coast of Europe will be similar in many respects. I believe that we will have many interests in common in the future as in the past. I believe these common interests would beget good relations.[8]

Such comments undermined Walshe's attempted placation of Hempel and soon afterwards the German Foreign Ministry instructed Hempel to protest against de Valera's remarks. Hempel had already aired his concerns to Walshe who expressed his regret and added the statement was a mistake and would not be repeated. De Valera's statement also served to strengthen British hopes that in appropriate circumstances, Ireland would be willing to consider proposals to join the Allied war effort.

Walshe has been adversely criticised for his seemingly over-friendly attitude towards Germany. De Valera's 'rare moral courage' in denouncing Hitler's invasion of Belgium and the Netherlands has been juxtaposed with Walshe's expression of admiration for German achievements.[9] De Valera's moral indignation might be construed as hypocritical though for if he was serious about the convictions revealed in his speech in Galway, then he could have chosen to have this view officially conveyed to Hitler's Third Reich. Instead, he allowed his diplomatic corps continue their work of appeasement towards Hempel. Self-preservation was the guiding principle of de Valera's neutrality and it was Walshe's task to carry out that policy. Walshe could neither afford the luxury of such condemnations, nor had he the authority to make them.

However to convey the image of Walshe restricting de Valera's desire to decide Irish wartime policy on the basis of moral principle is inaccurate. There was no such divergence. Both Walshe and de Valera agreed neutrality was the most appropriate policy for Ireland. It was part of Walshe's task to carry out this policy and if using language soothing to the German psyche was necessary, then he felt justified in doing so. In this exertion, Walshe was somewhat successful. Despite an obvious wave of anti-German hostility throughout Ireland, Walshe attempted to convince Hempel that Britain was Ireland's 'traditional enemy'. While the German minister correctly divined that de Valera's sympathies lay primarily with Britain, he believed that under the guidance of Walshe and Boland the possibility remained that the Taoiseach would come to realise the potential importance of German supremacy for Ireland.[10] This was an important achievement for Walshe, in particular when it came to deciding the diplomatic path to be pursued with Britain and the United States.

David Gray's preliminary reports from Ireland to the State Department indicated that while Ireland remained neutral there was growing realism among government members about the danger of their position and that they were responding by preparing public opinion for co-operation with the allies.[11] 'At last this Government is waking up to its danger' he reported, 'though doing nothing.'[12] Gray believed de Valera personally lacked the determination to remain neutral and tried to persuade him there could be no 'sitting on the fence'. In the years to come, through meetings with Walshe and de Valera, Gray repeatedly sought to alter Ireland's stance in the world conflict. He would alter his earlier statement that Irish policy was a 'beneficent neutrality' and described it as self-serving and cowardly. His argument was strengthened by several failed German espionage attempts to establish contact with the IRA and foment nationalist hostility against Britain. These attempts were of major concern to Walshe for their occurence alone led to difficulties in convincing some Allied representatives that Ireland was not a potential security threat.[13]

Consequently, to placate Allied concerns arising from these German espionage incidents, Walshe adopted a cooperative attitude in talks with British officials. On 23 May 1940, he and Col. Liam Archer of the Irish army's military intelligence section, G2, opened secret talks with British officials in London. The British Admiralty and the Air Ministry wished to discuss the possibility of mutual military co-operation between the British and Irish governments. Walshe outlined de Valera's stated position that while the Irish government welcomed British military assistance in the event of an attack by Germany, there was no question of allowing British troops on Irish soil before an actual invasion attempt had taken place.[14] This caused problems for the British who determined that any effective assistance would require troops to be mobilised before, or at the moment of, an Axis attack.[15]

Other matters dealt with at this meeting included a number of proposals advantageous to the Allied war effort. Walshe readily agreed, for example, that immediate measures would be taken to ensure greater security and all ships in and approaching Irish ports would be searched for troops, munitions, refugees and suspicious characters. Archer outlined specific steps, which the Irish government was taking to prevent enemy landings at aerodromes and seaplane bases. In return the British offered their expertise to aid Irish efforts to secure possible landing sites against German invasion. The minutes of the meeting concluded by listing the major points of agreement which included 'detailed planning to ensure the closest of mutual co-operation ...'[16] Thus Walshe, despite personal misgivings about Britain's relative strength against Germany, committed the Irish government to a level of co-operation which was in clear breach of her superficially uncompromising neutrality. This was the beginning of an unprecedented level of co-operation between the two governments, which was to last throughout the war.

In the meantime, Walshe continued his consultations with Hempel who insisted the German government respected Irish neutrality and hinted that the final outcome of the struggle would be significant for the fulfilment of Irish national aims. This was aimed at animating Walshe's expectations that a victory for Germany would lead to a united Ireland. Walshe, satisfied that Hempel had accepted his guarantees that Ireland would remain neutral, believed the German promises would remain intact, at least in the short term:

> The German minister was very friendly. He said he understood perfectly the difficulties of our position. I explained to him that the measures taken by you [de Valera] were essential for the establishment of the unity of the nation. You were desirous above all things to protect our people from the disastrous effects of the war being fought out in Ireland. You earnestly hoped that neither belligerent would violate our territory.[17]

Hempel's account of this conversation proves more substantial. The German minister also reported an amicable meeting saying: 'the conversation, in which Walshe expressed great admiration for the German achievements, went off in a very friendly way.'[18] Walshe aired the view that Britain was Ireland's most likely invader and he further hoped Hitler's recent statement that he did not intend to destroy the British empire did not imply the abandonment of German support for Irish ambitions.[19] Hempel did not accept Walshe's expressions of admiration for Germany's achievements as significant without first hearing the views of the Taoiseach. Surmising de Valera would wish to see him after Walshe had a chance to inform him of the conversation, he reserved the right to send a supplementary report. As predicted, de Valera promptly summoned Hempel. This meeting, held in the presence of Walshe but under the auspices of de Valera, had a distinctly different focus according to Hempel: 'De Valera listened to my statements with interest but obviously attached principal importance to assuring me of Éire's continued adherence to strict neutrality.'[20] Therefore, important differences existed between de Valera and Walshe in their approaches to Hempel. The difference is partly explained by the fact that since Walshe's first meeting with Hempel there had been significant proposals from the British which gave the Taoiseach good cause for adopting a more guarded approach towards the German minister.

Walshe's meetings with British officials in early May 1940, and his statements at that time on the possibility of compromise on the issue of neutrality, were significant in leading to discussions between Malcolm MacDonald and de Valera the following month. MacDonald, a former dominions secretary, was chosen to travel to Dublin with the intention of persuading de Valera to abandon neutrality.[21] MacDonald initially suggested 'a Joint Defence Council, on which representatives of the north and of the south would sit and consult and take decisions together.'[22] The proposal was couched in vague but optimistic terms: 'It might be only a first step to be followed by others. If the habit of co-operation on matters of common concern were established, it would be difficult afterwards to break it down.' De Valera reacted to the idea saying it would only serve to provoke Germany. He told MacDonald that the British government should announce an independent and united Ireland. Then, with the aid of British equipment, Ireland could defend herself against Germany.[23] Later that month MacDonald returned to Dublin with a new dimension to his proposal: 'that there should be a declaration of a United Ireland in principle.'[24] Again de Valera rejected the offer only to be faced with another version days later. This more definitive offer envisaged a British statement accepting the principle of a united Ireland. In return, Ireland was to enter the war on the Allied side.[25]

David Gray, who had anxiously encouraged some form of co-operation between de Valera and Stormont, was unaware of the proposal. When informed of it by Maffey he thought that Britain had approached the matter in the wrong way suggesting 'there should have been gestures preliminary of good will from Ulster'. He continued: 'the move the British have taken in promising a complete and immediate ending of partition I am afraid now will look like a trap'.[26] Gray, nevertheless, believed the offer was genuine and he hoped de Valera would accept it. He resisted offering any encouragement because he felt if de Valera knew that the United States were aware of the offer, it might give the impression that they were helping Britain to get Ireland into this 'trap'. He was annoyed at the position adopted by de Valera and mistakenly believed the isolating quality of neutrality would gradually make the Irish more congenial to Britain's demands.

The documentation within the Department of External Affairs at this time demonstrates little enthusiasm for the British proposal. These unity discussions were in themselves a breach of neutrality and a statement declaring strict adherence to that policy was now being sought:

> It is not sufficient to say that we want a Parliament for the whole of Ireland which will include among its rights that of going into war. Such a statement only sows suspicion in the minds of the Germans and of our own people, and makes the latter believe that we might possibly accept entry into a war, which, so far, is none of our concern, as the price of our neutrality.[27]

The timing of the proposition, as Britain's wartime chances looked bleak, was a crucial factor in Walshe's antipathy to the proposal. This view can be seen in a departmental memorandum, which pointed out that Ireland's entry into the war was the sole reason for the British proposals.[28] During the 1938 Anglo-Irish negotiations de Valera offered Britain the opportunity of a defence agreement in return for concessions on partition. Their desire to resurrect that offer in 1940 appeared purely opportunistic. Panic, in Walshe's view, was the driving force of this British proposal.

An unsigned analysis of the British initiative (which was most probably written by Walshe for de Valera) revealed further considerable doubts about the British motivations. It described the proposals as 'very vague and half-boiled'. Walshe was suspicious that the proposed joint committee, in the 'absence of any previous guarantee of the status of the Union as a whole', could be used by the British to establish 'a new state which would be far less independent than Éire'.[29] Walshe's pessimism regarding Britain's chances in the war was implied in his caution towards the plan, especially since it postponed any significant developments in uniting Ireland until after the war. The report recognised that, 'The truly appalling situation in which they now find themselves, fighting alone against the might of Germany, would be quite a sufficient excuse before the world for concentrating exclusively on the defence of these islands against Germany.'[30] John Maffey surmised it was on such an assessment of British hopes in the conflict that made the offer unacceptable. He mentioned his theory to Walshe who, according to Maffey, 'demurred at this unheroic suggestion' and argued the Irish refusal of the offer was based on 'distrust of the proposals' which relied upon British fulfilment of the deal after the war.[31] Maffey's intuition, however, was not unfounded. Document after document emanating from External Affairs at this time repeated the same Irish apprehensions over the war situation: 'It does not seem that there is a single organised State left in Europe or Asia which is not ready to profit by what they regard to be the impending downfall of Britain.'[32] The conclusion reached was: 'Britain's final folly was committed during the weekend, when Churchill by his accusations and his support of de Gaulle, threw France into the Totalitarian bloc and made England's defeat inevitable.'[33] This was not an uncommon view. In May, Belgium surrendered to German forces and French and British troops had to be evacuated from Dunkirk. In June, Italy declared war on France and German forces moved into Paris and occupied France for the remainder of the war. July saw Britain's sinking of French warships anchored off Oran in North Africa followed by the Vichy government breaking off diplomatic relations with Britain. The outlook for Britain was poor and Walshe's pessimism about the Allies would remain until the 'Battle of Britain' (which reached a climax in mid-August) encouraged him to reappraise the situation.

The decision to reject the offer of unity, therefore, was made on a number of criteria. The proposal itself was vague and did not guarantee Irish unity. Walshe told Gray that he and de Valera construed the proposals as 'a trap to be followed by strong arm stuff'. Walshe's fatalistic reports on Britain's wartime chances were of primary importance. The departmental memoranda, which confidently announced Britain's defeat was 'inevitable' and 'neither time nor gold can beat Germany', must have had a profound bearing on de Valera's decision.[34] While many believe de Valera's greatest political regret was not achieving a united Ireland, Frederick H. Boland, the assistant secretary in the Department of External Affairs, suspected de Valera was not quite so eager for such a resolution. In his memoirs Boland stated:

Dev had a very supple mind ... I could never find out exactly from him whether he really wanted the Six Counties in or not. My belief is, he didn't. He felt that we were not in a position to accept such a big Protestant adjunct to our population – especially, all of them hostile to Ireland.[35]

Perhaps Walshe's advice simply served to support de Valera's personal inclinations at that time.

Walshe further speculated Britain's desire to enlist Ireland to the Allied side was devised to reduce the cost of the war to Britain. He also noted in characteristic suspicious fashion:

It is natural that England should not cease ... to adhere to the policy of having a weak country on her western flank. Some day she might hope to take back the fortress, but she could never again hope to defeat an Ireland with a strong and prosperous population ... To all true Britishers it would constitute a weakening of Britain. That has been an elementary fact of British policy for centuries.[36]

Walshe alleged the British 'are now using against us all the tricks and wiles which they commonly use against small peoples' and he believed for a period that Britain was as great a threat to Irish security as Germany:

In view of recent events it is safer for us to make the assumption that the further and extraordinary means of communication being requested of us by the British are intended, not to meet the eventuality of a German invasion, but to facilitate the British Army in its task of re-occupation.[37]

These statements seem extraordinary considering the ongoing cooperation between the two sides. However, part of the problem was Walshe's dissatisfaction with Britain's lack of appreciation for Irish assistance, which held a considerable risk for Irish neutrality and security if Germany discovered it. Walshe referred to the First World War, pointing out the advantages of the new Anglo-Irish relationship for Britain's war effort: 'In the Great War British had 60,000 men keeping order here, now they have feeling of security about Ireland which would be complete if they gave us arms.[38] He was also annoyed by the manner in which Britain made its demands and noted the British 'will argue we should loosen censorship to convert those who are against war. (For them to be pro-Irish is to be pro-German).'[39] Walshe proclaimed 'we could not do more if we were in the War' and the list of co-operative efforts was indeed extensive. To receive credit was important for Walshe who saw his

government risking its neutrality while at the same time fielding a barrage of criticism from the British press. Walshe was under severe strain,
burdened by outwardly proclaiming strict Irish neutrality while inwardly
compromising that policy.

Walshe's ideas and attitudes towards Britain during these months of
the war were contradictory and difficult to decipher. Despite his apparently firm belief that Britain would lose the war he authorised extensive
cooperation with Britain and notwithstanding this extremely close collaboration he remained suspicious of British motives. While his assessment was that Britain would probably lose the war, he did not desire that
outcome. Ireland could not resist an assault from Germany so she had to
satisfy that quarter, but on the other hand Britain could not be alienat-
ed. Walshe was content, therefore, to continue covert assistance to Britain but within the remit of sustainable neutrality. In his memoirs, Boland explains that contradictions in Walshe's reasoning were not uncommon:

> To say that [Walshe] had a mercurial temperament is an understatement.
> His views and moods were liable to change at such short notice that it was
> often a task to keep them in any sort of precise focus. Joe himself was con-
> scious of his occasional inconsistencies, but he wasn't disconcerted by
> them; on the contrary, he tended as a rule simply to laugh them off as if they
> were inspired by no more than a spirit of mischief.[40]

Walshe's attitude in 1940 can be partially explained by his concern for
Ireland's position at the end of the war. He believed that even if Ireland
and the other European neutrals were invaded by Germany then 'neutrality at least has given them a right to the sympathy and good will of all
other peoples in their eventual effort to regain their independence'.[41] If
England won the war, Walshe believed Anglo-Irish relations would return to normal soon enough, though perhaps after 'a few years of un-
justifyable [sic] resentment' towards Irish neutrality. However, if Ireland
joined with Britain who then proceeded to lose the war, this would
result in the 'complete loss of our independence'.[42] These calculations
were central to Walshe's diplomatic strategy.

Another reason why Walshe's confidence in neutrality prevailed
was that he believed the United States would always support the Irish
government. The vast majority of the American people 'whose good will
we retain while we remain neutral can be a powerful – even a determin-
ing – factor in the restoration of our independence should we lose it during the war as a result of defending our neutrality.'[43] He argued that while

the possibility of a German invasion of Ireland existed it gave no excuse for the abandonment of neutrality. Rather, it made the maintenance of that policy all the more essential for he believed 'a neutral state has a better chance of resurrection in the final settlement'.[44] His estimation of the strength of the Irish lobby in the US sustained his conviction that Ireland would not be invaded or attacked by the Axis powers on the grounds that it would alienate public opinion in America. He stated: 'She knows how grievous a moral loss she would suffer if she attacked Ireland'.[45] Indeed, Walshe envisaged the use of American public opinion against British, rather than German, advances:

> American public opinion seems to me to be the only effective weapon left to us against an early occupation by the British Army as soon as British intrigues prove unsuccessful. It will be necessary to repeat to the American people that Irish neutrality is so fundamental a part of the Irish national position that to fail to defend it against all comers would involve the loss of our independence.[46]

Thus Walshe felt neither Germany nor Britain would attack Ireland as they did not wish to incur US hostility. Later in the war, Walshe re-evaluated this assessment as he did many of his early assumptions.

During the initial phases of the war, Edouard Hempel agreed with Walshe that neutrality was the best policy for Ireland but for different reasons: it met German interests best. He thought that if Ireland were to join the war she would most likely enlist with the Allies. The German minister believed the Irish government was endeavouring to do everything possible to maintain strict neutrality and in particular, he recognised that Walshe and Boland exerted a 'strong influence on de Valera in this direction'. Hempel was annoyed by the damaging effect of German espionage in Ireland. Therefore, he recommended that the German government issue a statement indicating its intention to respect Irish neutrality, in order to restore de Valera's confidence and to 'strengthen his power of resistance to British threats and to facilitate a possible future rapprochement with the Axis Powers'.[47] His superiors attempted to clarify the position and the German Foreign Minister, Joachim von Ribbentrop clearly instructed:

> In all conversations there please put most emphatically that in connection with Ireland we have exclusively the single interest that her neutrality be maintained. As long as Ireland conducts herself in a neutral fashion it can be counted on with absolute certainty that Germany will respect her neutrality unconditionally.[48]

Hempel quickly relayed this attitude to the Irish government. He had previously made assurances but believed both Walshe and de Valera remained suspicious of German intentions. The German representative now intimated to Walshe that the highest authority had reaffirmed his representations. Walshe recognised Hempel 'could now speak quite definitely and reaffirm in the strongest way' the previously expressed attitude towards Irish neutrality.[49] Hempel admitted to Walshe that German espionage attempts were damaging. However, he reassured Walshe that despite whatever suspicions were created in the past, 'he was now able to affirm without reservations (on account of the definiteness of his last instructions)' that Germany continued to respect Irish neutrality 'so long as we did not tolerate any violation of it by the other belligerent.'[50]

Nonetheless, German espionage agents continued to arrive and the case of Hermann Görtz in particular, who had landed in Ireland in May 1940 and was not captured until November 1941, inserted strain and mistrust into the Walshe–Hempel relationship. Walshe repeatedly exploited the matter with Hempel to give his defence of Irish neutrality a more offensive aspect. At a time when the country was under intense pressure to join the war, such German activities were unhelpful to Walshe who had to counter British arguments that Germany was planning to invade Ireland. Privately Walshe believed the assurances Hempel had given but this was of little assistance to him in his dealings with the Allies who cited these incidents as proof of concerted German activity in Ireland.[51]

At the end of July 1940, Hempel sent a report on the Irish situation to his ministry. Walshe had apparently suggested a certain amount of mutual benefit could be derived through co-operation between Irish and German elements in the United States. There would be obstacles to this however, as Hempel outlined: 'The difficulty is, as Walshe, too, pointed out, that if any German participation became known outside, it could easily lead to an undesirable effect in the opposite direction.'[52] This statement by Walshe had the advantage of appearing helpful without promising anything concrete on the grounds of neutrality. As Hempel noted: 'I assume that the Irish government because of well-justified anxiety about a possible unfavourable British reaction against Ireland must also avoid the appearance of co-operation with us.' Hempel also reported Walshe's hope that the unification of Ireland was a possible outcome of a German victory. Such attributed statements to the secretary can be read in a number of ways. It may have been a genuine aspiration of Walshe's to see the fulfilment of Irish irredentist aims in the event of German dominance; if Hitler was in control of Europe, and if Ireland remained on favourable terms with Germany, then why not at least mention this 'small request'. Walshe's articulation of such aspirations, however, may again have been part of the approach to persuade Hempel of the sincerity of his Irish impartiality. To speak of such Irish hopes in a post-war Europe dominated by Germany would surely serve to convince Hempel that the Irish government had nothing to gain in the event of a British victory and therefore Irish neutrality would not be flouted in favour of Britain.

However, Walshe might be accused of a certain 'tenderness towards the new masters of the continent'.[53] Indeed following a brief respite at a health spa in Germany in 1933 he was impressed by the initial achievements of Hitler.[54] He told de Valera of the dynamic atmosphere in Germany and of the 'great experiments' which were being carried out there, adding: 'the essentials of which we may well have to initiate in Ireland'. Walshe went considerably further when he advised: 'It seems to me inevitable that if you are to get leisure to think for yourself and your Ministers, as well as time to work you will have to give Parlt. [parliament] a holiday for an indefinite period.'[55]

As we have already seen, his initial assumption that Germany would win the war influenced External Affairs' policy for a number of months during 1940. To infer that Walshe was indeed pro-German is possible from limited analysis of some of the documentation, including Hempel's memoranda in which he reported Walshe's favourable comments. This, however, would lead to a somewhat one-sided conclusion.

The extent of Irish co-operation with the Allies – sanctioned and organised by Walshe – has previously been outlined. In his conversations with Hempel it cost nothing to be agreeable. This was also true in the case of his meetings with Maffey and Gray. Diplomatic conversations by their nature are inclined to be obliquely ambiguous. Coupled with this is the circumspection required when reading any of the memoranda produced by diplomats since diplomats are susceptible to portraying their input into any reported conversation as effective. If it was Walshe's task to convince Hempel of the uncompromising strictness and sincerity of neutrality then it was an assignment in which he was both resourceful and relatively successful. In a report to the German Foreign Ministry at the end of July 1940, Hempel concluded: 'Basically I have always given expression to a friendly and understanding attitude on the part of Germany toward Ireland.'[56] For the German minister to acquire such a helpful stance at this early stage of the war was an important achievement. To secure it for the future would be a more difficult task.

Parallel to his efforts to convince Hempel that Éire would not compromise its neutrality in favour of the Allies, Walshe tried to convince David Gray that the Irish government would not aid the Germans. Gray considered de Valera's recent refusal of the British offer of unity to be based on 'the very natural fear that England is going down and not wishing to be tied to the wrong horse'. However, he believed Walshe had gone one step further, that of not only fearing British defeat but 'going definitely pro-German. The Nuncio tells me so and I have noticed a change in his attitude to me.'[57] In August, Gray arranged a meeting with the specific aim of 'discovering how far Mr Walshe was pro-German and how far pro-British'.[58] He told Roosevelt: 'I like Joe [Walshe] very much but he has the reputation of being a suspicion monger and to some extent a trouble maker as he gets excited. I felt it was a good idea to get on a sound basis with him so we could talk turkey to one another.'[59] Walshe did not impress the US minister with the view that it was a distinct possibility that Britain would lose the war. While the prospect that 'England might create a stalemate with the aid of the dominions and the United States' was not ruled out, Walshe insisted Irish foreign policy could not be predicated on the assumption of a British victory. Indeed if Germany emerged victorious, Walshe believed it would be in Germany's interest to create and maintain, but not occupy, a strong Ireland. To Gray this was wishful thinking, Germany would surely occupy and exploit Ireland and develop the ports for its own use.[60] Walshe further revealed: 'If Britain won which he did not think possible or fought a draw which was a possibility then he thought Ireland would go on as before and that within the framework of the Commonwealth of Nations was Ireland's best chance.'[61] Gray, surprised by this thesis, thought it naïve to assume Germany would forego the opportunity of using Ireland to control Britain.[62] Walshe was told the attitude of the United States was pro-British and they were fearful of a German victory. From the US perspective, therefore, Walshe's stance and that of the Irish government was regarded as 'a stab in the back' for Britain. Gray opined Ireland genuinely feared Germany but insisted on implicating Britain as a possible invader. Walshe had referred to the recent British offer of unity claiming that following the breakdown in talks there was a real danger of a British invasion. Gray had received assurances from Maffey that this had never been their intention and he thought it unlikely as long as American opinion was against it.

Despite Gray's comments, Anglo-Irish relations at this time remained pleasant. The two governments were working together to procure arms for the Irish army and Walshe assured Gray that as soon as any invasion of Ireland by Germany had begun British aid would be immediately sought. He was anxious to point out Ireland would not be a liability to Britain. Gray, who believed Walshe's opinions represented very closely the government's attitude, concluded:

> I think they are all beginning to believe that we only want to be helpful in the long view of things, that we are now pro-British because we fear the results of a German victory, that we believe a German victory would be as bad for them as for us, and that appeals to anti-British feeling discredit them with us and are stupid because they do no good and only make the settlement of partition more difficult.[63]

Gray sought from Walshe assurances that Ireland was 'benevolently neutral', to which Walshe replied there could be no doubt this was the case but said as a matter of coincidence it happened to be of benefit to Germany also.[64]

In a letter Gray submitted to the censor he also enclosed a copy for Walshe admitting: 'one reason why I could never be a professional diplomat is that every time I write something secret and confidential I feel that I ought to tell your Government about it.'[65] Walshe would have readily agreed with Gray's diminution of his own diplomatic skills. Gray reported he was struggling to get Walshe 'straightened out' on a number of issues. He recognised Walshe's pivotal role in influencing Irish government opinion. He described Walshe as 'de Valera's eyes' and thought it important he remain as open and friendly as possible. This was of particular importance as he believed Walshe was 'personally defeatist on the War and not a good influence, though personally a very nice fellow.'[66] Gray expressed concern about the implications of the Irish foreign policy course for the Irish people and for Walshe:

> He is trying to frame a middle of the road policy for which I can't blame him, but it is helpful to point out to him that the Irish Government having condemned the invasion of Belgium, having jailed German agents and confiscated their money, having jailed the I.R.A. who have representatives in Berlin can only hope as individuals to be liquidated in a painless manner by the Gestapo when Hitler comes.[67]

Gray believed the British were sensible not to coerce the Irish on the ports issue as he felt the time would come when wartime circumstances would force the Irish to accede to the demands:

In various ways I have been letting Joe Walshe (External Affairs) get doses of American viewpoints. He gave me an opening by his complaints about American Correspondents suggesting that Éire was betraying her own interests in not throwing in with Britain. I told him that he probably hadn't heard the half of it, that what was to come would be worse than anything he had got thus far.[68]

Though Walshe was not in agreement with Gray's viewpoint, the US minister hoped he would finally realise the gravity of the situation. Later, he became more doubtful that Walshe could be convinced to join the Allied cause until a German invasion of Ireland was imminent. He adjudged Walshe to be naïve for not fearing that threat sufficiently:

We would be silly to wait till Hitler got the control of the British empire before we began to defend ourselves. Britain is our first line of defence just as she is yours. But you have never believed me. Now you see what has happened. You can speculate as well as I can as to what is likely to be the next step.[69]

For Gray, fear was the key to persuade Walshe that the Irish position was untenable. He asked Walshe: 'has it ever occurred to you that if you don't watch your step Éire might get left out of a front seat in the reshuffle, if that should take place?' Walshe could only reply, 'If there should be a great league of English speaking nations we should want to be in it.' He admitted to Gray that 'We want to stick close to the United States' and added: 'What we really want is to have an embassy at Washington and build an embassy building but we don't want to be turned down and so don't like to make enquiries there.' Gray, of course, was more than happy to make discreet enquiries but believed there would not be any definite answer until the outcome of the war looked more certain. As he informed Walshe: 'You may be a German province and not have any diplomatic representation at all.'[70]

Gray believed Walshe based his wartime foreign policy on the presumption of a German victory: 'Joe has been very defeatist, if not pro-Germanna [sic] and I think has been figuring out an Irish regime based on a German control of Europe. He has certainly been considering it a possibility if not a probability.'[71] As the likelihood of US involvement in the war increased, Gray's views on the Irish situation underwent some alteration. He became increasingly concerned to secure Allied access to the Irish ports. It was only a matter of time before open conflict and contention over this issue would materialise between Gray and the Irish government.

Meanwhile, Winston Churchill, in a statement to the House of Commons, strongly criticised the policy of the Irish government to remain neutral and deny use of the Treaty ports to Britain. Churchill saw this as a grave injustice describing it as a 'most heavy and grievous burden' on Britain's war effort. This attack and ensuing British press denigration of neutrality worried many Irish government officials. Hempel reported to his authorities that Walshe believed the latest attack was more a sign of British desperation rather than a reflection of any real intention to seize the southern ports. He maintained that the lack of defences at the ports undermined their value to Britain. Walshe also thought that any such aggression by Britain was unlikely because this would have serious repercussions for Anglo-American relations. The US government was strongly influenced by the Irish–American diaspora.[72]

Hempel, however, believed Britain would continue to pressurise Ireland in an effort to gain concessions. Therefore, he enquired of his superiors if de Valera should be informed of a possible German willingness to assist Ireland in the event of a British offensive. His superior, Ernst Freiherr von Weizsäcker, State Secretary of the German Foreign Ministry, replied there would be no objection to de Valera knowing that German assistance could be depended upon in this event. In light of this reply Hempel, therefore, made a number of efforts to sound out the Irish government's attitude to the idea of German aid but had found little opportunity to speak with de Valera. He approached Walshe to discuss this delicate matter.

Walshe revealed he had encountered anxiety in some Irish quarters concerning the possibility that Germany might sacrifice Ireland to Britain as a token in any future peace settlement. Walshe also intimated this hypothesis was unlikely due to 'Ireland's strategic importance.'[73] Hempel thought that while the ports were of major strategic importance Britain was unlikely to initiate an attack against Ireland unless as a pre-emptive move against German intervention in Ireland. Walshe, keen to impress on Hempel the importance of Ireland acting alone in the event of British aggression, admitted:

> Even the Irish army evidently considers avoidance of any first move by Germany of such fundamental importance that, referring to the possibility of holding out in the beginning with its own resources, it apparently envisages coordination with the hoped for German assistance only after an English attack has taken place.[74]

Ribbentrop cabled Hempel and suggested that any potential shipment of arms could be construed in such a way as not to represent a technical breach of neutrality.[75] Hempel believed the moment had now come to give some indication of Germany's continued interest in Irish neutrality. Some hints could be given to help persuade the Irish government that Germany would be of vital assistance in restoring a united Ireland. However, within a couple of days he reported having spoken with Walshe who now felt more definite than before that Britain would not attack Ireland. Walshe, citing detailed reasons for this belief, was preparing Hempel for an explicit rejection of the German proposals.[76] He previously indicated to Hempel that de Valera appreciated the offer but felt there was no way that arms could be covertly shipped to Ireland:

> If the English were to learn of the shipment, they would seize with both hands the welcome opportunity to assert the existence of a German–Irish plot; and, what was particularly dangerous, this would gravely jeopardise the freedom of movement secured in consideration of Ireland's neutrality by the vigorous efforts of the Irish–American community in the United States. The Irish government therefore had no other recourse at this time but to abandon acquisition of arms until a British attack, which was unlikely for the time being, had become a fact.[77]

In typical fashion, Walshe, while declining the opportunity of tangible cooperation, had nevertheless made it quite evident to Hempel that German assistance would be sought if a British invasion became a certainty.

Throughout 1940, and during the following years of the war, Walshe remained in regular contact with Gray, Hempel and Maffey. The policies pursued throughout the war revealed that while the Irish government actively supported Britain they would not countenance any active cooperation with Germany. Walshe did not deviate from such a policy and was willing to aid the Allies as long as the sustainability of Irish neutrality was not seriously threatened.

IRELAND, CANADA AND THE AMERICAN NOTE
Emma Cunningham

The study of Ireland's diplomatic relations with the wartime Allies has largely focused on Anglo-Irish and Irish–American relations. Consequently, the part played by Irish–Canadian relations tends to be overlooked and thus a major influence on wartime relations is missed. Irish–Canadian relations developed in the aftermath of the 1921 Anglo-Irish Treaty when the Irish Free State joined the Commonwealth with the same status as the oldest dominion, Canada. At this time, the Commonwealth was undergoing a dramatic transformation from an empire to an organisation of equal nations and it was in creating this new structure that the Irish Free State and Canada first forged a strong bond. This bond was strengthened further through their involvement in the League of Nations. With the outbreak of war, Ireland and Canada embarked on separate paths but the connections formed through the 1920s and 1930s were to prove beneficial. As Canada prepared for war, Ireland carefully developed her wartime position of neutrality. These differing policies meant the countries had very different concerns, priorities and policies for the duration of the war but the good relations existing between them were invaluable in mollifying the often harsher British and American attitudes towards Irish neutrality. This role was most clearly seen in the aftermath of the presentation of the 'American note' to de Valera by the American representative in Dublin.

With the onset of the Second World War, Irish–Canadian relations entered a new phase with the establishment of diplomatic links between the two countries. John Joseph Hearne was selected in August 1939 to act as Irish High Commissioner in Canada. He had served as legal adviser to the Department of External Affairs between 1929 and 1939 and was a major force behind the drafting of the 1937 constitution. In March 1940 Canada appointed John Hall Kelly, a lawyer of Irish decent, as Canada's first High Commissioner in Ireland. John Hall Kelly was succeeded by John Doherty Kearney in 1941. These men were to play a crucial role in the development of Irish–Canadian relations during the war. For John J. Hearne, newly arrived in Ottawa as Ireland's first High Commissioner to Canada, the outbreak of war was to be an early test of his, as yet unproven, diplomatic skills in the field. Canada's declaration of war on Germany was not greeted with manifest enthusiasm in Ottawa, but Hearne reported that recruitment progressed steadily:

> On the surface and underneath the surface, the unifying forces were identical – the belief that Canadian liberty was threatened, the belief that democracy was threatened, and the belief that, whatever the rights or wrongs of the situation in Middle-Europe, the continuous attempt at progressive re-settlement by violence and, of course the attempt to dominate the world by force struck at stabler things than the Treaty of Versailles. Add to that, the loyalty to the mother country and the allegiance to the King and the whole story of the striking unity of Canada is told.[1]

Despite this loyalty, Hearne found there was generally an understanding of Ireland's right to adopt a policy of neutrality and that it 'caused no embarrassment to this mission in the inauguration of its work'.[2] However, there was a widely shared view that Ireland's neutrality would not be sustainable. The Governor General in Canada, Lord Tweedsmuir echoed those views when he told Hearne that Ireland would not be able to keep out of the war. His view was 'not that Ireland was letting the democracies down, but that even Mr de Valera's skill and ingenuity would not succeed in sheltering her from the storm.'[3]

However, as Canada became more involved in the war and as increasing numbers of her men were killed on vessels approaching the British coast, Hearne found that criticism of the Irish policy began to surface. Canadians increasingly called for the Irish government to make bases available to the Allied war effort. *The Ottawa Journal* described de Valera's neutrality policy as 'impractical, impossible and dangerous'[4] and the *Toronto Globe* and *Mail* declared that 'the King's enemies would be perfectly justified in attacking one of the King's Dominions even though it elected to remain neutral'.[5] The call for access to Irish bases was further intensified in December 1940 with the torpedoing of the *Western Prince* steamship off the coast of Iceland. This was carrying the Canadian minister for Munitions and Supplies, C. D. Howe and his official party on a trip to London. Gordon Scott, the financial assistant to the delegation was killed. John Hall Kelly, the Canadian High Commissioner in Dublin, was astute enough to realise that little would be gained from public criticism of the Irish policy. He warned the Department of External Affairs in Ottawa of the perils of such press comments noting that such coverage was based on:

> [the] erroneous view that Ireland is anti-British because of the refusal to hand over the ports. Although Ireland is neutral, public opinion is certainly not pro-German and sympathy with Britain is constantly increasing. Any anti-Irish campaign can do no good and may prove detrimental. The fewer public statements and press comments made under the present circumstances about ports, the better it will be.[6]

As the war developed and both countries adopted very different policies which resulted in differences of opinion, Irish–Canadian relations continued to strengthen. By October 1941, John D. Kearney, the Canadian representative in Dublin, was able to report to Ottawa that de Valera's government was well disposed towards him and the British representative in Dublin, John Maffey. In contrast, Kearney reported that the American representative, David Gray, was not so popular. Joseph Walshe, the secretary of the Irish Department of External Affairs, had gone so far as to suggest to Kearney that he do all in his power to have some other American Minister appointed who would be more sympathetic to the Irish. Kearney did not agree and 'felt that Gray had dutifully carried out an unpleasant task. I gently but firmly declined to take any such action'.[7] On 20 February 1942, Kearney further reported that there was an 'exceedingly good relationship' existing between Ireland and Canada. He considered that his Irish ancestry perhaps aided this.[8] Kearney noted that it had been possible for him 'to bring before him [de Valera] moral issues without causing him to become annoyed and pound the desk, which sometimes occurs in his discussions with my colleagues.'[9] Over a period of ten weeks around the time of American entry into the war, Kearney had three meetings with de Valera. During these meetings, it was made clear to Kearney that American entry into the war would not cause any change to Ireland's neutrality policy. He learned that 'even a promise of unity of Ireland would not alter his [de Valera's] attitude'.[10] Kearney continued the conversation by contrasting the moral standpoint of the Allies with that of Hitler and by focusing on the increasing difficulties of staying neutral, particularly now that the Americans were in the war. Kearney reported to Ottawa that de Valera replied that 'he was morally sure that sooner or later Ireland would be in the war'.[11] The American representative, David Gray, on hearing this, described the meeting as historic but Kearney was not so enthusiastic, noting that despite de Valera's remarks he 'could only gather the impression that unless some new turn of events occurred Ireland would remain on the sidelines'. However, Kearney pointed out that it had to be acknowledged that Dublin's policy had shifted from one of neutrality to friendly neutrality and 'that it has been demonstrated that the Irish Government will do almost anything to help us short of involving themselves in the war'.[12]

By 1943, Canada was a major contributor to the war effort and she continued to watch with interest as Ireland's neutrality policy developed.[13] Canadian interest in gaining access to Irish ports and airstrips was renewed following the decision by the Axis powers to intensify submarine warfare in the Atlantic. In February 1943, Kearney reported to Ottawa that he agreed with Maffey and Gray that the time was right to approach de Valera on the issue of the Irish ports. Kearney's reasoning was that previous approaches had been made when the war situation looked bleak. Kearney did not doubt that there was widespread genuine support for neutrality in Ireland but he again reported that the attitude of the Irish government had changed from 'neutrality' to 'friendly neutrality'.[14] This trend, Kearney noted, was widely welcomed by the Irish population with the exception of the IRA. Kearney was convinced that there would be some support from both the public and the opposition at that point should a request be made for the use of the Irish air and sea facilities. He also noted that the threat of German air raids was now less likely and the Allies had stronger air power and could offer protection to Ireland. Therefore, it would be possible for the Irish government to modify the policy of neutrality in the knowledge that they were unlikely to be subjected to the devastating air attacks that would have been likely earlier in the war.[15]

Kearney stressed to Ottawa the importance of using 'good psychology' when dealing with the Irish and proposed that if they were to make a request it should not suggest that Ireland would become a belligerent though 'ultimately this is very likely to occur'.[16] Ireland should not be reprimanded for her neutrality, he wrote, but instead it should be stressed that this policy was respected although it was at considerable expense to the Allies. Kearney considered that the best way to approach the issue would be in the form of a public note from Roosevelt, speaking not just for the United States but for as many Allied countries as wished to become party to the request. He suggested that an appeal from the small, overrun Catholic countries in Europe would also be very effective. The crucial thing was that Britain's name should not predominate; she should simply be listed with the other countries in alphabetical order. Kearney also proposed that it might further help the situation if the government of Northern Ireland could be induced to send a letter stating it supported the request. He also noted that due to the hostility in Ireland towards communism, it would be better if the Russians were not party to the request. While realising the reasons behind Ireland's policy of neutrality had not disappeared, Kearney considered it would be 'to say the least, strange' if Ireland were not to help the war cause now that the threat of German attack had diminished.[17]

For Kearney, the success of the Allied request rested on their ability to justify their claim that the Irish bases were needed. However, Maffey had suggested to Kearney that even if the Allies could win the war without the facilities, a request should be made 'so that the reasonableness and moderation of the Allies with respect to Ireland would be recorded for history'.[18] The Dominion Office in London was not so enthusiastic, noting that:

> The most probable result of an approach would be to provoke from him [de Valera] a long and argumentative reply on the subject of partition, the value of which for publicity purposes would be at least doubtful. At present we are assured of American sympathy in ignoring Irish complaints, while we do receive certain minor but useful facilities. We might find ourselves in danger of losing these if we provoke a controversy on Irish neutrality.[19]

While no approach was made to de Valera at that time, the Allied diplomats in Dublin continued to hope that the Irish government would change her policy and play an active role on the Allied side. With the advancement of time, it became clearer that the fortunes of the belligerents had changed and Germany was no longer the formidable force she was in the early war years. An Allied victory now looked inevitable. From an Irish perspective, it also seemed that the worst was over. By 1943, it was unlikely that Ireland faced invasion from any quarter. The Allied diplomats in Dublin continued to assess the Irish ports issue. In May 1943 the American Minister, David Gray, warned his colleagues in Washington that certain Irish elements in the United States might seek to create trouble between the US and Britain in the post-war period.[20] Gray suggested that de Valera's government should be discredited before such a possibility arose. He proposed that the US government should request from the Irish government not only use of their air and sea facilities but also that they eject all Axis representatives from the state. However, following discussions between Gray and his superiors it was decided that the war effort no longer needed the ports; in fact acquiring them might slow down their plans, as they would have to divert personnel and equipment to occupy them.[21] Consequently, it was proposed in September 1943 that they would ask de Valera if the American government could count on the use of Irish air and sea facilities if the necessity arose, rather than requesting use of the ports and the ejection of the Axis diplomats. Kearney approved of this proposal because it focused on possible war needs and not on post-war politics. He had worried that the Irish government would refuse to accept the terms of Gray's initial proposal and the goodwill shown by the Irish authorities up to that point would be eliminated.[22] Again, however, de Valera was not approached. The US government was reluctant to act without the approval of the British, which to Gray's annoyance was not forthcoming.[23]

In December 1943, Maffey, on noticing Gray's disgruntlement, suggested to the Dominion Office that the issue of presenting a note to de Valera should be reconsidered. Maffey proposed that the issue of the German legation was 'the card to play with de Valera' noting that it was a reasonable request, which would not involve Ireland in the war.[24] The British raised no objection to this suggestion though they decided not to be party to it, opting instead to separately deliver their own note of support for the American request.[25]

On 21 February 1944, Gray delivered a note to de Valera that claimed that Irish neutrality was favouring the Axis powers, due to the fact that:

> Axis agents enjoy almost unrestricted opportunity for bringing military information of vital importance from Great Britain and Northern Ireland into Ireland and from there transmitting it by various routes and methods to Germany. No opportunity corresponding to this is open to the United Nations [Allies], for the Axis has no military dispositions which may be observed from Ireland.[26]

It requested that the Irish government as an 'absolute minimum' take immediate steps for the recall of the German and Japanese representatives in Ireland. They further hoped that there would be a complete severance of diplomatic links between Ireland and these two countries. On receiving the note from Gray, de Valera showed no anger but merely looked 'sour and grim'.[27] The following day, Maffey presented de Valera with the much shorter note, which simply said that the British concurred with the American request. De Valera reacted in a much more hostile manner to Maffey than he had to Gray, probably because he had a much better relationship with Maffey and thought that he would not be party to such action.[28] Kearney was not consulted prior to the delivery of the notes and first heard of their existence from de Valera. According to

Gray, Kearney was not informed of the notes because, 'we find the Canadian High Commissioner so disinclined to support the Allied Nations view as against Irish [sic] that we no longer take him into our confidence'.[29] This change of tone most likely resulted from Kearney's lack of enthusiasm for approaching de Valera with issues borne out of post-war planning rather than out of consideration for immediate war needs.

Kearney later questioned Maffey as to why he had not been informed about the notes. Maffey told him that 'all the Dominions had been notified of the intention of the United States of America and Great Britain to send notes to the Irish Government and until you hear direct from your Government I had no authority to inform you that notes had been sent or of the contents'.[30] The Department of External Affairs in Ottawa was informed but on 23 February, two days after the Americans delivered their note.[31] It was noted in Ottawa that had they been consulted they might have urged the adoption of 'less direct and formal methods'.[32] Kearney, in a report submitted on 28 March 1944, described how both Gray and Maffey were 'self-conscious' about the fact that they had not informed him of the notes. Maffey argued that as the initiative to send the notes lay with the United States it was not up to Britain to suggest that they should consult with the other dominions. Gray explained that the US government had consulted Britain because of her geographical position. If they were to consult with Canada they would have had to consult with all the other dominions and circumstances did not permit such a delay.[33] These arguments did not impress the Department of External Affairs in Ottawa. They considered that while Gray was not obliged to inform Kearney of his intention to deliver the note, he should have considered the fact that in the past Kearney had frequently acted with Gray and Maffey in making representations to the Irish government. Considering that Canada was the only dominion represented in Dublin, Gray could have informed their representative of his plans even if time did not permit him to consult the other dominions. Ottawa was even less impressed by Maffey's argument believing that his responsibility to keep Canada informed was greater than Gray's. While the British may not have felt free to advise Kearney of the intention to deliver the note without first consulting the US, there was no indication that they had ever sought such permission.[34]

Kearney, therefore, first heard of the notes on 24 February 1944, when de Valera requested a meeting with him. De Valera explained that while the request was from the American government, the British government had supported it. He explained that he saw the American note

as a threat and an attempt to force Ireland into the war. The use of the
words 'absolute minimum' in the text especially worried him and he saw
the note as a veiled threat of invasion. De Valera was also concerned
that such a formal note had been used rather than the more informal
verbal representations made on previous occasions. De Valera made it
clear to Kearney, however, that even if the request was made verbally, he
could not ask for the removal of the Axis missions but he would give an
assurance that he would take any measures suggested to eliminate any
possible espionage.[35] Kearney explained that while he did not know the
contents of the American note, he felt sure that de Valera was misin-
terpreting it and that the US and Britain, anticipating an Allied landing
in Europe, were simply taking all precautions possible to protect their
troops. De Valera hoped that through friendly intervention from Canada, the American and British notes would be withdrawn. In a telegram
to Ottawa on the issue, Kearney suggested that he could not see how
they could ask for the notes to be withdrawn but perhaps they could
suggest that they be kept secret.[36]

The Canadian Prime Minister, William Lyon Mackenzie King, at
first seemed willing to consider de Valera's request for intervention, but
reconsidered on receiving advice on the issue. The Under-Secretary of
State for External Affairs, Norman Robertson, in a memorandum to the
prime minister agreed with Kearney that the notes should be kept secret,
as there was no advantage to be gained by giving publicity to an unsuccessful diplomatic operation. He noted that it was 'not a comfortable
situation for de Valera, but even if we felt confident that we could help
him out of it I consider that we should not try to do so'.[37] Robertson advised Mackenzie King that the only way the Canadian government
could seek the withdrawal of the note would be if there was a chance
that the Irish government would take the initiative and expel the Axis
missions. As this was very unlikely, he suggested that the Canadians
could not act.[38] Canadian reluctance to become involved was strengthened following a communication from the British government. In a message for the Canadian government from the Secretary of State for Dominion Affairs, Lord Cranborne, it was noted that Churchill hoped that the
Canadian government would not agree to de Valera's request but would
associate itself with the United States and United Kingdom on the subject. The message pointed out that the security reasons behind the request applied as much to the Canadian forces as it did to the British and
American forces.[39]

The Canadian government decided that it could not be associated with the British and US request but they were anxious to secure the removal of the Axis missions. Their position was spelled out in a telegram to Kearney on 25 February 1944:

> We have a good deal of sympathy with Mr de Valera's objections to the form and timing of the United States–United Kingdom approach but having in mind the major issues involved we cannot help feeling that he would be well advised to comply with this request. We should be glad to intervene to secure the withdrawal of the notes if there were any assurance that such a step would make it easier for Ireland to expel the Axis missions, and come clearly over to our side. Since he has said to you that he is not prepared to do this, I do not think we would be justified in making an issue over the question of the way in which the views of the United States and United Kingdom Governments were brought to his notice.[40]

While failing to do as de Valera requested, the Canadians were sympathetic to the position in which he found himself. Robertson, in a memorandum to the prime minister, made a comparison between the case of Argentina and Ireland. In Argentina, the Americans had prepared a file of evidence on subversive activities carried out by Axis diplomatic agents to substantiate their claims. Britain had completed the case by arresting an Argentine consular employee who was acting as an Axis agent. These facts allowed the Argentine government alter her policy towards the Axis missions while continuing to act as a neutral power. In the Irish case, Robertson argued the British and American governments did not 'go out of their way to give Mr de Valera a plausible public occasion for modifying his policy'.[41]

Hearne first heard of the American and British notes on the morning of 26 February, when he was instructed to take the matter up with the Canadian government immediately.[42] That same day he met with Robertson who explained to Hearne that they were not forewarned about the note and while they would like to see Ireland in the war, they were not supportive of the approach used. Hearne was not convinced by the argument that the Canadians were not aware of the note prior to its presentation. He later speculated in a letter to Joseph Walshe that:

> [Mackenzie King] probably knew, in a general way, that something was to be done about the German legation and the Japanese consulate in Dublin. Very likely the British mentioned it in a 'casual' way sometime previously, and, having got no adverse reaction at the Canadian end, the way was clear for a formal American approach by whomsoever, i.e. whether the British Government, or the American military authorities, the initiative was to be taken.[43]

Hearne reported that during the meeting Robertson 'spoke with some embarrassment and an unusual tenseness'.[44] Robertson explained that the request was part of an effort to eliminate 'danger spots' prior to an invasion of Europe. In response to a question from Hearne, he said that he did not know what the consequence would be for Ireland if she did not comply with the request. Hearne suggested that 'as the Canadian Government had not been consulted about the note they might not be consulted about any subsequent action should that eventuate'. No other neutral country, Hearne claimed, had been as honourable in carrying out her duties as Ireland was in dealing with the Allied powers. In fact, Hearne argued, 'many might think we had carried the policy of benevolent neutrality too far'. Robertson said he knew that the Irish authorities had 'leaned back' in favour of the Allies and it was appreciated.[45] While Robertson made no commitment to Hearne, he suggested in a memorandum to his prime minister that while the Canadian government could not intervene in the matter he felt that a short word from Mackenzie King 'might help to steady Mr de Valera and prevent a bad business from getting worse'.[46]

On Sunday, 27 February 1944, Hearne spent almost two hours discussing the issue with Mackenzie King. Hearne began by stating that the policy of neutrality united the people of Ireland and made it impossible for the government to comply with the request in the American note. Hearne then proceeded to defend the Irish policy and the leadership of de Valera. He argued:

> This business of crying down Mr de Valera as if he were a dictator of some ideological school or other who held the Irish people in an iron rule went so far and went on so long that people here might have come to believe that he alone stood between the Irish people and their entry into the war. The fact was that Mr de Valera's leadership was unbreakable because at this moment he most fully and unequivocally represented the mind and heart of the whole people. He would never yield to the pressure now applied and, should he do so, he would not hold office for ten minutes after his surrender.[47]

According to Hearne, Mackenzie King listened 'very graciously and patiently'. Hearne continued with a complaint that Ireland had not received due credit for her friendly neutrality. Mackenzie King immediately interrupted explaining that while Ireland was looking for credit, Canada who was in the war had received none. He drew attention to Churchill's recent war summary in the House of Commons where he had not mentioned Canada, but Mackenzie King pointed out that he let it go, thinking that Churchill was too preoccupied 'with the whole war situation to bother about this or that contribution to the main effort'. On the subject of the note, Mackenzie King said that de Valera 'took more out of it than was intended'. Hearne then put the same question to the prime minister as he had put to Robertson the day before, regarding the consequence of non-compliance.[48] Mackenzie King noted his response in his diary:

> I said I could not say, but that I felt there would be disappointment naturally; that, could the step be taken, it would be warmly welcomed, not only by the United States and the United Kingdom, but by ourselves and I felt the other Allies. That there was a long future ahead of all of us after the war was over and that any and every step in the way of co-operation on anything which might lead to possible disaster or to serious ill consequence, would not easily be forgotten.[49]

Hearne then asked if Mackenzie King could assure de Valera that the notes were not designed to bring Ireland into the war. Mackenzie King was willing to give that as his own view, explaining that if such a policy existed the Canadian government would know about it.[50] By this, Hearne understood that 'if further action had been contemplated a serious Commonwealth of Nations issue would have arisen on which he as Prime Minister of Canada would have a view to put forward' and would therefore have been consulted.[51]

Hearne asked Mackenzie King if he could inform External Affairs in Dublin that the Canadian prime minister would help prevent a worsening of the situation and wished to be informed of any further developments. Hearne reported that Mackenzie King said he 'would be glad to render any good offices I can to prevent a dangerous situation from developing'. Mackenzie King, recording the conversation in his diary was not so enthusiastic:

> I said that I had no desire of being drawn into the matter beyond that of trying to clarify the situation and, naturally, would be gratified receiving any word which the Irish Government would wish to send, but that I would not wish, so to speak, to attempt to intervene in a matter which was one between the Government of the United States and the Government of Éire, or the British Government and the Government of Éire.[52]

While Hearne was attempting to ensure Canadian understanding for the Irish position, Kearney in Dublin was also playing a central role in persuading de Valera not to read too much into the notes. He reported on

28 February that Maffey seemed 'anxious that because of unique relations I [Kearney] keep in close touch with de Valera and act as "lightning-rod rôle" in this matter'.[53] On 2 March 1944, de Valera also expressed appreciation for the interest shown by the Canadian government and their contribution to 'keeping things on an even keel'.[54] Ottawa, while pleased that Kearney had helped steady a nervous situation believed that they could now cease their efforts.[55] On 7 March, de Valera replied to the American note. His tone was more composed than it had been in the aftermath of receiving it, perhaps indicating the role played by Canada in soothing a difficult situation. He expressed surprise that he had received so 'grave a note' but appreciated the assurance that the US did not intend to violate Irish territory. He defended Irish neutrality and argued that his government had done all that was possible to prevent Irish territory being used as a base for attack on Britain. He further outlined that while the German minister had a wireless set it had been in the custody of the Irish government for some months.[56] In keeping with the Canadian suggestion, it had not been intended to publish the notes but a leak to the press forced the issue.[57] On 10 March 1944, the American Department of State released the text of the American note to the press and on 11 March issued a press release containing the text of a message sent to de Valera in 1942 reassuring the Irish government that America did not intend to invade Irish territory or to threaten Irish security.[58]

On Monday, 13 March, Mackenzie King, in response to a question from the opposition, made a statement to the House of Commons on Canada's role in the American note affair. In his statement Mackenzie King explained:

> It may, perhaps, clarify matters if I say that the Canadian Government has not in any way endeavoured to mediate between the Irish Government and the United States, also that such representations as were received were in the nature of informal confidential conversations. Shortly after the presentation of the notes, Mr de Valera sent for Mr Kearney, our High Commissioner in Ireland, and told him that he considered it would be in the mutual interest of Ireland and the united nations if through the intervention of a friendly nation the notes might be withdrawn. He suggested Canada might be willing to assume this task and asked Mr Kearney to put his request before the Canadian Government. Subsequently Mr Hearne, the High Commissioner for Ireland, resident in this city came to see me personally. In my reply it was made clear that, as the Canadian Government was in full sympathy with the object of the approach made by the United States Government, we would not wish to intervene in the matter. I believe that the informal discussions which took place through Mr Kearney in Dublin and

with Mr Hearne here were of some help at the time in steadying a difficult situation.[59]

While a difficult situation may have been steadied, the issue was still not concluded. On 14 March 1944, Churchill made a speech in the House of Commons outlining plans to isolate Ireland. He declared that there was to be a travel ban and hinted at economic sanctions directed at Ireland. The press immediately picked up on the story and it seemed as if the action was being taken in reaction to de Valera's non-compliance with the American note. Churchill did nothing to stop such comments. On 19 March 1944 Churchill wrote to Roosevelt and informed him that it was still 'early days to start reassuring de Valera. There is not much sense in a doctor telling a patient that the medicine he has just prescribed for his nerve trouble is only coloured water. I think it would be much better to keep them guessing for a while.' While not planning to stop 'necessary trade' between Britain and Ireland, Churchill did propose stopping ships leaving Ireland for Spain, Portugal and other foreign countries until the invasion of Europe was launched. He also wished to control outward-bound airplanes and to cut telephone communications.[60]

On 15 March 1944, the Secretary of State for Dominion Affairs in London, Lord Cranborne, sent a telegram to Ottawa explaining that the recent reports of travel restrictions between Britain and Ireland were part of ongoing measures to provide security and were not in response to de Valera's rejection of the notes.[61] Ottawa responded by suggesting that the explanation given to them should also be given to de Valera. It was argued by Ottawa that if these steps were designed to prevent leakage of military information then the Irish government would have no cause for complaint 'as long as fear of ulterior political motives is not present in their minds'. It was further argued that if this fear were to lead to Ireland leaving the Commonwealth, it was a 'matter of serious moment' to the Canadian government and all the Commonwealth governments needed to be involved. The Canadians concluded by expressing the hope that they would be consulted before any further steps were taken:

> We wish therefore to empahasize [sic] that we are concerned over the position that has arisen. We have felt from the first that the approach looking to the removal of the Axis representatives was not made in the form best designed to achieve its object, but we at once did what we could to persuade the Irish Government to comply. We have also publicly supported the action taken. We hope that there will be full consultation before any further steps are taken which are likely to have repercussions on the position of Ireland in the Commonwealth.[62]

On 28 March 1944 Kearney submitted a comprehensive report on the effects of the American note, which resulted in a letter of congratulations from Ottawa for the credible way he had handled the situation.[63] In his report, Kearney described his visit to Walshe on the day Churchill delivered his speech to the Commons outlining his plans to isolate Ireland. Kearney reported that if Walshe's reaction was a reflection of the feelings of the government then it was 'an understatement to say that they were greatly excited, resentful and apprehensive'.[64] Walshe threatened to suspend co-operation with the Allies and Kearney reported how:

> I did everything I could to dispel the idea that Mr Churchill's 'Isolation of Ireland Speech' washed out, or even watered down the assurances which had previously been given to Mr de Valera. I said to Mr Walshe, with all the calmness I could assume, that if the situation were not so serious, to people placed behind the scenes like himself and myself, Mr Churchill's speech could not appear otherwise than amusing, he urged me to explain, and I added that Mr Churchill, when he made the speech must have had 'his tongue in his cheek'. I reminded Mr Walshe that, although your suggestion of no publicity had been agreed to by the parties concerned, unfortunately the secret leaked out and Mr Churchill, in my opinion had to improvise in order to meet the new situation. I said that, quite possibly, he used his 'Isolation of Ireland Speech' as a sop to British sentiment regarding the Irish refusal, at the same time knowing that Ireland should, and would, welcome any means taken by Great Britain to diminish Axis espionage in Ireland, thereby reducing the risk that Ireland was running of being the source of a possible espionage coup in connection with the impending European invasion.[65]

Walshe said such an angle had not occurred to him and he seemed 'considerable mollified'.[66] He intended to inform de Valera of Kearney's view.

Kearney later described the meeting to Maffey who approved of his line of argument. Kearney reported to Ottawa that Maffey was anxious that the British government should prevent a repetition of anything like Churchill's speech. Maffey attempted to assure de Valera that he could accept his 'previous representations as bespeaking the mind of the British Government, not withstanding the twist in Mr Churchill's speech and the British press comment thereon which might follow'.[67] Despite Irish public opinion being at 'fever height', Kearney reported that unless some unforeseen incident occurred, with careful handling they could continue to count on having the support of the Irish government. He saw one positive outcome of the whole incident: the Irish public were now in no doubt that their government wished to prevent Axis espionage activities.[68] This in turn would make people more aware of the prob-

lem and in turn more vigilant in preventing the workings of any espionage rings in the country.[69]

The American government considered sending a second note to the
Irish government. Lester Pearson of the Canadian embassy in Washington was shown a copy of the text. Pearson reported to Ottawa on 6 April
1944 that the draft note pointed out that the Irish response to the American note of 21 February 1944 was out of harmony with the traditional
friendship that existed between the two countries. It disputed the Irish
claim that to ask the Axis legations to leave Dublin would be the first
step towards war, pointing out that other nations had broken off diplomatic links without entering the war and it would still be possible to
maintain diplomatic relations with Irish representatives remaining in the
Axis capitals. The Americans further argued that while the good faith
of the Irish government was not being questioned, friendly intentions
were not enough. They could not believe that the people of Ireland, no
matter how much they desired to maintain neutrality, wished to see the
lives of American soldiers endangered.[70] This note was not sent as it was
feared that it would be counterproductive. De Valera called an election
on 9 May 1944. His subsequent victory convinced the American government that the plan to send a second note was undesirable.[71] The issue
was now considered over, a tense situation had passed without any significant long-term damage to relations. The focus switched from Ireland as
the belligerents attended to their preparations for ending the war, and
its aftermath.

The American note had tested Ireland's relations with the Allied
powers and had highlighted the importance of the Irish–Canadian relationship. Canada had helped to defuse a potentially damaging affair and
had managed to do so without antagonising anybody. In general, the war
years were a successful period in Irish–Canadian relations and Canada's
role in ensuring the success of Ireland's policy of neutrality favouring the
Allies has largely been undervalued. As Kearney wrote shortly before
the end of the war:

> There is a general feeling here that Ireland has done a great deal more for
> the cause of the United Nations than she is given credit for, and that per-
> haps Canada has been a little more conscious of it than some other coun-
> tries – in any event, the Irish consider that Canada has acted decently to-
> wards them during the emergency, notwithstanding the fact that Ireland
> was numbered among the neutrals.[72]

CON CREMIN, BERLIN AND 'DIE BILLIGE GESANDTSCHAFT'[1]
Niall Keogh

Con Cremin was in Germany for the last phase of the war, a period when the physical threat to Ireland had receded considerably.[2] Even though the threat of invasion had diminished, this did not reduce the importance of the Berlin mission for Dublin. Patrick Keatinge has argued that 'Ireland's diplomatic relations with the principal belligerents was the lifeline without which Mr de Valera would have been unable to explain or defend his policy of neutrality'.[3]

In investigating Cremin's work as a diplomat during his posting in Germany it is possible to examine his performance through a number of prisms. Firstly, there is his reporting from Berlin of the political, diplomatic and military events as they unfolded. Secondly, his personal experiences in Germany seen through his unpublished memoirs, official reports and the accounts of his diplomatic contemporaries. These provide valuable insights into the collapse of the Nazi régime and the problems this posed for the Irish diplomatic mission. It is then possible to trace Cremin's consular work on behalf of Irish nationals by looking at the cases of Francis Stuart and Mary Cummins, as well as his representations on behalf of many Jews. Finally we will look at the Irish legation's retreat from the Red Army, which posed a very real threat to its safety.[4]

In 1943 Cremin was aged 35 and Berlin was to be his first posting as head of mission. Originally from Kenmare, Co. Kerry, he had studied classics and accountancy at University College Cork before joining the Department of External Affairs in 1935. From 1937 he had served in France – in Paris and then Vichy – but wartime difficulties over accreditation dictated that Dublin would allocate him only with the status of *chargé d'affaires*. The Irish 'wanted to keep a lowish profile, in Berlin'[5], and so in choosing Cremin, who, unlike one of his predecessors – the infamous Charles Bewley (Irish Minister to Germany, 1933 and 1939) – 'had no sympathy for Hitler or National Socialism',[6] they made a wise decision. Moreover, Cremin's time in France after its fall in 1940 had shown him at first hand the Nazi occupation and exploitation of that country. His period in Vichy France had further reinforced his abhorrence of national socialism, and the Irish legation in Vichy distanced themselves from all unnecessary contact with Germans.

The Situation in Berlin

It was not the first time that Con Cremin had been posted to Berlin. His first term there was for two and half months in the late summer of 1942. William Warnock, the then Irish *chargé d'affaires*, had been injured in a motor accident and Cremin relieved him while he recovered. Warnock and Cremin had joined the service together in early 1935 and were good friends and colleagues.[7] They 'were members of a new generation of career diplomats who did not allow themselves to become personally involved in their assignments'.[8] Warnock 'reported competently from Berlin but his youthful enthusiasm may sometimes have got the better of him'.[9] However, by 1943 the strain became too much and in April he asked for home leave.[10] Warnock was informed that Cremin would replace him again immediately, but in August, the secretary of External Affairs, Joe Walshe, informed Warnock: 'Regret very much delay in this years holidays, crisis too grave for even temporary change in Berlin. Please remain at post.'[11] Warnock complained that he was not able to comment accurately on Irish affairs. He wrote:

> Two things have always puzzled the Foreign Office: 1. That despite the great importance of Berlin and the added interest attached to Ireland since the war, the staff of the Legation consists of only one diplomatic officer and one typist. 2. Why, in view of the bad state of communications between Ireland and Germany, I have not once been in Ireland during the past four years to report personally … Occasionally they refer to us as 'die billige gesandtschaft' (the cheap legation).[12]

The department took cognisance of the telegram, stating in October that they were awaiting word from the minister in Vichy, Seán Murphy, to see if he would allow Cremin to go to Berlin.[13] This was the biggest reorganisation of the Irish diplomats in service during the war.[14]

Cremin duly arrived in Berlin on 24 November 1943.[15] The simple task of handing over the mission was disrupted by the destruction of the legation in an air-raid on the night of 22 November; the raid killed 1,600 Berliners and destroyed the *Gesandschafts Viertel* (diplomatic quarter).[16] Warnock had:

ignored the air raid warning at eight o'clock in the evening and was working on his accounts in an upstairs room when a bomb set fire to the lower floor and walls. Warnock's files and archives were destroyed and he just had time to see the Legation's grand piano go up in flames before hurriedly leaving the building as the roof collapsed.[17]

Warnock gave a detailed account of the destruction, stating: 'I was entitled to go over to the bombproof bunker in the Government's Guest House across the road, but I felt that it was my duty to remain in the Legation'.[18] It is indeed a tribute to all of the Irish diplomats that none of them ever placed their personal safety ahead of their duty.

Cremin arrived at the shell of the legation, not knowing if Warnock was alive.[19] He found that Warnock had moved to *Schloss Staffelde*, the official Irish *point de repli*.[20] Warnock remained on as *chargé d'affaires* until he left for home on 28 February 1944. Cremin wrote:

> Warnock had had a difficult and probably lonely time in Berlin (for he was as yet unmarried) but he had a quite unusual command of German and seemed to have a host of friends. His experience of the 22 November must have been for him traumatic.[21]

The pressure was taking an increased toll on Warnock as he had served as *chargé d'affaires* since 1939, but 'owing to [a] total loss of records [Warnock felt] he must stay'.[22] Warnock telegraphed Dublin: 'Whole Legation quarter destroyed … In spite of strenuous efforts everything lost except code and key(s) of Bag 1 typewriter also saved. I have lost much clothing and most of my personal effects but escaped injury except for inflammation of the eyes caused during our fight against the flames.'[23] In the interests of security the code was considered one of the most important things to save. However, the Irish cipher *dearg* [red] was obsolete,[24] although it was used up to at least 1954.[25] O'Halpin argues that from mid-1941, Allied cryptanalysts were able to break Irish diplomatic cable traffic,[26] the Germans too were able to read whatever they wished.[27]

Cremin's posting coincided with the beginning of the heaviest raids on Berlin,[28] but he was fortunate in that *Schloss Staffelde* was located 30 miles north west of Berlin.[29] He tried to get all of his work done in Berlin on one day during the week and so conserve petrol and minimise the personal risk of going into the city.[30] The only official entertainment was lunches given at the Aldon Hotel, where 'the diplomatic corps was herded together and "treated with contempt"'.[31] They had little contact with leading Nazis.[32] These lunches sometimes coincided with the weekly visit of the US Air Force, which interrupted the proceedings.[33] At night the RAF bombed Berlin. Cremin in his memoirs records that some bombs landed near *Schloss Staffelde* and they had a further escape in Bremen.[34] He gave this account:

> The air raid Berlin Wednesday June 21st 1944 was manifestly heaviest American raid to date .... A cloud of smoke and dust over the city all day Wednesday gave impression of continuous twilight. After raid population seemed rather nervous but by 23 June when I was again in Berlin life seemed to be just as usual apart from certain disturbance in transport.[35]

In spite of the personal danger, Cremin continuously sent political reports back to Dublin on the developments within the Reich.

Political Reports and the July Bomb Plot

On 27 March 1944, Cremin reported on the German invasion of Hungary, Operation Margarenthe.[36] The Hungarian prime minister, Nicholas Kallay, had been attempting to negotiate a separate peace ever since the armistice granted to Italy in September 1943.[37] The occupation, however, destroyed the last bastion of European Jews and 570,000 of Hungary's 825,000 Jews ultimately perished in the Holocaust.[38]

The landings of the Allies north of Rome at Anzio on 23 January 1944 threatened Rome for the next six months. While the Allies were landing, Cremin received a surreal request from the Book Association of Ireland to give their 'catalogue what ever publicity you could'.[39] Ireland was truly in Plato's cave.[40] On 12 March 1944, Pius XII appealed for Rome to be spared and on 19 March de Valera sent an appeal to the belligerent powers pleading for the avoidance of the destruction of Rome, by making it an Open City.[41] On 23 March, Cremin was informed that only German military police were in Rome.[42] On 20 April, he sent the text of this 23 March German reply to de Valera.[43] Cremin informed Dublin that the German government would publish their response to the Allied demands for the evacuation of Rome. Throughout May efforts to establish a neutrality commission were fruitless.[44] Finally, Rome was declared an Open City on 3 June.[45] However on 6 June, Cremin reported the fall of Rome which the German press claimed was 'of no military value' adding that 'general opinion last September was that German main lines of defence are well to the North of Rome'. This was accurate; the main defensive line – the Gothic line – ran through Florence, although Rome could have been another Stalingrad. However, de Valera's initiative was perceived to have strengthened the 'special relationship' between the Holy See and Ireland.[46]

On 6 June 1944 the second Allied front opened in Normandy as expected. On 17 April Cremin had already reported expectations of an imminent Allied invasion of Western Europe.[47] Two *Auswärtiges Amt* (German Foreign Office) officials with whom Cremin spoke felt that the Allied invasion would fail,[48] while another contact felt that the sooner the invasion came the better, because elite German troops were being kept in the west,[49] which was not the case.[50] Cremin recalled in his memoirs:

> I remember at one lunch ... there were quite a few diplomats present and the date was the 5 June 1944. In the course of conversation a friend of mine from the Swiss Embassy asked me when I thought the invasion would take place. Although I naturally had no information at all I suggested within the next couple of days. In fact as we know it began the following day and my standing with my Swiss colleague soared enormously when the event happened.[51]

In mid-June, Cremin reported the German press reaction to Normandy: '[the] decisive phase of the war has now been reached and Germany has within her power attainment of final victory'.[52] German generals were not as optimistic and Hitler visited the western front to boost their morale.[53] Cremin's contact in the *Auswärtiges Amt* stated that the Allies had put 25 divisions in Normandy,[54] half the actual figure.[55]

Cremin reiterated on 4 July 1944 that government officials were seriously preoccupied by the military situation and 'many individual Germans are convinced that all is lost'.[56] It was the seriousness of the military situation that encouraged conspirators to make another – ill-fated – assassination attempt on Hitler. Led by Count von Stauffenberg, the plot was an attempt to wrest power back from the Nazis.[57] On 24 July, Cremin reported *Auswärtiges Amt* officials were still optimistic, and his contact ridiculed the idea that political change was needed in Germany. They still hoped that the English would compromise. Considering that the report came the day of the bomb plot itself indicates that the official line was still that Germany would fight to the end and indicates the secrecy surrounding the plot.[58]

Later that day, Cremin informed Dublin about the assassination attempt on Hitler, stating that the party was in control and there was no evidence of unrest. He reported:

> the armies abroad are in a more independent position. Much seems to depend on how deep the movement has gone among the officers in the field. The most serious defection at home is probably that of Fromm, head of the

reserve and as such controlling millions of men. I understand he has been arrested.[59]

The British intercepted this report and it was passed to Churchill who marked the following section in green:

> One aspect of the matter is that the Germans are now justified in believing on evidence of presumably competent officers rather than foreign propaganda that the military situation is very serious. This attempt was, I think, a complete surprise to officials. The Secretary of State, when he was out here Wednesday night, clearly had no inkling of the plot.[60]

One of the reasons that the British were interested in the Irish diplomat's reports was that they did not believe in the existence of an anti-Hitler movement. As late as July 14 the British intelligence chiefs doggedly concluded that any action against Hitler was unlikely.[61] Cremin's independent report was highly valued.[62] In late July, he gave a very accurate report on the bomb plot:

> One explanation I have however, from fairly well-informed non-party source is that plot was organised for purely military reasons by small group of officers in or close to headquarters who blame Hitler for having withdrawn troops too late on several occasions especially in Stalingrad, Crimea and Odessa with a loss of several thousand men.[63]

Major-General F. W. von Mellenthin in particular blamed Hitler for constantly refusing to retreat in time.[64] Cremin reported: 'A party member of the Propaganda Ministry told me episode is being deliberately used as pretext to introduce various changes, net result of which would be to make party still more identical with the State'. Cremin opined: 'I think it is safer to assume that episode will not in itself lead to weakening on fronts' and concluded by stating 'different sources affirm that Hitler will never agree to arrangement with Russia. If this is so, it may have played a limited role in the plot'.[65] Cremin's reporting was professional and accurate. On 11 August 1944, he wrote to Dublin: 'I think it is quite certain that German Government intend neither to capitulate nor to come to terms'.[66] In a report of 18 September 1944, he suggested the idea of the 'Southern Redoubt', from where the Nazis would fight on.[67] This possibility appeared solely in diplomatic reports and led the Allies to a cautious advance into Germany.[68] This particular report was shown to Churchill.[69] As the autumn approached, Cremin wrote that the Arnhem battle, the failed attempt by the British under Montgomery to capture the bridges over the Rhine, was being 'saluted as an important victory and the relative spectacle [at the present time] western front [seems to me to] prove German ability to [resist] successfully. All official pronouncements are a reiteration of Germany will not to give in'.[70] On the British intercept there is a blue tick on the bottom of the page, and the word 'Irish' was circled in red in 'Irish Chargé d'Affaires'.[71]

In November 1944, Cremin reported that Hitler might be suffering severe nerve damage. Himmler came to the fore and a new law decreed that party members could remain active even when in the military.[72] Cremin indicated that Himmler might try to make peace, but stated it was improbable that he would push Hitler aside.[73]

On 28 December 1944, Hitler launched the Ardennes offensive which saw the German army drive towards Antwerp.[74] Four days previously an unnamed colleague[75] had informed Cremin that the aim of the offensive was primarily political.[76] The diplomatic aim was the hope of destroying the US, British and Soviet alliance.[77] A week after the battle, Cremin wrote:

> I think the explanation is, in general, probable: it seems to me this must be objective of all German military operations in the future, as I do not think leaders here, apart from Hitler perhaps, really believe Germany can now impose her terms on her opponents by force of arms and her aim must therefore be to see that they do not impose theirs on her. I think, however, that, even if present offensive succeeds in sense that Germans can reach and maintain their goal, it may not be immediately followed by diplomatic initiative, as situation on Russian Front must first, it seems to me, become less unfavourable to Germany either by definite stabilisation of whole front at some point or by German victory, and such an improvement, if possible at all (as some here think it is) will take time.[78]

His *Auswärtiges Amt* source informed him that Antwerp was the objective and that two million tons of supplies had been lost.[79]

After the Battle of the Bulge, Cremin's main concern was to evacuate himself and his family from Berlin. However, before he could leave he had to fulfil both his professional responsibilities to Irish citizens trapped in Germany and a moral duty to alleviate some of the suffering of European Jews.

Consular Activities

Irish citizens in German-occupied Europe fell into three categories. The first were simple consular cases requiring exit visas and passports. These cases consumed a large amount of time, but were routine.[80] Second were the group that gave assistance to the Nazi régime: Francis Stuart, Charles Bewley and Frank Ryan.[81] Cremin had the most contact with Stuart. The third category was Irish citizens who fell foul of the Nazi régime, of whom Mary Cummins is an interesting sample case.[82]

The novelist Francis Stuart went to Germany in 1939, ostensibly to take up a university post, but also to act as a courier for the IRA.[83] Stuart quickly settled into life in Berlin,[84] and throughout the war worked as a broadcaster for Irland-Redaktion, the German propaganda service to Ireland. Dan Bryan, director of G2, wrote of Stuart's activities thus: 'I am convinced that he was active in the German IRA conspiracy from at least the outbreak of the war but see no hope of producing any legal evidence to that effect'.[85]

In August 1942, Cremin refused Francis Stuart a passport explaining to Stuart that he had, 'no inherent right to receive a passport and that the Government is free to act in regard to passports as it sees fit, taking into account of circumstances'.[86] Stuart again asked for a passport in late April 1944.[87] Walshe advised Cremin: 'Stuart's passport should not be renewed. For yourself he is regarded as having forfeited any claims to our diplomatic protection by unneutral and disloyal behaviour'.[88] In September 1944, Stuart and his lover, Fraulein Meissner, left Berlin for Munich.[89] On 24 February 1945, Stuart requested that Cremin write him a note allowing him to travel to Brenganz near the Swiss frontier.[90] Cremin wrote the note and gave Stuart hospitality in Brenganz.[91] Elborn states that from Stuart's point of view: 'Brenganz was a major disappointment, for although they met Cremin of the Irish Legation, he only offered a good meal'.[92] On 28 March 1945, Cremin again refused him a passport.[93] Stuart found lodgings in Dornbirn, south of Lake Constance, and was there when Germany surrendered in May 1945.[94]

When Stuart presented himself at the Irish legation in Paris in August 1945, 'Boland instructed Seán Murphy to give him £15. He was left in no doubt that "his conduct in 1940, at a particularly dangerous moment of our history", had not been forgotten in Dublin'.[95] Stuart lamented: 'I came under suspicion not because I was a Nazi, which God knows I never was, but because I was not on any side. There are those who argue ... that being in Berlin and broadcasting on Irland-Redaktion are proof enough of culpability'.[96] However, Stuart's culpability went further. As Dan Bryan stated: 'Stuart further indicated to him that if Russell's and Ryan's submarine mission [aborted attempt to land two IRA leaders in Ireland] was a success he, Stuart, was later to follow them with a cargo of arms'.[97] Bryan added: 'I was looking into this man's case and find that we have no legal evidence on any point associating him with illegal activities directed against this country ... His history and associations are, however of a very suspicious nature'.[98]

On the other extreme was the case of Mary Cummins, who was found guilty of espionage by the German authorities and was sentenced to death.[99] From April 1944, Cremin had been trying to visit Cummins and finally succeeded at the end of September 1944, although he was not allowed to ask questions about the details of the trial. He wrote:

> She does not look strong to me. She says however her health is generally speaking good but that she does not get enough to eat and is consequently somewhat weak. It is not permitted to send such prisoners food or clothing but I propose to raise the question with the foreign office.[100]

On 29 November 1944, he reported that he had succeeded in obtaining Cummins' release.[101] However by 16 December 1944 she had still not been set free.[102] In early January, Cremin, after a very persistent attempt to obtain her release, was told that she would be let go very shortly.[103] But on 16 January, he learned from the *Auswärtiges Amt* that:

> the case had been completely neglected by the official. That official had let the file lie on his desk for several weeks believing that it was just one of the several thousand pardon applications ... not realising that this was an exceptional case inspired largely, as Herr von Schonebeck put it, by political considerations.[104]

The next day Cremin was able to report: 'Cummins arrived here last night Tuesday and will stay with us for time being. She sends her family love and is most anxious to receive news'.[105] On 1 February, he sent the following telegram: 'Cummins is now much stronger and quite well. She admits being guilty of charge as stated. She says that she belonged ... to organisation financed from London'.[106]

The Cummins case was one of the reasons that Cremin had delayed leaving Berlin, and he left shortly after securing her release. He employed her as a maid, making it easier for him to bring her through Switzerland, as she would have been seen as a 'domestic' and not worthy of official scrutiny.[107]

Jewish Refugees
'Cremin did not share [Charles Bewley's, former Irish minister to Germany] prejudice towards the Jews', and during his time in Berlin he worked assiduously to intervene on their behalf.[108] This lack of prejudice

was important in the attempt by the Irish legation to try to protect some European Jews from extermination, although Cremin was ultimately unsuccessful.

On 5 January 1944, Walshe enquired whether '200 Polish Jewish families might be allowed to come to Ireland ... and would they allow specific Jewish families be transferred'.[109] Warnock and Cremin replied: 'You will also appreciate that German authorities are inclined to regard action by other countries as indirect criticism of their Jewish policy'.[110] On 16 March 1944, Cremin received a sinister reply from the German government and communicated this to Dublin:

> As regards Jews have been asked by internal affairs section of Foreign Office why we want them to go to Ireland whether it is intended that they become citizens or only remain there until the end of the war and whether any of them have relatives there. I gather no hope of visas except for such families as have relatives and even then I think little chance. Official concerned inclined to read political implications into our inquiry thinking it had something to do with Anglo–American refugee schemes.[111]

Cremin's information revealed that the German authorities had on occasion allowed Jews of British or Dutch origin leave Germany, but not German, French or Polish Jews. He repeated that the German authorities were anxious to know what would happen to the Jews if they went to Ireland. According to an unidentified official:

> If it was intended that these families should become Irish citizens the German authorities would, I was given to understand, 'gladly save us the inconvenience of having so many Jews' [Cremin's emphasis]; if on the other hand it was proposed that the families return to Europe after the end of the war it could be inferred that a German defeat was presupposed; if it was intended that they should later go to Palestine, the German government could not approve of an arrangement which would have for a result to introduce further Jewish elements into an Arab territory.[112]

Having read the statement the department could not be in any doubt as to what was happening to Europe's Jews. Cremin continued:

> I have thought it best to give you the above account of this interview so that you may see how enquiries touching on the Jewish question can be made to assume enormous proportions in the minds of certain German officials ... The official [to] whom I was referred is, I think, a member of the SS-organisation.[113]

He stated that this section in the Foreign Ministry was predominant when it came to the issuing of exit visas for Jews.[114]

On 20 April 1944, Cremin received a report from Walshe and de Valera asking if the granting of exit visas would prevent the deportation of Jewish children from the internment camp at Vittel in France.[115] Cremin knew that representations on behalf of Jews were useless, but he continued to make approaches to the German government.[116] On 27 April, he was told that persons interned in Vittel were not to be deported.[117] Two weeks later he was informed, having made further inquiries, that the Jews in Vittel had in fact been moved. He was assured however that: 'The measures for deportation had been suspended pending decision on our *démarche*'.[118]

This, however, was not so and on 6 June 1944 the Vittel Jews were transported to Drancy.[119] On 7 June, Cremin replied to queries from Dublin that he could not confirm their whereabouts. On 3 July he reported to Dublin that he was told that 'the 200 Polish families you have in mind cannot be traced. There were 77 individual Polish Jews in Vittel who are now in camp in eastern Europe'.[120] Cremin added that he was told by Eberhard von Thadden that: 'German authorities have been treating application with all possible good will because it comes from Ireland'. Von Thadden headed Department II of the Foreign Ministry, which was responsible for the crushing of attempts to obtain visas for Jews or information about the deportees.[121] On 27 August 1944, Cremin filed the following report:

> Official of Swiss Legation dealing with this question has now told me that there were originally 238 such Jews in Vittel; of these 163 removed in April ... in May some escaped some committed suicide. He says that the total in Vittel when he was there last month was 14.[122]

Cremin reported information received from the *Auswärtiges Amt* in relation to the Jews at Drancy, that the camp was disbanded and they did not know if the Jews were released or not.[123] On 5 October, he conveyed von Thadden's statement that inquiries had been sent to the authorities of the camp of Oswiecim/Auschwitz but no other reply had been received.[124]

On 21 October, Walshe telegraphed Cremin: 'Report that a rumour has reached the Jewish community in Dublin that the Germans plan to exterminate all Jews. Request for assurances from the F[oreign]. O[ffice]'.[125] Cremin replied that the *Auswärtiges Amt* official said: 'that rumour of intention to exterminate the Jews being spread by various enemy sources but that as it is pure invention and lacks all foundation the German authorities have no reason to make a statement on the subject'.[126]

In December Cremin presented an aide-memoire to the *Auswärtiges Amt* on behalf of Hungarian Jews which was not accepted.[127] His Swiss colleague, Dr Zehnder, believed: 'the USA have been using the Jewish question as a propaganda stick with which to beat the Germans'.[128] After January 1945 the file ended. It is clear, however, that Cremin did try repeatedly to break through the deception that obscured the Holocaust from the outside world, knowing all the time that the reports he was sending to Dublin were being read by the Nazis.[129] He continued to confront the German authorities about the deportation of Jews and bore witness to the Holocaust, even in the last stages of the Third Reich.

The 'Liberation' of the Irish Legation

As the Reich collapsed on all fronts, the remnants of the diplomatic community in Germany made arrangements to leave. As early as August 1944, Cremin was given complete discretion by de Valera to leave Germany when he thought it necessary.[130] On 28 October 1944, Walshe ordered Cremin to leave for Switzerland.[131] Cremin replied that he would leave when the situation merited it, but he would send his children to Switzerland,[132] as he and his wife, Patricia, 'thought it prudent in order to ensure greater mobility'.[133] Cremin reported that the papal nuncio was remaining in Berlin as he considered leaving would be tantamount to a split between Germany and the Vatican.[134] The main reason Cremin delayed his departure was the consular cases.

The Swiss minister had arranged visas for all diplomats on safety grounds so that they would be able to travel even if the frontiers were closed. Throughout November and December Walshe urged Cremin to leave for Switzerland.[135]

At the beginning of January 1945 the Soviets, under Marshal Zhukov, launched the Vistula-Oder Operation which by the end of the month brought them to within 40 miles of Berlin.[136] On 19 January, Cremin reported on the seriousness of the Russian offensive and stated that 'the situation looks very black' for Germany.[137] On 27 January, Walshe told Cremin to leave Berlin. Dublin had instructed Cremin 'not to get caught in Berlin'.[138] On 31 January, Cremin reported that massive numbers of refugees were flooding into Berlin and he had arranged with the *Auswärtiges Amt* to go to the Swiss frontier.[139] Next day he wrote that he was going to Salzberg.[140] Prior to his departure from Berlin, Cremin 'nominated Charlie Mills as *chargé d'affaires* and affixed certificates on various parts of the building to the effect that it housed the Irish Legation'.[141] Cremin's departure from Berlin was rapid and he did not have time to notify the Irish community in Germany.[142] He travelled with his wife to Salzberg,[143] and on 19 February, they left for the Swiss frontier.[144] They arrived in Bregenz on the shores of Lake Constance near the Swiss border on 23 February.[145]

Meanwhile, Dublin asked F. T. Cremins, the Irish Minister in Berne, for information about Cremin.[146] F. T. Cremins replied that Con Cremin was in Bregenz and could still reach Switzerland.[147] The department requested F. T. Cremins to get Cremin to Berne.[148] On 30 March, a report was received from Cremin stating that his telegrams were being delayed and that his only remaining function was to assist nationals within areas of German control.[149]

On 5 April 1945, on the recommendation of the Swiss embassy, Cremin and his wife moved to Babenhausen, where they stayed in the *schloss* with the Princess Fugger, who was from an old German banking family.[150] A diplomatic legation was a good form of insurance to protect one's property. Cremin wrote that a German diplomat was 'very active about looking after our welfare and security' and 'hoisted on the highest point of the *schloss* the Irish tricolour'.[151] The Burgermeister of Baben-hausen placed large signs in Irish, German, English and French indicat-ing the presence of the Irish legation. Their final size 'rather startled' Cremin.[152] On 17 April, Walshe ordered Cremin to leave Germany im-mediately.[153] On 25 April 1945 he still had not left and filed a report stating:

> Defeat certain and matter of at most a few weeks … The entire Foreign Office has now left Berlin, with the exception of Minister for Foreign Affairs, Secretary of State, Under Secretary of State and some others … The German government is to come south if, as everyone expects, things go badly in the north. I formed the impression Foreign Office is in some respects disbanded as many members have remained behind for private reasons and others from North Germany have gone there.

On the question of food Cremin reported prophetically that while the situation was not critical: 'it will certainly be worse and there will prob-ably be very serious situation in few months whatever evolution of mili-tary operations'.[154] Astutely he reported: 'The belief Western Powers and Russians will ultimately fall out is widespread: interest encouraging this belief as Germans see on such a development opportunity for Germany to play role in post war world'.[155] For many the origins of the Cold War date to 1942 when the tensions between the Allies were never resolved;

this was exemplified in Stalin allowing the Warsaw uprising to be crushed by the Nazis.[156]

On 25 April a telegram was sent to F. T. Cremins: 'Anxious for news of C'.[157] Dublin need not have worried as the *schloss* and the Irish legation were 'liberated' by a US Colonel from Limerick.[158] On 15 May, the department received a telegram from Babenhausen stating that Cremin would shortly proceed to Switzerland.[159] He also noted the conditions and attitude of the German people:

> Judging by this region, population, while not completely war-weary, are glad war is ended and that the Americans have got so far. They, of course, hope future attitude of Western Allies will allow of achievement of some freedom of political development and government. There is no doubt that England and America can profit by the dread of Russia felt by population and so consistently inculcated by Government propaganda and practice and that, in the circumstances, they will find no lack of collaboration originally.[160]

Simultaneously, the US government began to realise that world recovery depended on a strong, industrialised Europe and fought for a reindustrialised Germany under tight controls.[161]

By 7 June, Cremin was at his new posting in Lisbon and received word from Joseph Walshe:

> I should like to let you know how very much the Minister and all of us here appreciate your excellent work in Germany. We appreciate very fully the trials and difficulties which you and your wife had to overcome during the period of your mission in that country, and we are profoundly grateful that both of you took the whole experience as a great adventure which the Department will always remember as a bright and stirring page in the history of its early years of growth.[162]

The Second World War saw Ireland take the side of those countries that believed in the need to secure western democratic values and the 'country's new diplomatic élite made a strong contribution to help build up that fundamental commitment'.[163] This was especially true of Con Cremin and Seán Murphy. They did not allow their enthusiasm get the better of their judgement; both displayed a calmness under fire that saved Ireland from a dangerous misadventure of frolicking with Nazism during the dizzying days of 1940.

LIFE, POLITICS & SOCIETY ON THE IRISH 'HOME FRONT'

KEEPING THE TEMPERATURE DOWN:
DOMESTIC POLITICS IN EMERGENCY IRELAND
Donal Ó Drisceoil

Party politics flourished in wartime Ireland; paradoxically, however, the democratic context which gives such politics meaning was highly compromised in the cause of protecting and preserving the state. While the political temperature was kept down in 'the national interest' (a mantra that covered a multitude), Fianna Fáil simultaneously kept the party political pot simmering, turning it up to boiling point when it suited its purposes. The question of whether the ends (a 'successful' neutrality and an intact sovereign state) justified the means is not the main concern here; rather it is to detail and examine domestic political life in Emergency Ireland, and the fortunes of the main actors, within the context of the democratically 'challenged', governing politics of neutrality.

By the outbreak of war in 1939 Fianna Fáil already stood at the centre of Irish politics. Its programme set the national agenda. The Emergency witnessed a further contraction of the political field and a strengthening of the centrality of the dominant party. The Emergency Powers Act 1939 (EPA) gave the government a range of extraordinary powers deemed necessary for securing public safety, the preservation of the state, the maintenance of public order, and the provision and control of essential supplies and services. This was effectively a licence to rule by decree and the normal legislative functions of parliament were suspended; thus, parliamentary democracy continued in little more than a nominal way. The EPA also authorised powers of censorship that were used to achieve the 'neutralisation' of wartime political culture: this neutralisation involved not only the suppression of war-related material, but anything deemed a danger to internal political stability. A clear example was the attempted suppression of class politics, characterised as 'sectional' and anathema to the dominant conception of a national community. Neutrality was the overriding issue, and cross-party support for that policy carried with it a certain acquiescence in the national leadership role that de Valera lost at the time of the Treaty split but had, by the outbreak of war, partially regained.[1] In the dominant discourse, moulded and controlled by the state through its censorship/propaganda system, the survival of the state was synonymous with the survival of neutrality, and these twin objectives required the government to 'keep the temperature down', both between Ireland and the belligerents and internally.[2] When added to factors such as paper shortages and transport restrictions, and the virtual destruction of democratic local government, the damping down of political life was inevitable at one level.

An interesting feature of the Emergency, however, was that at other levels, political life was energised. Under the veneer of calm and control a lively and disparate culture of dissent and opposition asserted itself: the maverick parliamentarian James Dillon broke ranks with his opposition to neutrality; militant labour politics flourished at grassroots level and the Labour Party became fleetingly successful; a new farmers' party briefly broke the mould of rural politics; the controversial Oliver J. Flanagan emerged onto the political stage for the first time; and a small group of feminists made a precocious, if doomed, attempt to introduce gender politics into an alien and uninviting environment. However, the lack of overall common purpose, and any cohesion or co-ordination, together with the government's arbitrary powers, limited the impact of this opposition at a general level, while the various elements had their respective limitations exposed – all to the political benefit of Fianna Fáil. The Labour tide, for example, was stemmed by a combination of red scaring and self-destructiveness; the farmers' party failed to develop much beyond a protest movement, while the eternally dissident militant republican tendency was smothered by state repression and electoral humiliation. Fine Gael, the main opposition party, offered little: the war and neutrality placed it between a rock and a hard place and it went into brief electoral free-fall. On the fringes, the electorate was not ready to support the efforts to establish a women's party, the People's National Party was more a welcoming party-in-waiting for a Nazi invasion than a serious political organisation, while Ailtirí na hAiseirghe, Coras na Poblachta and independent republican candidates were all given short shrift by the electorate. The Communist Party of Ireland (CPI) dissolved itself in the south in 1941 and its members worked within the Labour Party, before providing a pretext for that party to be split.[3] Fianna Fáil took an electoral punch in 1943, but re-established its parliamentary majority in 1944.

The Politics of Neutrality

Neuhold has identified two major contributions a small state can make towards maintaining its neutral status in war: defence and political stability.[4] In wartime Ireland, the former was dealt with by secret arrangements with the Allies and clever diplomacy by de Valera; the latter was maintained by the prudent control of the state's finances, the repression of dissident and subversive forces and voices, and the foreshortening of the political field. The secret and extensive co-operation with the Allies and the diplomatic manoeuvrings are all treated in detail elsewhere in this volume but some related issues are worth noting with regard to domestic politics. The need for reliance on Allied defence arose from serious Irish defensive shortcomings. Censorship was used to hide this co-operation from the public, in line with the need to maintain the illusion of strict neutrality; a virtue was made of, and/or emerged from, necessity, in the shape of savings on defence and an emphasis on mass popular participation in the defence effort. All of these factors had the side-effect of benefiting Fianna Fáil. The maintenance of wartime economic stability was politically important to the government. The minimisation of economic disruption and shortages helped to lessen the appeal of radicals, while the many thousands who suffered unemployment because of the war's impact on the industrial economy – a potential source of political unrest – were facilitated in their emigration to Britain's war economy by the Irish state. The primary reason for Ireland's relatively comfortable war was economisation on defence, which was the basis of the unique achievement of reducing public expenditure as a proportion of gross domestic product between 1939 and 1945. The modest level of defence spending (less than half the proportion of public expenditure that it accounted for in other neutrals like Sweden and Switzerland) meant that tax rises were minimised.[5] This reduced the backlash against the government party, which had everything to lose as well as gain by the maintenance of party politics. Only a national coalition government (such as emerged in Sweden), could have inflicted the sort of financial burden, particularly on the middle-class, that a serious defence effort would have required. The Irish Times consistently pushed the all-party national government idea, and as it faced into the first wartime general election in 1943, the main opposition party, Fine Gael also asserted it as the most desirable arrangement in 'the national interest', but clearly in its own interests too. Fianna Fáil's emphatic success in the 1938 general election had signalled that party's dominance of Irish politics. The war and the chosen path of neutrality offered political dangers but also opportunities for the governing party; for Fine Gael, however, it offered mainly dilemmas and something of an identity crisis.

Neutrality was a popular policy for pragmatic and symbolic reasons. It meant avoiding the horrors of war and represented the clearest assertion since independence of Irish sovereignty. It was also the least divisive policy both within the population generally, and within Fianna Fáil. The futility of opposing neutrality while party politics continued resulted in Fine Gael support for a Fianna Fáil-led policy and an implicit abandonment of its Commonwealth position, its major distinguishing feature. The thawing of civil war divisions in the heat of a united defence effort further eroded the party's identity. The only payback for Fine Gael was participation with government and Labour Party representatives in a National Defence Conference, a poor substitute for national government which Fianna Fáil never took seriously. Following the fall of France in June 1940, fear of invasion gripped the country and Fine Gael privately suggested to the government that neutrality should be abandoned. It proposed an all-Ireland defence system consisting of British, French and Irish troops, under overall French command, as a pre-emptive move against a German invasion. Fine Gael leader W. T. Cosgrave privately made it clear to de Valera that if the government felt the need to abandon neutrality, it would have his party's 'fullest support'. In reply, de Valera stressed the government's belief that neutrality offered the best hope of preserving the state from invasion.[6] His prioritising of neutrality – and concomitantly 26-county sovereignty – over moves towards Irish unity in the context of participation in the war, was further illustrated by his dismissal of a British offer of unity in return for the ending of neutrality in June 1940.[7] For the remainder of the war Fine Gael fully supported neutrality as the only game in town. Deputy leader James Dillon, however, spoke out against it in the Dáil in July 1941 and again at the party's árd fheis in February 1942 (following the entry of the US into the war in December 1941). His reward was forced resignation from Fine Gael and isolation. His departure was a blow for a party already in trouble.

Despite the minimisation of wartime tax increases and the relative comfort of the Irish population in general, the war did have a negative socio-economic impact, and the working-class bore the brunt. Real wages fell by approximately 30%, profiteering and black-marketeering were rife, emigration and unemployment soared, and tuberculosis and infant mortality rates rose sharply. A senior civil servant admitted privately in 1941 that poverty and hunger were 'fairly widespread'.[8] The early years of the war saw an unusually high level of social conflict, manifested in strikes, housing agitation and street protests. Censorship was used to minimise publicity for these challenges to the notion of unity and consensus, and also to hide the fact that up to 200,000 Irish people joined the British forces and war economy. The scale of the exodus and official Irish facilitation of it compromised Irish neutrality, but was seen as essential to the maintenance of acceptable levels of unemployment and minimal levels of social disorder.[9] The contradiction between neutrality and the government's policy regarding migration to a belligerent economy and army was a feature of left-wing critique, but censorship and repression reduced its impact. (The need for 'economic defence', and the danger to neutrality of the government's policy, would, however, be part of the 1943 Labour Party general election programme.)[10]

However, it was not migration policy that provided the main focus for the growing discontent of the Irish working-class in the early years of the war, but two measures introduced in 1941: the Trade Union Bill and the Wages Standstill Order.[11] The large and militant campaign against these measures radicalised workers; the fact that the Labour Party rather than the Irish Trade Union Congress took a leading role led many to join the party, which grew from 174 branches in 1941 to 750 in 1943.[12] Some of the individuals who rose to prominence in Dublin, the core of the growth, had been members of the CPI and they – together with other left-wingers like the Larkins, Owen Sheehy Skeffington and socialist republican veterans – were active in Dublin, the cockpit of the campaign against the Trade Union Bill and wages freeze. The rejuvenated Labour Party had its first opportunity to reveal its potential as an alternative to Fianna Fáil for working-class voters in the 1942 local elections.

Local Elections
The need to keep the political temperature down meant a governmental aversion to elections of any kind. The avoidance of by-elections resulted in a total of nine Dáil seats remaining vacant between 1940 and 1943.[13] No local elections had been held since 1934, and the Emergency, together with the coincidental shift towards managerialism, further lessened Fianna Fáil's already minimal interest in local democracy. This attitude was shared by Cumann na nGaedheal/Fine Gael, and among the parties represented in parliament it was left to Labour to fly the flag for local government. The 1940 County Management Act became operational in August 1942; its thrust was to invest managers with executive

powers, thus reducing the authority of elected representatives and strengthening central control over local affairs. This trend had been in evidence since the foundation of the state. Between 1922 and 1942 rural
district councils were abolished, city managers were appointed in Cork,
Dublin, Limerick and Waterford, and ten county councils were suspended and replaced with commissioners. Local elections, which should have
taken place every three years, were repeatedly postponed and only
occurred three times: in 1925, 1928 and 1934.[14] Following the 1937 and
1940 postponements, the issue arose again in 1942. The Minister for
Local Government, Seán MacEntee, initially suggested a further postponement, citing the practical problems posed by wartime shortages as
well as the danger elections would pose to the 'spirit of comradeship'
that had marked the response to the 'common peril', especially in the
defence forces and voluntary auxiliary services. He subsequently relented in the face of opposition, citing the greater danger to the principle of
elective representation if the elections were indefinitely postponed.[15]
They were held on 19 August 1942, a week before the new local authority management system became operative.

   Fianna Fáil and Fine Gael agreed that the local elections should not
be marred by the introduction of 'politics', both to minimise divisiveness
and because, in any event, power had shifted decisively towards appointed managers and away from elected councillors. They failed to mount
nationwide party political campaigns and most of their candidates ran as
nominal 'independents' or 'ratepayers' rather than under party banners.
According to Labour, this was a mechanism to allow party loyalists from
both parties to vote for a candidate from the traditional enemy party and
against Labour, which, in line with its consistent championing of local
government and opposition to managerialism, refused to comply with
the depoliticisation of the elections. The restoration of the powers of
elected representatives was a major plank of its programme (making the
managers 'servants' and not 'masters'), which was a radical reformist one
of rent and rate reduction and improved services and housing. Fianna
Fáil accused Labour of breaking the 'no politics' *entente cordiale* and
using the elections to 'sabotage the government'. In a low turnout of less
than 50%, Labour was the major winner. It trebled its representation on
county councils and more than doubled it on urban councils and corporations, jumping from two to twelve seats on Dublin corporation,
where it became the largest party and secured the mayorship.[16] While
this was in part a victory for political commitment and organisation in
the face of apathy and arrogance from the larger parties, it also reflected

a growing disenchantment with Fianna Fáil and Fine Gael, especially in Dublin, and was a promising springboard for Labour in the general election that would be held the following year. Another threat to the two largest parties also emerged in 1942 in the shape of Clann na Talmhan, the recently established farmers' party, which won control of Roscommon and Kerry county councils.

1943 General Election

Fianna Fáil's majoritarian approach to democracy contained dangers of slippage towards authoritarianism. The operation of the Emergency censorship system, under the control of Minister for the Co-ordination of Defensive Measures, Frank Aiken (often accused of having dictatorial tendencies), contained many examples of such slips. In a memorandum entitled 'Neutrality, Censorship and Democracy', Aiken set out his view that 'the peace-time liberalistic trimmings of democracy', such as free speech and parliamentary democracy, needed to be set aside in order to preserve 'the fundamental basis of democracy', by which he meant the sovereignty of the state.[17] Aiken used censorship to protect himself politically, most significantly in banning criticisms of himself during his ill-fated mission to secure arms and supplies in America in 1941.[18] De Valera was also protected from party political criticism, and defended this by pointing out that criticisms and misrepresentations of the head of government were not 'in the interests of the State.'[19] Throughout 1942, with a general election on the horizon, opposition deputies began voicing concerns that censorship was increasingly being operated in a party political fashion. Interestingly, Dillon's árd fheis speech of February 1942 advocating full support for the American war effort, was allowed publication in full; Fine Gael accused Aiken of allowing it only to cause embarrassment to the opposition, regardless of the broader consequences for neutrality. These examples highlight the problems inherent in a situation where a single-party government effectively became the sole arbiter of the national interest, and the lines between government and state were blurred. The Taoiseach and his ministers, by virtue of their offices, were representatives of the state but they were also party politicians, and the use of state powers for party purposes was a more obvious danger than usual: this danger would intensify in the run-up to the first wartime general election.

A general election would have to be held in or before June 1943, unless there was all-party agreement on a postponement. Such agreement was not forthcoming from the opposition, to the chagrin of Fianna

Fáil which feared for its majority and let the Dáil run its full course for the first time ever. Senior minister Seán Lemass had pointed out that among the reasons for the 'considerable disquietude' within government regarding an election was the danger of leaving the country without effective leadership for even a short period.[20] This was partially over-come by not dissolving the Dáil, as was standard practice, on 26 May 1943, but merely adjourning it, thus leaving the old Dáil intact while the election for the new one took place. The election was bitterly fought and this, plus the fact that the number of candidates was the highest since 1927, gives the lie to the notion that domestic politics lacked vibrancy during the Emergency.

Fianna Fáil strategy was straightforward: it was the only party that could give stable government at this time of crisis, and voters should avoid the dangers inherent in 'changing horses when crossing the stream' (one of the party's slogans). It naturally sought to work both sides: claim party credit for the all-party supported policy of neutrality, but shirk and share responsibility for the economic stringencies and social inequalities of the Emergency; the other parties were accused by de Valera of capital-ising on grievances caused by 'inevitable' wartime hardships.[21] Claims and counterclaims about who was primarily responsible for neutrality had been denied publicity since late 1942: a Labour Party advertisement which read: 'Labour's Foreign Policy: Labour is the keystone of the Na-tional Arch of Neutrality' had been altered by Aiken's censorship to read 'Labour's Foreign Policy: Neutrality', and another which read simply that 'Labour policy is the people's policy of strict neutrality' was stopped in its entirety. The censorship authorities also retained the right to censor election speeches that were 'likely to weaken or compromise Ireland's position as a neutral State'.[22] The Fianna Fáil position was that neutrality was a Fianna Fáil achievement and its maintenance could only be guar-anteed by keeping it in power: 'In times like these – safety first'; 'If you vote Fianna Fáil, the bombs won't fall'. Its speakers and canvassers were instructed to highlight Fine Gael's flawed pedigree on the issue and that it only came behind the policy when it became clear how popular it was.[23] Fine Gael campaigned for a national government; Fianna Fáil claimed that it alone could provide a truly national government as it represented 'all sections of the community'.[24] In the absence of a na-tional government, a coalition was the only alternative to Fianna Fáil, and the latter continually stressed the dangerous instability of such an outcome. It used Fine Gael's past resistance to coalitions to oppose the idea, while the Fianna Fáil newspaper, the Irish Press, ran features on the failures of coalitions elsewhere in the run-up to the election.

The main threat to a Fianna Fáil majority came not from Fine Gael, however, but from the resurgent Labour Party in Dublin and the new farmers' party, Clann na Talmhan, in rural areas. Despite grassroots radicalism, the Labour Party's programme remained relatively conservative, reflecting the continuing control of a tame leadership and the disproportionate influence of the ITGWU, the country's largest union, whose leadership was supportive of government policy. Fianna Fáil dismissed Labour's aspirational social democratic electoral promises as 'outlandish', inflationary and unworkable: taxes would need to be doubled to improve social services as promised by Labour and its programme was described by MacEntee as 'a declaration of war on every thrifty, industrious household in this country'. It was MacEntee who spearheaded the lurid and ludicrous red-scare campaign against Labour in 1943, claiming that the party was controlled by communists. This was despite the fact that none of the communists who had joined the party were election candidates. However, former communists Jim Larkin and his son, 'Young Jim', were put forward in controversial circumstances and with fateful consequences. MacEntee extended his smears to include the rural electoral threat of Clann na Talmhan – Galway 'totalitarians' in league with the Dublin 'Muscovites' in a bizarre Nazi–Soviet pact of convenience.[25] Clann na Talmhan had been formed before the war to represent the interests of small farmers, particularly in the west, who felt betrayed by Fianna Fáil and unrepresented by the big farmer-dominated Irish Farmers' Federation (IFF). In 1942, however, it merged with the IFF-established, Leinster-dominated National Agricultural Party, which featured prominent figures like Independent Wicklow TD, Patrick Cogan. By 1943 the Clann had developed into an impressive grassroots organisation, with Michael Donnellan, a former Sinn Féin and Fianna Fáil councillor from Galway, as leader and Cogan as deputy leader.[26] The party, and Donnellan in particular, engaged in populist anti-establishment, anti-'party system' rhetoric, which prompted MacEntee to dub him 'Herr Von Donnellan'. Its attempt to represent often conflicting class interests among farmers and its lack of a coherent political strategy would ultimately finish Clann na Talmhan, but in 1943 it offered an opportunity to register dissatisfaction with Fianna Fáil's (and Fine Gael's) agricultural and rural policies that many farmers were happy to grasp.

The general election was held on 22 June 1943. The vote for the two biggest parties dropped by over 10% each, which translated as a loss of 10 seats for Fianna Fáil (from 77 to 67) and 13 for Fine Gael (a calamitous drop from 45 to 32). Labour's vote increased by 5.7% to 15.5, which meant an increase of 8 seats (from 9 to 17), its best ever performance. Clann na Talmhan won 10 seats, while independent farmer candidates claimed another 5. Fianna Fáil lost most heavily in the most agricultural areas – to the Clann where it had candidates, and to independents where it had not. Fine Gael also lost out to the new party. Of Labour's gain of 8, half were in Dublin, including Jim Larkin Senior and Junior. Emergency repression, including censorship, internment, imprisonment and executions, as well as its own lack of political engagement, had virtually eliminated the IRA from the political landscape. On the electoral front, the 5 candidates from the militant republican Coras na Poblachta (formed in 1940) all lost their deposits, as did the 4 from the fascistoid cultural nationalist/republican party, Ailtirí na hAiseirghe.[27] Four women, including Hanna Sheehy Skeffington, who ran on a feminist ticket in the hope of laying the foundations for a women's party, all lost badly and the number of women in the Dáil remained at 3 (1 Fianna Fáil and 2 Fine Gael, all widows of former TDs who never showed any interest in issues affecting women and were known affectionately as 'the Silent Sisters').[28] There were 43 new TDs in all, including Oliver J. Flanagan, who was elected on a Monetary Reform ticket and got himself noticed with his sweeping attacks on all parties, his IRA and Nazi sympathies and his outrageous anti-Semitic outbursts.[29]

Fianna Fáil was in a minority of 5, but Clann na Talmhan and Labour abstained in the vote for Taoiseach rather than precipitate another election, resulting in a minority Fianna Fáil government. Fine Gael, which had lost a number of its leading TDs, lost its leader in January 1944 when W. T. Cosgrave stood down. In the absence of Dillon (who rejected a Fine Gael offer to return to the party as leader in the Dáil), Cosgrave's designated successor Mulcahy (who had lost his seat in 1943) took over the leadership, with T. F. O'Higgins as leader in the Dáil.[30] While Fine Gael's problems brightened the government's spirits, those in the Labour Party were even more welcome at that particular juncture. The key to the success of the new red-scare that now engulfed that party was that, unlike MacEntee's smears, this one came from within. William O'Brien, general secretary of the ITGWU, picked up the red card from MacEntee and applied it to justify his splitting of Labour (which had more to do with his long-standing vendetta against Larkin), claiming that Larkinites had plotted with former CPI members to take over the party. Having failed to have these 'undesirable elements' excluded, the ITGWU disaffiliated in December 1943 and in January 1944 five of the union's eight TDs formed the National Labour Party (NLP), committed to Catholic nationalist (Fianna Fáil-friendly) politics and free from communist, or even socialist, infestation. It received clerical endorsement and encouragement from Fianna Fáil, with whose approach it so closely harmonised that one historian has dubbed it 'Fianna Fáil's Labour Party'.[31]

1944 General Election

William Norton and the rest of the Labour leadership attempted to limit the damage by launching an inquiry into communist infiltration, against the background of McCarthyesque witch-hunting articles in the Catholic *Standard*, penned by an influential champion of the NLP, Alfred O'Rahilly (with the connivance of William O'Brien and information from Garda Special Branch, the same source as MacEntee's).[32] This resulted in the expulsion in April 1944 of six members for attending a CPI conference in Belfast the previous October and the effective silencing of the left in the party. With Fine Gael dispirited and Labour split and in disarray, Fianna Fáil seized an early opportunity to call a snap election in order to regain its majority (as it had done in 1933 and 1938). Following defeat on a vote on a transport bill on 9 May 1944 (amid accusations of Fianna Fáil-connected corruption in railway share dealings), the Dáil was dissolved and an election called in the face of united opposition from all other parties and independents. The government's arguments about the inadvisability of wartime elections were forgotten in the face of the prospect of a majority. The *Irish Times* noted sarcastically that de Valera had once again found the statesman in conflict with the politician, and the politician had prevailed.[33] Besides Fianna Fáil's better-prepared election machine and the problems besetting the opposition, de Valera had the further advantage of his recent popular 'triumph' in the American note affair, and an attractively packaged rural electrification scheme to offer the electorate.[34] In a short campaign of only 18 days, Fianna Fáil reiterated the need for stability and strong government (a renewed concern among many following the American Note episode) and made hay while Labour split.[35] MacEntee praised the NLP, calling it a labour party in the true 'Pearse and Connolly' tradition, in contrast to the 'Internationale Labour Party'.[36] The NLP increased its anti-communist rhetoric, focusing its attention on the Labour Party rather than offering opposition to the government. The Labour Party fell into the trap, asserting its own anti-communism and fealty to Catholic principles and Church authority in public affairs (to little avail), rather than maintaining its focus on the oppositional politics that had served it well in 1943.

In the lowest turnout since 1927 (68.5%), Fianna Fáil won back its majority, winning 76 seats (a gain of 9, mainly at the expense of Labour) against a combined opposition total of 62. All the opposition parties fared worse than in 1943, except for Clann na Talmhan, which, despite a marginal increase in its vote, still lost a seat.[37] Fine Gael's weakness was evident in its fielding of only 55 candidates (32 less than the previous year), an admission of its inability to offer a single-party governmental alternative. Its vote dropped a further 2.6% and it lost another 2 seats. The losses included 'safe' seats like Cosgrave's former one in Cork. Only one new Fine Gael TD was elected and internal party transfers had dropped to a paltry 62%. Virtually the only consolation was the return of party leader, Richard Mulcahy. (In five by-elections in 1944–45, the party failed to nominate a candidate in three and was beaten into third by Clann na Talmhan in another.) The two Labour parties won fewer votes and seats than the united party in 1943. The NLP won 4 former Labour seats, but lost one, while the Labour Party lost a further 5, reducing its representation from 17 to 8. NLP transferred well to Fianna Fáil, but more Labour transfers went to Fine Gael than Fianna Fáil for the first time.[38] De Valera comfortably won the vote for Taoiseach, but in a break with the past, the Labour TDs voted against him. Fianna Fáil recognised that it could no longer rely on others to gain a parliamentary majority and set out to underpin its 'team' performance through vote management and internal transfers.[39] It was now more clearly than ever 'Fianna Fáil versus the rest', and the rest would twice manage to coalesce in the following decade to temporarily break the dominant party's stranglehold on government.

Conclusion: Emergency Politics and their Aftermath
De Valera's famous reply to Churchill's attack on Irish neutrality at the war's end put the seal on Fianna Fáil's success in the politically crucial war of perception: it copperfastened the idea that Ireland had been responsible for the success of its neutrality (despite the highly compromised nature of the policy and the heavy role that good fortune played in its survival); it struck the right emotional notes against the old enemy (the final shots in a phoney war, given the extensive wartime co-operation and Irish *de facto* reliance on Allied defence); and it crowned de Valera as national leader and Fianna Fáil as the triumphant architects of a successful and popular policy. The risk of maintaining party politics during

the Emergency had paid off – the government party had strengthened its stranglehold on Irish politics. The other main parties were outmanoeuvred, forced to support the government's policies 'in the national interest' and gain few political rewards in return. Fine Gael had been decimated, ending the war with 15 fewer seats and its role as an alternative government party buried. It lacked a strong party identity and national organisational infrastructure (only in Dublin and Cork did it possess any semblance of a party machine). Fianna Fáil's increasing conservatism lessened the counter-appeal of its main challenger on the right. On the other wing, the Labour Party had been neutered and the hopes of socialists for a party that would challenge Fianna Fáil hegemony over the working-class and help shift Irish politics in a leftward direction (as was occurring in Britain), lay dead on the Emergency landscape. The splits in the political and industrial wings of the labour movement represented a major political coup for Fianna Fáil, to the extent that it had played a not insignificant role in helping to bring them about; they simultaneously removed an electoral threat and facilitated a close and fruitful long-term alliance between the party and the dominant sections of the trade union movement. The red-scare vaccine had banished socialist and secular class politics to the outer extremities of the body politic yet again, and when the electorate next expressed its dissatisfaction with Fianna Fáil, a major beneficiary was the new (relatively) radical Clann na Poblachta (formed in 1946), which was sufficiently Catholic/nationalist to survive a lash of the red brush. That party gained support from potential Labour voters and also from republicans who had lost all faith in Fianna Fáil, particularly following its use of the opportunity afforded by the Emergency, and the danger to the state represented by militant republicanism, to turn the screw on the IRA and temporarily eliminate a persistent political (albeit not electoral) irritant. The electoral threat of Clann na Talmhan had peaked, though its medium-term persistence, together with the brief success of Clann na Poblachta, allowed the first two inter-party governments to be formed (which helped rescue Fine Gael from continued decline and created a context for the reunification of Labour in 1950), before 'normality' was restored in 1957.

Neutrality was, according to Frank Aiken, the only policy compatible with the security of the state: there was no room for flexibility in the context of an evolving and fluid situation, no dissent or questioning was allowed publicity. This 'neutrality' became less a policy than a dogma as the war proceeded. In this form it was used to herd the opposition and the public into line with the Fianna Fáil position across a range of domestic issues. A clear illustration of the political utility of the neutrality card was the branding of British-based unions and their allies in Ireland (such as Larkin's Workers' Union of Ireland) as enemies of and threats to the policy, and thus to the state, which provided the background to the creation of a labour movement far more amenable to the Fianna Fáil approach. If the object of the government policy of neutrality was, as it stated, the preservation of the state and the democratic structures and procedures that theoretically defined it, then its role was paradoxical. The concept and principle of democracy was reduced to its pragmatic simplification: it was not even a fully functioning parliamentary democracy, as we have noted, but a functioning electoral system, extending to the parliamentary election of Taoiseach. Even this truncated system existed in a highly compromised democratic context: free speech, a free press, the right of the minority to challenge the majority and so on were mere 'liberalistic trimmings' that could be, according to the ruling ideology, and effectively were, swept aside. It was not these fundamentals that were the basis of democracy, according to the government, but rather the 'sovereignty of the state': *salus rei publicae suprema lex* (the safety of the state is the supreme law) is a concept rooted in absolute monarchism rather than in democracy. A democratic concept of national security, whereby civil, political and economic rights are fundamental, was not up for discussion. Not only was democracy diminished by the restriction of political debate and discussion, but the more general information vacuum created by the Emergency censorship undermined the ability of Irish citizens to make informed choices in relation to Ireland's position on the war and the issues at stake. Finally, the shift in power at local government level from elected representatives to appointed officials which was completed during the Emergency (and which harmonised with the more general trend towards centralisation, which is normal in wartime) should also be borne in mind when considering the question of wartime democracy. This argument about the politics of neutrality is not centred on the question of whether the ends justified the means, but on whether it is meaningful to characterise, consider and analyse Irish wartime politics as democratic at all. Given the democratic deficit, and the (not unrelated) copperfastening of the dominance of a party that had left its youthful radicalism behind, it is hardly suprising that conservative continuity rather than radical change was the primary political feature and outcome of the Emergency.

AILTIRÍ NA hAISEIRGHE: A PARTY OF ITS TIME?

Aoife Ní Lochlainn

Labelled fascist by its contemporaries and by present-day commentators,[1] Ailtirí na hAiseirghe,[2] has become a shadowy organisation, barely meriting a footnote in most accounts of Ireland during the Second World War. The major texts on twentieth-century Irish history and politics have little to say about it. Yet, despite its omission from the history books, Ailtirí na hAiseirghe and its founder, Gearóid Ó Cuinneagáin, were well known in political and cultural circles in Ireland during the 1940s.

Ailtirí na hAiseirghe the political party, grew out of an Irish language organisation, Craobh na hAiseirghe,[3] which had its beginnings in Conradh na Gaeilge (the Gaelic League). From its inception in the late 1880s Conradh na Gaeilge had been to the forefront in the drive to revive the Irish language. While the language revival movement had benefited from its identification with revolutionary nationalist politics, by the late 1930s much of the energy generated by this association had dissipated. With the formation of the new state, the Irish language had become institutionalised. Conservative in its views and pedestrian in its approach, Conradh na Gaeilge had little to offer the new generation of language enthusiasts. Craobh na hAiseirghe, on the other hand, with its street marches, *ceilís* and cultural events, quickly established a firm and visible presence in Dublin social and cultural life. Ailtirí na hAiseirghe, though just as visible, proved less successful in terms of public support than its parent organisation. A political party committed to an autocratic corporate state, it seemed to have a limited appeal to Irish voters. It did, however, gain some notoriety for its campaigning style and Gearóid Ó Cuinneagáin himself belonged to the network of pro-German individuals and groups which was active during the war years. Ailtirí na hAiseirghe was born out of the commitment of one man to his idea of a Gaelic, Catholic Ireland, yet its policies and ideology found many contemporary echoes and resonances which rescue it from the obscurity of the historical anachronism.

Origins

On 26 September 1940, a group of people gathered at 55 Lower O'Connell Street, Dublin in the offices of Uí Chuinneagáin & Cooke, Accountants, with the intention of forming a new *craobh* (branch) of Conradh na Gaeilge, which would have a fresh approach to the language question. The objective of Craobh na hAiseirghe – to have Irish spoken countrywide as soon as possible – was spelled out that night by Gearóid Ó Cuinneagáin, who chaired the meeting. Through the use of modern propaganda – advertising, film, radio, records, newspapers and magazines – he believed this could be achieved quickly. Its members invested a lot of time, energy and hope in its future, and in the early stages they were not disappointed; Craobh na hAiseirghe's activities increased rapidly as its members tried to prove that Irish could be a modern, fashionable language. While Conradh na Gaeilge was weighed down with older, conservative activists, Craobh na hAiseirghe was run by young, energetic and culturally adventurous enthusiasts, who were embracing modern times and modern methods. *The Spectator* referred to Ó Cuinneagáin as a 'Go ahead Gael' and commented on how the 'young people were forcing the language out of the backroom to the street corners'.[4]

Born in Belfast on 2 January 1910, Gearóid Ó Cuinneagáin was committed to the realisation of a Gaelic, Christian Ireland. Educated by the Christian Brothers, he entered the civil service as a tax clerk in 1927. He was promoted to Junior Executive Officer and served in this position in the Department of Defence until 31 July 1932 when he resigned in protest at the refusal by the civil service to grant him three months' leave to study Irish in Rath na Feirste, Co. Donegal. This resignation on principle was characteristic of Ó Cuinneagáin. Dedicated, single-minded and idealistic, he spent his life in pursuit of the goal of Gaelicisation.[5]

By the beginning of 1941, Craobh na hAiseirghe was thriving. Outdoor meetings were held twice a week, often with invited speakers from outside the *craobh*. Sometimes they would be accompanied by pipers as they marched to the meeting-point at the corner of Lower Abbey Street carrying with them the Irish flag and a banner inscribed with their motto, *Téid focal le gaoith ach téid buille le cnáimh* (Words go with the wind but a strike hits the bone). In October 1941 the *craobh* held the first showing of the film *Aiseirghe* produced by member, Liam Ó Laoghaire.[6] It was a short propaganda film on the activities of the *craobh*. This was followed by a photographic exhibition on the 1916 rising and the

War of Independence by the photographer Joseph Cashman entitled Ár gCúig Bliana Glórmhara (Our Five Glorious Years). An exhibition of books published in Irish was also organised. To entice people in to such events, music was played loudly outside the premises. Irish classes proved increasingly popular, especially the ranganna cois teaghlaigh (classes at home) – where locals would gather in a neighbour's house to learn Irish – and the night classes for shift workers which were taught in factories. The demand for Irish teachers was now so high that they were unable to meet it. In August 1941 the craobh published its first pamphlet, Aiseirghe. This was quickly followed by the publication of Parnell and A Handbook of Modern Irish for Adult Beginners, written by Proinsias Mac an Bheatha for use in the Irish classes.[7] Regular social nights were held, with music and ceilís, debates, study circles, marches and cultural outings and inter-craobh hurling and camogie blitzes. One of the more curious activities was the holding of a Ceilí Oráisteach on 12 July 1941, in memory of the battle of the Boyne.[8] Denis Ireland from Belfast gave a lecture and everybody in attendance wore orange lilies.[9] In spite of their unequivocal nationalism, craobh members hoped that they could forge a common bond and promote friendship and understanding with unionists through the Irish language. The activities of the craobh were funded through regular collections, contributions from members and advertising revenue from its publications.

Craobh na hAiseirghe held its first AGM on 3 December 1941. At that meeting, Gearóid Ó Cuinneagáin, on his own recommendation, was given complete control of the organisation and finances and was elected as ceannaire (leader) for another year. The only check on his power would be the election of two auditors whom he could not dismiss. While many involved saw this as an undemocratic move, they were willing to accept it in order to achieve their ultimate aim, the promotion of the Irish language. Gearóid Ó Cuinneagáin was viewed as a man with a vision and the will and talent to realise it. Although members of Craobh na hAiseirghe were comfortable with the leadership of the craobh, the Coisde Gnótha (the executive committee of Conradh na Gaeilge) was becoming more and more uneasy with the situation. It was apprehensive about some of Ó Cuinneagáin's outspoken views on the government's Irish language policy. There were many in the upper ranks of Conradh na Gaeilge, including some prominent Fianna Fáil supporters, who did not think it appropriate to comment on national politics even if it related directly to the language.[10] Thus, it seemed inevitable that Gearóid Ó Cuinneagáin and Conradh na Gaeilge would come into conflict.

The conflict was quick to arrive. In March 1941 Ó Cuinneagáin informed the executive committee of Conradh na Gaeilge that he had secured a large quantity of paper, at no cost, for the purpose of publishing a pamphlet commemorating the rebellion of 1916. The paper was donated by ex-Cumann na nGaedheal TD, J. J. Walsh, of Clondalkin Paper Mills. However, the executive committee and Ó Cuinneagáin could not agree on an editor. Ó Cuinneagain wanted Ciarán Ó Nualláin, a member of Craobh na hAiseirghe, to edit the pamphlet.[11] The executive committee, wary of Ó Cuinneagáin's influence on Ó Nualláin, proposed that two others of their choice edit the pamphlet with him. This was unacceptable to Ó Cuinneagáin and a brief dispute between the two parties ensued. Finally, the executive decided not to publish the pamphlet. Ó Cuinneagáin was furious; the idea of refusing free paper at a time when it was heavily rationed angered him. He decided to secure the paper for Craobh na hAiseirghe instead, and used it for the first copy of *Aiseirghe*, published in 1941.[12] Ó Cuinneagáin then sent a letter to every branch in the country berating the organisation for putting the publication in jeopardy in order to allow two 'old men' co-edit the pamphlet. The members of the executive committee were incensed; they issued a retaliatory circular disputing Ó Cuinneagáin's claims and accusing him of insulting old people.

By 1942, Craobh na hAiseirghe had made striking progress. Sub-branches continued to form in the suburbs of Dublin and in towns throughout the country. It now boasted over 1,200 members, an impressive figure for a branch of Conradh na Gaeilge.[13] It continued to publish and sell pamphlets and papers on such diverse topics as Joan of Arc, the Young Irelanders and the film industry. However, members such as Proinsias Mac an Bheatha began to notice a change of focus in the branch from matters cultural to political. This change of focus was highlighted at a commemoration held in Rath Cáirn, Co. Meath to celebrate Thomas Davis and other patriots of the nineteenth century. Three papers were read: one on Robert Emmet, one on Irish women, and the main paper was read by Gearóid Ó Cuinneagáin. It was expected that Ó Cuinneagáin would give a talk on the activities of the branch and on the difficulties faced by the inhabitants of Rath Cáirn in preserving their Gaeltacht. However, in a speech he was later to publish, he spoke of his vision for a free, Gaelic and Christian Ireland, and his intention to found a new political movement called Ailtirí na hAiseirghe.[14]

While a free, Gaelic and Catholic/Christian Ireland had long been an aspiration of Craobh na hAiseirghe, it was never the intention of its members to enter the political arena. Proinsias Mac an Bheatha and other leading members of the organisation now began to question the future of the branch and their place in it. One leading member of the executive body of the branch had already been dismissed by Ó Cuinneagáin because he left a lecture early, and now it looked as though others would resign. While Mac an Bheatha was willing to accept Ó Cuinneagáin's dictatorial style if it was in service of the Irish language, he was not so keen on it where politics were concerned and he did not have much respect for Ó Cuinneagáin as a political thinker.[15]

Mac an Bheatha was not the only member of the branch to show concern at the direction the movement was taking. Many of the founding members were civil servants and were uneasy with both themselves and the Irish language being identified with this new political party. Conradh na Gaeilge, also unhappy with the events at Rath Cáirn, seized the opportunity presented by the failure of the branch to pay their fees to the Coiste Teanga (the language committee) and banned the branch from the *árd fheis* (their annual conference). Following this, in November 1942, Craobh na hAiseirghe formally left Conradh na Gaeilge. Ó Cuinneagáin resigned as leader of the branch in order to concentrate on his new political party but, against Ó Cuinneagáin's wishes, Proinsias Mac an Bheatha was elected in his stead as *ceannaire* of Craobh na hAiseirghe.[16]

Having accepted the post, Mac an Bheatha was now faced with repairing the damage done to the *craobh* by Ó Cuinneagáin's recent exploits. Finance was tight and they could no longer expect support from Conradh na Gaeilge. It continued to share a building with Ailtirí na hAiseirghe with whom it was constantly being confused. Mac an Bheatha felt that the branch now needed a new direction and a fresh input of energy. A new constitution was written and the *craobh* was renamed Glún na Buaidhe.[17] Still dogged by Ailtirí na hAiseirghe, Glún na Buaidhe issued a circular to concerned bodies including government departments, stating that it was, and always had been, a completely autonomous body and that its interests were entirely cultural.[18]

In terms of its impact, Craobh na hAiseirghe proved to be a resounding success and did much to lift the cloud of apathy that hung over the Irish language movement. It was Gearóid Ó Cuinneagáin's ability to motivate people and infuse Craobh na hAiseirghe with vitality and creativity which made it a success. Now, he was hoping to harness some of the energy that had made the *craobh* so unique for his new organisation, Ailtirí na hAiseirghe.

A *New Party*

The innovative and unorthodox methods which had characterised Craobh na hAiseirghe continued under the new party. Marches and open-air meetings were held regularly. Keen to retain a cultural dimension, Ailtirí na hAiseirghe also formed a *cumann culturga* (cultural society), which held *ceilís*, debates and camogie and hurling blitzes. In 1943 and barely one year old, the party embarked on the campaign trail. Ó Cuinneagáin cycled from town to town attending open-air meetings and ceremonies. At these meetings he placed a strong emphasis on the northern question and flag days were held for the dependants of those republicans imprisoned in Northern Ireland. Ailtirí na hAiseirghe protested against what it saw as any residual British influence in Éire. Typical of such protests was one held outside Dominick Street Church in Dublin to demand the banning of the newspaper, the *Sunday Dispatch* until such time as it printed a defence of Irish neutrality. It appears the party was offended by a picture of a British Royal Air Force vehicle which appeared in the newspaper.[19]

Ó Cuinneagáin, a frequent agitator at Dublin corporation meetings, railed at the retention by the state of monuments to the British empire. True to their motto: *Muinighím as Dia. Dochas as Éirinn. Misneach i Gníomh* (Confidence in God. Hope in Ireland. Courage in Action), members decided to take some 'positive' action. When, during an Ailtirí na hAiseirghe march, the British flag flying above Trinity College in support of the British war effort was pointed out, one young member scaled the building and replaced it ceremoniously with the Irish one.[20] Particular criticism, however, was reserved for Nelson and General Gough.

> With the Nelson Pedestal in O'Connell St. still in existence what can we do? What can we do while a traitor is honoured in Talbot St.? What can we do when the decapitation of the Gough monument in the Phoenix Park is described as vandalism?"[21]

General Gough sat proudly on his golden horse in the Phoenix Park until late 1944/early 1945, when a botched attempt to blow up the monument resulted in his decapitation and the shattering of the rear of his horse. Ailtirí na hAiseirghe was the main suspect. Even though Gearóid Ó Cuinneagáin publicly denied responsibility for the explosion in the national press, the gardaí were in no doubt that Ailtirí na hAiseirghe members were the culprits. Two leading members of the party were arrested but released after 24 hours due to lack of evidence. In search of

incriminating evidence, detectives raided Ó Cuinneagáin's flat. In the
presence of his fiancée, they searched the room thoroughly, leaving only
the contents of a small suitcase unchecked. After a few attempts of
trying to unlock the suitcase, they grew impatient and left. Had they
stayed a little longer and requested Ó Cuinneagáin to unlock it, they
would have found the evidence needed to prosecute him. Ailtirí na
hAiseirghe had indeed caused the explosion, Ó Cuinneagáin had kept a
few pieces of the shattered monument in his suitcase and the rest was
thrown in the Liffey at Islandbridge.[22] In an article intended for *Aiseirghe*, Ó Cuinneagáin wrote a mocking piece on the fruitless search of
his flat entitled *Cuartú agus Ransú* (Search and Ransack) in which he
sarcastically wondered whether the gardaí considered that the last of
Ailtirí na hAiseirghe's blasting powder was indeed contained in the
case.[23]

Ailtirí na hAiseirghe expected the same commitment from its
members as Craobh na hAiseirghe. In addition to paying their annual
fees, members were expected to contribute as much of their weekly pay
as possible to the party. Members were also expected to purchase imita-
tion-gold badges bearing the Ailtirí na hAiseirghe emblem. Pamphlets
and posters were sold to members and non-members alike to offset the
cost of printing. Volunteers searched relentlessly for advertisers.[24] While
this was often a thankless job, they did have some success. Among the
companies who advertised regularly were Rowntrees and Mackintosh,
the confectionery companies, and Smithwicks, the brewery. It is interesting to note that An Gúm, the government-owned publishing company, was also a regular sponsor. While the selling of pamphlets and
badges and collection of membership fees would have yielded a respectable sum of money, the income from these sources alone would not
have been sufficient to keep Gearóid Ó Cuinneagáin in full-time employment. Ailtirí na hAiseirghe had some high-profile contributors.
Ernest Blythe, who had already publicly expressed his admiration for the
new party, was a regular donor. The former Cumann na nGaedheal
minister, J. J. Walsh, however, was its most substantial contributor.
Walsh was also a supporter of Córas na Poblachta, a small republican
party active in the 1940s to whom he also offered financial assistance.
Córas na Poblachta declined his financial backing because it feared he
wanted too much control over policy-making. Ailtirí na hAiseirghe
seemed to have no such fears.[25] There is some evidence to suggest that
at one stage a merger was being considered by Ailtirí na hAiseirghe and
Córas na Poblachta. This apparently was seriously considered by

Gearóid Ó Cuinneagáin and his committee, but, 'owing to the strength of J. J. Walsh's backing they could not take the chance at present'.[26] Whether their reservations were due to a fear of alienating J. J. Walsh or Córas na Poblachta, is not clear.

Ailtirí na hAiseirghe's organisational structure reflected its autocratic ethos. In common with Craobh na hAiseirghe, the *ceannaire* was endowed with almost total control. The *ceannaire*, elected every three years, was advised by a committee, the *Árd-Comhairle* (executive committee). Members of the *Árd-Comhairle* were appointed by the *ceannaire*. The *Árd-Comhairle* would be an advisory and administrative body only; all decision-making would lie with the *ceannaire*. Below the *Árd-Comhairle* existed a complex network of committees, sub-committees and officers to cover every region of Ireland. The structure of the party was designed to work on a corporate basis with advisory committees for every region and sub-region. However, there was no element of vocational organisation; all of the committees corresponded to geographic location. Despite these provisions, at the end of 1942 Gearóid Ó Cuinneagáin was still the only full-time officer working for the party and all work was being carried out by him, assisted by a few members of the organisation working in their spare time. According to a garda report, the total strength of the organisation in Dublin at that time was believed to be between 30 and 40 members.[27]

Ideology and Policy

Based on its ideas of a Gaelic, Christian Ireland, the policies of Ailtirí na hAiseirghe, were, in the main, neither revolutionary nor original. Many of its economic policies, such as the strong emphasis on full employment, would have been shared by other political parties at the time. Its corporate and authoritarian ideology and policies, however, distinguished it from other political parties during the 1940s. Fine Gael had all but abandoned the idea of a corporate state. Corporatism now, more than ever, was associated with fascism and the regimes of Hitler and Mussolini. During the heyday of the Blueshirts in the early 1930s, corporatism was never fully embraced by the Irish electorate and few seemed to regard it as a serious alternative for Ireland. By the 1940s the number had dwindled further. Thus, Ailtirí na hAiseirghe's appeal to many people would have to come from its other policies, many of which were ill-considered and over-ambitious: the purchase of two national banks for example. Its pamphlets were full of general statements on patriotism and history, and lacked much substance. In many cases, it neglected to say how it intended to carry out its ambitious proposals. At its hustings speakers were prone to digression, alternating frequently between policy and spiritual rhetoric on the state of the nation. Michael Gallagher claimed that they 'resembled a sect rather than a political party, and [their] often mystical visions were far removed from the every-day concerns of the Irish people'.[28]

Between the years 1942 and 1946, Ailtirí na hAiseirghe published a number of pamphlets and articles outlining its ideology and general policy. Central to all of its policies and founding ideology was a total commitment to a free, Gaelic and united Ireland. Its fundamental na-tionalism coloured every aspect of its ideology including the govern-mental and financial systems. In an effort to break Ireland free from the 'tyrannical' influence of Britain, Ailtirí na hAiseirghe looked to Catho-licism and the Catholic states of Europe for inspiration. In Portugal they found the perfect example of a nationalist, Catholic and corporate state, and in Salazar, the perfect leader.

All of Ailtirí na hAiseirghe's policies were based on a single pre-mise, that Ireland would be united in the near future. It was a basic assumption which was taken for granted in both its ideology and policy. As soon as the new Aiseirghe government reclaimed the north of Ire-land, it could begin to rebuild the country and put its policies in place. While many politicians at the time embraced the idea of a united and independent Ireland, most would not have publicly advocated a full scale invasion of Northern Ireland during the sensitive war years. How-ever, Ailtirí na hAiseirghe was not as tame or guarded in its proposals. At its most extreme, Ailtirí na hAiseirghe displayed its nationalism in a call to arms against the 'occupiers' of the northern state, while at its most farcical it suggested moving the seat of government from Dublin to the Hill of Tara. Although it was the most fundamental element in its ideology, it showed an almost childish lack of sophistication in its think-ing. In common with many Irish nationalists, it saw Irish identity as in-extricably linked with Catholicism. It believed the Irish people posses-sed a spirituality which separated Ireland from other nations. This spiri-tuality was also an element of the ancient Gaelic culture, to which the Irish must now look in order to increase morale and take on the monu-mental task of building a Gaelic, Catholic nation. The first step in com-pleting this task would be the unification of Ireland.[29] Ailtirí na hAis-eirghe believed that Northern Ireland could be taken in a night. Ó Cuinneagáin estimated that it would take little more than 60 minutes to defeat the British army if Irish defence forces were strengthened and adequately organised and trained. National military service for all males would be a requirement if this Northern Ireland policy was to be fulfilled.

Naïvely, he was also under the impression that he could persuade the vast majority of unionists to join a 32-county Ireland. He would ask them to partake not in a Gaelic Ireland, but in an Irish Ireland. They would unite under the Christian banner and be a pawn of Britain no more:

> We will tell the doped, duped and misled non-Catholics of the North East the truth about England's unchristian exploitation of their religion for Imperial ends. The next time they catch on their enslavement at the hands of die-hard vested interests directed from Whitehall, the bogy (sic) of the Pope will not work because they will be educated into full national consciousness.[30]

In the run up to both the elections of 1943 and 1944, Ailtirí na hAiseirghe produced little of substance on the 'partition problem' and failed to provide any details as to how it proposed to end partition. However in December 1944, six months after the election, it published two pamphlets devoted to the question of Northern Ireland.[31] While both of these contained the usual diet of rhetoric on the injustice of partition and the honour of dead patriots, it also provided some specifics on policy:

> Our first step will be use of the modern weapon *par excellence* – propaganda. It alone can work an incredible transformation in the political situation in the North ... unrelenting daily propaganda of the most vigorous and modern character. Radio Éireann will tell the world each day the whole story of British injustice in Ireland. As the Aiseirghe Government will establish a film industry immediately, the Cinema shall be used persistently.[32]

If staunch unionists could not be swayed by propaganda to join in a united Ireland, then they must be swayed by the economic performance of the south and by the promise of investment in the north. Ailtirí na hAiseirghe was sure that if it could boost the economy in the south and ensure a Christian standard of living there, then the people of the north whatever their political persuasion would wish to end partition. This economic reform policy and substantial financial aid for the northern counties would form part of a 'Passive Resistance Campaign', inspired, it claimed, by the Sinn Féin policies of 1918. Ailtirí na hAiseirghe believed that its Christian corporate system would also attract many northern unionists to a united Ireland. Christian ideology and policies coupled with the prospect of representation in the proposed provincial assemblies would be sufficient to persuade unionists to join the south under an Ailtirí na hAiseirghe government. God would also have an important role in the ending of partition. Gearóid Ó Cuinneagáin solemnly believed that the power of prayer and a truly Christian outlook would help them in achieving their goal, a united Ireland. However, Ó Cuinneagáin conceded that God might require some assistance:

> When all is said and done – when propaganda, passive resistance and prayer have been resorted to unremittingly – there is one stark fact that stares us in the face … it is impossible to talk the English out of Ireland. Pressure propagandist economic, etc.! Moral force! Yes certainly! But physical force as an inevitable addition, if necessary.[33]

Ailtirí na hAiseirghe's nationalism went much further than the simple aim of unification; it was their ambition to 'Gaelicise' the entire island and the population's way of life. Of supreme importance was the national language, the restoration of which was imperative to national morale. Without national morale Ireland would never fulfil her true destiny and would fall behind other European nations:

> Without national morale as a people in the world of today we are betrayed, stranded and lost. Bereft of the Irish-Ireland mentality we cannot but lose our national morale, our racial consciousness, confidence and convictions.[34]

If Gaelicisation was to be successful and national morale boosted, an entire cultural revival must be initiated. Irish games, dances, music, literature and drama must be encouraged, but above all, an Irish philosophy. It never explained exactly what it perceived Irish philosophy to be, aside from its obvious Catholicism. It also believed that inherent in the Gaelic tradition and therefore in the Irish psyche, were notions of leadership, courage and other qualities which should be promoted in society by the government. It also proposed to Gaelicise the legal system by re-establishing the Brehon laws. Ailtirí na hAiseirghe was resolute in its commitment to the Irish language. Given its genesis, this is hardly surprising. However, while many might have been sympathetic to their views on the importance of culture, it is doubtful whether Ailtirí na hAiseirghe would have garnered much support for their idea that Irish society would benefit from a return to medieval and Celtic ways.

    Whilst claiming to shun the individualistic and material world, Ailtirí na hAiseirghe was fully prepared to use and manipulate it to achieve its aims. Its Irish language policy demonstrates a strong awareness of the

power of the media, especially radio and film. It was among the first of
the Irish language organisations to recognise that if it was to be successful in accomplishing its aims, it must be prepared to embrace new, and
increasingly popular technologies. If the national language was to be
restored, people must be exposed to it. To facilitate this, Ailtirí na hAiseirghe proposed that the government found a nationally controlled film
industry and over a period of years 'the talkie film and stage shows, and
the drama, and the newspapers and all publications will be entirely
Gaelicised'.[35] Gaeltacht areas would benefit from increased funding and
investment in order that they might expand and the increasing tide of
emigration from these areas be quelled. As part of the dramatic overhaul
of the civil services both north and south, civil servants would be required to give priority to the restoration of the Irish language. Stormont
officials would be given more time to adapt to this policy, but in time,
all civil servants retained by the new government would be compelled
to study the language. Thus, through the use of propaganda, financial
investment and direct legislation, the Irish language would be restored.

In keeping with its policy of Gaelicisation, Ailtirí na hAiseirghe
proposed the introduction of Catholic principles into the social and
political life of Ireland. This would manifest itself in a variety of ways.
The family, seen as the social fibre of the country, would gain even greater prominence than it did in de Valera's 1937 constitution. The financial system was to be reorganised in order to reflect this with greater
accessibility of financial institutions and a wider availability of credit. It
scorned the exploitation of workers and demanded that a dignified
family wage be legally enforced. This emphasis on Christianity would
boost morale and render the country 'unconquerable'. Strengthened by
its Celtic spirit, Ireland would exemplify the modern Christian state and
thereby become a world leader:

> Briefly then the task of our young men today is the establishment here of
> the exemplary Christian state, ultimately to subject the whole world to the
> spiritual influence of a reinvigorated and vitally Christian Ireland. To make
> Ireland mistress of the Atlantic as is the wish of Japan to become mistress
> of the Pacific. With the difference that we shall become masters in the
> Pacific Ocean also. Dictators are plentiful both in eastern and western
> worlds in 1942. Should we play our cards carefully and cleverly, it will be
> possible for us from the capital of Ireland, to dictate to the dictators.[36]

As part of its aim to purge Ireland of alien influences and institutions, it
prioritised the system of government. In place of the traditional British

party system Ailtirí na hAiseirghe would substitute corporatism. The governmental system, which was advocated by the pope in his encyclical in 1931, satisfied both its nationalist and religious views. Like many others at the time, Ailtirí na hAiseirghe felt disheartened and let down by the first two governments in Ireland since independence. The only remedy in its eyes was to dispense with the corrupt, bureaucratic, ineffective and alien parliamentary system. It felt that as the party system was imposed on the country, and had not developed organically from Irish society, it was not suitable to address the needs of Ireland. In order for the country to reach its potential, a system of government must be found which was compatible with Irish culture. In corporatism Ailtirí na hAiseirghe thought it had found such a system.

Corporatism, Corporativism and the Influence of Salazar

Although Italy was the more notorious exponent of corporatism, it was the Portuguese system, often known as corporativism, and its leader Dr Antonio de Oliveira Salazar, that attracted Ailtirí na hAiseirghe's attention. Salazar preferred to use the term corporativism when referring to the Portuguese system in order to differentiate it from the Italian system.[37] Ailtirí na hAiseirghe used the term corporativism in its writings, further emphasising its preference for the Portuguese model. In the pamphlet *Ireland Looks at Portugal*, Feargus Ó Mordha, a leading ideologue of the party, extolled Salazar's virtues and spoke in glowing terms of his achievements.[38] According to Ó Mordha, Salazar had saved Portugal, changing it from a state spiralling into chaos and anarchy, to an exemplary Catholic state with economic and political stability. He had returned the Catholic church to its prior state of influence and wealth, and abandoned the liberal party system. The Salazar régime had many admirers during the 1930s and 1940s amongst the conservative, Catholic right both in Ireland and across Europe. Unlike the Italian system which was considered more autocratic and secular, Salazar's Portugal afforded a more important position to the Catholic church and retained a veneer of democracy.[39] It also remained neutral throughout the Second World War and did not draw the degree of international censure that Mussolini's régime did.[40]

Ó Cuinneagáin's vision of government was greatly influenced by Salazar, and he used Portugal as a model for his own system. It would comprise two chambers, an Economic Council and a National Council. The Economic Council would be elected by all grades of workers on an occupational or individual basis and would deal solely with economic

policy and legislation. National affairs, as they put it, would be dealt
with by the National Council.[41] This council would comprise 100 deputies. Vocational bodies – farmers, professional men, trade unions, manufacturers, etc. – would elect 50 deputies. From the National Party 35
deputies would be elected. These 85 deputies would then elect the head
of state or national leader, to be named the *Ceannaire Stáit* (Head of
State), for a period of seven years. The *Ceannaire Stáit* would nominate
an additional 15 deputies from amongst men[42] of outstanding merit not
otherwise selected, 'and thus his independence [the *Ceannaire Stáit*] of
all parties and cliques and vested interests will be emphasised'.[43] However, even though the National Council would be designed to deal with
national issues, it would in fact have no legislative power as Ailtirí na
hAiseirghe intended that the council would merely be a forum for discussion and an advisory body for the head of state. The powers of the
Ceannaire Stáit would remain unrestricted for his period of office. This
autocratic structure, Ailtirí na hAiseirghe claimed, would allow the
government to operate more efficiently and without interference from
various 'vested interests'. In this sense, the Ailtirí na hAiseirghe system
of government veered more towards Mussolini's corporatism than Salazar's corporativism.[44] Ireland would be a completely autocratic state.
Ailtirí na hAiseirghe also advocated the establishment of parish councils, voted for by the heads of families and with both economic and
social responsibilities.[45] This, it believed, would give the rural population
some input into the administration of the state.

Feargus Ó Mordha admired not only Salazar's public policies, but
also his frugal private life. Ailtirí na hAiseirghe was very disapproving of
the lavish lifestyles of those in public life. According to Ó Mordha, the
party shared the same policy on private property as Salazar: one had a
right to the ownership of private property only if it did not impinge on
the common good. Similar constraints would be placed on freedom of
speech and expression, which was guaranteed unless it threatened the
stability of society. These policies reflected their mutual opposition to
liberalism and individualism. The strong position of Catholicism in
Portugal and the abandonment of the liberal party system was, for Ailtirí
na hAiseirghe, a major achievement. Throughout its publications it
continued to extol the achievements of the Portuguese state. Its theory
of corporativism however, never developed past a mere pastiche of Salazar's governmental system.[46] Under Ailtirí na hAiseirghe, Ireland would
be unashamedly a completely autocratic state.

Encouraged by its endorsement by the pope, and the ideology's compatibility with Catholicism, Ailtirí na hAiseirghe saw in corporativism a system which struck a blow at liberalism and British influences at once. Corporativism, it claimed, was also compatible with Ireland's heritage.[47] In her glorious Gaelic past, Ireland's chieftains led the country with strong central leadership; that was the Celtic way. Corporativism, it also believed, would help appease the unionists who would be brought into the state through the establishment of provincial assemblies, they would have a voice in government also. How the establishment of powerless provincial assemblies in an avowedly Catholic state would solve the sectarian divide one can only imagine. Moreover, Ailtirí na hAiseirghe never clarified how it would reconcile its Gaelic Ireland ideology and anti-liberalism with the appeasement of northern unionists.[48] While it advocated a Christian society, it was clear that Ailtirí na hAiseirghe specifically envisaged a Catholic one, influenced heavily by Vatican thinking and edicts.

'Vested Interests'
Ailtirí na hAiseirghe's fervent nationalism displayed an intolerance and latent racism which was characteristic of the period. The party shared its anti-semitism and a fear of foreigners with much of the population. However, it would have been rare to find pronouncements from political parties and public figures which compared to those of Ailtirí na hAiseirghe.[49] While criticisms of the Jewish section of the population were mostly tempered by protestations of Christian tolerance, the racism was difficult to disguise:

> Since Aiseirghe is a Christian movement which must carry the stamp of Christianity in all its actions, it should go without saying that the methods we intend to employ in dealing with this very important, and, I think I may say advisedly, delicate problem, must be characterised by Christian charity and justice. Having said this and made it clear that we intend to employ none of the unjust and inhumane tactics which have been rightly condemned elsewhere, I must not be taken as saying that we are going to do nothing. The failure of Laissez-Faire is as disastrous to Jew and non-Jew alike as is the failure of Anti-Semitism. Christianity alone can guide us in what we must do as well as what we must avoid.[50]

While being careful not to ally itself with Hitler and the Nazis, Ailtirí na hAiseirghe made it clear that it viewed the Jewish population with suspicion. It confirmed its belief in all of the old anti-Jewish stereotypes: immoral money-lending, control of the financial and credit institutions, monopolies and the secret manipulation of the economy and politics:

To most Irishmen who talk openly of the Jews, the name is associated with finance, business and industry and unscrupulousness … Secrecy – this very odd characteristic of the Jewish problem turns up everywhere and in many forms. We know it in the anonymous press agencies in the unseen hand in politics and finance, and in the subterfuge of the false name. To recognise it is to despise it, and to fear that, while it persists, peace with Israel is in danger. To see Jews wearing the names of Irish patriots must naturally arouse suspicion in the minds of the people.[51] It serves no useful purpose, but only irritates and stirs up anger.[52]

Its mistrust of Jews bordered on the paranoid. Throughout its writing, references are made to 'vested interests'. Ailtirí na hAiseirghe believed that secret, unseen 'vested interests' were impeding Ireland's development and hampering both the economy and the government for their own gain. Though never unmasked, these 'vested interests' probably referred to the Jews, accompanied by the masons and the English. The idea that Ireland's path was not in her own hands, the hands of the real Celtic Catholic Irish people, runs through Ailtirí na hAiseirghe's writings. It took for granted that Irish meant Catholic, and if not Catholic, at the very least, Christian.

Ailtirí na hAiseirghe's fear of 'vested interests' was also reflected in its financial and fiscal policies.[53] These 'vested interests' had questionable motives and contributed to Ireland's economic backwardness. Ailtirí na hAiseirghe proposed to reorganise Ireland's financial institutions and seize control from these 'vested interests'. In *Aiseirghe Says* and *Aiseirghe 1942*, it puts forward its policies on finance and the economy. The capitalist system, influenced by British ways, in its view, did not reflect either the natural Celtic culture or the productive capacity of the country. Moreover, it was stifling the country's economy. To rectify this situation, it planned to bring the financial institutions under centralised state control. It would sever the link with sterling in accordance with its de-Anglicisation policy and abandon the alien and archaic coinage system for the European metric system. Ailtirí na hAiseirghe proposed a number of restrictions on the banks. They would be obliged to give any profit they made over 5% to the state. The new, reorganised and state-controlled Central Bank would be given extra powers, among them the power to fix interest rates, the overseeing of the use of credit throughout the country and control of international payments and investments. The latter would be strictly monitored in order to ensure that wealth remained in the country. Ailtirí na hAiseirghe would also insist on the repatriation of Irish capital invested abroad, which it calculated to be approximately £500 million. It would use some of this capital to purchase assets owned by non-nationals.

The authoritarian nature of Ailtirí na hAiseirghe allied with the pro-German sympathies of supporters such as J. J. Walsh, ensured that Gearóid Ó Cuinneagáin was subjected to surveillance by both the gardaí and the G2 intelligence unit of the army during the war years. He also featured regularly in a series of British intelligence reports entitled 'Secret Reports on the situation in Ireland, 1942–1944'. Ó Cuinneagáin was among a number of people active at that time with pronounced pro-Axis sympathies. As the war in Europe escalated, pro-German groups such as the People's National Party and An Cumann Náisiúnta began to form in the city and suburbs of Dublin. It was as a member of Cumann Náisiúnta, also known as the Irish Friends of Germany, that Gearóid Ó Cuinneagáin first came to the attention of G2.

Promoting German Interests

The Irish Friends of Germany was founded in early 1940 by Liam D. Walsh. Walsh, who was employed at the Italian legation, was a prominent fascist and Nazi supporter and was active in promoting anti-semitism in Dublin before the war. The People's National Party, which broke away from the Friends of Germany in the summer of 1940, also boasted some renowned local fascists such as George Griffin, and the former leader of the Blueshirts, Eoin O'Duffy.[54] Alex McCabe, another former Blueshirt and a former Cumann na nGaedheal TD, was also a principal member of the Friends of Germany, and when in June 1940 both Walsh and McCabe were interned, Maurice O'Connor took the mantle as leader of the organisation. According to O'Connor, the Friends of Germany had the support of the German authorities, the IRA and internees at camps such as Gormanstown. He planned to organise supporters in readiness for an invasion by German troops. O'Connor is said to have claimed that those who took an active role in the assistance of German troops, 'would be assured of good positions when the occupation was complete'.[55]

In autumn 1940, Gearóid Ó Cuinneagáin was reported to be attending Friends of Germany meetings on a regular basis. At this stage both McCabe and Walsh had been interned and the meetings recorded a small attendance. It was at a Cumann Náisiúnta meeting that Ó Cuinneagáin announced his intention of forming a Hitler youth movement through the medium of the Irish language. He stated that he already had a membership of 30 and would hold the classes twice a week with one night 'being reserved for Nazi lectures'.[56] It was later confirmed by the gardaí that Ó Cuinneagáin had indeed held Irish classes under the auspices of Conradh na Gaeilge at 45 Dawson Street, and a lecture on Germany was given in Irish by someone invited there by Ó Cuinneagáin.[57] According to garda sources, Ó Cuinneagáin also intended to form a Gaelic organisation for adults in conjunction with a pro-German and IRA acquaintance, Joseph O'Kelly, for the purpose of promoting the Irish language. This organisation would be used as a pretext for the holding of lectures on Germany and the dissemination of German propaganda.[58] Ó Cuinneagáin also planned to run a Hitler youth organisation under the auspices of Córas na Poblachta with the aid of Joseph O'Kelly, and the support of Maurice O'Connor, Roger McHugh, and T. A. O'Gorman, who were well known in pro-German circles.[59] British intelligence believed that:

> Ernest Blythe and J. J. Walsh, co-operating with Cunningham, have formed 23 clubs for school children in Dublin. Rooms have been taken in private houses and fitted up for physical exercise. Lectures are given to the youths on Nazi lines ... The Roman Catholic clergy are visiting schools warning the teachers to stop their pupils joining the clubs.[60]

Many of the prominent pro-German individuals and republicans took an active interest in Conradh na Gaeilge, and at its AGM in 1941, they and others ousted the sitting president and Fianna Fáil supporter, Liam Ó Buachalla. Ó Cuinneagáin also stood for election as president, but was eliminated at the first count. Following his elimination, Ó Cuinneagáin ensured that his transfers went to another candidate, Seán Óg Ó Tuama who was an internee at the time. According to Proinsias Mac Aonghusa – author of *Ar Son na Gaeilge*, an official history of Conradh na Gaeilge – Ó Tuama was an anti-Fianna Fáil and an anti-establishment candidate.[61] There is evidence of an organised anti-Ó Buachalla campaign in this election. Roger McHugh, who was interned in the Curragh at the time, received a letter from a man thought by intelligence sources to be Seán MacBride, chief of staff of the IRA in 1937 and subsequently leader of Clann na Poblachta. In it he wrote:

> I suppose you have heard that Seán Ó Tuama is the new president of the Gaelic League, something attempted, something done. Ó Cuinneagáin refused to stand down in spite of all pleadings (had I got your vote I would not have given it to him). He had some bee in his bonnet that it was between him and Ó Buachalla and no amount of explaining that he was causing a split and ensuring the election of Ó Buachalla (as we thought then) would move him ... To give a dog his due Gearóid must have swung his 13 votes over to Ó Tuama so we are not feeling too badly towards him now.[62]

Ó Cuinneagáin's involvement with the individuals and groups such as the Irish Friends of Germany introduced him to many Germans residing in Dublin, a number of whom were connected to the German legation.[63] They attended some of his lectures, *ceilís* and social events held in the city. With the internment of McCabe and Walsh and the arrest of O'Connor, the Friends of Germany faded away and was defunct as an organisation by mid-1941. Ó Cuinneagáin then focused his attention on Craobh na hAiseirghe. While he was not considered to be of great importance, the authorities did consider him to be a threat, if only a mild one, to the security of the state, as this army intelligence report illustrates:

> Gearóid Ó Cuinneagáin appears to be of the sincere fanatical type who, by reason of his leanings towards the authoritarian form of Government and his anti-British bias, might become a danger to the state in the event of an attempted invasion of this country by the AXIS powers.[64]

The security forces continued the surveillance on Ó Cuinneagáin, monitoring both his movements and his correspondence. Within army ranks however, there was some interest and support for Ailtirí na hAiseirghe. A young Kilkenny soldier joined the party and expressed an interest in forming a branch in Urlingford, Co. Kilkenny. He also managed to persuade a few of his colleagues to join. The army intercepted his letters and reminded the soldiers that they were forbidden by law from joining any such organisation.[65] The army continually refused Ó Cuinneagáin's application to show films to internees. However, more sinister allegations that Ailtirí na hAiseirghe were intending to develop an armed unit surfaced. An ex-IRA internee released in July 1944 claimed that it was the intention of elements in the IRA to hand over weapons to Ailtirí na hAiseirghe.[66] There were also indications from other quarters that Ailtirí na hAiseirghe might be contemplating arming themselves; to what end it was not stated. On further investigation however, these allegations remained unsubstantiated.

In 1945 Captain Ryan, who investigated Ailtirí na hAiseirghe on behalf of the army, wrote:

> In spite of a lack of any apparent success in the development of the organisation both as to membership or acceptance by the public, the enthusiasm and zeal of the officials in Dublin at any rate continues to a marked degree. They appear to have good organising ability and drive but lack co-operation or effective support from their provincial agents, some of whom appear very callow in the political sense. Since the last election in May 1944 a

number of rumours have reached this branch suggesting subversive approaches to or by the organisation. None of these have been substantiated as a result of what check in that regard was practicable. One report received of an approach by the organisation was entirely exploded on investigation. Approaches to the organisation might in the nature of things, be expected, it (the organisation) being possibly the only remaining political movement that is not entirely discredited. Observation is being maintained re: this aspect but to date there has been nothing in that connection to come to grips with.[67]

Ó Cuinneagáin's speeches do suggest that he considered that violence might be inevitable if their programme was to be carried out in full. While Ailtirí na hAiseirghe had demonstrated by the bombing of the Gough monument that it was not adverse to the use of violence, it is questionable whether Ó Cuinneagáin or any other senior member of Ailtirí na hAiseirghe ever seriously considered establishing an armed movement.[68]

Despite its failure to make a significant impact on the political scene, Ailtirí na hAiseirghe did provoke a response from other political activists and from the Dublin media. It drew both censure and bemusement in equal measure but from different quarters. Left-wing organisations and commentators were vocal in their opposition; some were even threatening. Members of the Labour party would attend Ailtirí na hAiseirghe meetings in order to disrupt them and then challenge Gearóid Ó Cuinneagáin to a debate on street corners.[69] An intelligence officer present at a Communist Party meeting reported that:

> The Party in Dublin are about to take active steps against Ailtirí na hAiseirghe and the Green Front as pro-fascist and tending to bring disunity between the working masses of North and South. Open opposition will be carried out against these organisations.[70]

Left-wing publications such as *Torch* and *Irish Freedom* wrote scornfully about fascists in Gaelic clothing. In an article 'Same Shop, Different Counter', Ó Cuinneagáin is referred to as the 'Irish Fuhrur' (*sic*) and compared to every fascist leader in Europe:

> Conceived in Rome, suckled in Lisbon, educated in Berlin and well-fed in Madrid, the ugly brat of Fascism now openly walks the streets of Dublin. Dress Cunningham in a Black shirt, give him a German accent and he would have talent enough to join the lesser fry who curry favour with the Fascist dictators now seeking to crush democracy throughout Europe.[71]

Not all reaction to Ó Cuinneagáin and his followers was solemn. They were a favourite topic of Myles na gCopaleen in his column 'An Cruiskeen Lawn'. He regularly reported on their progress in prose oozing with irony. However, while gaining much amusement from their exploits, he also recognised the dangers inherent in their preachings:

> I was recently held up again at a Dublin Street corner by a small crowd who were listening to a young man with a strong North of Ireland accent who was aloft on a little Irish Scaffold. 'Glún na Buaidhe' ,he roared, 'has its own ideas about the banks, has its own ideas about amusements, has its own ideas about dancing. There is one sort of dancing that Glún na Buaidhe will not permit and that is Jazz dancing. Because Jazz dancing is the product of the dirty nigger culture of America, the dirty low nigger culture of America.' Substitute Jew for nigger there and you have something new and modern. But what pained me was the fact that nobody present laughed.[72]

Political Failure and the Arrival of Clann na Poblachta

Ailtirí na hAiseirghe ran candidates in both the 1943 and 1944 general elections. Campaigning in 1943 was difficult due to wartime shortages of items such as paper and petrol, yet it was the most closely fought election since 1927. Despite these wartime conditions Ailtirí na hAiseirghe published prolifically. It continued to receive funding from interested individuals such as Ernest Blythe and its printing cost was subsidised by a printer in Clondalkin who was willing to print its material at cut price. The party spent heavily on advertising and its posters were to be seen all over Dublin. It also continued to publish many pamphlets on political and cultural topics.[73] Ailtirí na hAiseirghe conducted meetings and campaigned vigorously throughout the country. On 10 June 1943 Gearóid Ó Cuinneagáin was arrested in Belfast at a *ceilí* and held for a week and ordered never to enter the Northern Ireland state again. *The Belfast Telegraph* told the tale of the 'fascist who failed'. Other newspapers were not so harsh and dutifully reported on its regular campaign meetings. However despite this publicity, Ailtirí na hAiseirghe, running on its nationalist, corporativist ideology, failed to make much of an impact in either election and could not capitalise on the general disillusionment felt by much of the country. In 1943 it ran four candidates and all lost their deposits.[74] Among them was the nephew of Cathal Brugha, Tomás Ó Dochartaigh who ran in Waterford. In 1944 it ran seven candidates and, while it practically doubled its total first preferences from 156,533 in 1943 to 302,700 in 1944, its nationwide percentage remained at 0.49% of total first preferences polled. Ailtirí na hAiseirghe's performance was only slightly less miserable than that of Córas na Poblachta. It did gain support however, from persons of some notoriety such as Dan Breen, who remarked in his speech at the close of counting in Tipperary in 1944, that he was sorry that Ailtirí na hAiseirghe had not done better.

Despite two indifferent receptions by the Irish electorate, Ailtirí na hAiseirghe continued to campaign on various issues until the end of the 1940s. By the end of the decade it was clear that they would never find success as a political party. Gearóid Ó Cuinneagáin continued to campaign on the Irish language and to publish *Aiseirghe* on a monthly basis until the mid-1970s. While the paper consisted mainly of political commentary and news items, the nationalist, Gaelic, Christian ethos which characterised the Ailtirí na hAiseirghe party was still very much in evidence. To those disillusioned with the main parties and seeking a united Ireland, restoration of the language and a more aggressive social policy, a more promising prospect now was Clann na Poblachta, a new republican party that also focused on partition, emigration and other social issues.

Touting many of the same aims as Ailtirí na hAiseirghe, Clann na Poblachta offered more realistic policies, especially on Northern Ireland. It had as its leader a staunch republican and ex-IRA chief of staff, Seán MacBride. Clann na Poblachta resembled Ailtirí na hAiseirghe in more than its republicanism; many of their social and fiscal policies were almost identical. Like Ailtirí na hAiseirghe, Clann placed great emphasis on the family unit and the Christian state. Reduction of emigration, full employment, repatriation of Irish currency and the protection of rural life also featured highly in the programmes of both parties. Ailtirí na hAiseirghe and Clann na Poblachta both campaigned on the same educational issues, the raising of the school leaving age to 16, free second and third-level education and the establishment of technical and agricultural courses for school leavers. Their solutions to unemployment were very similar. Both parties proposed to eliminate unemployment though the establishment of government schemes such as afforestation, hydro-electrification and house building.

Clann na Poblachta also included an element of corporatism in their programme. It stated that it was its policy to provide 'co-operative organisations on elevated parish councils with statutory powers for the purpose of providing agricultural machinery [and] co-operative marketing'.[75] It also shared with Ailtirí na hAiseirghe some of its views on alien influences on Irish life. In statements reminiscent of many made by Ailtirí na hAiseirghe warning against alien influences which were corrupting society, Clann na Poblachta warned against 'alien, artificial and unchristian concepts of life' which 'are being constantly pumped into and absorbed by our people'.[76] In its proposals to combat these influences, Clann proposed to establish a national theatre and film industry; Ó Cuinneagáin had put forward the same proposals. Both Seán Mac-Bride and Gearóid Ó Cuinneagáin were highly aware of the power of the modern media and technologies and used them to their own advantage.[77]

While there were many similarities between both parties, they differed in one major way, their respective views on autocracy. Clann na Poblachta was an avowedly democratic party, committed to the principles of democracy. Ailtirí na hAiseirghe, on the other hand, was not. Yet despite this fundamental difference in ideology, Clann na Poblachta drew much support from members of Ailtirí na hAiseirghe.[78] Ailtirí na hAiseirghe's poor showing in the elections of 1943 and 1944 meant that there was still room for a strongly republican party. The fact that so many members of Ailtirí na hAiseirghe were willing to transfer their allegiance to Clann na Poblachta, poses the question of how serious were most members about the corporativist policies of Ailtirí na hAiseirghe in the first place. While the main ideologues of the party saw corporativism and the establishment of an autocratic state as central to their project, it seems likely that it was the party's republican views and commitment to the Irish language which attracted the majority of its followers.

Considering the ready defection of many members to Clann na Poblachta, one could also question the extent to which Ailtirí na hAiseirghe had ever developed beyond the personal crusade of its founder and leader. Craobh na Aiseirghe was born out of the passionate commitment of Gearóid Ó Cuinneagáin to the Irish language and it was he who was the driving force behind the transition from cultural movement to political party. While there were a few other members who contributed to the writing of *Aiseirghe* and to the running of the party, from the outset it was Ó Cuinneagáin who formed the main policies and made all of the major decisions in the party. Yet, if Ailtirí na hAiseirghe could be characterised as 'one man's obsession' it would be a mistake to reduce it to this. As a party, its ideas and its policies were firmly rooted in the context of its time, a Europe which was riven by anti-semitism, by ideological and physical conflict and which was home to the autocratic and authoritarian corporate state. Furthermore, the striking similarities between Ailtirí na hAiseirghe and Clann na Poblachta in terms of their national policies and methodology would suggest that Ailtirí na hAiseirghe articulated a viewpoint which was representative of public opinion to some extent. It is arguable that as a party, Ailtirí na hAiseirghe responded to a desire for action and committed leadership within a section of the republican population disillusioned with the stagnation of post independence Ireland, and that while its response was unsuccessful, Ailtirí na hAiseirghe was very much a party of its time.

A TALE OF TWO ACTS: GOVERNMENT AND TRADE UNIONS DURING THE EMERGENCY
Finbarr O'Shea

Speaking in the Dáil on 2 September 1939, between Germany's invasion of Poland and Britain's declaration of war, the Taoiseach, Éamon de Valera, outlined the historical conditions that determined Ireland's attitude to a European war:

> We, of all nations, know what force used by a stronger nation against a weaker one means. We have known what invasion and partition means; we are not forgetful of our own history and, as long as our own country, or any part of it, is subject to force, the application of force, by a stronger nation, it is only natural that our people, whatever sympathies they may have in a conflict like the present, should look to their own country first and should, accordingly, in looking to their own country, consider what its interests should be and what its interests are.[1]

Given the partition of Ireland and the continued British presence in Northern Ireland, the government believed it had no option but to remain neutral during the Second World War.

Non-involvement, however, did not mean that Ireland would remain unaffected by the war. Due to its strategic position, it was inevitable that Ireland, too, would have to endure exceptional circumstances and resort to exceptional measures to survive. The stockpiling of essential supplies had been ongoing for some time; the Dáil passed the Emergency Powers Act 1939 on 3 September; a major cabinet reshuffle saw Seán Lemass move from the Department of Industry and Commerce to a new Department of Supplies, which de Valera declared to be 'the central planning department for our economic life';[2] and on 8 November, the government introduced an emergency supplementary budget, raising the standard rate of income tax by a shilling (from 5s 6d to 6s 6d in the pound) and increasing custom and excise rates on tobacco, beer, spirits, tea and sugar.[3]

The Wages Standstill Order

The Minister for Finance, Seán T. O'Kelly, used the opportunity of this supplementary budget to outline the government's attitude to the question of wage increases during wartime. Shortage of supplies, he said, were already leading to price increases, which in turn were leading to demands for wage rises. If successful, these demands would lead to further price increases, which would be followed by further wage demands. This inflationary spiral, if unchecked, would lead to an 'artificial price structure' being built up, which, O'Kelly said, 'would inevitably collapse at the end of the war, if not before, leaving behind widespread unemployment and depression'. Consequently, the government, he declared, 'was determined to set its face against the efforts of any class to obtain compensation for the rise in prices at the expense of the community'.[4] This, in essence, was a call for wage restraint, necessitated by an emergency situation, with the threat of government intervention if the call went unheeded. But go unheeded it did. Through late 1939 and 1940, the cycle of rising prices and wages continued. Consequently, in May 1941, the government issued an order under the Emergency Powers Act to impose a wage freeze on the country. Announcing this order, which became known as the Wages Standstill Order, Seán T. O'Kelly justified it by reference to the 'mad race' of 'higher wages followed by higher costs, higher prices and again higher costs – all in rapid movement'.[5]

Though he announced the introduction of the Wages Standstill Order, O'Kelly was not its author. The suggestion of a general wage freeze had been put to the government by the Minister for Industry and Commerce, Seán MacEntee, in August 1940. MacEntee had moved from Finance to Industry and Commerce in the September 1939 cabinet reshuffle, and through 1940 he and his new department grappled with the question of how to deal with rising wage demands. The policy of containing wage rates had more fundamental objectives than the immediate though crucial one of survival in a world at war. In two memoranda in March and July 1940, Industry and Commerce set out its interpretation of the decisive long-term connection between the level of wages and economic development.[6] The starting-point was a statement of what was regarded as the correct level of wages: 'wages should not be higher, and if anything, lower, in this country than Great Britain'. But, according to the department, wage movements during the inter-war period had resulted in the reverse being the case: 'broadly speaking, the wage level for both skilled and unskilled workers, outside agriculture, as compared with Great Britain, was unduly high'.[7] This situation was 'disastrous for the general economy in this country', increasing the cost of agricultural production, reducing the level of agricultural exports and hindering the development of an industrial sector capable of competing on the international stage: 'The future of the national economy both in respect of agriculture and industry would, therefore, appear to turn on the possibility of redressing the existing disequilibrium between town and country remuneration [and] between the wage level in this country and in Great Britain.'[8]

The task, therefore, was clear: the level of industrial wages in Ireland had to be reduced in real terms as compared with Irish agricultural and British industrial wage rates. The problem for Industry and Commerce was that those with primary responsibility for addressing the task – employers – were incapable of doing so. Indeed, they were part of the problem: 'The absence of organisation and real effort on the part of employers generally has permitted the present uneconomic wage level to come into existence.'[9] This organisational weakness on the part of employers was exacerbated by their mind-set: 'employers generally, instead of regarding the duty of combating unreasonable wage demands as their own, persist in looking to the Government for action by legislation or otherwise to check unreasonable demands on the part of labour'. Consequently, according to Industry and Commerce, government intervention was unavoidable: 'in view of the necessity of safeguarding the national economy, there seems no alternative for the Government but to consider what steps should be, and can be, taken by the Government to check the threatened upward movement of wages in industrial and allied occupations'. The first step, Industry and Commerce suggested, should be 'to give effective support in whatever way is practicable to any large employer, e.g. the Railway Companies, the Electricity Supply Board, etc., if any of these bodies is prepared to combat unreasonable wage demands'.[10]

At the end of February 1940, 2,000 workers at Dublin corporation went on strike over a claim for a wage increase of eight shillings a week. The strike, which lasted 20 days, was particularly bitter, and, initially at least, very effective. It affected many public services, including water works, street cleaning, sewerage and the fire brigade. Both the army and the gardaí were brought in, the former to run the fire services and the latter on telephone duty. Led by the Irish Municipal Employees' Trade Union (IMETU), the strike was notable for the level of trade union solidarity it attained, eventually involving no less than 11 unions. The strike was eventually called off following the intervention of the Auxiliary Bishop of Dublin, Dr Wall; however, the subsequent settlement negotiations turned sour, and the dispute ended in 'dismal and depressing failure' for the union.[11] Part of the reason for this outcome was the active role the government played in the dispute. When the IMETU submitted its eight-shilling-a-week wage claim in late January 1940, Dublin corporation was initially willing to offer 3s 9d and to link this to future variations in the cost of living; but before making the offer, it sought the opinion of the government. At a meeting on 26 January, the government decided to encourage a more intransigent stance. The city manager was to be informed that 'no increases in the wages of Dublin corporation workers should be granted without full regard being had to the prevailing rates of wages in comparable employment outside the corporation and to the consequences which any increases in the wages of corporation workers might have on wage rates generally'. Furthermore, 'in the event of a strike of corporation workers the Government would give such assistance as might be necessary with a view to the maintenance of essential services'.[12] Consequently, the corporation revised its earlier decision and offered the IMETU an increase of two shillings. This was unacceptable to the workers, and the bitter dispute ensued.

Interventions of this kind caused resentment in the trade union movement. At the annual conference of the Irish Trade Union Congress (ITUC) in July 1940, delegate after delegate recounted stories of ministerial interference in wage negotiations. Gilbert Lynch of the Amalgamated Transport and General Workers' Union (ATGWU), for instance, claimed:

> we find that in every industry where the Minister has direct or indirect control he has exercised that control to prevent wages going up. Where we have been able to induce or convince in many cases reactionary local bodies that it was necessary to make some concession to the workers to meet the increasing cost of living the responsible Minister has exercised his authority and has withheld sanction for such increases.[13]

Yet despite the government's calls for wage restraint, its active support for employers who were willing to counter wage claims and its introduction of a wage freeze for civil servants in May 1940, the upward trend in wage rates continued.[14] In July 1940, Industry and Commerce stated that 'Since the beginning of the year … there has been a definite acceleration in the direction of increasing wages' and claimed that 70% of Dublin workers had received a wage rise since the outbreak of the war.

And while outside Dublin 'the tendency towards increased wages has been slower and less in extent … There is but little doubt that in time the tendency will be for other districts to move upwards.'[15] These contentions were confirmed by an unusual source: the trade union movement. According to the Irish Transport and General Workers' Union (ITGWU), 'In the closing months of 1939 some increases in wages to meet the increased cost of living had been secured, and from January 1940, wage movements gathered momentum and continued steadily all through the year.' And the crux of the issue, from the government's point of view, was also identified by the ITGWU, which claimed that, while ministerial pronouncements in opposition to wage increases influenced employers to some extent, 'generally in industries and services not coming directly under the authority of State Departments the Union's wage campaign succeeded'.[16]

It was in this context that Seán MacEntee brought proposals for a general wage freeze to cabinet on 2 August 1940. He asked the government to approve in principle the making of a general standstill order under the Emergency Powers Act 1939 '(a) making it illegal for an employer to pay, or for a worker to strike in support of an application for, increased remuneration after the date of the Order and (b) suspending the Trade Disputes Act, 1906 in relation to such an illegal strike'.[17] Proposing this radical measure, Industry and Commerce recognised that there were two key issues to be decided: first, whether the prohibition on wage increases should be absolute or should allow for some minimal increases by means of a wages tribunal; and second, whether the order should be general, that is, apply to all workers, or scheduled, that is, apply only to workers in certain named industries. In relation to the first, the department argued against the establishment of a tribunal or industrial court mainly on the grounds that the history of such arbitration machinery in countries like Australia and New Zealand suggested that it tended – and was intended – to lead to wage increases. And in relation to the second, the department favoured a general standstill order, arguing that, though the primary objective of any order would be to prevent wage increases in protected industries, the widespread nature of these industries and the danger of complications inherent in a scheduled order meant that it would be best to proceed on the basis of a general order, from which certain named industries or categories of workers, such as agricultural workers, could be exempted.[18]

The government, however, was not convinced of the necessity of such a drastic measure, and at its meeting on 2 August it accepted the principle of a general order on wages 'subject to the establishment of a tribunal to deal with applications for increased remuneration'.[19]

MacEntee returned to the cabinet table in October with a draft of the wages order, but his proposals in relation to a tribunal were very limited. A tribunal would be established to which only workers who had not received a wage increase since September 1939 would have recourse. This, obviously, maintained the essentials of Industry and Commerce's original position; as the department itself stated: 'When the Tribunal had dealt with all pending applications in accordance with the terms of the Order, the position would ultimately be reached when no increases in wages could be obtained by any worker on an assumption that all workers who had not earlier got increases in wages had been before the Tribunal.'[20] In November, the government yet again instructed Industry and Commerce to dilute the absolute nature of its proposals, suggesting that the wages tribunal should be empowered to sanction increases for any group of workers once the increase had been agreed by the workers concerned and their employer.[21]

MacEntee was adamant in his opposition to the tribunal being granted such powers, however, and consequently resubmitted the same draft order to the government in December with a memorandum explaining his position. The 'whole character of the present proposal would be altered', he argued, if the tribunal was given power to grant wage increases to any group of workers. 'The Order would cease to have any "stand still effect".' Indeed, such an order would be counterproductive, since 'the provision of machinery in the form of a Tribunal accessible to all workers would inevitably result in fomenting applications for increased wages so that the making of the Order would bring about the result which the Order itself was originally designed to avoid'.[22] MacEntee's cabinet colleagues were equally adamant, however, and again rejected the draft order in December.[23] This impasse was finally resolved the following February when MacEntee submitted a new draft order that was restricted to certain named industries – protected industries and essential services – and made no provision for a wages tribunal. The government, perhaps wearying of the issue at this stage and certainly preoccupied with other concerns, approved the draft order at a meeting on 7 February, and the Minister for Finance announced the introduction of Emergency Powers (No. 83) Order 1941 – the Wages Standstill Order – in his budget speech in May.[24]

After six months of debating, therefore, Seán MacEntee had secured cabinet approval for the type of wage control that he had sought.

Admittedly, the scope of his original proposals had been restricted from general to scheduled. Industry and Commerce had always held the view, however, that the principal aim of the government's wages policy was to control wages in protected industries. The immediate object was to control inflation, and in this respect protected industry was seen as crucial because of its central role in the economy. The long-term object, on the other hand, was to reduce the differential between protected industry and both Irish agricultural and British industrial wage rates. Thus the immediate and the long-term purposes of the government's wages policy coincided in the necessity to control wages in the protected sector of the economy. Consequently, the change from a general to a scheduled order did not entail any compromise on the part of Industry and Commerce. And in relation to the second basic issue involved, whether the order was to impose an absolute wage freeze or provide for a system of moderate wage increases, MacEntee's view had prevailed. Despite objections from some colleagues, he had succeeded in excluding any provision for a wages tribunal, thereby maintaining the order's standstill effect. The Wages Standstill Order was essentially MacEntee's order.

The Trade Union Bill
The Dublin corporation strike of early 1940 had a major influence on the government's labour policy in the early war years. As has been seen, it was the active encouragement of the government that initially led the corporation to adopt a more intransigent approach to the IMETU's wage claim, and as the effects of the strike intensified, so too did the government's involvement. On 8 March, amid rumours that the dispute was to be extended to Dublin Port – thereby threatening the crucial livestock export trade – the cabinet approved a package of measures aimed at defeating the strike. While the Minister for Local Government and Public Health, P. J. Ruttledge, was to 'do everything in his power to encourage the City Manager in the adoption of an unyielding attitude in regard to the strike', MacEntee was to meet the ITUC and the Dublin Trade Union Council (DTUC) to 'warn them that the government would not acquiesce in the extension of the dispute to other essential services and would ask the Oireachtas for special powers to deal with such a position should it arise'. Furthermore, MacEntee was empowered to concert, in consultation with transport undertakings and relevant government departments, 'the steps which it might be necessary to take in order to ensure that the normal import and export trading of the country would continue as far as possible'.[25] All these measures had been suggested to

the government by MacEntee, as had a proposal (rejected by the government) that the striking corporation workers be issued with an ultimatum that if they did not return to work by Monday, 11 March, their jobs would be declared vacant and steps would be taken to fill them.[26]

These measures had their intended result, and, as has been seen, the strike ended in defeat. MacEntee, however, was not content to let the matter rest there. For him the Dublin corporation strike had wider implications; there were lessons to be taught, and he intended to do the teaching. At the cabinet meeting on 8 March he sought and got approval for the drafting of legislation to deal with the issues raised by the strike, and Industry and Commerce immediately set about preparing the draft heads of a bill. Dissatisfied with his officials' first proposals, on 17 March MacEntee penned a lengthy minute to the secretary of his department, R. C. Ferguson, setting out his views on workers, trade unions and industrial disputes.[27] His starting-point, which underlay his entire approach to industrial relations matters, was startling, as much for its honesty as for its jaundice:

> the party in [strikes] which is numerically the stronger is composed very largely of individuals whose every-day occupations tend to make them more reliant upon physical strength rather than upon mental processes for the solution of their difficulties. Accordingly, in every strike it is natural for the men engaged in it to tend to resort to force and violence to secure their ends, and it is from this fact that the danger to civil order and, indeed, the stability of the State, which is inherent in every major labour dispute, lies.

MacEntee expressed his dissatisfaction with traditional approaches to regulating the right to strike, which in his view proceeded on the assumption that responsibility for strike action was not a corporate but an individual responsibility 'for which Trade Unions, as organisations, are not to be held accountable'. The result? That old familiar bogey – the powerful but unaccountable trade union:

> Thus we have come to the position in which a body of Trades Union members can do here what no Government would dare to do, that is, at their own sweet will to paralyse our whole productive economy without any advertence whatsoever to the loss and suffering which may be inflicted upon other sections of the community and with no regard for the public interest.

MacEntee believed the stakes to be very high: 'Quite clearly, if the State and our economic system here are to survive, the most effective measures that can be devised to defeat this accelerating tendency on the part of workers to irresponsible action must be taken by the State.' But he also believed the time to be ripe: 'I believe that public opinion is now such that it would welcome any measure, no matter how apparently restrictive, which would make Trade Unions, as such, responsible for the acts of their members.' And while he emphasised the corporate responsibility of trade unions for the actions of their members, MacEntee was not about to absolve trade unionists of their individual responsibility; on the contrary: 'if an individual engaged in an essential industry chooses to engage in an unjustifiable strike and thereby inflicts loss upon the whole community, the community in retribution for such action may and should relieve itself, for a definite period, of its social obligations to such an individual'; the form of 'retributive action' he had in mind was exclusion from the benefits of social welfare legislation. MacEntee's instructions were clear: 'the present favourable conditions of public opinion' were to be used to secure the acceptance, in legislative form, of two key principles – trade union responsibility for the acts of their members and the state's entitlement to retributive action.

Industry and Commerce officials returned to the drawing-board and came up with revised draft heads of a bill to regulate the exercise of the right to strike. The purpose of the draft heads was to eliminate what was regarded as the irresponsible use of the right to strike. They were based in part on two pieces of British anti-strike legislation, the Emergency Powers Act 1920 and the Trade Disputes and Trade Union Act 1927, from which acts respectively the draft heads took provisions giving the government the necessary powers to deal with what it declared to be an emergency situation resulting from a strike and outlawing political and sympathetic strikes. Building on these borrowed provisions, Industry and Commerce proceeded to do justice to the lead offered by MacEntee. What were termed 'irresponsible' or 'arbitrary' strikes (strikes in which the customary strike notice had not been served) were added to the list of illegal strikes, while the principle of compulsory arbitration – though it was not called that – was introduced for disputes in essential services. The penalties for breach of these provisions also bore the imprint of MacEntee: exclusion from the benefits of the Unemployment Insurance, Unemployment Benefit and Home Assistance Acts and possible loss of pension rights for those guilty of an offence, and fines for their trade unions even if they did not support the actions of their members.[28] Evidently, MacEntee believed in a short cut to industrial peace: reduce the level of strikes simply by outlawing certain categories of them.

The imprint of MacEntee, however, was too draconian for his cabinet colleagues. Seán Lemass wrote to MacEntee to express his opposition to the proposals; saying that he was 'strongly of opinion' that the legislation 'should be as simple as possible in character and aimed to do no more than the minimum immediately required', Lemass suggested that it should be confined to lightning strikes in essential services.[29] Even the Department of Finance, which could hardly be accused of being soft on unions, objected to the proposals, on the basis that they were unworkable and likely to be self-defeating.[30] Not surprisingly, then, in late May the government rejected MacEntee's proposals and decided that, as Lemass had suggested, the legislation should be restricted to lightning strikes in essential services.[31] MacEntee duly returned to the cabinet table in June with a revised scheme, which, though aimed at eliminating lightning strikes in essential services, retained many of the drastic, cumbersome and highly contentious provisions of the earlier proposals; among these were the penalties relating to exclusion from the provisions of the state's social legislation, which MacEntee insisted on retaining despite the advice of his departmental secretary, R. C. Ferguson.[32] Like the April proposals, the June draft heads proved too contentious for MacEntee's cabinet colleagues, and they were withdrawn in early July.[33] By summer 1940, therefore, MacEntee had twice sought cabinet approval for proposals to severely curtail the right to strike and had twice failed.

Faced with this impasse, Industry and Commerce broadened its approach to the question of how to deal with industrial disputes. The focus shifted from penal anti-strike legislation to addressing what was perceived to be one of the major causes of strikes – demarcation disputes between trade unions. This led Industry and Commerce to consider the issue of trade union reorganisation, or rationalisation and culminated in the 1941 Trade Union Act. There were two main parts to this act. First, it required all trade unions to obtain a negotiating licence before they could negotiate wages and conditions of employment, and in order to qualify for a licence a trade union would have to comply with various requirements, including paying a deposit of between £2,000 and £10,000 depending on the size of the union. Second, the act set up a trade union tribunal which would have the power to grant a union sole rights to negotiate for a category of workers where that union already represented a majority of those workers. Explaining the measure to the Dáil during its second reading, MacEntee gave a very clear exposition of its objectives:

It is hoped that the Bill, by requiring each union to lodge a deposit of at least £2,000, will lead to the disappearance, by amalgamation with or absorption into the sounder and stronger unions, of a number of fissiparous and weaker unions before the licensing provisions begin to apply, six months after the passing of the Act. After that date we believe that the tendency will be for unions to have recourse to the machinery of the trade union tribunal to regulate the enrolment of new members in particular unions and to regulate the activities of trade unions *vis-à-vis* each other. This, we think, should reduce very considerably the present overlapping and rivalry of trade unions and thus remove an unnecessary and senseless cause of industrial disputes.[34]

Put simply, the deposit requirement would eliminate many of the smaller trade unions, and the tribunal, through its determinations, would gradually reorganise the trade union movement into a small number of large trade unions, each with its own sphere of activity. By this circuitous, and, it was anticipated, largely uncontentious, route, inter-union disputes would be eliminated and industrial peace would be promoted.[35]

That, at least, was the theory. The reality proved to be otherwise. In the middle of May 1941, little over two weeks after the Trade Union Bill was published, a special conference of the ITUC passed a resolution registering 'its emphatic opposition' to the bill, which it said was 'an unwarrantable invasion of the constitutional and historic rights' of trade unions.[36] In late May, the DTUC set up a Council of Action to campaign for the withdrawal of the bill, and this became the principal agent for mobilising and giving expression to the deep opposition that the bill aroused within the ranks of the trade union movement. Through early summer protest meetings and rallies were organised throughout the country, and the Department of Industry and Commerce received, almost daily, letters and resolutions from trade union branches and other organisations calling for the bill's withdrawal. Criticism and condemnation of the bill filled the pages of the Labour Party's weekly, *The Torch*, and a petition protesting against the bill and the Wages Standstill Order was signed by over 70,000 people in Dublin alone. This ground swell of opposition reached its climax with a mass demonstration in Dublin on 22 June, which attracted an estimated 20,000 people, including representatives of 53 unions. James Larkin senior, rejuvenated by this display of solidarity, ignited the crowd by holding aloft and burning a copy of the bill. Hailed as the biggest labour movement demonstration since the 1913 lockout, it was an impressive show of strength, especially at the height of the Emergency.[37]

The higher echelons of the labour movement, initially moot in their response to the bill, were forced to review their stance. On 17 June, the general secretary of the Irish Seamen's and Port Workers' Union,

Seán O'Moore, took part in a deputation from the Council of Irish Trade Unions (a caucus within the ITUC) that met MacEntee. The deputation requested the withdrawal of the bill but did so, not on the grounds of principle, but rather 'in the interests of Irish trade unions'; they argued that the deposit requirements would unfairly affect small Irish unions and suggested that an alternative procedure, such as a fidelity bond, might be adopted.[38] Six days later, in the wake of the 22 June demonstration, O'Moore wrote to Industry and Commerce to explain that the situation had been transformed: 'My considered opinion ... after yesterday's demonstration is that the question of amending the bill is now out of official hands. The mandate given yesterday was clear and unmistakeable and demands that the bill must be withdrawn.' Declaring that never before during his 30 years' involvement in the labour movement had it staged such a monster demonstration, O'Moore warned bluntly that if the government persisted with the bill it 'will have to fight a United Trade Union Movement'.[39] The Parliamentary Labour Party too underwent something of a conversion, the contrast between its moderate, 'responsible' opposition during the bill's second reading and its defiant obstructionism during the later stages of the bill's passage through the Dáil being graphically illustrated by Richard Corish, who, having stated on 5 June that 'I am not one of those who would advocate that there should be disregard of the law', proceeded to declare on 24 June that 'I for one ... will advocate that the law will not be observed when this bill is passed, and I will take the consequences.'[40]

In the event, the demonstration of 22 June proved to be the high point of the campaign against the bill. Through the second half of 1941, the wave of opposition dissipated in a welter of confusion and manoeuvrings far too complex to address here.[41] The Trade Union Bill became law in September 1941, and the unions, however reluctantly, complied with its provisions.[42] Yet the fact remains that the summer of 1941 had witnessed the worst crisis in government–trade union relations since independence, and they had been brought to this juncture by Seán MacEntee. However much a desire to abide by traditional economics and refrain from state intervention in the economy characterised his tenure at the Department of Finance, the same cannot be said of his time at Industry and Commerce. He brought to the department an entirely new approach to the handling of labour issues, one which had a very narrow view of the rights of trade unions and showed little appreciation of the dynamics of industrial relations. In its public presentation, his approach was, like his style of politics, uncompromising, aggressive and confrontational, while its underlying philosophy was excessively legalistic. It was a view of industrial relations which saw regulation of the trade union movement through restrictive and often penal legislation as the means to industrial peace, but which resulted instead in the politicisation of industrial relations and confrontation.

Lemass' Amendments

In a minor cabinet reshuffle in August 1941, MacEntee was moved to the Department of Local Government and Public Health. Lemass resumed responsibility for Industry and Commerce, and quickly set about the work of bridge-building. In October he announced his willingness to consider amending both the Trade Union Act 1941 and the Wages Standstill Order, and the following July he introduced the Trade Union Bill 1942. The terms of the amending bill were not particularly significant and need not be addressed here.[43] What was important was the bid for legitimacy Lemass made when announcing the changes. Explaining that the amendments were the result of meetings between himself and 'representatives of various trade unions', he said that the bill was 'largely an agreed measure'; and he added, tellingly, that 'its passage through the Dáil may, in fact, be fairly described as the formal termination of the controversy which took place last year'.[44] The bid was successful, too, since the ITUC's official estimation was that 'the Bill substantially carried out the undertaking given by the Minister and in several details removed some of the objectionable provisions of the Act of 1941 and made important, and on the whole more satisfactory, alterations in others'.[45]

This new emphasis on moderation and conciliation was even more evident in the evolution of the government's wages policy. During the winter of 1941–42 Lemass discussed the amendment of the Wages Standstill Order with the ITUC, and in April 1942 he got cabinet approval to replace the order with a new order, Emergency Powers (No. 166) Order 1942.[46] This decision marked a reversal of the outcome of the government's deliberations on the Wages Standstill Order during the winter of 1940–41: the principle of a wage freeze was abandoned and was replaced by a system of regulated, moderate wage increases. Under the order, wages tribunals, made up of workers' representatives, employers' representatives and an independent chairman, were established. The procedures were cumbersome, and the scope for wage increases was limited. But the important point was that the possibility of wage increases now existed – and could only be secured by the active participation of the trade union movement in the implementation of the government's wages policy.

Despite initial reservations about Order 166, the trade unions could not resist the temptation to get back to the business of wage negotiation. At the ITUC's annual congress in July 1942, for example, Leo Crawford, one of the leaders of the opposition to the Wages Standstill Order the year before, complained of 'the unseemly scramble among Unions … for seats on the Tribunals', while the ITGWU declared that the introduction of the new wages order led to 'one of the most active phases in the Union's history'.[47] Any residual reservations were removed the following March when Lemass introduced another amending wages order, Emergency Powers (No. 260) Order 1943, simplifying the wage negotiation machinery's procedures. By this stage even the ITUC's formal denunciations of the principle of wage control had diminished and the movement was preoccupied with securing the best results it could within the established machinery.[48] This situation had been brought about, moreover, without any alteration to the fundamental objectives of the government's wages policy. When Lemass first proposed the making of a revised wages order, he emphasised that the required changes could be introduced 'without injury to the principles of Government policy':

> it is a condition of economic health in this country that the industrial and town wage level generally should not in normal circumstances be higher than the corresponding level in Great Britain. It is a guiding consideration, therefore, in putting forward the recommendations in this memorandum that it is in the general interests not to permit the wage level in this country to follow, as in the last European war, the English wage movements but to be so stabilised and controlled as to be in keeping with the general economic circumstances of the country. The adoption of a policy based on this principle would, apart from helping to prevent inflation during the emergency, be of assistance in coping with post-emergency problems.[49]

This was precisely the rationale used by MacEntee to justify an emergency wages order in 1940. The principles of the policy, therefore, were consistent. The strategy of the respective ministers, however, was different. MacEntee believed that a wage freeze was necessary, while Lemass adopted the more pragmatic approach of providing for strictly controlled, moderate wage increases. The significance of the difference was seen in the results: MacEntee provoked widespread hostility and resentment in the trade union movement, whereas Lemass secured not only the acquiescence but also the active participation of the trade union movement in the administration of the government's wages policy.

The Industrial Relations Bill

Participation in Lemass' wartime wage negotiation machinery was palatable to the trade union movement because it was always understood to be temporary. In the closing years of the war, trade unions looked forward to and the government feared the ending of emergency wage controls, one looking forward to a return to free collective bargaining and the prospect of negotiating wage increases to compensate for losses suffered during the war, the other fearing serious industrial unrest at a time when, though the Emergency might be over, emergency conditions might still prevail. Mindful of the need to address the issue constructively, in July 1944 Lemass suggested the establishment of a public commission of inquiry to examine the question of developing a wages policy for the post-war period; he told his departmental secretary, R. C. Ferguson, that what he had in mind was a body, composed mainly of representatives of trade unions and employers' organisations, that would have 'a general authority to investigate methods of wage adjustment with a view to the avoidance of industrial stoppages through trade disputes whilst permitting of the evolution of a consistent wage policy for all workers'.[50] Lemass drafted the terms of reference for the commission, which, despite the strenuous objections of the Department of Finance (the principal one being that 'the result of establishing new machinery … would be to move the wage level upwards'[51]), secured cabinet approval on 5 December.

Two days later Lemass approached the ITUC, and immediately made clear the importance he attached to their involvement, stating: 'I would hesitate to propose the establishment of a Commission if the Trade Union Congress felt, for any reason, unable to participate in its work.' Congress reciprocated in kind, stating that they 'fully realise the great importance' of the proposal and had set up a subcommittee to examine it.[52] Exposing the inner workings of wage negotiations to the full glare of public opinion was too daunting a prospect for the ITUC, however, and they told Lemass so when a deputation met him to discuss the proposal in mid-February 1945; while they agreed that it was desirable to establish some negotiation machinery to reduce the likelihood of strikes arising from wage claims, they felt that, rather than a lengthy public commission of inquiry, 'discussions on a less formal basis under departmental auspices with representatives of employers' organisations and without publicity would be more likely to yield satisfactory and speedy action'.[53] Lemass immediately adopted this suggestion, and dropped the idea of a commission of inquiry.[54] The speed with which Lemass abandoned his plans for a commission of inquiry, plans he had forced through cabinet in the face of Finance objections, is striking – all the more so in view of his earlier comment that 'I regard, as the most important aspect of this proposal, the public participation of the Trade Union movement in the consideration of methods of avoiding disputes, the relationship of wage policy to economic development, etc.'[55] – and is testament to the primary role he accorded the ITUC in the process. Equally testament to the subsidiary role of employers' organisations was the fact that the first they heard of the proposals was when Ferguson met a deputation from the Federated Union of Employers (FUE) in late February; the FUE agreed to enter into negotiations with the ITUC under the auspices of Industry and Commerce, and there was no mention of a commission of inquiry.[56]

Plans were under way to set up these round-table discussions when the ITUC split into two rival congresses, the ITUC and the Congress of Irish Unions (CIU), in April 1945. Aware that representatives of the two congresses would hardly sit in the same room as each other never mind discuss new wage negotiation machinery, Lemass put the process on hold. But by the following December, with the expiry of the Emergency Powers Act – and with it the ending of the system of wage controls – only nine months away, he could wait no longer. Realising that round-table negotiations were still a non-starter, Lemass himself drafted detailed proposals for new wage negotiation machinery.

The core of the proposals was the suggestion that a permanent industrial relations body, to be called the Labour Court, be established. The remit of this body, which would consist of an independent chairman and an equal number of trade union and employer representatives, would extend to all workers except agricultural workers, civil servants and employees of local authorities and statutory corporations. It was suggested that, in addition to taking over and extending the functions of the Minister for Industry and Commerce regarding the establishment and monitoring of trade boards (bodies with the power to set legal minimum wages in trades where trade unionism was weak and wages were low), the Labour Court would be given a role in the assessment and registration of agreements between employers and trade unions, the investigation and settlement of inter-union disputes and disputes in essential services, and the prescribing of minimum weekly wages for any area other than a county borough or large town. The fundamental principle underlying the proposals was that of voluntarism: there was to be no compulsion other than that knowingly and freely entered into. A registered agreement on wages or conditions of employment, for instance, would be legally binding, but such an agreement could only be registered in the first place with the consent of all parties to it; likewise, in the case of an inter-union dispute, the Labour Court would have the power to issue an award having investigated the matter but this award would not be legally binding; likewise also, payment of the prescribed minimum weekly wages would not be compulsory.[57]

Circulating these proposals to the ITUC, the CIU and the FUE in late December, Lemass emphasised their provisional character and welcomed alternative suggestions and discussions. In response, the two congresses submitted their observations in February 1946 and requested meetings with the minister. These took place in early March, and in their wake Lemass drew up preliminary draft heads of the Industrial Relations Bill 1946.[58] Lemass' original proposals had by now been altered in two significant respects. First, and most immediate, the suggestion that wage control be continued temporarily (for one or two years) in essential services had been dropped. Second, and of more long-term significance, the proactive role of the Labour Court as a mediating influence in industrial disputes had been extended. The court was to be given the power to appoint conciliation officers, who would try to secure a settlement in an industrial dispute by bringing both sides to negotiations and acting as mediator. If conciliation failed, the Labour Court would then itself be able to investigate the causes and merits of a dispute and make a recommendation on how it should be resolved. This recommendation would not be legally binding on the parties to the dispute, but it was hoped that the moral authority of the court would secure acceptance in most cases. Finally, if both parties to a dispute agreed, the Labour Court would be able to constitute itself as an arbitration court and make awards that would be legally binding.[59]

This expansion of the proposed new body's facilitative functions in the prevention and resolution of industrial disputes was entirely in keeping with Lemass' own voluntarist thinking and contrasted sharply with the views of the employers. In early March 1946, the FUE submitted its detailed response to Lemass' December proposals and bemoaned their lack of compulsion and enforcement:

> in view of the known reluctance of many parties on both sides of Trade and Industry to avail of or submit to outside interference in their affairs, any legislative machinery envisaged should be supported by such necessary measures of compulsion and enforcement as will obviate the danger of its falling into disregard or disuse.

It is noted with regret that the memorandum received does not appear to contemplate any far-reaching provisions for such compulsion and enforcement.[60]

The FUE's preference for a legalistic approach to industrial relations was also evident in its suggestions that sympathetic and unofficial strikes be outlawed and picketing be strictly curtailed. And the FUE was not alone. Some officials within Lemass' own department also displayed a fondness for a bit more stick. For instance, D. Sullivan, a principal officer of considerable experience, said he felt the use of the word 'conciliation' by the CIU was 'unfortunate' and that the Labour Court 'should be, for all practical purposes, an Arbitration Board'.[61] Sullivan's former minister, Seán MacEntee, also availed of the opportunity to revisit the scene of some old battles. Noting that 'there is no provision ... to prohibit strikes affecting essential services or the supply of essential commodities', the Minister for Local Government and Public Health suggested that such strikes should be prohibited altogether or that at least local government officials involved in strike action should lose their pension rights.[62] But the most serious opposition to Lemass' proposals came from the Department of Finance. It will be recalled that Finance had opposed the establishment of a commission of inquiry in 1944, primarily because of fears about its likely effect on wage rates. Nothing, apparently, had changed in the interim, and the department again argued that no action should be taken which would 'add further to the volume of purchasing power'; indeed, for Finance, the situation was, as always, dire and merited not the creation of new wage negotiation machinery but the introduction of legislation to extend the emergency wage controls for a year after the expiration of the Emergency Powers Act.[63]

Lemass' response to these suggestions was resolute: the one principle on which he would not compromise was voluntary participation. Ironically, one of the more telling expressions of this response came in Industry and Commerce's reply to the department of its erstwhile minister, Seán MacEntee:

The Minister notes the observations of your Minister as to the position of strikes in essential services. In this connection I am to point out that the proposed Bill represents a new departure in dealing with industrial disputes, and that if it is to be successful it will need the goodwill and cooperation of organised labour. He [Lemass] considers that legislation on the lines suggested [that is, prohibiting strikes in essential services], while it may be desirable in itself, would lead to opposition to the whole Bill and accordingly would negative any prospects of its successful working.[64]

Lemass' proposals came before the cabinet in late April 1946 and, despite the urgings of Finance, were approved. In mid-June, the Industrial Relations Bill was introduced in the Dáil, where Lemass once again emphasised his opposition to any element of compulsion on the practical grounds that 'compulsory arbitration decisions are not enforceable against a body of workers who are opposed to their terms, at any rate in a free society'.[65] The bill rapidly passed all stages, in time to come into effect on the expiration of the Emergency Powers Act in September. The Labour Court was set up and the wartime system of emergency wage controls came to an end. The act was endorsed by both trade union congresses, and the Labour Court was welcomed by the secretary of the CIU, Cathal O'Shannon, as 'a great landmark in our industrial history and in worker–employer relations'.[66] Despite problems in its early years, the Labour Court soon established the moral authority on which, in the absence of any compulsion, its success depended. Now, well over a half-century later, it is something of a venerable institution on the industrial relations landscape. The contrast with Seán MacEntee's unproductive and turbulent two years at Industry and Commerce could hardly be starker.

VOCATIONALISM IN EMERGENCY IRELAND
Don O'Leary

Introduction

Vocationalism featured prominently in Catholic social teaching in the 1930s. Set against the background of economic depression and the overthrow of democratic regimes in Europe, it proposed the creation of a new social order based on organisations comprising employers and workers. Politically, vocationalism promised to consolidate democracy by diminishing the power of the state. It offered the prospect of a Catholic *via media* between the extremes of communism and fascism which were gathering strength throughout Europe in the inter-war years. On the economic front, its appeal was enhanced by the widespread loss of confidence in capitalism after the Wall Street Crash in 1929. Co-operation, rather than competition, was to be the most outstanding feature of a reformed economic system. Pope Pius XI, in his encyclical *Quadragesimo Anno* (1931), declared that vocational organisations promoted harmony between all social classes when they functioned on the basis of Christian principles. Furthermore, they relieved the state of an excessive number of duties so that it could adopt an overall co-ordinating role in society in accordance with the principle of subsidiarity which stated that power should be devolved to the lowest level of organisation consistent with efficiency. The state had a crucial role to play in the creation of a new vocationalist order.

Quadragesimo Anno stimulated widespread interest in papal social teaching among Roman Catholics, especially in Ireland. But Fianna Fáil, in power since 1932, had done nothing substantial to promote the development of vocational organisations. By the summer of 1938 the vocationalist lobby had become impatient with the lack of progress. A policy of appeasement seemed to be the most appropriate response. With the threat of war hanging over Europe the disruptive potential of the vocationalists was enhanced. This probably influenced the Taoiseach, Éamon de Valera, to concede to their demands and set up a commission (the Commission on Vocational Organisation) to examine and report on the most appropriate and efficient means of promoting the creation and development of vocational organisations. With such an extremely difficult task before them the vocationalists would have little opportunity to create problems for the government. The burden of responsibility would be put on the self-declared experts to devise a practicable scheme of comprehensive socio-economic reforms on the basis of Catholic social principles. It is most likely that these considerations accounted mainly for de Valera's decision to set up the commission.[1] The vocationalists were deeply suspicious about his intentions but they could not, with credibility, decline to co-operate with such an apparently benevolent act.[2] The personnel and terms of reference of the commission were formally approved by the government on 10 January 1939.[3] It comprised 25 members under the chairmanship of Dr Michael Browne, Bishop of Galway. Trade unions, employers, the agricultural sector, the churches and the universities were all represented, although not formally. Those who served on the commission included James Larkin (Senior), General Secretary of the Workers' Union of Ireland; James J. Walsh, industrialist and former Cumann na nGaedheal Minister for Posts and Telegraphs; Algernon A. Odlum, President of the Irish Flour Millers' Association; Fr Edward J. Coyne, President of the Irish Agricultural Organisation Society; and the university professors Michael Tierney and Alfred O'Rahilly.[4]

De Valera's Address to the Commission

When war broke out in Europe in September 1939, Bishop Browne was quick to realise the implications it had for the work of the commission. The nation faced great uncertainty and he anticipated that some of the members might not be able to maintain their commitments due to pressing business difficulties. In view of the rapidly changing circumstances he wanted the government to decide whether or not the commission should suspend its activities for the duration of the war. On 23 September Browne wrote to de Valera expressing some of his concerns. On a visit to Dublin a few days previously he had observed that those who worked on government commissions were demoralised due to the outbreak of war. However, he believed that the war made it even more urgent to coordinate social and economic activities.[5] This implied that there was a greater need for vocational organisation in time of war than in peacetime. The Taoiseach was invited to address the commission and Browne believed that this would galvanise the members. The chairman indicated he would agree to any decision reached by de Valera and his ministers because, in his opinion, they were in the best position to judge the needs of the country and the dangers facing it.[6]

De Valera attended a plenary session of the commission on 5 October 1939. He expressed concern that the war would create major economic difficulties, exacerbating existing problems such as unemployment. The government would have to take action but the measures adopted might be ineffective if they were not implemented in accordance with an overall plan. Furthermore, some of the adjustments might prove to be extremely counterproductive in the post-war era. De Valera aspired to 'a system with the least possible evils'; no system could be perfect.[7]

Existing conditions presented de Valera with a dilemma. He believed that *laissez-faire* was not an option for the state. However, the difficulty with state intervention was that it might become so extensive that over-centralisation could result. The outcome could be an overburdened state unable to efficiently perform it duties. Implicit in the Taoiseach's speech was the principle of subsidiarity so espoused by the vocationalists. He declared himself 'a believer … in the greatest possible amount of de-centralisation'. The best means to achieve this was the creation of parish organisations commanding support from the different sections of the community. He had already called for the creation of these bodies on a voluntary basis in the course of parliamentary debates in both Dáil Éireann and Seanad Éireann.[8] Parish organisations, he hoped, would bring about a high level of self-sufficiency at local level and a concomitant reduction of dependency on the state.

The opinions de Valera expressed to the Commission on Vocational Organisation indicated a convergence of government objectives and vocationalist aspirations. Co-operation between the various sectors of Irish society was vital for decentralisation. De Valera hoped that a scheme devised by the commission could help to bring this about. He urged Browne and his colleagues to press ahead with their research and if possible to intensify their efforts.[9] His statements, taken at face value, indicated that the commission's findings would have a profound influence on government policy. But there was still a lingering suspicion about his motives for establishing the commission. Fianna Fáil had a poor record of acting on the reports of government commissions and tribunals and this did not escape the attention of the commission. Government inaction gave rise to the widespread belief that 'the appointment of a commission is merely a convenient means to shelve an inconvenient problem.'[10]

The Threat of Suspension

Vocationalists frequently emphasised their commitment to democratic forms of governance. Democracy, they argued, could be enhanced by reducing the power of bureaucracy which was equated with the civil service. Civil servants were not indifferent to such criticism. Understandably, some of them were opposed to the commission's work. The secretary of the Department of Finance, J. J. McElligott, was particularly unsympathetic towards the commission and its objectives. When T. F. Hennessy, secretary of the Irish Banks' Standing Committee, refused to co-operate fully with the commission McElligott argued in support of his position. McElligott wrote to Maurice Moynihan, secretary of the Department of the Taoiseach, outlining the view that the banks were for years being 'grilled' by the Commission of Inquiry into Banking, Currency and Credit (1934–38) and were now entitled to 'a little respite'.[11] This was not granted. Browne wrote to de Valera and argued his case trenchantly. On 3 May 1940 his wishes were complied with when Hennessy and Lord Glenavy appeared before the commission to give oral evidence.[12]

On 30 May, Joseph Brennan, a close friend of McElligott's and chairman of the Currency Commission, attended a session of the commission for the same purpose but made it clear that he did not do so willingly. It seems this provoked McElligott to write to his minister, Seán T. O'Kelly, the following day urging the suspension of the activities of the Commission on Vocational Organisation.[13] He also pressed for the suspension of a number of other commissions, tribunals and committees then active.[14] The two main commissions were those concerning vocational organisation and agriculture. McElligott argued that these two commissions, in particular, were making heavy demands on staff which could be ill-afforded and were examining conditions which were likely to be completely changed in the near future.[15] O'Kelly wrote to de Valera on the same day, reiterating McElligott's recommendations. and giving a third reason: the pressure of urgent work on government ministers and their officials was so great that it precluded the possibility of giving attention to any report that a commission of inquiry might submit in wartime. The first point was not sustainable, the third point was questionable, but the second one was eminently defensible and was vindicated by subsequent developments.[16]

De Valera gave serious consideration to O'Kelly's recommendation. On 5 June he telephoned Patrick A. O'Toole, secretary of the Commission on Vocational Organisation. He inquired about progress and was informed that intense efforts had been made to speed up the work after his address to the commission on 5 October. On that occasion Browne had informed de Valera that the commission was about midway through its study. However, the chairman had grossly underestimated the magnitude of the task. O'Toole informed the Taoiseach that, despite the best efforts of Browne and his colleagues, progress was slow. A huge amount of data had accumulated and it was proving difficult to analyse the vast quantity of documents. De Valera believed the commission might take years to complete its assignment. It now seemed unlikely that the commission would be able to offer the expert guidance that might prove useful to the government during the Emergency.

O'Toole's reply to the Taoiseach's inquiry added weight to the demands made by the Minister for Finance. De Valera informed O'Toole that he was contemplating suspending the work of the commission and that he would contact Browne in relation to this. Browne adopted a confrontational stance. On 7 June he wrote to O'Kelly alleging that, because of the examination of 'the Banks' and of Joseph Brennan, McElligott regarded the commission as 'a most inconvenient body' and that 'there would be a certain grim satisfaction in getting rid of the Bishop of Galway, on the ground of war economy.'[17]

O'Kelly wrote to de Valera on 13 June, enclosing a copy of Browne's letter. He repudiated the allegation of ulterior motives and asserted, with exaggeration, that 'the demands for additional staff and the pressure on officials have now reached such a pitch that the Government must decide in a big way to suspend peacetime activities unless the new activities of Departments such as Defence are to be rendered nugatory.'[18] On the same day de Valera met Browne in Dublin. The Bishop of Galway was no longer prepared to acquiesce to the Taoiseach's judgement about whether or not the commission should continue with its work. Evidently, Browne persuasively argued his case because de Valera decided that the commission should continue its inquiries with the same number of staff.[19]

O'Kelly was, apparently, unaware of the Taoiseach's decision and on 19 July he pressed for the redeployment of staffs of government commissions and special inquiries as a matter of urgency so that the 'difficult staffing position' created by the Emergency could be alleviated.[20] He argued that staffing requirements for some government departments, such as the Department of Defence, were becoming increasingly difficult to meet and that where possible 'normal' activities should be suspended so that staff could be released for emergency services.[21] O'Kelly's recommendation was discussed at a cabinet meeting on 23 July and was rejected. The only concession to the Department of Finance was that the Commission on Agriculture was to be suspended on the completion of its Interim Report on Silage.[22] De Valera was not persuaded by the arguments put forward by O'Kelly. Furthermore, he had acknowledged that the Commission on Vocational Organisation was the most important one since the foundation of the state.[23] Suspending it would have risked adverse publicity and the summer of 1940 was a most inopportune time to antagonise the vocationalists.

Emergency Parish Councils and Muintir na Tíre

After the defeat of Poland, Germany had invaded Denmark and Norway. From May to June 1940, Holland, Belgium and Luxembourg were overrun by the armies of the Third Reich and by the end of June the French had surrendered. Adolf Hitler controlled the continent from eastern Poland to the Pyrenees. The future was never more perilous for the two island democracies on the western fringe of Europe. As the war moved westwards de Valera spoke again about the need to form parish councils. After his advocacy of these organisations in the autumn of 1939 there had been much discussion of the subject in the press but very little action.[24] On 17 June 1940 the Taoiseach spoke with a much greater sense of urgency. He feared some unforeseen catastrophe might paralyse the functioning of central government. In these circumstances local organisations, acting on their own initiative could, he hoped, be able to maintain essential services.[25]

The state had a role to play in stimulating and facilitating the growth of local organisations. It seemed that the parish was 'the most natural unit' of local organisation. Nevertheless, there were some complications with this approach; for example, some parishes extended across county boundaries and a question of fundamental importance was how local organisations, based on self-reliance and co-operation, would interact with the administrative system of the state. De Valera had delegated the task of examining these issues to Patrick J. Ruttledge, Minister for Local Government and Public Health. However, the first and most pressing objective was to stimulate the formation of voluntary parish councils.

On 15 July the Cabinet Committee on Emergency Problems decided that an inter-departmental conference on parish councils should be held on the following day. Those who attended included: John Leydon, secretary of the Department of Supplies; S. A. Roche, secretary of the

Department of Justice; John Hurson, secretary of the Department of Local Government and Public Health; R. C. Ferguson, acting secretary of the Department of Industry and Commerce; Dr J. H. Hinchcliff, assistant secretary of the Department of Agriculture; J. Blunden, Department of Defence; and P. Kennedy, assistant secretary of the Department of the Taoiseach. Hurson informed his colleagues that all the county council secretaries had been requested to attend a meeting at the Department of Local Government and Public Health scheduled for 19 July.[26] On that date, Ruttledge told those present at the meeting that the most effective method of organising parish councils was to request the help of each parish priest, who would then call a meeting so that council members could be selected.[27] The parish councils were to be created primarily for the emergency. Their functions in a system of local government after the emergency would depend on future legislation as envisaged in the Local Government Bill (1940) which had been introduced to the Dáil at the end of May.

Ruttledge informed the county secretaries that parish councils should: 1. ensure that there is adequate supplies of food and fuel for the parish; 2. distribute, on an equitable basis, food and fuel in emergency conditions; 3. assist in the prevention of unnecessary evacuation and, when evacuation is deemed necessary by the military authorities, to support it; 4. maintain communications with other areas as much as possible if existing transport systems fail; 5. encourage citizens to co-operate with, and to join, the emergency services, such as the Local Security Force and the Red Cross; 6. survey parish facilities suitable for accommodating people evacuated from other districts.[28]

On 27 November 1940, when the Local Government Bill was in its second stage, Ruttledge informed the Dáil that the response to the government's appeal for the setting up of parish councils was good. Voluntary local councils, commonly known as parish councils, were set up in every county. There were no formal links between these councils and statutory bodies but the minister hoped local councils would give assistance to statutory bodies because their knowledge would be advantageous in dealing with local problems.[29]

Some of those who were active in the creation and functioning of local councils argued that these bodies should be given statutory powers. It was claimed that local organisations would not endure for long if they relied totally on voluntary commitment. Without statutory powers, it was contended, little could be achieved.[30] Ruttledge did not agree with this opinion. He believed that 'the great majority' of those who were active in local organisations were opposed to the granting of statutory powers.[31] He declared that it was not the desire, nor the intention, of the government to create statutory parish councils.[32] Nevertheless, provision was made in the Local Government Bill (1940) for county councils to delegate some functions or powers to local councils.[33] The duties and powers delegated were intended to be of a 'very limited character'.[34]

Ruttledge stated in the Dáil that he had no wish to replace existing parish councils with those set up specifically to deal with the emergency. He instructed the secretaries of the county councils that they should co-operate with existing local organisations and that these bodies could obviate the need to set up parish councils for emergency purposes.[35] Ruttledge had in mind the parochial branches of Muintir na Tíre; like de Valera he recognised the potential of this rural development organisation.[36] Muintir na Tíre served as a good example of what could be achieved by voluntary action. It had endeavoured for several years to bring alive the vocationalist ideal through the working of its parochial guilds and councils. Its founder and chairman, Fr John Hayes, was also a member of the Commission on Vocational Organisation. Muintir na Tíre was very much in touch with local needs and problems and this enhanced its efficiency. Its varied projects included food production, turf-cutting schemes and charitable activities.

Hayes was prepared to co-operate with government policy, but within limits. He was adamant that the independence and voluntary nature of Muintir na Tíre should not be compromised. He believed that Muintir na Tíre's long-term sustainability would be endangered if it became too closely associated with the government scheme of parish councils.[37] These councils were to be created for the emergency and were only intended to have functions consistent with the exigencies imposed by the escalation of war to Ireland. A representative of Muintir na Tíre made it clear to Ruttledge that the organisation did not want statutory powers and that its policy was to develop on a voluntary basis.[38]

The local councils that were set up as a result of the government's initiative – some of them in urban areas – varied greatly in how long they lasted and in the quality of their work.[39] Some councils gave valuable service to their communities in connection with fuel and food production and they assisted with the provision of emergency services.[40] However, many councils were set up under the auspices of the local authorities, often in great haste and, all too frequently, did not win widespread support from the local population. Some members of these emergency bodies were inexperienced in committee work and were unsure about how to proceed. There was a shortage of civic-minded people with good leadership skills at local level. A writer for the *Irish Independent*, Louis J. Walsh, observed that 'provincial' Ireland was never so deficient in leadership. In reference to the National University of Ireland he maintained that 'it was thought at one time that the University and its constituent colleges would provide us with "local leaders of thought and action." Instead they have given us only good bridge players.'[41] There was a tendency to look to Muintir na Tíre for guidance – its parish councils provided the best examples of community initiative. A letter to Fr Hayes from a newly appointed secretary of a parish council provides a good example of the lack of experience amongst committee members. The author informed Hayes:

> In a rash and irresponsible moment the newly-formed Parish Council of Coolock-Raheny appointed me their hon. sec. We are all in a quandary as to procedure. The general feeling of the members is that we should endeavour to function as a permanent council, and not merely as an emergency body. For that reason they are anxious to have your opinion and advice … If we could be affiliated to Muintir na Tíre, we would consider ourselves privileged.[42]

The popular support for Muintir na Tíre was quite evident to de Valera. He wished to emphasise that government policy was in harmony with the ethos of the organisation. This was facilitated by an invitation to address Muintir na Tíre at its Rural Weekend meeting in Lucan in early November 1941. Hayes addressed the meeting first and reiterated some of the basic principles of vocationalism. Class conflict had to give way to a new spirit of co-operation. The aim was to build a new social order based on Christian moral principles and voluntary effort. The application of Christian values to the social and economic life of the community would lead to a greater decentralisation of decision-making as parishes assumed more responsibility for their own affairs and became less dependent on government assistance. Hayes made it clear that he was opposed to the incorporation of voluntary parish organisations into the administrative system of the state. He made reference to the Local Government Bill which made provision for county councils to delegate certain powers to voluntary bodies. Parish guilds and councils, he declared, should be voluntary. The spirit of self-reliance and self-help would be ruined by a statutory policy which would only reinforce the attitude of dependence on the government.

In response to Hayes' concern that local voluntary organisations should remain free of state control, de Valera stated:

> At no time was there a question of the State desiring to do that. That desire
> has come, unfortunately, from people forming parish councils or groups who
> have been trying to bring the State in and organise them, and give them
> statutory functions. We have resisted that and agree with Father Hayes that
> it would destroy the whole movement. It is precisely because it is a volun-
> tary coming together, with full independence of action, that this movement
> promises so well.[43]

The option to grant statutory powers to local councils was not implemented. Provision was made in section 74 of the 1941 Local Government Act for county councils to delegate statutory powers and duties to
officially 'approved' local councils. The purpose of this section of the act
was to permit county councils to delegate functions in circumstances
where these could be most effectively performed through local organisations. But the local councils, which were formed as a response to the
Emergency, remained 'purely voluntary' bodies and did not receive official status. Furthermore, the act specified that a county council could, at
any time, revoke the delegation of statutory functions.[44]

De Valera stated that Hayes and the government were in 'complete
agreement', but this was not quite true. Although Hayes was adamant
that the independence and voluntary nature of Muintir na Tíre should
be upheld, this did not mean that parish councils should not benefit
from government assistance.[45] He had stated in his speech that his organisation requested funding from the Department of Finance to undertake a turf-cutting enterprise. Financial assistance was granted but there
was some difficulty in reconciling this with his earlier statements which
praised local self-reliance. De Valera took issue with Hayes on this matter, declaring that if the application had come before him it would have
been turned down because the people, if they had sufficient confidence
in their own work, should have raised the money themselves. Some
assistance would be given to local initiatives but this would be 'as little
as possible'.[46]

The Taoiseach evidently embraced some of the principles of *Quadragesimo Anno* which so strongly underpinned the ethos of Muintir na
Tíre. However, his vision of vocational organisation was extremely
limited.[47] The merit of his outlook was that the state would be freed from
an excessive burden of responsibilities by the promotion of self-sufficiency at local level. Contrary to the message of *Quadragesimo Anno* the
Irish state gave little, if any, assistance to the formation of vocational

organisations. De Valera relied totally on spontaneous or 'organic' growth to promote their development. He warned Hayes against the hasty establishment of a central national council because he felt that this might prevent natural growth. Possibly he felt that a highly organised and numerically strong Muintir na Tíre might pose political problems for Fianna Fáil in the future. De Valera's heavy emphasis on spontaneous growth and voluntary commitment indicated that his government looked unfavourably on any ambitious scheme to create an elaborate system of vocational organisation which entailed the devolution of statutory powers. This was difficult to reconcile with the third and fourth terms of reference of the Commission on Vocational Organisation which seemed to envisage the creation of some vocational organisations on a statutory basis requiring legislative and administrative changes.[48]

Centralisation or Subsidiarity?

The principle of subsidiarity, so central to vocationalist ideology, was not compatible with the views of the leadership of Fianna Fáil, despite de Valera's declared abhorrence of over-centralisation. Seán Lemass' outlook was radically different from that of the commission's. He held two ministerial portfolios at the time: Industry and Commerce, and Supplies. He believed that democratic governments extended their powers only when it was in the public interest to do so. Economic developments, at home and abroad, indicated to Lemass that there was very little scope for decreasing government intervention in economic matters. In a speech to the Philosophical Society, Trinity College Dublin, on 28 October 1943, he referred to the imposition of new controls over imports and exports by the belligerent states in support of their war efforts. He was of the opinion that these regulatory measures would not be terminated when hostilities ended. This implied that if Ireland was not to be singularly disadvantaged it would have to conduct its trade with tight government controls in place. The severe unemployment problem also seemed to dictate an expansion rather than a contraction of state intervention. Lemass believed that if unemployment was to be dealt with effectively then the government, rather than private enterprise, would have to take up the challenge. Therefore, after the war, the government would have to be given extensive powers in economic matters 'not far short' of the powers given to it in wartime.[49] The publicly expressed opinions of Lemass indicated the findings of the Commission on Vocational Organisation would not be favourably received by the government.

The commission, despite the difficulties it encountered, managed to complete its work and formally submitted its report to the Taoiseach on 1 August 1944. It was extremely critical of politicians and civil servants. It recommended an extremely complicated hierarchical network of vocational organisations to reverse some of the bureaucratic centralisation which had occurred since the foundation of the state, especially since the onset of the Emergency. Vocationalist recommendations provoked scathing criticism from civil servants who were not reticent about communicating their opinions to government ministers. They exposed numerous inaccuracies and errors of judgement in the report. Fianna Fáil's opposition to vocationalist proposals became evident shortly afterwards.

In October 1944, Bishop John Dignan of Clonfert, chairman of the National Health Insurance Society, published his *Outlines of a Scheme of National Health Insurance*. Seán MacEntee, Minister for Local Government and Public Health, dismissed the vocationalist scheme as impracticable. Later that month, the Minister for Agriculture, Dr James Ryan, spoke out against the criticisms directed at his department by the Commission on Vocational Organisation. He argued that vocationalism was not the vigorous force for constructive change and local self-sufficiency which it was claimed to be and that people frequently failed to organise on a vocational basis even when it was in their interests to do so.[50]

Ryan had been moderate in his criticism. Lemass was uncharacteristically intemperate. On 21 February 1945 he told the senate that he did not find it easy to speak about the *Commission on Vocational Organisation Report* because of 'the querulous, nagging, propagandist tone of its observations'. He alleged that it was a 'slovenly document' containing an 'extraordinary number' of inaccuracies and certain self-contradictory recommendations. This outburst gave rise to an acrimonious controversy with Bishop Michael Browne through the medium of the national press in March. Browne was the clear winner of the debate but it was an empty victory.[51] The bishop's final response to Lemass was published in the *Irish Press* on 28 March 1945. In the same issue of the newspaper Lemass outlined his thinking about economic reforms to eliminate unemployment. It was conspicuously devoid of vocationalist recommendations and it envisaged a central role for the state in economic development.

Lemass indicated the government would seek to extend its powers of intervention in economic activities which entailed monitoring prices and imposing sanctions where necessary. Profit restrictions and other

controls would be imposed on monopolistic enterprises. A state organisation would help to build up industrial exports. In agriculture a state
organisation would control the market and regulate poultry, egg, butter
and bacon exports.[52] There was no role for the national vocational
assembly or any of the other major vocational bodies proposed by Bishop
Browne and his colleagues.

De Valera did not make any conciliatory statements in reference to
Lemass' harsh criticism of the commission. Instead he made it clear, in
Dáil Éireann on 18 April 1945, that the commission had 'failed practically completely' in its task because the scheme it proposed for the organisation of the rural community was not satisfactory.[53] The ideal of participation in voluntary organisations, which were devoted primarily to
serving the welfare of the entire community, was a core principle of
vocationalism. There was never a greater need for the activation of this
principle than in wartime. De Valera had tested its potential and he was
not favourably impressed. Most of the parish organisations which were
created as a response to the Emergency had ceased to function.[54]

The advocacy of parish councils was an essential element of vocationalist proposals. James J. Walsh, who had served as a member of the
Commission on Vocational Organisation, believed that attempts to promote the proliferation and development of parish organisations had
ended in abysmal failure because no statutory powers had been granted.[55]
However, de Valera consistently opposed demands for the granting of
statutory powers, arguing that the implementation of such a policy would
be counterproductive. The Department of Local Government and Public Health concluded that the parish was unsuitable as an administrative
unit for local government purposes. The department found that most of
those who were active in the creation of parish organisations did not
wish to be subject to official control. Administrative costs for such a
small area would be prohibitive. Furthermore, the provision of some
essential services, for example those pertaining to roads and hospitals,
would not be practicable on the basis of parish units.[56] Therefore, from
either a statutory or a voluntary perspective, a vital element of the vocationalist scheme was untenable.

There was now little reason for optimism amongst those who wished for a new social order. When Dr James Ryan spoke at the Mansion
House on 20 November 1945 he was critical of the commission's scheme
of vocational organisation. His speech was one of a series of lectures
which had been organised by the National Executive of Fianna Fáil.
Ryan dismissed the commission's report as impracticable. He assured his

audience that the extremes of rampant capitalism, condemned by Pope Pius in 1931, were no longer threats to the welfare of society. Unrestrained capitalism was declining and the squalid living conditions of the poor were being eradicated. His opinions strongly implied that *Quadragesimo Anno* and vocationalism were obsolete. In the new post-war era state intervention in the economy was to increase rather than decrease.[57]

The vocationalist movement lacked the ability to bring about constructive changes on the basis of voluntary action. Government assistance was vital but this was not forthcoming in the months which followed Germany's unconditional surrender in May 1945. The time for grand conciliatory gestures to the vocationalists had passed. Their aspirations were effectively buried with the report of the Commission on Vocational Organisation.

BLUEPRINTS FROM BRITAIN:
IRISH RESPONSES TO POST-WAR PLANS
Robert McNamara

> Our standards must approximate to British standards, or our people will go.
> – Seán Lemass[1]

Of the British plans for a post-war world – often described as 'Blueprints from Above' – four in particular stand out: the Beveridge Report on Social Security; the 1944 White Paper on Full Employment; the 1944 Butler Education Act, which introduced free secondary education; and the plans for a comprehensive National Health Service (NHS) agreed during the Second World War but built by Aneurin Bevan in its aftermath. The influence of all four can be traced in Irish politics and society but the greatest impact was from two in particular: the Beveridge Report and the 1944 White Paper on Full Employment.[2]

The Beveridge Report
It is clear that Britain in the period 1939 to 1945 underwent considerable political and social change thanks to the collective mentality engendered by the war. Irish politics and society did not change to the same extent owing to her neutrality. In British domestic politics the Labour Party dominated the Home Front ministries by 1942. Its participation in Churchill's coalition government formed in May 1940, and its distance from the pre-war policy of appeasement, garnered the party a surge in popularity. On the other hand, the events of 1940 with its exposing of the inadequacy of Britain's war-readiness discredited a generation of Conservative politicians and their ideals. H. G. Wells spoke derisively of the war aims of Chamberlain's government in the early months of the war as hoping 'to paralyse Germany in some as yet unspecified fashion and then to go back to their golf links or the fishing stream and then doze by the fire after dinner'.[3] The collapse of France, the seeming

imminence of German victory and its talk of building a 'new order' in Europe were important spurs to the planners of post-war Britain. The wartime mobilisation of Britain contributed to a growing sense that the state was required to take an unprecedented role in the economy and the lives of the people not only to win the war but also to win the peace afterwards. Pinpointing the exact point at which the electorate of Britain moved decisively in a leftward direction is difficult. But Paul Addison argues that by 1942, Conservatism was in retreat and a Labour victory in a post-war election was, if not assured, likely.[4] Upon this fertile ground was thrown the Beveridge Report.

In May 1941 William Beveridge, at various times a social scientist, senior civil servant and university head, was asked by the government to undertake 'with special reference to the inter-relation of the schemes, a survey of the existing national schemes of social insurance and allied services ... and to make recommendations'. By December, Beveridge had circulated an outline. Social insurance would be designed to create a national minimum (safety net), and would involve three fundamental assumptions: an NHS, family allowances and the maintenance of employment.[5]

The report compiled evidence over the first nine months of 1942.[6] The Labour Party, the Trades Union Congress (TUC) and the Liberals all supported the extension of social services. Industrialists did not, fearing that the increased costs would force British exporters out of world markets. Beveridge campaigned in advance that his new scheme would be revolutionary and popular interest was intense. The initial hope of some Conservatives that the report could be buried was doomed to failure. Instead it was agreed that the report should receive major publicity. Indeed with its emphasis on social progress the report became part of the war effort; an astonishing 600,000 copies were sold. All social classes, according to public opinion surveys, welcomed the report even though it was conservative in many ways. Social insurance at a flat rate is of course a regressive tax as it takes no account of ability to pay. It assumed that the rate of unemployment would not exceed 8.5%. To save money family allowances were to be paid only to the second and subsequent children and the old age pension was to be phased in over 20 years before being paid in full.[7] In fact its assumptions of full employment and an NHS were far more radical than the report itself.

While public reaction was enthusiastic, Conservatives in the government were not. Chancellor Kingsley Wood declared that the plan involved an impracticable financial commitment and would give benefits to people with savings who would not need them, while paying for it would require an intolerably high tax burden. Churchill feared that the plan would take away from more pressing resources and would raise expectations. They both feared that the post-war world would not be a very welcoming place, politically or economically.[8] A secret committee of Conservative backbenchers drew up a plan that would have nullified the proposals. When the plan came before the Reconstruction Priorities Committee in 1943, Labour members (particularly the Home Secretary, Herbert Morrison), took the Conservative pessimists to task, arguing that fears for a post-war world beset by economic woes and the need to maintain a consistently heavy burden of armaments were not the only possibilities. Economic and political prospects might be better than expected. The cabinet agreed that they would accept the plan in principle, but that it would be deferred until after the war along with the introduction of family allowances and a comprehensive medical service. In the final analysis, a Labour minister pointed out that the report provided the vital stimulus that ministers and officials needed 'to quicken our steps and leap over obstacles placed in our path by timid, short-sighted or sinister persons'.[9]

It is likely that the Beveridge report would not have got through the bureaucratic and political obstacles placed in front of it without the presence of the Labour Party in government to argue for it. Furthermore the report helped legitimise the Labour Party's programme. The battle over Beveridge in Ireland would show how a bureaucracy and a political culture that had become convinced of its own rightness and righteousness could be fiercely resistant to change.

Irish Reaction

In Ireland the war had not brought the same amount of social cohesion as in Britain. Ireland had, by many countries' standards, a relatively easy war. While she suffered some deprivation, she did not suffer invasion or protracted bombing. The draconian censorship provided the government with the opportunity to suppress debate about the war. The innate conservatism of the Irish people, demonstrated by the failure of left-wing parties to lead any Irish government since independence, aided the lack of debate. This is not to claim that the Fianna Fáil government was adverse to some social progress. Until 1942 Irish social welfare provision, based mainly but not entirely on pre-1914 British legislation, had kept pace with Britain.[10] Indeed it followed closely the diffused nature of British social welfare provision with a variety of different bodies, regulated but theoretically not run by the state, administering the system.

Clearly some ministers were more enthusiastic than others about the new concept of the welfare state. This division of opinion was most evident in the lengthy internal government debate about whether or not to provide family/children's allowances.[11] The debate had begun in 1939 when Seán Lemass, Minister for Industry and Commerce, after some prompting from the opposition TD, James Dillon, had proposed that family allowances be instituted. The directive social principles of Article 45 of the 1937 constitution seemed to countenance the provision of family allowances. One of the reasons offered for putting forward these family allowances was the need to maintain population because of the late marriage age in Ireland. There appeared to be an underlying assumption that emigration, like the poor, would be always with Ireland and population problems would best be handled by making marriage and childbearing more attractive.[12]

Another problem for the Irish government was the assumption that Irish emigrants to Britain during the war would be repatriated at the end of the hostilities. This raised the spectre of over 100,000 workers returning in one go (and imbued with 'leftism' according to Freddie Boland).[13] Once this spectre of mail-boats in Dun Laoghaire spewing out tens of thousands of returning radicalised workers from their holds to spread the doctrine of social revolution was removed by the British decision to allow Irish people to remain in Britain, Irish government thinking about the post-war world loses all sense of urgency. Indeed as J. J. Lee notes, the high-powered Committee on Economic Planning comprising senior ministers and established in 1942 to deal with radical proposals from Seán Lemass regarding wartime economic measures was concerned with parochial matters more worthy of a county council than a cabinet committee.[14]

However, the publication of the Beveridge Report did set alarm bells ringing in the government.[15] It was realised that a well-founded system of 'cradle to the grave' welfare was a potent weapon in the hands of the Irish Labour Party. Hugo V. Flinn, the Parliamentary Secretary to the Minister for Finance, wrote to de Valera in December 1942 stating that 'Every wildest claim made by them [the Irish Labour Party] may be made to seem possible of accomplishment: "if this can be done by England after a horribly costly war, what could not be done by a country that has remained at peace".'[16] Flinn clearly recognised the danger of Beveridgeism to Fianna Fáil's political hegemony. Meanwhile press reaction was muted. The Irish Press, echoing Fianna Fáil, was cautious and dubi-

ous. The *Irish Times*, pro-British and pro-Allies, argued that as the 'immediate preoccupations of this country, at their worst, are smaller than
those of Great Britain, and if the British can find time to look ahead,
Ireland ought to have even more leisure for that purpose'.[17]

It would appear however, that certain Fianna Fáil ministers and the
Department of Finance used much of this leisure time not to further, but
to frustrate, social progress in Ireland. Standing watch at the Zion Gate
and prepared to block any Irish entry to the New Jerusalem were the
secretary of the department of Finance, J. J. McElligott, and the Minister
for Local Government and Public Health, Seán MacEntee. They were
to be the two strongest opponents of Beveridgeism in Ireland. They also,
of course, were strongly opposed to the family allowance scheme that
was proposed by the interdepartmental committee and most enthusias-
tically promoted by the Minister for Industry and Commerce, Seán
Lemass. In their attacks on children's allowances and Beveridgeism,
both MacEntee and McElligott used the traditional and understandable
Finance rhetorical weapons: the country could not afford it and it would
involve the raising of taxes and therefore cut back on individual initiative.

They also distorted Catholic social teaching as propounded in papal
encyclicals by selectively citing some negative Catholic opinion on
Beveridge and family allowances. In fact, such was their distortion of the
evidence that one can only conclude that they were deliberately trying
to mislead their cabinet colleagues. MacEntee, in a lengthy March 1943
memorandum for the government, drew on his own readings of the
papal encyclicals. He warned that eminent Catholic opinion:

> holds that in order to give effect to the Beveridge proposals it is necessary
> for the State to control and regiment industry, labour, the sick, and, of
> course, the children and the Family, the authentic teaching of the Church
> would confine the functions of the State in such matters to 'directing,
> watching, stimulating, restraining as circumstances suggest and necessity
> demands'.[18]

The Department of Finance, in a memo written by McElligott, broadly
reiterated the above warning of the dangers of increasing state control
over the individual and the deleterious effect on charitable giving caused by state control. McElligott also made the quite astonishing observation 'that degrees of poverty here were not at all as acute as in industrialised countries like Great Britain, France and Belgium, where conditions of acute poverty and squalor prevail in urban slums', suggesting

perhaps that the secretary of the Department of Finance led a rather cosseted existence.[19] In 1945 Erskine Childers, Parliamentary Secretary to MacEntee at Local Government, sent a memorandum on the operation of Employment Schemes to MacEntee. This very revealing document noted that in:

> many urban homes the wife is unaware of her husband's gross earnings and is frequently ignorant of how best to spend the sum given to her. In 1939 the consumption of tea, white bread and potatoes as almost exclusive diet was a common feature of such households.

The same memorandum quoted a report from a medical officer attached to the Turf Development Board, which described in some detail the living conditions of those who worked on the Clonsast Bog Labour Camp in the years before the war. Its description of urban squalor is worth quoting at length:

> It may be stated at once that as a whole the prevalent type of this series was wretchedly poor. To anyone without previous similar experience such a demonstration might well suggest the hopelessness of any effort to bring about improvement in economic level. In my view such an opinion would be ill-informed and short sighted. Evidence of abject poverty there was in abundance, incredible bodily filth was the rule and not the exception. I found, except in a few cases, little evidence that the clothing had been removed for years and certainly in a majority neither the feet nor the bodies had been washed for many months. It is almost incomprehensible how any normal person could tolerate, even in himself, such nauseating uncleanliness. The depressing side of these cases is that they do not seem to be personally conscious of this and clearly they have never known any other. It does not need to be emphasised that no advance, mental, physical, or economic, is possible while they themselves find such conditions tolerable. That there is at least an element of personal responsibility in this matter all who have had contact with the problem will admit and it is, in my opinion, largely an individual reaction to the atmosphere of hopelessness which surrounds their economic position.[20]

Most damning of all, James Deeny, the state's chief medical officer in the 1940s and 1950s, leaves us an account of his and McElligott's visit to a centre for screening and disinfecting Irish emigrants to Britain. So squalid was the scene that McElligott 'a man with proper sensibilities, promptly came over faint and had to be taken outside and revived in the fresh air'.[21]

A few days after this extraordinary paper from Finance de Valera delivered perhaps his most contentious radio address as Taoiseach. His

1943 St Patrick's Day speech is notable for its call to Irish people to be more interested in the spiritual than the material and for people to be sated by 'frugal comfort'.[22]

The Lemass plan for family allowances was finally accepted and introduced in 1944, ironically before Britain implemented their scheme. In all other areas, Beveridge was not to be on the Irish agenda. Implementing it fully would have involved the generation of approximately £25 million extra in tax revenue.[23] To do this would have required the widening of the tax base (particularly to include medium sized farmers) and/or tax increases for the urban middle-income earners. Both groups were key components of the Fianna Fáil grassroots organisation.

The effects of Beveridge in Ireland are hard to quantify. While Fianna Fáil realised that Beveridgeism was a potent weapon for a party of the left such as the Labour Party, the Labour Party itself made no use of this potential and did not even mention Beveridge in its 1943 election programme.[24] Labour registered a 50% increase in its vote but this was gained at the expense of putting up more than twice as many candidates as it had in 1938. Fianna Fáil, by its standards, posted a poor showing in the election (41.9% of votes cast). Its vote in the west was dramatically cut by Clann na Tamhlan, a party of rural disgruntlement and protest against Fianna Fáil's growing detachment from the small farmer. Tired Fine Gael fell back to just over 20% of the vote.

The Labour Party's descent into internecine warfare and Fine Gael's increasing 'lack of fight' combined with nationalist reaction to the American note incident and the appealing issue of rural electrification, all aided Fianna Fáil's handsome victory in the 1944 election. 33% of the electorate did not even bother voting or had voted with their feet and gone to Britain. Even so, the 1944 election sealed Fianna Fáil's domestic political hegemony. The electoral influence of the Beveridge Report appears to have been limited.

Full Employment

Ideological divisions in Fianna Fáil were also apparent in the reaction to the 1944 British White Paper on Full Employment but they were kept secret.[25] The British civil servants who drew up the White Paper were initially hamstrung by a treasury which remained fiercely resistant to demand-management techniques, such as deficit financing to sustain employment during a depression. However, the Conservatives and Churchill were less resistant in general to what now seems an unexceptionable, some might say moderate, programme.[26] Churchill understood that what was proposed was increased public expenditure in a recession to counteract the contraction of private output, investment and spending. In recessions, Churchill supposed, in his usual atavistic manner, that 'it would be helpful to have a series of cabinet banquets, a sort of salute the Stomach Week'.[27] The White Paper was approved with hardly any trouble.

The Irish reaction to the White Paper demonstrated the increasing divisions in the Irish government and the upper echelons of Fianna Fáil about what course to pursue in the post-war world. It brought forth a critical paper from Finance, which did not see the White Paper as an adequate model for Ireland. Its key point was the following:

> It would be contrary to the national interest to endeavour to expand employment by methods which would reduce the general standard of living or prevent it from rising in sympathy with the standard in other countries. The White Paper is, of necessity, far more suited in its general terms to an industrial economy than to a country with an agricultural economy.

It suggested that rather than simply employment, the primary drive behind Irish emigration was the seeking of a higher standard of living. In other words taking control of the 'commanding heights of the economy', in the parlance of the day, might threaten the prosperity of those who were already relatively comfortable. Finance, unsurprisingly, was most in favour of the conservative aspects of the White Paper's proposals, particularly those which emphasised that private enterprise would continue to play the major role in the provision for unemployment. In spite of increasing evidence that suggested agriculture was unable to even absorb the natural increase in the rural population, it suggested that the 'easiest and most obvious avenue' of employing returning emigrants and the demobilised defence forces personnel was through 'an expanding agriculture'.[28] Finance also urged the reconsideration of any plans for an expansion of welfare on the grounds that the country could not afford them. In essence it was arguing that a full employment policy would have required immense economic disruption and would damage the incomes of those who were doing reasonably well.[29]

Lemass replied with two memoranda. His first was a direct riposte to Finance in which he argued that unemployment, not living standards, was to blame for emigration. He noted that most of the emigration was concentrated in the urban and rural working-classes.[30] Furthermore he recognised that even 'a very substantial increase in agricultural output would not result in full employment for all born on the land'. His second

memorandum, dated 17 January 1945, saw his department take on the
ideas of Keynes and especially Beveridge whose book on full employment was far more radical and prescriptive than the British White Paper.
Lemass' paper advocated large-scale state intervention and contained
material about directing labour that would have upset trade unionists as
much as conservatives.[31] For agriculture, he proposed: '(1) the elimination of the incompetent or lazy farmers who fail to maintain a reasonable
output from their farms; (2) the reduction of farmer's costs; and (3) the
provision of long term capital.' Lemass certainly made clear the political
difficulties of following his policy: 'It is probable that the aspects of a full
employment policy which will arouse the greatest political difficulties
will be those which deal with wage regulation, mobility of labour (as between occupations), and the maintenance of factory discipline.' He suggested that trade unions might be bought off with workers' councils
which would give them some input into the running of their firms. He
also urged the regulation of price levels to wipe out inefficient industry.
Any industrial expansion required capital, the paper argued. Dr Jim
Ryan, the Minister for Agriculture, strongly objected to Lemass' proposals for agriculture.[32] Finance did not submit a memorandum on the
paper.[33]

It would appear that the Cabinet Committee on Economic Planning deferred consideration of the paper and in April the issue was
brought before the full cabinet, where Lee suggests that Lemass 'was
swamped'. By June the matter was off the agenda, suggesting that the
cause had been lost.[34] Indeed the cabinet committee never met again.
However, the sketchy nature of the cabinet's and the committee's
minutes tell us very little about the actual discussions. The public battle
that broke out between Lemass and MacEntee about full employment
indicates that the debates were robust. Lemass propounded the need for
economic change and reorganisation. However, he was by no means a
whole-hearted enthusiast for the original Beveridge Report and the
sanctity of planning, which begs the question of how much input he had
into the two memoranda referred to above. In November 1944 he was
dismissive of the view, held by many, that the post-war plan was 'something almost sacred, and it may be denounced as next to blasphemy if I
suggest that there is a danger that many a post-war plan will prove to
have a close resemblance to a "mental rut"'. He continued by suggesting
that we 'should be seriously perturbed, because for very many people
post-war planning seems primarily a matter of devising new methods of
dividing up the national income – by increased social services, higher

wages for the same performance, shorter hours and longer holidays, by the putting of the cart before the horse'.[35]

MacEntee, now the leading conservative in cabinet, had no inhibitions about making coded attacks on Lemass' radical proposals. As early as May 1944 he raised questions about planning and its dangers in public.[36] However, his strongest attacks on Beveridge's report, his views on full employment and by implication an attack on Lemass' blueprint for full employment were made at a speech on Beveridge to a Fianna Fáil cumman in March 1945. MacEntee attacked Beveridge's *Full Employment in a Free Society* (1944), which as we have seen underpinned the Lemass paper:

> The Plan for Full Employment inexorably requires the enforced mobility of labour, the imposed ascription of men and women to whatever occupation the State selects for them; the drastic restriction, not only of the right to strike, but even of the right to look for higher wages; the regulation of individual spending; the control of industrial investment; and the nationalisation of private enterprise to the extent to which that may be necessary to make the plan work. All these as I have shown you are foreshadowed, either explicitly or by implication, in Sir William Beveridge's book.

MacEntee was perhaps implying that they were foreshadowed in the Industry and Commerce paper as well. He also contended that the compulsory contributions necessary to make the scheme work would have the effect of increasing dependence on the state: 'They will not call this system Totalitarianism: they will not even call it a "planned economy"; they will call it "Full Employment". But the substance of totalitarianism and crude materialism from which it derives will be there all the same.' Fianna Fáil or the Irish people, he claimed did not need Beveridge to eradicate poverty, sickness and unemployment. He concluded with a rallying call against statism and for freedom worthy of Fredrick von Hayek or Milton Friedman:[37]

> [We] shall be careful to ensure that whatever be the consequences the State that will function here will be constituted by a community of free men and women, whom the State will exist to serve, and not they to serve the State. We want no stamp-licking Irish serfs.[38]

A Lemass speech in Cork two weeks later was almost a complete rejection of MacEntee. While unafraid to declare his commitment to full employment he did retreat from some of the more intemperate language from his memorandum to government on full employment. He questioned whether the mechanisms to guarantee full employment would work in an agrarian economy suggesting that he had accepted the views of the Department of Finance.[39] Clearly MacEntee and the forces of conservatism were temporarily victorious. The clash between the conservative and radical wings of Fianna Fáil ended in stasis. Lemass, as he would frequently do again in the future, put party unity before what one assumes he perceived to be the economic interests of the country. By 1946 he appears to have completely lost his ardour for battling for full employment and argued strongly for the defeat of a motion at the Fianna Fáil *árd fheis* calling for large-scale government intervention for a full employment policy.[40] Seán T. O'Kelly, the Minister for Finance, officially pronounced that Ireland would not pursue British welfare and full employment policies in his 1945 budget statement, after first warning that 'State Control carried far enough is totalitarianism'. He concluded that while he did not want to dismiss these dreams of social services, social security and full employment as entirely utopian, 'having regard to the economic structure of this country and, I think, with the present constitution of the average individual here we must make do with the less perfect instruments which the above outlay provides for'.[41]

Post-war Effects

MacEntee and the opponents of radical measures were able to prevent a move towards a welfare state. However MacEntee was to lose influence over the policy area during the 1945–48 period as many of the functions of his department were removed from his portfolio to the newly created departments of Social Welfare and Health.[42] The 1945 and 1947 Health Bills were notable for their centralising and statist tendencies.[43] Expenditure on social welfare and health services would grow significantly over the next decade in Ireland despite MacEntee's efforts. Indeed by 1955, thanks to the disastrous performance of the economy and a general increase in government expenditure – much of it wasted on projects that never saw the light of day – Ireland had among the highest central government expenditure percentages in the OEEC.[44] However, Irish health and social welfare provision lacked the universality of the British system. Indeed the means-tested nature of the 1953 Health Bill that was introduced after the failure of Noel Browne's Mother and Child Scheme, particularly in relation to medical cards, indirectly reinforced the clientist nature of the relationship between TDs – who spent a great deal of time procuring medical cards – and their constituents.

MacEntee's resistance to socially progressive policies was a consistent feature of his career. During the 1943 election his vitriolic attacks on the newly left-wing agenda of the Labour Party soured his relationship with Lemass.[45] Criticism from Lemass, and others, prompted him to write a resignation letter to de Valera, which was not accepted. His acerbic manner was evident in his treatment of those he clashed with; his withering dismissal of the Bishop of Clonfert, Dr Dignan's 1944 radical (if uncosted) plan for National Insurance and his subsequent engineering of Dignan's removal as Head of the National Health Insurance Society is a case in point.[46] J. J. Lee expresses surprise at MacEntee for clashing with Dignan as he had expended so much energy invoking Catholic theology in the battle with Lemass over family allowances,[47] but the fact that Dignan's plan was even more expensive than the Beveridge proposals was probably the main reason for his views.[48] In the end MacEntee may well have lost politically because of his conservative zeal. It was Lemass rather than MacEntee who was appointed to the position of Tánaiste on Seán T. O'Kelly's move to the presidency in 1945. Indeed, in that election the independent republican, Pat McCartan, received around a fifth of the vote suggesting that there might be reasonable electoral prospects for a more radical agenda. Clann na Poblachta were briefly to garner this support.

MacEntee's Parliamentary Secretary, Erskine Childers, seemed prepared to countenance more radical measures than his boss. In April 1945 his submission to the Interdepartmental Committee on Special Employment Schemes seemed to contemplate the use of labour camps and an element of compulsion to make people work in them.[49] He also seemed to believe that a much greater effort needed to be made with regard to social welfare. He warned that the tendency to imitate English and American ways of living and the inducement offered by the British government's Social Insurance Scheme when carried out in full would 'have an effect on emigration' and that the application of the British welfare state to Northern Ireland might cause unfavourable comparison between the two portions of the island. He concluded: 'It may be taken as an absolute fact that the threat of insecurity is no longer accepted by the modern world in a fatalistic spirit and no Government can afford to ignore this trend of opinion.'[50] It is not clear what effect this memorandum had on MacEntee. As it does not seem to feature in the Department of the Taoiseach's files on social welfare, it appears that it did not receive much, if any, distribution outside his own department. Childers, greatly alarmed by the rise of Clann na Poblachta, noted the growing disillusionment with Fianna Fáil even among its own supporters by 1947. He began to fear electoral meltdown and blamed a lack of social welfare provision and the maintenance of the old guard for the problems. Sometime in 1947 he wrote to MacEntee: 'We may be too late. It is probable that we should have founded a new Party at the end of the Emergency embracing National Labour, FG and ourselves.' Perhaps he feared that Fianna Fáil would face a landslide defeat like the Conservatives had in Britain in 1945.[51] As it was, Fianna Fáil was easily the largest party after the 1948 election, only being denied office by an unlikely coalition of all the other political groupings.

The Inter-Party Government from 1948 to 1951 tended to bear out Childers' view that there were few policy differences between the parties.[52] It would appear to have been as ideologically committed to protectionism and the promotion of agriculture as the most ardent Fianna Fáil minister. Thanks to the infusion of a small amount of Marshall Aid, this government did make some moves towards Keynesian policies. Its investments, however, mainly benefited agriculture (due to the advocacy of the Minister for Agriculture, James Dillon) but this investment did not pay dividends as agricultural commodities faced stagnant prices because of the British 'cheap food' policy. Furthermore, as many in the civil service already knew and had articulated to the highest levels including de Valera, agriculture was next to useless at providing extra employment.[53] When the Inter-Party Government fell in 1951, Fianna Fáil returned to office with MacEntee as Minister for Finance, where he pursued a vigorous deflation policy and continued to attack full employment as inflationary.[54] Lemass, backed by Frank Aiken, forced MacEntee to introduce some Keynesian public works (the National Development Fund) in 1953 against his will.[55]

MacEntee's overly prudent, some might say overly zealous, stewardship of the exchequer's purse strings at Finance in the 1951–54 Fianna Fáil government doomed his chances of ever becoming Taoiseach.[56] Lemass, between 1945 and 1957, in government and in opposition, struggled to articulate a coherent economic policy. His legislation for industrial efficiency fell by the wayside with the Fianna Fáil defeat of 1948. His protectionist structure might have been appropriate before the war, but in the newly open world economy it was disastrous.[57] The vested interests which he had helped create – particularly the uncompetitive and sometimes incompetent, protected industrialists – were not confronted.[58]

Lemass required the intellectual stimulus of T. K. Whitaker to create a new direction after 1958. Whitaker's blend of free market/free trade economics with Lemass' shrewd social conscience at last imposed a framework that would see sustained economic and social progress for the first time since independence. Indeed there was a perceptible shift in Irish politics from the mid-1950s with policy being framed not by politicians but by technocratic civil servants, versed in economics, exemplified by people such as Whitaker and Patrick Lynch. This was a trend evident in countries such as France since 1945. However the relative radicalism of Lemass and Whitaker should be put into perspective; at this time even Franco's Spain moved away from the policies of protectionism and autarky, which had proved such an unambiguous failure towards planning and free trade.[59]

The Consequences

The battles over these two blueprints from Britain exposed fissures in the Fianna Fáil cabinet but produced no serious political fallout. The effects were more demographic than political; the welfare state and the affluent society that Beveridgeism and full employment created in Britain were to be key factors in the greatest exodus of Irish emigrants since the 1880s. More than one-fifth of the population left in the period from 1945 to 1960. Emigration seems an inadequate term for such a movement; the emotive 'population transfer' seems more appropriate. Most of those who left were from the rural undereducated peasant-class from the west and the unskilled working-class – the landless peasantry and the proletariat – so often the engine of revolution and social change elsewhere. It is notable that these two groupings were among the biggest economic losers since Irish independence. If Ireland had remained part of the United Kingdom, the full employment and welfare policies implemented by the Labour government between 1945 and 1951 would have massively benefited those sectors of the population.

Since the widening of the franchise in the 1870s, Ireland had been dominated politically by a Catholic petite bourgeoisie, which had managed to maintain power against all challenges despite a questionable economic and social record. This grouping comprised those who were in reasonably secure employment and covered a wide range of social strata encompassing such occupations as civil servants, shopkeepers, merchants, publicans, skilled tradesmen (who used a strict quota of apprenticeships to protect their wages which the Department of Finance and the Commission on Emigration claimed bore close comparison to British wage rates), those employed in the protected industries and those who held reasonable amounts of land.[60] This 'respectable class' gained most from independence and were not insignificant in number.[61]

A full employment and social welfare policy comparable to Britain's would have required major increases in taxation and would have directly impacted on this 'respectable class'. It would have necessitated the implementation of proper planning and the pursuit of more dynamic economic growth in Ireland in the period from 1945 to 1960, and the abandonment of protectionism. It was not until the more well-off sections of society began to join the exodus to England in the mid-1950s that significant change was made to economic policy. Fifteen years of the greatest economic boom Europe had ever seen had been wasted, and this in a country virtually debt free and undamaged by war.

Tom Garvin persuasively argues that many in the ruling elite in Ireland were not interested in economic development and growth and feared that it would sap 'the national spirit, lead to shoneenism, rootless cosmopolitanism and spiritual emptiness'.[62] This ruling elite maintained its dominance because it shared vital cultural aspirations with the lower classes: the same nationalist aspirations, the same religion and conservative values. Most importantly, the most disaffected in Ireland had the safety valve of emigration. Those who migrated to Britain invariably voted for the British Labour Party. They did not have an opportunity to remain at home and vote for the Irish Labour Party. The total of those who emigrated between 1932 and 1959 exceeded the Fianna Fáil vote at every election of the period. It was and remains a rather distressing vote of no confidence in Éamon de Valera's Ireland.[63]

In 1952 the then Fianna Fáil government set up an interdepartmental committee to examine how British policy since the war had been detrimental to Ireland's economic interests. Generally the report suggested that little damage was being caused apart from that 'British policy in regard to social welfare, full employment and wages has set headlines which have stimulated demands for similar standards here and thus imposed serious strains on our economy. These, however, are matters of domestic policy in which individual countries claim to exercise sovereign rights.'[64] Ireland, as a nation, had exercised her sovereign right to say no to such policies. Hundreds of thousands of Irish people said yes, and moved to Britain.

NORTHERN IRELAND, AND THE IRISH IN THE BRITISH ARMY

THE BELFAST BLITZ, 1941
Jonathan Bardon

During the autumn of 1938 letters from Austria began to appear on Ministry of Commerce desks in Belfast. When civil servants opened them they were made vividly aware of the Nazi tyranny in central Europe. A maker of artificial flowers in Vienna, Dorothea Both, explained that an article had appeared on 29 August in the *Zionistische Rundschau* indicating that the Northern Ireland government 'would be disposed to receive emigrants from Austria which would establish manufactures or trades and offer work and gain to workless people'. As a result nearly 300 letters arrived in Belfast from Jews appealing for permission to settle in Northern Ireland. Along the margin of Frau Both's letter, in which she further explained that her husband was no longer permitted to practise as a barrister, a civil servant had written just one word, 'regret'. The *Zionistische Rundschau* had been mistaken: the government was not about to make Northern Ireland a haven for the persecuted Jews of the Third Reich. Altogether 244 letters seem to have been rejected after only brief consideration and then marked in blue pencil with such curt comments as 'no reply', 'no opportunity', 'no opening', and 'not written to'. Jews, or those of Jewish blood, had already made a remarkable contribution to Belfast's economic development, including Gustav Wolff in shipbuilding, and Sir Otto Jaffe in linen manufacture (he had been Lord Mayor) – a contribution out of all proportion to their numbers. Northern Ireland lost the opportunity to offer help to fellow humans in peril and to draw on the genius of a remarkable people.[1]

As war approached Lord Craigavon, Prime Minister of Northern Ireland since its inception in 1921, claimed: 'Ulster is ready when we get the word and always will be.' On Monday 4 September 1939, Tommy Henderson, the independent unionist MP for the Shankill, asked the prime minister if the government realised 'that these fast bombers can come to Northern Ireland in two and three quarter hours'. Craigavon evaded the question and replied in general terms: 'We here today are in a state of war and we are prepared with the rest of the United Kingdom and empire to face all the responsibilities that imposes on the Ulster people. There is no slackening in our loyalty.' Lady Londonderry, who had corresponded with Hitler and entertained foreign minister Joachim von Ribbentrop at Mountstewart, wrote to her husband in London: 'All sorts of rot going on here. Air raid warnings and black-outs! As if anyone cared or wished to bomb Belfast'.[2]

Actually almost no one in authority believed that Belfast was in any danger. During the 'phoney war' such an attitude was understandable enough, though it was not shared by municipal authorities on the other side of the Irish Sea. There is ample evidence that the political leaders lacked the will, energy and capacity to cope with a major crisis when it came. 'He is the one politician who can win an election without leaving his fireside', the *Daily Express* had observed of Craigavon just before his 1938 election victory.[3] Sir Wilfred Spender, the cabinet secretary, thought he was a premier whom 'true friends would advise to retire now' for he was incapable of doing 'more than one hour's constructive work' in a day. Lady Londonderry confided to Sir Samuel Hoare, the Home Secretary, that Craigavon had become 'ga-ga'. According to Spender, Richard Dawson Bates, the Home Affairs Minister, was 'incapable of giving his responsible officers coherent directions on policy' – actually, by this time, he was drunk for most of each day.[4] Bates' Parliamentary Secretary, Edmond Warnock, for all his righteous indignation later, showed little energy in preparing people for civil defence. He had informed the Northern Ireland cabinet on 19 June 1939 that: 'an attack on Northern Ireland would involve a flight of over 1,000 miles ... the enemy planes must twice pass through the active gun, searchlight and aeroplane defences of Great Britain ... it is possible we might escape attack.'[5]

After a brief flurry of activity, the regional government's attitude to civil defence soon lapsed back to being as soporific as before. Dawson Bates simply refused to reply to army correspondence and when the Ministry of Home Affairs was informed by imperial defence experts that Belfast was a certain Luftwaffe target, nothing was done. The only member of the government recognising the nature of the crisis was Sir Basil Brooke, the Minister of Agriculture, who threw himself into the task of making Northern Ireland a major supplier of food to Britain in her time of danger. Brooke ordered that potatoes, carrots and cabbage be grown in lazy beds on the Stormont estate, got golf clubs to plant corn on the fairways and persuaded Queen's University to cultivate its front lawn.

Neither the regional government nor Belfast corporation had done much to protect the city's citizens in peacetime. In the whole inter-war period Belfast corporation built only 16 houses by direct labour and subsidised the construction of only 2,600 more. The city's economy had been severely affected by the protracted depression following the 1929 Wall Street Crash – 29.5% of insured industrial workers were unemployed in February 1938, the highest figure for any region of the United Kingdom. Still, the corporation was obsessively concerned to keep the rates down and, when it did exert itself, its activities were surrounded by outrageous scandal, particularly in the corrupt awarding of contracts to cronies who did shoddy work.[6] Belfast's public health record was just about the worst in the United Kingdom. When compared with six British cities in 1938, Belfast had the highest infant mortality rate, 96 per 1,000 live births compared with, for example, 59 in Sheffield. Maternal mortality actually *rose* by one-fifth between 1922 and 1938. Malnutrition arising out of poverty, lack of hygiene, and inadequate medical care largely explained why in Belfast 51% of all deaths of children under 15 years were caused by infectious diseases, 25% higher than in English county boroughs. Pneumonia was the deadliest disease but the main killer of young adults was tuberculosis, responsible for 49% of all deaths in the age group 15 to 25.[7]

By the beginning of 1941 there were only four public air-raid shelters made of sandbags round the City Hall, together with underground toilets at Shaftesbury Square and Donegall Square North. Only some houses in the harbour area had domestic shelters and not a single one had been provided anywhere else in Northern Ireland. Only 8,800 children had been evacuated and more than half of these had returned by the spring of 1941. Belfast corporation was so lacking in any real sense of urgency that vital pipe fittings for fire-fighting appliances and building materials for shelters were not available when Hitler turned his forces westward in 1940.

The Northern Ireland government also failed to make adequate preparations: much vital time was lost while the government argued that civil defence in the region was Westminster's financial responsibility. Warnock considered that it would be 'illogical for the Government to provide Anderson shelters for private houses'.[8] The city had no fighter squadrons, no balloon barrage and only 21 anti-aircraft guns when the war began, and only around 2,000 civil defence volunteers had been trained.

Craigavon had a habit of beginning many of his speeches with the words 'We here in Ulster', but he was only speaking for two-thirds of the population of Northern Ireland. About a quarter of Belfast's citizens were Catholics who had been given few incentives to put themselves out on behalf of the war effort. During the first two days of the war, the RUC logged 12 anti-war incidents, including: the lighting of bonfires and gas street lamps; the burning of gas masks; two soldiers stripped of their uniforms; the shooting of an army reservist in the stomach; and the painting of hostile slogans, one of which declared 'ARP [Air Raid Precautions] for English slaves, IRA for the Irish'.[9] Clearly the people of Northern Ireland were not united in common defence as the war got under way.

In the spring of 1940 the vortex of total war suddenly swung westwards. Then, as the shattered remains of the British army gathered on the Dunkirk beaches, Churchill is said to have remarked gloomily in his map room that the only properly armed and disciplined force left in the United Kingdom was the Ulster Special Constabulary. As Britain's plight became ever more desperate Churchill sought drastic political solutions including an offer of a declaration in favour of the reunification of Ireland in return for British use of the Treaty ports. Craigavon fired off a series of apoplectic cipher telegrams before de Valera rejected the offer on 7 July 1940. Éire's neutrality and the German occupation of France forced Britain to divert its convoys around the headlands of Co. Donegal and into the North Channel. Northern Ireland now had a crucial role to play as U-boats continued to wreak havoc on merchant shipping in the western approaches.

'I have heard speeches about Ulster pulling her weight but they have never carried conviction,' Warnock said, announcing his resignation from the Northern Ireland government in May 1940. A fortnight later, Lt. Col. Alexander Gordon, Parliamentary Secretary to the Ministry of Finance, also resigned, explaining to the Commons that the government was 'quite unfitted to sustain the people in the ordeal we have to face.'[10] The Labour MP, Jack Beattie, described the prime minister as having reached his 'doting stage'. It is likely that several unionist backbenchers agreed with him. The cabinet secretary was understandably irritated that his valuable time was being used to telephone London to order marmalade from Fortnum and Mason for Lady Craigavon or to run out to buy tobacco and cigarettes. In September, Warnock introduced a vote of censure, calling for a complete change in the government's composition. Craigavon's simple response to all the demands to revamp his government was: 'My answer is that I am not going to do it.'[11]

On Sunday 24 November 1940, just after listening to the six o'clock news on the wireless, Craigavon died peacefully in his armchair. John Andrews had often deputised for Craigavon and there was no dispute when he was chosen to succeed as prime minister. The only new face in the government was Lord Glentoran. The old guard, therefore, remain-ed in office and under the direction of Andrews it was no more capable than before of coping with the exigencies of war.

On a fine Saturday afternoon, 30 November 1940, a single, unob-served German plane flew high across the Ards Peninsula towards Bel-fast. The crew brought back photographs of suitable targets, identified by the Luftwaffe's Section 5 photo-reconnaissance unit, including, *die Werft Harland & Wolff Ltd, die Tankstelle Conns Water, das Fleugzeugwerk Short & Harland, das Kraftwerk Belfast, die Grossmuhle Rank & Co, das Wasserwerk Belfast, die Kasernlagen Victoria Barracks*.[12] The entire city of Belfast, the Germans discovered, was defended by only seven anti-air-craft batteries.

Back in June, to fend off criticism, Craigavon had appointed John MacDermott, QC, as Minister of Public Security. The new minister quickly appreciated the fearfully inadequate defences in the region but again and again his efforts were frustrated by lack of support from his colleagues. As the bombing of British cities commenced it was clear that Belfast was the most unprotected city in the United Kingdom. On 24 March 1941 MacDermott expressed his anxiety in a letter to Andrews: anti-aircraft cover was less than half the approved strength in Belfast; the city did not possess a single searchlight; and no other town in Northern Ireland had any defence at all. He concluded:

> Up to now we have escaped attack. So had Clydeside until recently. Clyde-side got its blitz during the period of the last moon ... at present the enemy could not easily reach Belfast *in force* except during a period of moonlight. The period of the next moon from, say, the 7th to the 16th of April, may well bring our turn.[13]

On the night of 7–8 April a small squadron of German bombers, led by a pathfinder Heinkel III from Kampfgruppe 26, raided Belfast, and com-pletely destroyed the four-and-a-half-acre Harland and Wolff fuselage factory, reduced a major timber yard to ashes, and delivered damaging blows to the docks. Compared with the horrifying assault on London, Liverpool, Glasgow, Bristol and Great Yarmouth the same night, the attack was a small one, but the people of Northern Ireland now knew they were vulnerable after all.

The sky was clearing on the evening of Easter Tuesday, 15 April

1941, as 180 German bombers, predominantly Junkers 88s and Heinkel IIIs, flew in formation over the Irish Sea. As the raiders approached the Ards Peninsula they dropped to 7,000 feet. On the Castlereagh Hills ground crews manned anti-aircraft guns; Hawker Hurricane Mark IIs sped down the runway at Aldergrove aerodrome; and at 10.40 p.m. sirens wailed in Belfast. Casting intense light, hundreds of flares drifted down, then incendiaries, high explosive bombs and parachute mines rained on the city. It was not the industrial heartland but the congested housing north of the city centre that received the full force of the attack. This may not have been the German intention: perhaps the Belfast Waterworks at the Cave Hill was mistaken for the harbour; perhaps a hastily contrived smoke screen at the shipyards confused the pilots; or perhaps the instruction to take a bearing on the twin spires of St Peter's pro-cathedral on the Falls Road caused the Germans to overshoot their targets. The result was a fearful carnage in the New Lodge, the lower Shankill and the Antrim Road. Suspended from green artificial silk parachutes, 76 landmines slowly drifted down; designed to rend apart the reinforced concrete and steel of factories and workshops – their existence was not acknowledged by the British government until 1944 – more than half of these fell on decaying kitchen and parlour houses. In Veryan Gardens and Vandyck Gardens 130 homes were destroyed and in one house eight members of the Danby family were killed. York Street Spinning Mill, the largest of its kind in Europe, was sliced in two; the collapsing six storeys obliterated 42 houses, and damaged 21, in Sussex Street and Vere Street. A bomb struck one house in Ballynure Street and nine people were killed. In the Ulster Hall, Delia Murphy, the popular singer, kept performing through the raid. Some of her audience were later forced to take refuge in a shelter in Percy Street; when a parachute mine fell next to it, 30 people were killed. HMS *Furious* was the only vessel to add to the anti-aircraft barrage but she sheared loose from the recoil of her guns.

At 1.45 a.m. a bomb fell at the corner of Oxford Street and East Bridge Street, wrecking the city's central telephone exchange. All contact with Britain and the anti-aircraft operations room was cut off. The guns on the ground fell silent for fear of shooting down the Hurricane fighters, which, with cruel irony, had been withdrawn shortly before by fighter command. For another two hours the Luftwaffe attacked Belfast completely unopposed. Altogether 203 metric tons of bombs and 800 firebomb canisters were dropped on the city. After the raid a Luftwaffe pilot gave this description on German Radio:

We were in exceptional good humour knowing that we were going for a new target, one of England's last hiding places. Wherever Churchill is hiding his war material we will go ... Belfast is as worthy a target as Coventry, Birmingham, Bristol or Glasgow.[14]

Around 140 fires now raged in Belfast and several of these spread into conflagrations. Just as the Auxiliary Fire Service arrived to fight the inferno sweeping across the Antrim Road, the water pressure fell away – the mains had been cracked in 20 places. The Ministry of Public Security requested help from civil defence regions throughout Northern Ireland and the War Office responded promptly to a call for aid, sending a total of 42 pumps and 400 firemen from Glasgow, Liverpool and Preston.

From his house near Stormont, MacDermott watched the flames enveloping the city. At 4.15 a.m. he crawled under his desk and telephoned Brooke who was staying nearby. The line was still working. MacDermott asked for permission to request fire engines from Éire. 'I gave him authority as it is obviously a question of expediency', Brooke noted in his diary.[15] At 4.35 a.m. a telegram was sent by railway telegraph, because the telephone lines to Dublin had been cut. De Valera agreed without hesitation to send help. Altogether 70 men and 13 fire engines from Dun Laoghaire, Dublin, Drogheda and Dundalk sped northwards. 'I had to sit on my hands to keep them from getting numb,' one volunteer remembered; 'There were no landmarks on the way up; we reached our destination by following the telephone lines.'[16]

As they approached the city outskirts the southern firemen saw smoke and flames rising hundreds of feet into the air. Horrified at the carnage, John Smith, Belfast's chief fire officer, was found beneath a table in Chichester Street fire station, weeping and refusing to come out. There was little the firemen could do to fight the flames – hoses were cut by falling buildings, fittings were often the incorrect diameter, and the water pressure had fallen too far. There were numerous individual acts of heroism but both Spender and MacDermott felt that firemen and civil defence workers had performed badly. An American, seconded to the Short and Harland factory by the Lockheed Aircraft Corporation, was not impressed by his fellow workers; in a letter to his parents in California he wrote:

You have heard how tough the Irish are – well all I can say is that the tough Irish must come from S. Ireland because the boys up in N. Ireland are a bunch of chicken shit yellow bastards – 90% of them left everything and ran like hell. Short and Harlands the Aircraft factory that builds Stirlings here had 300 Volunteer fire fighters in the plant, after the raid they were lucky to get 90 of them.[17]

Outside of Belfast the Germans struck at targets that lay within their flight path, including Newtownards, Bangor and Derry.

At dawn on Wednesday 16 April a thick yellow pall covered Belfast. People tore at the smouldering rubble to bring the trapped, dead and injured to the surface. Sam Hanna Bell remembered: 'We wrestled with street doors blown halfway down hallways. From under the stairs of a house we extracted an old woman still clutching a miniature Union Jack.'[18] The Reverend Eric Gallagher, then minister of Woodvale Methodist Church, helped to dig out the bodies of 14 members of his congregation from the ruins of houses in Ohio Street. On the Crumlin Road army lorries were piled high with corpses and severed limbs. Many of the dead were brought into the Falls Road Public Baths. As more arrived the pool had to be emptied in order to lay out over 150 corpses; an attendant remembered: 'One coffin contained – all open – a young mother with her two dead children, one in each arm. One lovely girl of sixteen lay in a coffin in her white confirmation robe with blue silk ribbon and black hair.'[19] There the bodies lay for three days as relatives attempted, often in vain, to identify them. In St George's Market, 255 corpses were laid out. Emma Duffin was one of the nurses on duty. She recorded in her diary:

> No attendant nurse had soothed the last moments of these victims, no gently reverent hand had closed their eyes or crossed their hands. With tangled hair, staring eyes, contorted limbs, their grey-green faces covered with dust, they lay bundled into the coffins, half-shrouded in rugs or blankets or an occasional sheet, still wearing their dirty, torn, twisted garments.[20]

Of the bodies taken here, 151 were identified and only 92 taken away by relatives and friends for burial. On Monday 21 April the unclaimed dead were buried in mass graves: Protestants at the city cemetery and Catholics (identified by rosaries and emblems) in the Milltown cemetery close by. The official figures were 745 people dead and 430 seriously injured. The actual total was at least 900 dead. No other city in the United Kingdom, except London, had lost so many lives in one air raid. Some 6,000 people arrived in Dublin from Belfast and tens of thousands left the city for the countryside. Of those who remained, 40,000 had to be put up in rest centres and 70,000 had to be given meals every day in emergency feeding centres. The military authorities were deeply unimpressed by the unco-ordinated rescue work and troops were disgusted by widespread looting and the refusal of young men sightseeing to lend a hand.

At 9.45 p.m. on Sunday 4 May 1941 the first squadrons of a total force of 204 German bombers took off from northern France and about an hour after midnight another attack on Belfast began. In the words of one pilot, 'visibility was wonderful. I could make out my targets perfectly'.[21] Until 1.55 a.m. the pathfinders of Kampfgruppe 100 dropped 6,000 incendiaries almost exclusively on the harbour, the aircraft factory and the shipyards; then the rest of the bombers were led in by the rapidly spreading conflagration. Three corvettes nearing completion were destroyed; the transport ship *Fair Head* sank at her moorings; three ships received direct hits in the Abercorn yard; and altogether Harland and Wolff suffered the devastation of two-thirds of its premises. Much of the densely inhabited area about the Newtownards Road was burning fiercely.

The German crews reported a 'picture of destruction none of us will forget'. A war correspondent, Ernst von Kuhren, flying with one squadron, broadcast his impressions back in Germany later that day: 'when we approached the target at half-past two we stared silently into a sea of flames such as none of us had seen before ... In Belfast there was not a large number of conflagrations, but just one enormous conflagration which spread over the entire harbour and industrial area.'[22] This time much damage was inflicted on the city centre: the area around St Anne's Cathedral burned intensely; almost the whole northern side of High Street was ablaze down to the Albert Memorial; and Arnott's store, the Bank Buildings, the Athletic Stores, the Ulster Arcade, Thornton's, the Co-operative Timber Stores, Dunville's Stores, Gallaher's tobacco factory, the Water Office, Rosemary Street Presbyterian Church and the banqueting room of the City Hall were either destroyed or severely damaged. Two parachute mines landed in the Barbour Street–Whitewell Road area and killed 30 people. That night almost 300 people, many from the Shankill, took refuge in Clonard Monastery in the Falls Roads, whose *Domestic Chronicles* record:

> The crypt under the sanctuary, also the cellar under the working sacristy, has been fitted out and is opened to the people, women and children only, as an air-raid shelter. This act of ours is very much appreciated by all, Protestants included. Prayers are said and hymns sung by the occupants during the bombing.[23]

Andrew McFall remembered: 'Before the raids the Shankill was the

Shankill and the Falls was the Falls and ne'er the twain did meet. But after that big raid at Easter half the Shankill spent their nights at the Clonard Monastery and it was amazing the transformation that came over people.'[24] In fewer than three and a half hours the bombers had dropped 95,992 incendiaries and 237 tons of high explosives. As dawn came Emma Duffin stepped into the garden of the hospital where she was working on the Stranmillis Road:

> The smell of burning was in the air. The grass was strewn with blackened and charred papers. There was a sheet from a child's essay book. On the top of the page, I read, 'The End of the World'. It seemed appropriate. It was the end of the world as we knew it.[25]

Early on Monday morning a lone German aeroplane flew over Belfast to make a photographic record of the results of the raid. *Der Adler* published aerial views of the city and gave a full page to analysing the successful outcome of the attack. For the first and only time in the war, Northern Ireland made headline news in the German press. *Völkischer Beobachter* began its report 'Strong Air Fighter Units Bomb Belfast' and 'Back from Belfast: Fires Everywhere'.[26] By now 53.5% of Belfast's housing stock had been destroyed or badly damaged. The death toll for this May raid was 191 – a surprisingly low figure largely explained by two facts: that in this Sabbatarian city the centre was largely deserted when the attack began; and a very large number of people had already fled to the countryside.

The exodus from Belfast during and after the May air raids was on a huge scale. Towns close to Belfast were overwhelmed. This mass migration from Belfast brought into the open the extreme deprivation of those now bombed out of congested streets who had endured two decades of unemployment and neglect. Emma Duffin's middle-class sensibilities were offended by 'the incredible dirt of the people, of children crawling with lice, not even house trained, who destroyed mattresses and stuffed clothes down W.C.s in order to get new ones'. Moya Woodside recorded that the 11 evacuees staying with her mother were 'all filthy, the smell of the room is terrible, they refuse all food except tea and bread, the children have made puddles all over the floor, etc.' Her sister, living 30 miles from Belfast, complained of:

> the appalling influx from the slums the day after the raid. They were totally unprepared for such numbers and the type of people arriving. The whole town is horrified by the filth of those evacuees and by their filthy habits and

take-it-for-granted attitude … The smell is awful … They don't even use the lavatory, they just do it on the floor, grown-ups and children.[27]

The day before the May raid Spender estimated that 100,000 people – around one-quarter of the population of Belfast – had fled to the Northern Irish countryside. Yet well over half those killed on the night 4–5 May were women and children, and next morning, as railway and bus stations were once again besieged, a fresh exodus began. By the end of May some 220,000 had left the city, thus creating acute congestion in the rural towns and farmhouses.

And what was the government doing? The ministers had a previously-scheduled meeting the day after the May raid. In the cabinet minutes, only 5 lines are devoted to the air attack and there are 23 lines on whether or not the Northern Ireland government should respond to an offer by what is described as the 'Eire Electricity Board' to sell them 6,000 kilowatts; the decision on the latter, incidentally, was no, because of 'political difficulties of making any such arrangement'. Andrews did ask some of his ministers to prepare memoranda on what were described as 'Post-Blitz Problems' for a cabinet meeting on 13 May. MacDermott's paper was detailed and elegantly composed, entitled 'Memorandum by the Minister of Public Safety on Questions of Government raised by recent air raids on Belfast'. He praised the Ministry of Education for so rapidly making schools available as rest centres but went on to observe that 'there was a very considerable degree of confusion and disorganisation'. Not enough had been done by Belfast corporation:

> I have gained the definite impression that the presence on the scene of the Central Government tends to encourage an abatement of local effort and a reduction in the sense of responsibility under which all local bodies should be working. The policy adopted should, I feel, be to strengthen the local authorities increasingly …

The corporation should play a more active role in civil defence. He continued: 'It might well be the function of the corporation but as at present constituted I do not think this body would be likely to deal with it successfully.' Too much was being left to the troops:

> During the first heavy raid the military worked with much enthusiasm and devotion to duty. At the end of the second heavy raid … it was apparent that the military had not the same zest in the work. I heard several complaints of soldiers at work being watched by large crowds of idle but able-bodied men … the difficulty in getting the Council to develop the civil

defence services with sufficient promptitude led to the transfer of civil
defence functions to a separate body [the Advanced Government Head-
quarters]. Had the municipal authority been able to deal satisfactorily with
A.R.P. the distinction between civil defence functions and the other functions ... would never have arisen in practice ... I suggest that much difficulty would be avoided and that efficiency would be promoted if the whole
powers of the Council were put in commission, assuming that say three
capable men can be found to act as commissioners.[28]

He admitted that he had made upbeat speeches in public but here, in
the privacy of the cabinet room, he warned that 'it is impossible to resist
the conclusion that the morale of the city as a whole is not first class.
Indeed it is in some ways definitely disappointing. There is much fear.
Many are still leaving the town nightly to stay in the fields or walk on
the roads till the danger of a raid is thought to have passed'. He ended
by recommending protection for the buildings at Stormont and by advocating the imposition of conscription: 'This country has suffered and
is suffering from being only half in the war ... Its introduction would
cause difficulties with the minority but I would doubt if they would be
as great as they were at the beginning of the war.'

Sir Basil Brooke, now Minister of Commerce, in his memorandum
had a bleak view of the future:

> There is every reason to anticipate further raids of at least equal severity in
> the future. It is true that the shortening of the hours of darkness should
> normally result in some reduction in enemy activity. It is by no means cer-
> tain whether this will redound to the advantage of Belfast, however, on
> account of the ease with which enemy aircraft can approach Belfast along
> either the East or the West coast of Éire without risk of interception.

It was a problem to persuade those remaining in the city to evacuate:
'Working-class areas in both East and North Belfast have suffered with
exceptional severity ... It is the policy of the Government to evacuate
women and children from these areas, but wives are reluctant to leave
because no provision is being made for their husbands'.[29] He wanted the
army to make 200 Nissen huts available for these essential male war
workers.

Richard Dawson Bates in his brief memorandum tersely outlined
the desperate situation:

> The position now is that the country accommodation is completely full.
> There are 900 people in the Lisburn Halls, 2,000 in Dunmurry, and 330 in
> Dublin Rest Centres which we have promised to remove at the earliest

possible moment, and for which there is no accommodation whatever.

The position is therefore as urgent as it can possibly be. We must start clearing arrangements at once and we must start from the Belfast end. It is, therefore, absolutely essential that we should have Government House, Hillsborough, without delay ...

We must have large houses, institutions or camps for respectable families who are at present billeted in the country in some cases at the rate of 30 to small houses, under conditions which they definitely cannot be expected to tolerate and which will lead to an outbreak of disease ...

Then, in what could have been the most liberal observation of his career, he added: 'My officials inform me that various authorities in Éire are, they believe, prepared to co-operate very generously ... In the event of an immediate emergency co-operation with these authorities would appear to be the only course available and we should take advantage of it.' What about those citizens who were not so respectable, those his ministry had done so little to protect? Dawson Bates continued: 'There is in the country probably about 5,000 absolutely unbilletable persons. They are unbilletable owing to personal habits which are sub-human. Camps or institutions under suitable supervision must be instituted for these.'[30] At the bottom of this memorandum, in the copy of the cabinet conclusions, is a doodle, a cartoon of the Home Affairs Minister. Was it executed by Sir Wilfred Spender whose wife Lilian had a special loathing of Bates, as she confessed to her diary?

A fortnight later, the retiring Moderator of the Presbyterian Assembly, the Reverend Dr J. B. Woodburn, gave this warning in his sermon:

After the big blitz of a few weeks ago I was inexpressibly shocked by the sight of people I saw walking the streets. I have been working 19 years in Belfast and I never saw the like of them before – wretched people, very undersized and underfed down-and-out looking men and women. They had been bombed out of their homes and were wandering the streets. Is it creditable to us that there should be such people in a Christian country? ... We have got to see that there is more talk of justice; we have got to see it enacted, and the work will have to begin immediately. If something is not done now to remedy this rank inequality there will be revolution after the war.[31]

Radio Paris, under German direction, informed its listeners in the middle of May: 'Fearing air raids, 20,000 women and children escape every evening from Belfast to the outskirts of the city.' This was a considerable underestimate. Nearly 30 years ago I persuaded my colleague, Jim McConville, to write down his memories of the Blitz. He remembers:

The exodus began around 10 p.m. Hundreds went as far as the Falls Park; thousands felt safer another mile out of the city. Parents and children 'well happed up' against the cold night air would sit around on folding stools, or lie on ground sheets; some could and would sleep; most of us talked, joked and bantered as only the Belfast working man can; someone would light a cigarette and immediately from all around would come: 'Put out that match! Do you want Jerry to see us!'

Though rumours circulated in Protestant areas that Catholics had help-ed guide German bombers by shining torches from the rooftops, the shared experiences of fear, hardship and bereavement did seem to reduce intercommunal tensions for a time. Jim McConville continues:

This nightly journey 'up the road' to the safety of the countryside, and the return in the early hours of the morning, helped intensify the feeling of togetherness that had grown up as the war progressed ... New friendships were forged; old acquaintances and long-time neighbours were seen in a new light; kindness and a helping hand appeared from the most unexpected quarters.[32]

Protestants and Catholics were also united in their contempt for the government's ineptitude and complacency. Tommy Henderson, the flam-boyant house painter and independent unionist MP for the Shankill, said bitterly at Stormont on 13 May: 'I broke down after the things I saw. I broke down when I saw lying dead men I had been reared beside. When I saw the whole district where I roamed in my bare feet razed to the ground.' Then looking angrily towards the prime minister, he asked:

Will the Right Hon member come with me to the hills and to Divis Moun-tain? Will he go to the barns and sheughs throughout Northern Ireland to see the people of Belfast, some of them lying on damp ground? Will he come to Hannahstown and the Falls Road? The Catholics and Protestants are going up there mixed and they are talking to one another. They are sleeping in the same sheugh, below the same tree or in the same barn. They all say the same thing, that the government is no good.[33]

Henderson's fury would have been all the more intense had he known how much time the Northern Ireland government would devote to arranging camouflage for the Stormont Parliament Buildings (they were heavily painted all over with bitumen and the approach roads covered with black cinders) and to protecting the bronze statue of Carson in its grounds from possible bomb damage. On three occasions the protection of the statue was discussed as a major item at cabinet meetings. At the

first, on 17 June, Andrews said it would cost 'an expenditure of some
hundred pounds ... to provide protection by sandbags, etc., over the entire monument'. A confused correspondence between ministers and civil
servants followed over whether or not a decision had been made. The
topic was debated again with enthusiasm on 19 August. The most protracted discussion on the issue took place at the cabinet meeting of 23
September:

> The Prime Minister said he had consulted Lady Carson as to the measures
> which might be taken to protect her late husband's statue from air-raid
> damage.
>   He thought the statue, which it would be difficult if not impossible to
> replace, should be removed for safe storage elsewhere, and that the pedestal
> could if necessary be either repaired or renewed should be left in its present
> position.
>   The Ministers of Labour and Education supported this view and on the
> proposal of the Prime Minister the Parliamentary Secretary to the Minister
> of Commerce undertook to communicate with Mr Merrifield, the sculptor,
> and ascertain his views as to the steps which should be taken to safeguard
> the statue from bomb damage and also as to the best method of dismantling
> and removing the statue, should it be decided to adopt this course.[34]

This was during a period when tens of thousands of Belfast citizens were
still without the protection of air-raid shelters.

Fortunately for the people of Northern Ireland the Germans did not
return. On 26 June 1941 the Wehrmacht crossed the borders of the
Soviet Union and by the end of the year Hitler sealed his fate by casually
declaring war on the richest nation on earth – the United States. The
cabinet had turned down MacDermott's proposal to put Belfast into commission (which would have been a government secretariat with full
authority to act to ensure rapid response and order on behalf of the
government in the aftermath of a major air raid), but the noxious odours
of corruption had become so stomach-heaving that the decision had to
be reversed. Soon after Andrews was ousted by Brooke, who came to
power as the Americans practised for the Normandy landings by acci-
dentally running over Ulster dolmens in their tanks, when unemployment virtually disappeared in Northern Ireland for the first time since
1919, and when Northern Ireland was indeed becoming an arsenal of
Allied victory.

NEUTRALITY, IDENTITY AND THE CHALLENGE OF THE 'IRISH VOLUNTEERS'
Geoffrey Roberts

In *Dividing Ireland: World War I and Partition*, Thomas Hennessey argued that the First World War posed a series of acute challenges to the Irish and Britannic identities which co-existed within Ireland on the eve of 1914. The interaction and development of these identities in the circumstances created by the war resulted in a transformation of the Irish Question. Ireland was divided psychologically before it was partitioned politically, says Hennessey, and the particular way in which identities changed and clashed during the war resulted in a separatist rather than a home rule Ireland.[1]

The Second World War also posed a series of challenges to Irish identities. The different responses to these challenges in Ireland did not result in any great crisis nor any great rupture comparable to that of the First World War. But there was a definite outcome to the identity questions and issues posed by the war – an outcome that had an important bearing on the post-war development of the Irish state, politics and society. At the same time the diversity of responses to the identity question produced a series of political and cultural contradictions and tensions which are still evident 60 years later.

What was the impact on that process of identity formation of the large number of Irish citizens who volunteered for service in the British armed forces between 1939 and 1945?[2] During the war an estimated 70,000 citizens of neutral Ireland served in the British armed forces, together with 50,000 or so from Northern Ireland.[3] Virtually all who served were volunteers and, unlike the First World War, Irish volunteering during the Second World War was not primarily a process of collective mobilisation. In southern Ireland, at least, decisions to volunteer and serve were mainly individual. No doubt individual decisions were influenced by family and friends and sometimes the process of enlistment was aided and abetted by various organisations, but there is no sign of the 'logic of collective sacrifice' evident in Irish recruitment to the British armed forces during the First World War.[4] Nor was there any general political mobilisation for war even remotely comparable to what happened in Ireland between 1914 and 1918. In that light the figure of 120,000 recruits north and south, if at all accurate, compares well with the estimated 210,000 Irish volunteers during the First World War.[5]

The idea that the Second World War was a crucial period of Irish identity formation is not new. In his treatment of the war period Terence Brown cites Clifford Geertz's distinction between 'essentialism' and 'epochalism' in the process of national identity formation and nation-building. 'Essentialism' refers to the utilisation of local traditions and symbols in the construction of new identities (in the Irish case various aspects of the Catholic and Gaelic tradition), while the concept of 'epochalism' concerns the public political narrative of the nation-state's relationship to the outside world. Brown argues that for the first 20 years of independent Ireland's existence essentialism predominated in the process of identity formation, but that from the Second World War onwards epochalism came much more to the fore.[6]

What was the emergent 'epochal' narrative of the Irish state during the war? De Valera in his wartime speeches told a story of a small state trying to survive and maintain its independence in a dangerous world dominated by big powers, a small state which stood for certain principles of international behaviour and for national rights, including the right to remain neutral.[7] Notwithstanding the occasional gesture in the Allied direction, de Valera's public stance on the war combined strict political neutrality with a moral distancing of Ireland from both sides of the conflict. The only time he deviated from this position was in May 1940 when he expressed opposition to the German invasion of the Low Countries: it 'would be unworthy of this small nation if ... I did not utter our protest against the cruel wrong which has been done to them.'[8]

De Valera's statement coincided with the publication of Pope Pius XII's expressions of sympathy for the plight of Belgium and Holland.[9] But, much like Pius, de Valera was to maintain his silence thereafter. As Joseph Walshe, secretary of the Department of External Affairs, told the German minister in Dublin, the speech was a mistake which would not be repeated.[10] And it wasn't. Not until long after the war did de Valera acknowledge the virtue and justice of the Allied cause.

There were some challenges to de Valera's nationalistic neutralist narrative – above all by James Dillon, deputy leader of Fine Gael until 1942.[11] Dillon argued that there was a great struggle against evil unfolding in the world, a struggle which Ireland should be part of. But de Valera's viewpoint was the one accepted by Fine Gael and the rest of the Irish political elite. Moreover, the policy of neutrality and the definition and identity of the state that it embodied was a consensus attitude and policy at the popular as well as the elite level. These populist under-pinnings of the evolving identity of the Irish state were themselves the product of a political strategy by the Fianna Fáil government to neutra-lise public opinion on the war. The main mechanism for the implemen-tation of this strategy was the censorship régime imposed during the war. As Donal Ó Drisceoil has shown elsewhere in this volume that censor-ship was more than just an instrument for safeguarding the formal or legal neutral position of the state; it was also a form of propaganda, the aim of which was to foster a neutral public outlook on the war, i.e. the view that there were no strong moral grounds for supporting one side or the other and that Irish neutrality was a morally superior stance to that of any and all the combatants.[12]

Fianna Fáil's political manipulation of the censorship régime was but one aspect of its domination of the domestic politics of Emergency Ireland. Another salient aspect of Fianna Fáil's hegemony was its success in establishing the centrality of its definition of the nature of Irishness and of identifying the national interest with its own party interests.[13] More generally, John M. Regan has recently summarised the position thus: 'Ireland's experience of war helped foster a new consensus within Irish nationalist politics after the travails of the civil war (1922–3) and the internecine politics of the 1920s and 1930s.' At the same time, the war 'should be properly seen as a catalyst accelerating the restoration of an older consensus within nationalism rather than a new beginning'.[14] In December 1940 the Irish correspondent of The Round Table reported on the unifying effects of the national mobilisation to protect Éire's neu-trality: 'Men who fought on opposite sides in the Civil War are now drilling and working together. British veterans of 1914 are serving in the local security forces side by side with men who fought against the British.'[15]

Another aspect of this wartime consensus was highlighted by James Hogan in his book Election and Representation, published in 1945: Fine Gael's strong support for neutrality amounted de facto to an abandon-ment of its distinct identity as the 'Commonwealth party'. During the war Fine Gael made numerous reaffirmations of its support for Irish par-ticipation in the Commonwealth, but, as Hogan pointed out, standing aside when the very existence of the Commonwealth was at stake was tantamount to its abandonment.[16] In this connection it cannot be without significance that it was a Fine Gael-led coalition government that took Ireland out of the Commonwealth and established the republic in 1948.[17]

But while Fianna Fáil conceptions dominated definitions of Irish identity they did not monopolise them. As Alvin Jackson notes in his recent history of modern Ireland: 'while most Irish people endorsed neutrality, there was broad sympathy for the Allied cause; massive recruitment to the British army was compatible with popular support for de Valera'.[18] Others have pointed to the significance of the fact that between 1939 and 1945 nearly 200,000 workers from Éire migrated to work in the British war economy – most of whom remained in the country after the war.[19]

In relation to the issue of neutrality versus Ireland's participation in the war Brian Girvin quotes Fine Gael leader Richard Mulcahy's summary judgement in July 1940:

> Dev would have to swerve his party away from their present road. He could only get half. Cosgrave two-thirds. We would be left with a divided front. One-third of the country opposed to us. This would be a matter of terrible difficulty. The one-third of the country would be that part with the greatest possible capacity for nuisance and damage.[20]

Mulcahy's pessimism about the possibly dire consequences of a break with neutrality explains why in mid-1940 the Fine Gael leadership began to distance itself from talk of Ireland aligning itself with Britain. The exception among Fine Gael leaders was James Dillon who continued to emphasise the moral issue of the war and the prospects for a transformation of political attitudes in Ireland, particularly after the American entry into the war in December 1941.[21] This point is endorsed by Girvin, who also emphasises the potential political capital of the British offer in July 1940 to end partition in return for Irish support in the war.[22]

Girvin and Jackson's questioning of the extent and solidity of the pro-neutrality consensus is confirmed by the evidence of a series of wartime British political intelligence reports on 'The General Situation in Éire'.[23] A major theme of these remarkably even-handed bi-monthly reports is the impact of the course of the war on Irish public opinion. The summary for March–April 1942 reported:

> During March sources throughout Éire reported a troubled feeling on account of disasters and losses suffered by the allies ... In spite of anti-British

opinions aired in public, the overwhelming majority of the people are clearly pro-British at heart in the present struggle.

On the other hand, 'opinion continues to harden in favour of neutrality'. Commenting on the 1943 election campaign, the report of 1 July 1943 noted:

> The successful prosecution of the war and the money flowing into the pockets of the working-class families from England has produced a wave of pro-British feeling throughout the country, thus neutralising the efforts of most of the Fianna Fáil candidates to increase their polls by speeches calculated to stimulate the old nationalist and anti-British issues.

The summary of 1 November 1943 noted:

> It has been aptly said that *Éire's neutrality is her own private war*. It satisfies her spirit of defiance and independence and she is determined to show that she can win. It seems that Éire will abandon neutrality only if she becomes involved in a quarrel of her own with the Axis powers. A responsible official of the Department of External Affairs was recently asked whether Éire would abandon her neutrality if the Pope were persecuted or taken prisoner. He replied quite seriously: "Who knows? That is the only question which might set things moving" (emphasis in original).

The American equivalent of these British intelligence reports, produced by the Office of Strategic Studies (OSS), are less upbeat about pro-British and pro-Allied feeling but still contain plenty of evidence of the fluidity and cross-currents of Irish identity formation during war. In January 1943 the OSS reported:

> All the parties are genuinely committed to the policy of Éire's neutrality, and in so doing reflect quite accurately the sentiments of the vast majority of the population ... [but] despite the existence of very rigorous news, movie and radio censorship, which prevents the population ... from having any real understanding of the true nature of Nazi-ism and Fascism, it can be said quite truthfully that the sympathies of the vast majority of the people are on the side of the Allies. This is especially true since America's entry into the war, and the turning of the tide of battle in favour of the Allies.[24]

Another source of evidence on Irish attitudes during the war are the articles, reports and stories of the novelist Elizabeth Bowen. One of Bowen's concerns was the impact of Irish isolation and neutrality on popular attitudes, including those of the pro-Allied element in Ireland. In 1941 she wrote:

It is true that a thinking minority in Éire holds that the country would, in her own interests, have done better to enter the war, on the British side, in the autumn of 1939. This reflective opinion, quietly held, is distinct from the emotional opinion of former Unionists, with their tradition of service under the British flag. But this minority recognises its own extreme small-ness. It also holds that Éire, having declared for neutrality, is at this stage in no position to alter her policy. So this minority has to be ruled out; it does not now hope or wish to effect a change.

Later in the same piece she laments the impact of the Irish censorship régime:

But the general effect is – the sense of a ban on *feeling*, in a country in which feeling naturally runs high. And, more serious, there is an inhibition of judgement that cannot be good for human development. No fact (with regard to Europe) is withheld, but facts are denied moral context ... On the whole, Éire's sequestration from Europe is (for her) the principal ill of her neutrality: it may go to create a national childishness, a lack of grasp on the general scheme of the world.[25]

One group that escaped Bowen's censure were those Irish citizens who enlisted in the British armed forces during the war. But what did this enlistment mean in Irish identity terms?

One angle is suggested by Terence Brown who argued that the war and Irish neutrality led to a further alienation of the so-called 'Anglo-Irish' community in Ireland who felt that Éire should have fought along-side Britain.[26] This suggestion may be linked to the idea that the Irish volunteers came predominantly from the surviving Protestant-cum-unionist community in the Irish Free State. This was certainly the view favoured by Northern Ireland politicians just after the war. In a speech in October 1946 Northern Ireland's prime minister, Sir Basil Brooke, said: 'I have heard it said in a boasting manner that Éire men went forward to the war. Of course they did, but they were our men, they were our people who thought as we did.'[27] The context of Brooke's remark was the embarrassing fact that recruitment rates in neutral Ireland had been almost as great as those in 'loyalist' Northern Ireland.

It is probably true that proportionate to their numbers, Protestants were over-represented among the southern Irish volunteers in British armed forces. Of the 100 or so Irish veterans of the Second World War interviewed/questioned by the Volunteers Project about 20% identified themselves as coming from a Church of Ireland background.[28] But join-ing up was only one response of members of the Protestant community to the outbreak of war. Another, not uncommon, response was for in-

dividuals to use the opportunity of the Emergency to integrate themselves into the broader community by supporting neutrality and by taking part in the local defence forces and other home front activities.[29]

But most of the southern Irish volunteers were Catholic and together with their Protestant compatriots they were representative of the
social, political and religious diversity of Irish society.[30] The volunteers'
reasons for joining up were as varied and diverse as one would expect
from any cohort of young people: adventure, employment, money, family
tradition, a sense of patriotic duty. Explicit political motives for volunteering – anti-fascism, for example – did not figure prominently in most
cases but it seems clear that the volunteers were not unsympathetic to
the cause they were fighting for and that they did not share the hostility
to Britain of some of their compatriots. As to Irish neutrality, most
volunteers supported it and saw no contradiction between their service
for the Allied cause and other patriotic obligations. The defeat of Hitler
was seen as no less in Ireland's interest than in Britain's.[31] As Denis
Johnston, who served as a BBC war correspondent, noted in his diary in
April 1942: 'it is my belief in Ireland's neutrality that has so largely sent
me forth. Only those who are prepared to go into this horrible thing
themselves have the right to say that Ireland must stay out.'[32] In retro-
spect one can see the volunteers as symbolising and personifying a patriotic Irish nationalism which permitted a multiplicity of allegiances and
loyalties – to Ireland, Britain, the Allied cause – and as indicating the
continuing possibility of combining elements of Irish and British identities.[33]

Contemporary echoes of this retrospective reading of Irish volunteer identity can also be found. The prime example is R. M. Smyllie,
editor of the *Irish Times* during the war. Smyllie was the first to put
forward the pragmatic defence of Irish wartime neutrality that figures so
predominantly in historical literature today. Smyllie argued that for various political reasons neutrality was a necessary policy, but it was one that
suited the Allies as much as Ireland. He pointed to the various forms of
Irish aid to the Allied cause, above all to the many thousands of volunteers in the armed services. Smyllie's message was that Ireland was *de
facto* on the side of the Allies – 'Unneutral neutral Éire' was the title of
an article he wrote for *Foreign Affairs* in 1946 – and that the Irish volunteers acted on behalf of the best interests of Ireland.[34] Implicit in his
arguments, too, was a much more diverse and cosmopolitan concept of
Irish identity and of Ireland's place in the world than that being propounded officially at the time.

Another contemporary example of a lauding of the volunteers' role is an editorial by Peadar O'Donnell in *The Bell* in 1947. This was an editorial replying to Russian objections to Irish membership of the UN on the grounds that Éire had aided the Nazi cause. O'Donnell argued:

> It would startle even the best informed among ourselves to have accurate figures of the recruitment of Irish men and women into the British armed forces and war industry ... soldiers home on leave were welcomed by their neighbours. An air raid in Britain brought anxiety to every parish in Southern Ireland. One met the joke often ... that what the Irish were doing dare not be told because the facts would embarrass both the Belfast Government who wished the world to believe their people were in the war, and Mr de Valera who wanted the Southern Irish to believe they were out of it.[35]

The Irish state and government itself maintained an official silence on the question of the volunteers. During the war it could hardly do otherwise within the confines of the rigid public policy of neutrality and of the severe censorship régime which strove to maintain a balance between the Allied and Axis causes.[36] But even after the war this official silence continued. One reason for this continuing official silence was undoubtedly the hostility to the volunteers in some republican quarters, including Fianna Fáil.[37] Another reason was that official recognition of the role of the volunteers would have put the policy of neutrality under critical scrutiny, including the fact that 'unofficially' the Irish state had co-operated with the British state in numerous ways. No doubt, too, such recognition would have provoked considerable resentment among those who loyally served in the Irish armed forces and LDF.[38]

Perhaps most important, the volunteers lacked a spokesperson in the Irish political context. The only real possibility was Fine Gael, and many individual members and TDs did speak out on behalf of the volunteers after the war – an example being James Dillon – but officially Fine Gael tended to be as silent as Fianna Fáil.[39]

These local political difficulties aside, there were perhaps some more profound reasons for the complete exclusion of the volunteers from mainstream discourse about Ireland's role in the war. First, there was the impact of the war on Ireland's southern Protestant community. The war was a watershed in the further diminution of a distinct and separate Protestant identity in independent Ireland. As Kurt Bowen notes, 'it was not until after World War II that the well-entrenched communal boundaries of the [Protestant] minority began to crumble'.[40] This post-war development was the culmination of the long-term historical trends detailed in Bowen's book, but the war definitely acted as an accelerant. The integration of many Irish protestants into military and civil defence structures has already been noted; those protestants who left Ireland to fight in the war by and large never returned;[41] and, as Elizabeth Bowen noted, the wartime isolation of neutrality had a corrosive effect on the loyalty and identity of the so-called West Brits. The combined effect was the further fragmentation of the social-cultural group most likely to be supportive of the volunteers in post-war Ireland.

The second fundamental problem of the volunteers was that their actions did not fit into the epochal narrative of Ireland then being constructed.[42] They represented an alternative moral stance to the official neutrality of the war period. While the Irish state had distanced itself from the Allied crusade against fascism and retreated into isolationism, the volunteers had – at least symbolically – embraced the anti-fascist cause. It was a deeply embarrassing tension given the democratic values that the Irish state itself proclaimed.

In the post-war period Irish politicians often used the excuse of partition for Éire's non-participation in the war. But the truth was that neutrality reinforced partition and accentuated the polarisation of identities in Ireland. In this respect Dublin's rejection of the British offer of July 1940 was an historic turning point in north-south relations. As Dennis Kennedy argued:

> After de Valera's rejection of the overtures of 1940, Ulster's loyalty became of crucial importance to the British war effort. In early June 1940 the Unionist position was more vulnerable than at any time since 1921. Had de Valera taken up the British offer and agreed to some measures of joint defence of the two islands, then the Northerners would have come under irresistible pressure. But the danger to Unionist Ulster was only as real as the chances of de Valera abandoning neutrality ...
>
> In effect the war years, and Irish neutrality, were a confirmation of the complete gap that had opened up in Ireland between North and South. They were also, in Unionist eyes at least, proof that ... Irish nationalism ... was somehow inherently anti-British, that the new Irish identity consisted in a large part in rejection of a British identity and therefore in rejection of Northern Unionists.[43]

Irish citizens who had served in the British armed forces during the war, often alongside their Northern Irish compatriots, implicitly resisted and refused this polarisation. In Northern Ireland their diverse identity as Irish–British patriots was denied while in the south they were marginalised socially, politically and culturally, and excluded from the ongoing process of identity formation. One example of this exclusion was the boycott by successive post-war governments of Remembrance Sunday commemorations. That began to change in the 1980s but official representation at remembrance services and ceremonies was patchy until the mid-1990s. Symbolically, the National War Memorial at Islandbridge was allowed to decay into a state of considerable disrepair. As well as official apathy there was popular hostility towards the volunteers which was summed up by the furore created by Gay Byrne's announcement in 1988 that he would wear a remembrance poppy on his show. He backed down in the face of protests and threats.[44]

But the problem of the place of the volunteers in Ireland's epochal narrative remained, particularly as republican–nationalist dismissals of them came to have less and less purchase in public and political opinion.[45] One obvious solution was to revise the narrative itself, to argue that Ireland wasn't really neutral at all during the war, that it was a non-belligerent on the side of the Allies, that the country did as much as it could to aid the Allied side during the war. Within that framework the volunteers could be lauded as heroes who made a significant contribution to the Allied cause, a not to be forgotten Irish dimension of the anti-fascist struggle during the Second World War. This revised narrative of the role of Ireland and the Irish in the Second World War came in the 1980s and 1990s to form the backbone of most historical works on the topic. In press coverage of anniversaries of the war, articles and editorials defending Irish neutrality stood side by side with features on the exploits of Irish volunteers. It is a viewpoint exemplified by, among others, Kevin Myers – a staunch defender of Irish wartime neutrality, but one who spent many years campaigning for public and official recognition of the Irish veterans of the Second World War.[46] In November 1999, Myers wrote:

> Ireland now officially remembers its lost sons of the Great War without embarrassment or shame. It would be no bad thing if people also freely recalled the purely personal and voluntary sacrifice made by many individuals, unsupported by any political campaign and rigorously concealed by the censor – even in their deaths – those whose fight for freedom helped to give us a free Europe.[47]

But Myers underestimated the extent to which the Irish volunteers of the Second World War had already been fully rehabilitated – politically, historically, and in popular opinion. The contemporary consensus which views both the volunteers *and* wartime neutrality in a positive light is, of course, largely an updated version of R. M. Smyllie's position, which is basically an attempt to harmonise the Irish neutralist position during the war with support for the Allied cause.

Officially, the long government silence on the volunteers began to be broken in 1994 when Bertie Ahern (then Minister of Finance) formally opened the renovated and completed Islandbridge war memorial. Kevin Myers commented that Ahern's presence signified 'a change in attitude towards Irishness, in definitions of what it is to be Irish and how many forms of Irishness there can be without betrayal of anybody or anything.'[48]

In April 1995, Taoiseach John Bruton spoke at Islandbridge and paid tribute to the 150,000 Irish people north and south who 'volunteered to fight against Nazi tyranny in Europe, at least 10,000 of whom were killed while serving in British uniforms ... In recalling their bravery, we are recalling a shared experience of Irish and British people ... We remember a British part of the inheritance of all who live in Ireland.'[49] Bruton's speech was interesting because of its implication that there is more to the issue of the volunteers than simply assimilating their role as an aspect of neutral Ireland's contribution to the Allied cause. His words were uttered in the context of the unfolding peace process in Northern Ireland and in front of representatives from northern and southern Irish political parties. His allusion to a shared Irish and British experience and to the British inheritance were an obvious gesture in the direction of a concept of Irish identity or identities incorporating a plurality of loyalties, experiences and traditions.

From being a marginal and excluded group in Irish society in the 1940s the Irish volunteers of the Second World War had by the 1990s come to represent historically and symbolically an aspect of a refashioned and broader concept of Irish identity.[50] There is a certain poetic justice in all this since the most frequently reported volunteer experience of loyal service in the British armed forces was that it made them feel more Irish and more patriotic. Notwithstanding this strengthening of their Irish identity, most volunteers did not feel very welcome when they returned to post-war Ireland, nor for many more years to come.

CONCLUDING THOUGHTS
Mervyn O'Driscoll

This collection represents an effort to unveil much new work undertaken in Irish archives and elsewhere to illustrate Irish policies and experiences during the Second World War. Various contributors, each in their own way and from their own perspective, illustrate the diversity of approaches that can be taken to understand the origins, implementation and implications of Ireland's neutrality. Their focused analyses highlight the multidimensional nature of neutrality and draw the reader's attention to the considerable complexities and challenges of examining Ireland during the Second World War.

The case studies contained in this volume demonstrate that Ireland, in spite of its neutrality, did play a role in the global conflict and in this sense was very much 'in' the Second World War and affected by it. Rather than remaining in 'Plato's cave', untouched by the war, all elements of national life were shaped by it – politics, economics and society. Ireland also performed a significant service in aiding the Allied war effort in numerous ways, at least indirectly.

It is now possible to reflect on the general nature of Irish neutrality during the war, consider what has been revealed by the foregoing pieces, and raise questions regarding possible directions for future research.

A 'middle-of-the road' policy was never going to win wartime Ireland friends or influence externally, but de Valera, and a considerable section of nationalist opinion, had long aspired to it. Of course this policy might be open to accusations of cowardice, opportunism and a sense of betrayal but such charges ignore the radicalisation of Irish nationalist politics since the First World War. Neutrality is unpopular during any conflict, more especially with one's neighbours if they believe they have shown special consideration in the past, e.g. 'granting' Irish independence, accepting de Valera's reinterpretation of Ireland's Commonwealth status, returning naval bases on Irish territory, etc. The Fianna Fáil objective of making Ireland a republic externally associated with the British Commonwealth-empire was clearly unacceptable to British imperialists, notably Winston Churchill.

There was no self-delusion about the difficulty of the path of neutrality being embarked upon as this excerpt from Frank Aiken's memorandum on 'Neutrality, Censorship and Democracy' to cabinet colleagues in January 1940 shows:

> [I]t is not like a simple mathematical formula which has only to be announced and demonstrated in order to be believed and respected ... Instead of earning the respect and goodwill of both belligerents it is regarded by both with hatred and contempt. 'He who is not with me is against me.' In the modern total warfare it is not a condition of peace with both belligerents, but rather a condition of limited warfare with both ... In cold economic and military fact it is becoming more and more difficult to distinguish between the seriousness of the two emergencies called war and neutrality.[1]

Nonetheless, neutrality was at least theoretically possible. De Valera had repeatedly publicised Ireland's intention to remain neutral by insisting that he could not join with Britain in a war against Nazi Germany because of Britain's 'maintenance' of partition. Rather Ireland would grant a 'certain consideration' to Britain. He ensured that Berlin accepted this conditional neutrality, informing the German minister to Ireland, Hempel, at the end of August 1939, that he could not maintain unimpeachable neutrality. He baldly stated that Irish economic dependence on Britain and the latter's vital security interest required no German exploitation of Irish territory or nationalism for its own ends.[2] The diplomatic groundwork had already been laid in the previous 20 years.

The establishment of a modest but strategically positioned Irish diplomatic corps serving in London, Washington, Berlin, Paris, Ottawa, Berne and the Holy See during the inter-war period was important. Together with membership of multilateral organisations, notably the League of Nations, it provided the country with a mechanism to distinguish itself from Britain. The country operated under its own flag.

The External Relations Act (December 1936) together with the new Irish constitution (1937) and the return of the Treaty ports of Queenstown (Cobh), Berehaven and Lough Swilly cumulatively eliminated the crown from Irish domestic affairs, limiting its role to rubber-stamping consular and diplomatic appointments. This confirmed the creation of the 'republic in all but name' by the Irish electorate, and ensured that the state had complete control over its territories. The result by 1938 was the achievement of a revolution in the Anglo-Irish constitutional connection. The implications of this transformation are central to understanding Irish neutrality and Anglo (and by extension Allied) -Irish relations during the Second World War.

As a result of it both sides had made a tacit agreement that their respective territories would never be used as a launch pad for aggression, or invasion. There was also the agreement that Dublin and London would be mutually supportive in time of war. That was a measure of the confidence in 1938 that the British government had in Éamon de Valera, and in his government, to act responsibly at a time of unprecedented international crisis.

The legislation for an 'Emergency' had been drafted and fine tuned in the months immediately after the Munich crisis (September 1938). It drew upon the British government's preparations for the apparently unstoppable and rapidly-approaching European war.[3] The experience of the Anglo-Irish 'Economic War', though damaging to the Irish economy in many respects, aided some industrialisation, and more importantly, ensured that the economic sacrifice of neutrality was not a major trauma.

As Joe Lee has commented: 'It needed no supreme act of statesmanship to declare neutrality. Most European countries, to say nothing of the United States, did so in 1939 ... Nor did neutrality require exceptional skill in purely domestic political terms. All Dáil parties supported the policy.'[4] With the Nazi conquest of neutral Belgium and the Netherlands in May 1940, and with Hitler turning his attentions to Britain after the conquest of France, was it rational to join the beleaguered British then? At this stage German control of the western coast of France made the southern Irish ports of Berehaven and Cobh largely redundant. So why did the new prime minister, Churchill, obsess about them? This needs to be examined in future research.

The challenge for Ireland was to establish a credible working neutrality appealing to both belligerents. To many external commentators with limited knowledge of the Irish situation and mentality at the time this seemed improbable. The mindset of the government is suitably captured in de Valera's statement on the outbreak of the Second World War: 'We, of all nations, know what force used by a stronger nation against a weaker one means.' It revealed a distrust of larger states in light of Irish nationalist perceptions and its small state status. De Valera also invoked Irish self-interest, i.e. look to one's own country first.[5]

During the war, de Valera, his government and diplomatic service were involved in playing a multi-level game, pitting several players against one another. On the one hand the Allies were played off against the Axis as both sides feared the other would gain a foothold in Ireland. On the other hand, the Allies and the Axis were informed that domestic opinion was incompatible with joining either side in the conflict. Domestically, Fianna Fáil appealed to national solidarity but refused to create a national coalition despite emotive appeals from the opposition, Fine Gael in particular, to do so. Yet, Fianna Fáil did not reap electoral benefits by identifying itself as solely responsible for neutrality.

Meanwhile, neutral Ireland remained virtually defenceless in terms of modern warfare. Massive financial outlay might have remedied this but it could probably only be achieved by a national coalition.[6] A military buildup would have necessitated large armament shipments from the Allies but the latter would not make these available without Ireland joining their war effort or providing access to the Treaty ports. Conversely, it was not only difficult for the Axis to provide armaments, but diplomatically undesirable from the Irish government's perspective, as it would provoke the Allies, the closest belligerents. Therein lies the quagmire of Irish neutrality during the Second World War.

In the light of Allied insinuations that Ireland was pro-German during the war, a major question still needs to be addressed: Did Irish neutrality cause the deaths of members of the Allies by denying Washington and London access to the Treaty ports – ports freely returned to the jurisdiction of Dublin in 1938? That is a problematical question. But the answer will be provided in part by a careful evaluation of the strategic role played by Northern Ireland in the Second World War and by detailed analysis of military and naval records for the war in the Atlantic. Ironically, though partition was deployed by de Valera as a central reason for Ireland's objection to joining the Allies, it made neutrality possible. With the Fall of France in 1940, Northern Ireland's bases were needed instead of the now vulnerable southern ports. These northern bases were assets to the Allied war effort, notably after American entry into the war in Europe, but the Stormont government was embarrassed that the number of volunteers for British military service from neutral Ireland easily exceeded those originating from Northern Ireland.[7]

Other questions also need to be answered on the basis of comparative work in archives in London, Washington, Ottawa, Canberra and Auckland: did the Irish government at any point after the outbreak of war make its policy of friendly neutrality conditional on gaining certain concessions from London and from Washington? It is clear that both London and Washington penalised neutral Ireland during the war. But did the Irish government ever seriously threaten a shift away from benign neutrality to a pro-Axis stance? The temptation was particularly acute in the summer of 1940 when the Secretary of the Department of External Affairs, Joseph Walshe, concluded that Germany might win the war. There is no convincing evidence to prove that a reorientation of Irish neutrality was seriously considered even at this most desperate juncture in the war, despite the temptation to do so. Countervailing forces in the higher civil service and Irish military proved too strong.

Another major question needs to be answered. What was the nature and degree of Irish government cooperation with London during the war years? Much work has already been done in this area, but it ought to be stressed that the Irish government did nothing to hinder the fighting of the war on the British home front. There was no barrier to Irish people going to work in Britain. The mechanisms set in place were mutually executed through a policy of cooperation between Dublin and London. Despite the problem of desertion from the Irish to the British army, there was strong cooperation between the two governments in order to permit Irish men and women to join the British and Allied forces in Northern Ireland or in Britain.

The experience of the Commonwealth countries in the alliance should also be evaluated. This research would have a major impact on the assessment of the evolution of Irish neutrality. New Zealand and Australia could prove, initially, to be the most relevant and important dominions for this purpose. To what extent was the sovereignty and autonomy of these two powers respected in that alliance system?[8] This exercise would highlight the fact that histories and accounts of Irish conduct during the Second World War lack context. Why was Ireland the only Commonwealth member to remain neutral?

At the outset it needs to be borne in mind that Ireland was the only dominion of the British Commonwealth in Europe and in immediate geographical reach of London at the outbreak of the war. It was the only one with such immediate implications for British security during a general European conflict. Ireland was also a state dissatisfied with its enforced dominion status and Commonwealth membership. It was the dominion most closely linked to continental Europe through strong historical, religious and cultural ties. Its governments were determined to loosen Commonwealth constraints and exercise national free will. They had unceasingly forced the pace of change in the Commonwealth-empire since 1921.

Wartime neutrality must be viewed as a continuation of Irish pre-war foreign policy with regard to partition, Britain and the British

Commonwealth. This nationalist agenda was the primary motivation for the Irish government's foreign policy. Joining in an international war could undermine what had already been achieved. Therefore de Valera exhibited no willingness to be coerced into a decision to provide bases for the British in the summer of 1940. He would not erode the sovereignty won through force of arms less than 20 years before. The most he was willing to offer was benevolent neutrality towards Britain. It was also a policy designed to further differentiate Ireland from Britain. Allied public opinion saw matters differently. For it, the Second World War evolved into a conflict between democracy and fascism. It became a fully-fledged people's war rather than one concerned with old-fashioned great power politics in the Allied mind. This process created a perceptual gap between the two neighbours. It meant that as Ireland maintained a position of 'friendly neutrality', Britain and the United States perceived it to be unfriendly.

Another question also arises at this juncture: how did Ireland's behaviour compare to that of other neutrals during the war? To a certain extent Ireland was unique as it was the only surviving European neutral that lay within the Allied sphere of influence but this should not obscure neutrality as a general phenomenon practised by more states than Ireland. Useful parallels and differences might be drawn with Finland in particular, bearing in mind that in history, unlike natural science, there are no directly identical phenomena. Only tentative analogies are possible. Nonetheless, a Finnish–Irish comparison could prove revealing in many respects.

The role of Ireland in the Second World War should not be confused with the overlapping but distinct question of the role of first-generation Irish in the Allied armed forces during the war, an area which requires considerable detailed research as Professor Geoffrey Roberts has indicated in this volume. Who were the Irish who served in the British armed forces? What were their motivations for joining those forces? How did this wave of Irish emigration differ from previous waves of Irish emigration? How did they reconcile their individual decisions with Irish state policy?

Of the total number of Irish nationals in the British armed forces between 1939 and 1945 what proportion were normally resident in Britain prior to 1939 and for how long? Did pre-war residency affect their decision to enroll in the British armed forces? It can be tentatively hypothesised at this point in time that Irish recruits to the British forces were drawn from diverse backgrounds. Simplification of Irishmen's motives

for joining needs to be avoided until detailed quantitative and quali-
tative research reveals whether identifiable categories of Irish nationals
had a greater or lesser tendency to join the British forces. Furthermore
to what extent did Irishmen 'joining up' after 1939 represent the continuation of a pre-existing trend? Next, how were Irish men and women
who contributed to the war effort, either directly in the Allied armed
services or indirectly providing labour to the British war economy, viewed by their hosts? What was the role of Irish organisations in the United
States and Britain during the Second World War? These are just a few
of the questions that must be confronted as part of a major scholarly
study of the Irish diaspora.

There is further need to study the role of Irish chaplains during the
Second World War, a subject on which my co-editor, Professor Dermot
Keogh, has commenced research. Finally, there is a need to explore the
pro-Axis role of Irish people in German-occupied Europe, in Vichy, in
Italy, in Spain and Portugal, in Latin America and in South Africa.

So what is the legacy of the 'Emergency' for Irish foreign policy and
Irish identity? Wartime policy became a considerable source of collective pride, but it was seen uncritically as a testament to Irish resilience
and determination. A self-indulgent interpretation perhaps, but taking
account of its constraints, Ireland played a very positive role in the
Allied war effort both covertly and by turning a blind eye. It provided
substantial reserves of manpower to the British armed services and
economy, it ensured a regular flow of agricultural produce to Britain, and
it provided protection to Britain's flank preventing the use of its territory
as a base for attack or subversion of its neighbour. Had Ireland joined the
Allied war effort it could have been subject to civil unrest and devastation from German aerial bombardment which would have undermined
its contribution to the Allied war effort.[9] It did not hinder the defeat of
the Axis, rather it assisted constructively in this endeavour despite its
small vulnerable status. The evidence for this is incontrovertible.

To adopt alternative views such as that German espionage was rampant, or that there was no subversive risk, or argue that neutral Ireland
was pro-German or that Ireland should have wholeheartedly joined the
Allies, is problematical. As Roy Foster has commented: 'Much of Éire's
wartime experience simply provides harmless diversion for counter-
factual speculation (or the writers of might-have-been thrillers).'[10]

In the early stages of the war, declaratory neutrality was a hardheaded policy from the Irish state's point of view, despite the somewhat
confusing mythology that has been fostered around it. All states are

pragmatic and seek survival using the means at their disposal in time of war. New states, in particular, tend to be prickly about preserving their newly-won sovereignty and are reluctant to surrender any part of it, even temporarily, especially to a former ruler. From the perspective of the Fianna Fáil government, neutrality signified the rightful exercise of recently-won independence in foreign affairs and its right to declare peace or war.

Prevalent generally in Irish nationalist foreign policy was an innate disapproval of *realpolitik*, or the use of naked power to achieve international ends. This was especially true since the Irish nationalist interpretation of the causes of the Second World War was at odds with that of the so-called Anglo-Saxons. Moderate republicans, moreover those of de Valera's Fianna Fáil party, were highly critical of the Allies' conduct of the Congress of Versailles after the end of the First World War. Irish nationalists read the Treaty of Versailles as a product of power politics which failed to aspire to the principles of democracy and self-determination as propounded by US President Woodrow Wilson's Fourteen Points. From this perspective, Germany's enforced demilitarisation, reparations, forced admission of 'war guilt', and reduction of its national territory, were both unjust and ingredients for further conflict.[11] Wartime neutrality exploited the sentiment that Ireland had played no part in fomenting conditions conducive to the outbreak of war. In any case it was hoped that Nazi Germany was too distant to be a threat.

In that atmosphere, Irish neutrality became identified with Irish sovereignty and independence, to Britain's dismay. Neutrality metamorphosed into a state of mind. This latter was underlined, in no small part, by Churchill providing an opportunity for de Valera to express appreciation, albeit sarcastically, to the British prime minister for effectively resisting his overwhelming urge to invade Ireland.

Churchill, as part of a self-congratulatory broadcast to the British on the defeat of Nazi Germany, had pronounced that the lack of access to the southern Irish bases had threatened to strangle Britain but:

> ... with a restraint and poise to which, I say, history will find few parallels, His Majesty's Government never laid a violent hand upon them, though at times it would have been quite easy and quite natural, and we left the de Valera Government to frolic with the Germans and later with the Japanese representatives to their hearts content.[12]

This opening permitted de Valera to critique Churchill's position of moral superiority and self-righteousness by showering him with faint praise for barely respecting Irish sovereignty and distinguishing the Allies from the Axis who had no respect for neutrals. Such rhetoric played well with the domestic audience but it did not rescue the impression that de Valera had created internationally a few days previously.

He had paid a visit to the German minister's house to pay his respects on the death of Germany's head of state, Adolf Hitler. At this time Nazi Germany's genocide of the Jews was evident to the world's media. De Valera's visit, defended on the basis of diplomatic protocol, was one of the greatest errors of judgement in de Valera's political career and it coloured international opinion to an inordinate degree for decades. It appeared to substantiate Allied allegations that 'neutral Ireland' was pro-German.

Yet de Valera rescued his domestic standing as a statesman in his dignified response to Churchill a few days later. During his broadcast reply to the prime minister he made allowances for Churchill's 'unworthy' statement 'in the first flush of victory'. Nonetheless he had to indicate that the implication of Churchill's speech was that 'Britain's necessity would become a great moral code and that when this necessity became sufficiently great, other people's rights were not to count'. While he gave 'all credit' to Churchill for resisting the temptation to invade neutral Ireland, he then proceeded to attempt to explain the misunderstood Irish neutrality to Churchill:

> Could he not find it in his heart the generosity to acknowledge that there is a small nation that stood alone for not one year or two, but for several hundred years against aggression; that endured spoliations, famines, massacres in endless succession ... a small nation that could never be got to accept defeat and has never surrendered her soul?[13]

Both men claimed in their own ways the moral high ground and clearly neither held a monopoly on self-righteousness. Both also provided the requisite leadership for their respective countries during the Second World War, but it was the normal citizen in both jurisdictions which ultimately accepted, implemented and made a success of those policies. The respective electorates of both states ultimately decided that both political leaders had outlived their usefulness at the first opportunity to vote after the war. Like Churchill, de Valera lost his first general election after the conclusion of the war (1948). In the final analysis, once the Second World War ended, domestic socio-economic concerns dominated politics and past foreign policy 'victories' and grandstanding were no substitutes for success in bread and butter issues.

NOTES

Abbreviations
AHC (American Heritage Center), DFA (Department of Foreign Affairs),
DGFP (Documents on German Foreign Policy), DIC (Department of Industry and
Commerce), DJ (Department of Justice), DT (Department of the Taoiseach),
FA (Franciscan Archives), FDRL (Franklin D. Roosevelt Library), IPA (Institute of Public
Administration), MA (Military Archives), NAC (National Archives of Canada),
NAI (National Archives of Ireland), NAUS (National Archives of the United States),
NLI (National Library of Ireland), OSS (Office of Strategic Services), PRO (Public Records
Office), PRONI (Public Records Office of Northern Ireland), SPO (State Paper Office),
UCDAD (University College Dublin Archives Department), UP (University Press)

❖ INTRODUCTION

1 T. Desmond Williams, 'Study in Neutrality', *The Leader*, January–April, 1953; 'Neutrality!', *Irish Press*, 6 June–17 July 1953.

2 Patrick Keatinge, *The Formulation of Irish Foreign Policy* (Dublin, IPA: 1973).

3 Patrick Keatinge, *A Place Among the Nations: issues of Irish foreign policy* (Dublin, IPA: 1978); *A Singular Stance: Irish neutrality in the 1980s* (Dublin, IPA: 1984); *Ireland's Foreign Relations in 1990* (Dublin, RIA for the National Committee for the Study of International Affairs: 1991).

4 Joseph Thomas Carroll, *Ireland in the War Years, 1939–1945* (Newton Abbot, David and Charles: 1975).

5 Carolle J. Carter, *The Shamrock and the Swastika* (California, Palo Alto: 1977).

6 T. Ryle Dwyer, *Irish Neutrality and the USA, 1939–47* (Dublin, Gill and Macmillan: 1977), *Strained Relations, Ireland at Peace and the USA at War 1941–45* (Dublin, Gill and Macmillan: 1988); *Éamon de Valera* (Dublin, Gill and Macmillan: 1980), *De Valera's Finest Hour: in search of national independence, 1932–1959* (Dublin, Mercier: 1982); *De Valera: the man and the myths* (Dublin, Poolbeg: 1991); *Guests of the State, the story of allied and axis servicemen interned in Ireland during World War II* (Dingle, Brandon: 1994).

7 Ronan Fanning, *The Irish Department of Finance, 1922–58* (Dublin, IPA: 1978); *Independent Ireland* (Dublin, Helicon: 1983).

8 Deirdre McMahon, *Republicans and Imperialists: Anglo-Irish relations in the 1930s* (New Haven, Yale UP: 1984).

9 I am grateful to my colleague, Dr O'Driscoll, for his help in tracing the many references cited in this introduction. While in no sense exhaustive, it is a comprehensive list of the main research published in the related fields over the past 30 years.

10 The former Ombudsman of Northern Ireland and chairperson on the Forum for Europe, Senator Maurice Hayes, recently described this book as: 'a well-focused and well-researched study ... and a valuable contribution to our understanding of how a small state, emerging into independent nationhood, and without a serious defensive capability, was able to survive in the shark-infested waters of European politics.' Senator Maurice Hayes, 'Swimming in shark-infested wartime waters', *Irish Independent*, 29 May 2004.

11 Ireland and Europe, 1919–1948 (Dublin, Gill & Macmillan: 1988); published in paperback: *Ireland and Europe 1919–1989* (Cork & Dublin, Hibernian UP: 1989). ARTICLES: 'Origins of Irish Diplomacy in Europe, 1919–1921', *Études Irlandaises*, 7, 1983, pp. 145–64; 'Éamon de Valera and Hitler: an analysis of international reaction to the visit to the German Minister, May 1945', *Irish Studies in International Affairs*,

Autumn, vol. 3, no. 1, 1989, pp. 69–92; 'The Treaty Split and the Paris-Irish Race Convention', *Études Irlandaises*, 12, December 1987, pp. 165–170; 'Profile of Joseph Walshe, Secretary of the Department of Foreign Affairs 1922–46', *Irish Studies in International Affairs*, Autumn, vol. 3, no. 2, 1990, pp. 59–80; 'Ireland, the Vatican and the Cold War: the Case of Italy, 1948', in *The Historical Journal*, vol. 34, no. 4, 1991, pp. 931–52; 'L'Irlande et de Gaulle', *Espoir, revue de L'Institut Charles de Gaulle*, no. 80, March 1992, pp. 65–74; 'Ireland and the Historiography of European Integration', *Historians of Contemporary Europe Newsletter*, vol. 7, nos. 1–2, June 1992, pp. 37–62; 'An Eye Witness to History: Fr Alexander J. McCabe and the Spanish Civil War, 1936–1939,' *Breifne – Journal of Cumann Seanchais Bhreifne*, *Cavan*, 1994, pp. 445–88; 'The Diplomacy of "Dignified Calm" – An Analysis of Ireland's Application for Membership of the EEC 1961–1963', *Journal of European Integration History*, vol. 3, no. 1, 1997, pp. 81–101.
CHAPTERS IN BOOKS: 'Ireland, de Gaulle and World War II' in Pierre Joannon (ed.), *De Gaulle and Ireland* (Dublin, IPA: 1991), pp. 23–52; 'Irish Department of Foreign Affairs' in Zara Steiner (ed.), *The Times Survey of Foreign Ministries of the World* (London, Times Books: 1982), pp. 276–96; 'Sources for the Study of European History in Ireland' in Walter Lipgens (ed.), *Sources for the Study of European Integration (1945–55)* (Leyden, Sijthoff: 1980), pp. 51–9; 'Jewish Refugees and Irish Government Policy in the 1930s and 1940s' in *Proceedings of Conference – Remembering for the Future*, Conference pre-print, vol. 1 (Oxford, Pergamon Press: 1988); 'Ireland, Vichy and de Valera, de Gaulle' in Bernard Tricot, *Charles de Gaulle* (Paris, Institut Charles de Gaulle: 1991); 'Ireland and the Single European Act' in Clive Church and Dermot Keogh (eds), *A Handbook on the EEC and the SEA* (Canterbury: 1990); 'Argentina and the Falklands (Malvinas): the Irish Connection' in Alistair Hennessy and John King (eds.), *The Land that England Lost: Argentina and Britain, a Special Relationship* (London, British Academic Press: 1992); 'Federalism, the Irish State and the Challenge of European Integration' in Franz Knipping (ed.), *Federal Conception in EU Member States: Traditions and Perspectives* (Baden-Baden, Nomos Verlagsgesellschant: 1994); 'The Irish Free State and the Refugee Crisis, 1933–1945' in Paul Bartrop (ed.), *False Havens: The British Empire and the Holocaust* (New York, University Press of America: 1995); 'Ireland and the Holocaust' in David S. Wyman (ed.), *The World Reacts to the Holocaust* (Baltimore, John Hopkins UP: 1996).
MONOGRAPHS: *The Vatican, the Bishops and Irish Politics* (Cambridge, Cambridge UP: 1986); *Romero: Church and State in El Salvador* (Dublin, Dominican Publications: 1981); *Twentieth Century Ireland: Nation and State* (Dublin, Gill and Macmillan: 1994); *Ireland and the Vatican: The Politics and Diplomacy of Church and State, 1922–1960* (Cork, Cork UP: 1995); *Jews in Twentieth Century Ireland: Refugees, anti-Semitism and the Holocaust* (Cork, Cork UP: 1998) [awarded the 1999 James S. Donnelly, Snr, Prize by the American Conference for Irish Studies in the History/Social Science Category].
12 Monograph in preparation: *Diplomatic Recognition in Irish Foreign Policy, 1949–1963*.
13 Mark M. Hull, *Irish Secrets: German Espionage in Ireland, 1939–45* (Dublin, and Portland, Oregan, Irish Academic Press: 2003).
14 Robert McNamara, *Britain, Nasser and the Balance of Power in the Middle East, 1952–1967: from the Egyptian Revolution to the Six-Day War* (London, and Portland, Oregan, Frank Cass: 2003).
15 Don O'Leary, *Vocationalism and Social Catholicism in Twentieth-Century Ireland : the Search for a Christian Social Order* (Dublin, Irish Academic Press: 2000).
16 Donal Ó Drisceoil, *Censorship in Ireland, 1939–1945: Neutrality, Politics and Society* (Cork, Cork UP: 1996).

17 David Ryan, *US–Sandinista Diplomatic Relations: voices of intolerance* (Basinstoke, Macmillan: 1995). Other titles from Ryan are: *The United States and decolonisation: power and freedom* (Basinstoke, Macmillan: 2000); *US Foreign Policy in World History* (London, Routledge: 2000)

18 Bernadette Whelan, *Ireland and the Marshall Plan, 1947–57* (Dublin, Four Courts: 2000). Other titles from Whelan are: ed. with Michael Holmes & Nicholas Rees, *The Poor Relation: Irish foreign policy and the Third World* (Dublin, Trocaire: 1993); ed., *The Last of the Great Wars: Essays on the War of the Three Kings in Ireland 1688–91* (Limerick, University of Limerick Press: 1995); ed., *Clio's daughters: essays on Irish women's history, 1845 to 1939* (Limerick, University of Limerick Press: 1997); ed., *Women and paid work in Ireland, 1500–1930* (Dublin, Four Courts: 2000).

19 Submitted to the University of Florence (Political Science).

20 See, for example, Catherine Manathunga's doctoral study, 'The Evolution of Irish United Nations Policy 1957–61: "Maverick" diplomacy and the interaction of "possession" and international "milieu" goals', Department of History, University of Queensland, Australia, 1995. See also Greg Thomas Spelman's 'Reconciling a Policy of Neutrality with the Prospect of Integration – Ireland, the European Community and Ireland's United Nations Policy, 1965–1972', School of Humanities and Human Services, Centre for Social Change Research, Queensland University of Technology, Australia, 2003.

21 The project has moved forward under the editorship of Dr Michael Kennedy, Ms Catriona Crowe, Prof. Eunan O'Halpin and Prof. Ronan Fanning. I am also a member of that editorial team. See, with Ronan Fanning, Michael Kennedy & Eunan O'Halpin, *Documents on Irish Foreign Policy, Vol. I, 1919–1923* (Dublin: 1998); *Vol. II, 1923–1925* (Dublin: 2000); *Vol. III, 1926–1932* (Dublin: 2002), *Vol. IV, 1932–1936* (Dublin: 2004).

22 H. Dickel, *Die Deutsche Aussenpolitik und die Irische Frage von 1932 bis 1944* (Wiesbaden, F. Steiner: 1983). Besides co-editing *Documents on Foreign Policy*, Eunan O'Halpin has published *Defending Ireland: the Irish state and its enemies since 1922* (Oxford, Oxford UP: 1999, republished 2000); *Ireland and the Council of Europe: from isolation to integration* (Strasbourg, Council of Europe: 2000); *The Geopolitics of Republican Diplomacy in the Twentieth Century* (Dublin, Institute for British–Irish Studies, UCD, 2001); *MI5 and Ireland 1939–1945: the official history* (Dublin, Irish Academic Press: 2003).

23 John P. Duggan, *Neutral Ireland and the Third Reich* (Dublin, Lilliput: 1989); R. Fisk, *In Time of War: Ireland, Ulster and the price of neutrality, 1939–45* (London, Paladin: 1983); Sean O'Callaghan, *The Jackboot in Ireland* (London, Alan Wingate: 1958); Enno Stephen, *Spies in Ireland* (London, Macdonald: 1963); Andreas Roth, *Mr Bewley in Berlin: Aspects of the Career of an Irish Diplomat, 1933–1939* (Dublin, Four Courts: 2002); W. J. McCormack (ed.) *Charles Bewley, Memoirs of a Wild Goose* (Dublin, Lilliput Press: 1989); John Bowman, *De Valera and the Ulster question, 1917–1973* (Oxford, Clarendon Press: 1982); Paul Canning, *British Policy Towards Ireland, 1921–1941* (Oxford, Clarendon Press: 1985); Mike Cronin and John M. Regan (eds.), *Ireland: The Politics of Independence, 1922–49* (London, Macmillan: 2000); Richard Doherty, *Irish Men and Women in the Second World War* (Dublin, Four Courts: 1999); Richard Doherty, *Irish Volunteers in the Second World War* (Dublin, Four Courts: 2002); John P. Duggan, *A History of the Irish Army* (Dublin, Gill & Macmillan: 1991); Brian Girvin and Geoffrey Roberts (eds.), *Ireland and the Second World War: politics, society and remembrance* (Dublin, Four Courts: 2000); Douglas Gageby, *The Last Secretary General: Sean Lester and the League of Nations* (Dublin, Town House & Country House: 1999); Michael Kennedy, *Ireland and the League of Nations, 1919–1946: International relations, diplomacy and politics* (Dublin, Irish

Academic Press: 1996); Michael Kennedy, and Joseph M. Skelly (eds.), *Irish Foreign Policy, 1919–1966: from independence to internationalism* (Dublin, Four Courts: 2000); David O'Donoghue, *Hitler's Irish Voices: the story of German radio's wartime Irish service* (Belfast, Beyond the Pale: 1998); Michael Kennedy and T. Geiger, *Ireland, Europe and the Marshall Plan* (Dublin, Four Courts: 2004); Seán Ó Lúing, *Celtic Studies in Europe and other essays* (Dublin, Geography Publications: 2000); Trevor Salmon, *Unneutral Ireland: an ambivalent and unique security policy* (Oxford, Clarendon: 1989); G. R. Sloan, *The Geopolitics of Anglo-Irish Relations in the Twentieth Century* (London, Leicester UP: 1997); Eunan O'Halpin, *Defending Ireland: the Irish state and its enemies since 1922* (Oxford, Oxford UP: 1999, reissued 2000); Michael Kennedy and Eunan O'Halpin, *Ireland and the Council of Europe: from isolation towards integration* (Oxford, Oxford UP: 2000); Eunan O'Halpin, *The Geopolitics of Republican Diplomacy in the Twentieth Century* (Dublin, Institute for British–Irish Studies, UCD, 2001); Eunan O'Halpin, *M15 and Ireland 1939–1945: the official history* (Dublin, Irish Academic Press: 2003).

24 A selection of the best includes: Carolle J. Carter, 'The Spy who Brought his Lunch', *Éire-Ireland*, 10:1, 1975, pp. 3–13; C. Cox, 'Wir Fahren Gegen Irland', *An Cosantóir* May 1974, March 1975; C. Cox, 'Militar Geograpahische Angaben uber Irland', *An Cosantóir*, March 1975; J. P. Duggan, 'Celtic Cloaks and Teutonic Daggers', *An Cosantóir*, May 1978, pp. 143–4; J. P. Duggan, 'The German Threat – Myth or Reality', *An Cosantóir*, September 1989, pp. 6–12; Michael Kennedy, 'Our Men in Berlin: some thoughts on Irish diplomats in Berlin, 1929–39', *ISIA*, 10, 1999; M. O'Driscoll, 'Inter-war Irish–German Diplomacy: continuity, ambiguity and appeasement in Irish foreign policy' in M. Kennedy and J. M. Skelly (eds.), *Irish Foreign Policy, 1919–1966: from independence to internationalism* (Dublin, Four Courts: 2000); Eunan O'Halpin, 'Intelligence and Security in Ireland, 1922–45', *Intelligence and National Security*, 5:1, 1990; Paul Canning, 'Yet Another Failure for Appeasement? The case of the Irish ports', *International Historical Review*, 4:3, 1982; Michael Kennedy, '"Nobody knows and ever shall know from me that I have written it": Joseph Walshe, Éamon de Valera and the Execution of Irish Foreign Policy, 1932–8', *ISIA*, 14, 2003, pp. 165–83; '"It is a disadvantage to be represented by a woman": the Experiences of Women in the Irish Diplomatic Service', *ISIA*, 12, 2002, pp. 215–35; '"This tragic and intractable problem": The Reaction of the Department of External Affairs to the Outbreak of the Troubles in Northern Ireland', *ISIA*, 12, 2001; (with Till Geiger) 'Select Documents L: "The lost origins of Ireland's involvement in Europe: the Irish response to the Briand Plan, 1929–30"', *Irish Historical Studies*, vol. XXXII, no. 126, November 2000, pp. 232–45; 'In Spite of all Encumbrances, the Development of the Early Irish Foreign Service', *History Ireland*, Spring 1999; 'Charting Irish Diplomacy', *Foreign & Commonwealth Office Newsletter for Editors of Diplomatic Documents*, no. 12, June 1998; '"Publishing a Secret History", The Documents on Irish Foreign Policy Project', *ISIA*, vol. 9, 1998, pp. 103–17; 'Towards Co-operation: Seán Lemass North–South economic relations: 1956–65', *Irish Economic & Social History*, XXIV, 1997, pp. 42–61; '"Civil Servants Cannot be Politicians": the professionalisation of the Irish foreign service 1919–22', *ISIA*, vol. 8, 1997, pp. 95–109; 'Prelude to Peacekeeping: Ireland and the Saar 1934–1935', *Irish Historical Studies*, May 1997; 'Principle Seasoned by the Sauce of Realism: Joseph Walshe, Sean Lester and Irish policy at the League of Nations towards the Japanese invasion of Manchuria', *ISIA*, vol. 6, November 1995, pp. 79–94; 'Candour and Chicanery: The Irish Free State and the Geneva Protocol 1924–25', *Irish Historical Studies*, vol. 115, no. XXIX, May 1995, pp. 371–84; 'New Perspectives on Irish Foreign Policy', *Review of Postgraduate Studies*, Spring 1993, pp. 42–8; 'The Irish Free State and the League of Nations, 1922–1932: The Wider Implications', *ISIA*, vol. 3, no. 4, 1992, pp. 9–24;

'"We will not be suckled by the Russian Bear": Neutral Ireland and the Cold War in the 1970s', *Proceedings of the sixth international conference of the editors of foreign policy documents* (Canberra), 2003; 'The Emergence of East Asia as an Issue in Irish Foreign Policy', *Documenting diplomacy in the twenty-first century* (Washington), 2001.

❖ DEFENCE AND THE NEW IRISH STATE

1 Maurice Moynihan (ed.), *Speeches and Statements of Éamon de Valera, 1917–73* (Dublin, Gill and Macmillan: 1980), p. 32.

2 Trevor C. Salmon, *Unneutral Ireland* (Oxford, Clarendon: 1989), p. 89.

3 *Ibid.*

4 The earl of Longford (Frank Pakenham), *Peace by Ordeal: an Account from First-hand Sources of the Negotiation and Signature of the Anglo-Irish Treaty 1921* (London, Hutchinson: 1972 edn), pp. 146–8.

5 *Dáil Debates*, 72, col. 696–703, 1938.

6 Memorandum on the development of the forces in the period 1923–1927 prepared by the general staff (MA, A/0876).

7 Request for direction in defence policy submitted by defence council to Executive Council, 22 July 1925 (MA, A/1478).

8 *Ibid.*

9 *Ibid.*

10 *An t-Óglach*, January 1930, p. 8.

11 Memorandum on the defence forces 1944 (MA, Emergency defence plans [EDP], p. 26). This document was basically a blueprint for the future, based on the experience of the defence forces since 1922. The Emergency defence plans are the documents of the planning and operations staff established in October 1940.

12 MA, DEF/POL/0005.

13 MA, G2/0057.

14 MA, EDP 65, p. 58.

15 *Ibid.*, p. 61.

16 *Ibid.*, p. 62.

17 *Ibid.*, pp. 62–4.

18 *Ibid.*, p. 64.

19 *Ibid.*, p. 67.

20 *Dáil Debates*, 18, col. 400, 1927.

21 *Ibid.*, col. 392.

22 *Ibid.*, 51, no. 4, col. 1667, 1934.

23 *Ibid.*, 72, no. 7, col. 733–5, 1938.

24 *Ibid.*, 79, no. 5, col. 1549–51, 1940.

25 *Ibid.*, col. 1601, 1604 and 1607.

❖ PREPARING LAW FOR AN EMERGENCY

1 NAI, DT S.10454, n.d. (between October and December 1937).

2 NAI, DT S.5864, O'Duffy to secretary of the Department of Justice, 10 August 1931.

3 NAI, DJ Offences Against the State Act file, January 1939.

4 NAI, DT S.10454, n.d. (c. October 1937).

5 Roche suggested that members of the Dáil might be appeased if unlawful associations were given an opportunity to challenge proclamations in the courts.

6 NAI, DT S.10834.

7 Section 2 (1): 'The Government may, whenever and so often as they think fit, make by order (in this act referred to as an emergency order) such provisions as are, in the opinion of the Government, necessary or expedient for securing the public safety or for the preservation of the State, or for the maintenance of public order, or for the

provision of supplies and services essential to the life of the community.'
8 Section 2(2).
9 'Suspend the operation of or amend or apply (with or without modification) any enactment (other than this act) for the time being in force or any instrument made under such enactment.'
10 NAI, DT S.10834, Ó hÓgáin to Moynihan, 8 April 1939.
11 NAI, DT S.11039, Ó hÓgáin to Moynihan, 22 November 1938.
12 NAI, DT S.10834B, 6 October 1938
13 NAI, DJ D.42/37, O'Donoghue to Moynihan, 30 September 1938.
14 NAI, CAB G.C. 2/17, 18 October 1938.
15 'Nothing in this Constitution shall be invoked to invalidate any law enacted by the Oireachtas which is expressed to be for the purpose of securing the public safety and the preservation of the State in time of war or armed rebellion, or to nullify any act done or purporting to be done in the pursuance of any such law.'
16 NAI, DT S.10834B, Moynihan (on behalf of de Valera) to the attorney general, 20 October 1938.
17 NAI, DT S.11039, Matheson to the attorney general, 25 October 1938.
18 NAI, DT S.11039, 16 November 1938.
19 The Parliamentary Draftsman wrote: 'On a strict construction, Northern Ireland is the only territory neighbouring to ours; if a wider construction is adopted, difficulties arise at once – for instance, is France a neighbouring State, and would a Franco–Italian war be a war in a neighbouring State? It might even be argued that events at present taking place in Spain constitute an armed rebellion in a neighbouring State'. Matheson to the attorney general, 25 October 1938.
20 NAI, DT S.10834, Moynihan to the attorney general, 20 October 1938.
21 The constitution could be amended in four ways:
   a.   Completely rewriting Article 28.3.3 as appropriate;
   b.   inserting a new subsection;
   c.   inserting appropriate additional words in Article 28.3.3; or
   d.   by a definition in a new subsection 4 of the expression 'time of war' contained in Article 28.3.3.
   They suggested: 'A national emergency arising out of a war in Europe in which Ireland is not engaged as a belligerent but which emergency is declared by Dáil Éireann (or, alternatively, both Houses of the Oireachtas) to threaten the vital interests of the Community.'
   Ó hÓgáin preferred suggestions c and d (a and b would require new and independent provisions in the constitution) adding it would be easier to justify an amendment under Article 51 of the constitution if it related directly to the existing provisions of Article 28.3.3.
22 In conflict with Article 25.4.2, any attempt to apply the provisions of this section to offences committed against the Emergency Powers Order prior to the passage of the Emergency Powers legislation, would be repugnant to Article 15.5.
23 A draft prepared by the Draftsman was rejected as 'verbose and complicated', and the Taoiseach later agreed in principle with Ó hÓgáin's recommendation of 22 November 1938, which itself was based on the earlier suggestion of O'Donoghue and Hearne. Ó hÓgáin to M. Moynihan, 29 December 1938. Ó hÓgáin's proposal:
   'For the purpose of the foregoing subsection of this Article and for that purpose only, the expression 'time of war' shall be deemed to include a national emergency which (a) arises out of a war waged between European Powers in which this State is not a Belligerent (b) is declared by Dáil Éireann to threaten the vital interests of the State.'
24 Under Article 51.2.

25 NAI, DT S.11039, Ó hÓgáin to Moynihan, 3 December 1938.
26 NAI, DT S.11039, Ó hÓgáin to Moynihan, 29 December 1938.
27 M. Moynihan, P. Ó Cinnéide, G. P. Ó hÓgáin, P. P. O'Donoghue and J. Hearne attended.
28 NAI, DT S.11039, Hearne to Ó hÓgáin, 19 January 1939.
29 P. P. O'Donoghue's view on whether this limitation should be retained or not depended on the amendment's 'legislative navigability' through the Dáil (to use O'Donoghue's words). NAI, DT S.11039, O'Donoghue to Ó hÓgáin, 17 January 1939.
30 Of the 22 December 1938 draft.
31 Delete Article 28.3.3. Insert: 'Nothing in this Constitution shall be invoked to invalidate, or to nullify any act done or purporting to be done in pursuance of, any law enacted by the Oireachtas which is expressed to be for the purpose of securing the public safety and the preservation of the State in time of national emergency, provided that the President shall have signified by a message addressed to Dáil Éireann and Dáil Éireann shall thereupon have declared by resolution, that a national emergency exists which threatens the vital interests of the State.'
32 Insert after Article 28.3.3 '4': 'For the purpose of the next preceding subsection of this section the expression "time of war" shall be deemed to include a national emergency arising from an armed conflict in which the State is not a participant provided that the President shall have signified by a Message addressed to Dáil Éireann and Dáil Éireann shall thereupon have declared by resolution, that such armed conflict threatens the vital interests of the State.'
33 NAI, DT S.11039.
34 'In this subsection "war" includes an armed conflict in which the State is not a participant, but in which –
(i) the President shall have signified, in a message under his hand and seal addressed to the Chairman of each House of the Oireachtas, and
(ii) each such House shall, after receipt of such message by its Chairman, have resolved, that such armed conflict creates a national emergency which threatens the vital interests of the State.'
35 'In this subsection "war" includes an armed conflict in which the State is not a participant and in respect of which each House of the Oireachtas has resolved that such armed conflict creates a national emergency affecting the vital interests of the State.'
36 NAI DT S.11039, Matheson to Ó hÓgáin, 21 March 1939.
37 NAI DT S.11039, Matheson to Ó hÓgáin, 22 March 1939.
38 'There is a period of three years in which an opportunity will be given, if they are small matters of drafting and not constitutional principles, to change them, if the President agrees' (*Dáil Debates*, 67, col. 47–8, 11 May 1937).
   'Once the Constitution is adopted by the people as a whole it ought to be changed only by their direct and immediate will' (*Dáil Debates*, 67, col. 1901, 4 June 1937).
   'If some minor, some verbal, amendments reveal themselves as necessary during the period laid down, I think it is only right that it should be possible to make them easily … [The next Dáil] will be charged with seeing that any minor amendments that are necessary to fill up any gaps that may not have been averted to, will be made' (*Dáil Debates*, 68, col. 2–5, 10 June 1937)
   'I think, that, once we have settled it [the Constitution], it ought to be the people alone who would change it and I think that the provision for a three year period (Deputy McDermot had proposed an eight year limit to Article 51 during the Report Stage) ought not to be availed of lightly. I do not know what views would be taken of it under the powers to be given to the President under the Constitution but my own view would be that matters of principle certainly should go to the people, and that any other changes should be only changes of a minor character which were necessary

in order to deal with some oversight' (*Dáil Debates*, 68, col. 288, 10 June 1937)

39 Note by Ó hÓgáin to Moynihan, 23 March 1939.

40 'In this subsection war includes an armed conflict in which the State is not a participant but in respect of which each House of the Oireachtas shall have resolved that, arising out of such armed conflict, a national emergency exists affecting the vital interests of the State.'

41 Ó hÓgáin to P. P. O'Donoghue, 17 April 1939.

42 The bombing campaign began in January 1939.

43 NAI, DT S.10454B, memorandum by Roche, January 1939.

44 He wrote in his observations: 'The logical end of this line of thought would be to regard the Court as a permanent body of high authority charged generally with the duty of preserving the State from internal disruption – a committee of Public Safety second in importance only to the Government itself. Under such a scheme emergency powers which have formerly been vested in Ministers, Courts, and police would be concentrated in the hands of the Special Court and it would perhaps be less difficult to induce the Oireachtas and the public to view the existence of such powers without apprehension if the body entrusted with such powers had the full status of a permanent Court, independent of the Executive.' It was felt that the additional powers exercised by the Constitution Tribunal could be transferred to the gardaí.

45 The Public Safety (Emergency Powers) Act, 1926 was still in force, and technically the government could (following the making of a proclamation) intern persons.

46 NAI, DT S.10454, draft memorandum, n.d. (c. December 1938).

47 More often than not persons with knowledge of the commission of offences incriminated themselves.

48 NAI, DT S.10454, draft memorandum, December 1938.

49 NAI, DJ Offences Against the State file, Department of Justice observations on revised drafts of legislation.

50 NAI, DT S.10454B, Roche to Moynihan, 10 February 1939.

51 The office of the attorney general compared forfeiture to disqualification and felt it would only generate strong criticism – it agreed that the closing of premises by Chief Superintendents was a better proposal.

52 Eventually section 25 of the act.

53 He assured the government that there was no need to fear giving the court the 'most extensive powers', and that there was no reason to fear 'undue severity', in any case the government had the powers of pardon and remission. NAI, DJ Offences Against the State Act file, 1939, Observations by the Department of Justice and office of the attorney general.

54 The attorney general's office claimed it could find no case where the ordinary law was exceeded by the Constitutional Tribunal, adding the most serious of offences were punished by long terms of penal servitude, though in practice two years' imprisonment was the most practical and appropriate maximum punishment.

55 On the margin Roche noted, 'I think the Courts Bill must be a separate Bill'.

56 Roche wrote that little could be 'gained by comparison to the Emergency Power Bill which deals with a war situation and which so far as I am concerned was never really discussed thoroughly so far as the Special court … is concerned. It is better to consider the present Bill on its own merits and in relation to its own problem. It should be a model for war time legislation rather than *vice versa* (Roche's emphasis).'

57 Section 30 of the act.

58 NAI, CAB G.C. 2/43, 44, 45, 47.

59 *Dáil Debates*, 74, col. 1283, 2 March 1939.

60 See J. Bowyer Bell, *The Secret Army: The IRA 1916–1979* (Dublin, Poolbeg: 1990), pp. 145–63, on the IRA's 'S-Plan' and its bombing campaign in England in 1939.

61 *Dáil Debates*, 74, col. 91, 8 February 1939. The Minister declared 'That is a position which the Government is not going to tolerate.'

62 *Dáil Debates*, 74, col. 91. Deputy Norton argued that there was 'no set of circumstances within the country which justifies the introduction of this unusual type of legislation and the exceptional type of court which the legislation foreshadows.'

63 *Dáil Debates*, 74, col. 1292–3, 2 March 1939.

❖ REACTING TO WAR: FINANCE AND THE ECONOMY, 1939–1940

1 UCDAD, MacEntee Papers, P 67/169/2, Finance memorandum for cabinet on Budget Prospects, J. J. McElligott, 28 February 1938. Circulated for cabinet meeting 1 March.

2 NAI, DT S.10581, MacEntee to Brennan, 30 March 1938.

3 *Ibid.*, MacEntee to de Valera, 22 March 1938; de Valera to MacEntee, 29 March 1938.

4 *Ibid.*, MacEntee's notes of conversation with Jacobsson, 4 April 1938.

5 *Ibid.*

6 UCDAD, MacEntee Papers, P 67/563/20, McElligott to Jacobsson, 1 October 1938; Jacobsson to McElligott, 15 October 1938.

7 *Ibid.*

8 NAI, DT S.10868A, Finance memorandum on action in Emergency, 24 September 1938.

9 UCDAD, MacEntee Papers, P 67/563/6, 'War Finance': paper delivered by MacEntee's to Economics Society of Queen's University Belfast, 28 October 1938. For reaction, see *Irish Times*, 29 October 1938.

10 MacEntee, 'War Finance'.

11 *Ibid.*

12 *Ibid.*

13 UCDAD, MacEntee Papers, P 67/563/20, Jacobsson to McElligott, 15 October 1938.

14 NAI, DT S.11466, Cabinet Committee on Emergency Measure, Meeting, 20 May 1940; Irish Banks Standing Committee Note of interview, 4 June 1940.

15 MacEntee, 'War Finance'.

16 The extent of discontinuation is unclear. The treasury informed John Redmond that while there was no more money for the Congested Districts its grant would not be reduced during the war. See NLI, MS 26,156, Edwin S. Montagu to John Redmond, 22 March 1915.

17 MacEntee, 'War Finance'.

18 NAI, DT S.10913A, G C 2/14, 27 September 1938.

19 *Ibid.*, Finance memorandum, 6 January 1939.

20 *Ibid.*, p. 1.

21 *Ibid.* Some 42 money votes – over half the total – were considered.

22 Andrew McCarthy, 'Financial Thought and Policy in Ireland, 1918–45' (Unpublished PhD Thesis, UCC, 1996), p. 202 and table 4.1, p. 189.

23 NAI, DT S.10913A, Finance memorandum, 6 January 1939, p. 5.

24 *Ibid.*, cumulative total of 6 page table annexed to memorandum.

25 See J. J. Lee, *Ireland 1912–1985: Politics and Society* (Cambridge, Cambridge UP: 1989), pp. 236ff, for an enlightening discussion of de Valera's mind on such matters.

26 NAI, DT S.10913A, Minutes of meeting of Committee on Emergency Measures, 13 April 1939.

27 *Ibid.*, G C 2/68, 4 July 1939.

28 *Ibid.*, Finance memorandum on Government Services in time of war, 24 July 1939.

29 *Ibid.*, G C 2/87, 1 August 1939.

30 *Ibid.*, S. Moynihan to M. Moynihan, 16 July 1939.

31 *Ibid.*, M. Moynihan to S. Moynihan, 22 July 1939.

32 *Ibid.*, G C 2/94, 5 September 1939.

33 *Ibid.*, S. Moynihan to secretary, Taoiseach's Department, 9 September 1939.

34 *Ibid.*, Ó Cinnéide to secretary, Finance, 12 September 1939.

35 The Finance memorandum in January was ten pages, whereas their new proposals were restricted to four pages. See NAI DT S.10913A, Finance memorandum, 9 September 1939.

36 *Ibid.*

37 NAI, DF S.101/7/39, Minutes of first meeting of Economy Committee, 15 September 1939.

38 NAI, DF S.101/7/39, Minutes of second meeting of Economy Committee, 19 September 1939.

39 This was an all-party Committee of the Dáil founded in the late 1920s and was distinct from the Economy Committee. See Ronan Fanning, *The Irish Department of Finance* (Dublin, IPA: 1978), p. 201.

40 NAI, DT S.11441, Fine Gael submission to Economic Committee, 19 September 1939.

41 *Ibid.*

42 *Ibid.*

43 NAI, DT S.10913B, Economy Committee Interim Report, 12 October 1939.

44 *Ibid.*, p. 1.

45 *Ibid.*, p. 4.

46 NAI, DF F.43/3/39, Finance memorandum on Exchequer position, 1939–40, 13 October 1939.

47 NAI, DT S.10913B, Economy Committee Second Interim Report, 2 November 1939, p. 4.

48 NAI, DF S.101/7/39, Minutes of Economy Committee meeting, 19 September 1939.

49 NAI, DT S.10913A, Minutes of meeting of Committee on Emergency Measures, 13 April 1939.

50 NAI, DT S.10913B, Economy Committee Second Interim Report, 2 November 1939, p. 4.

51 *Ibid.*, p. 6.

52 *Ibid.*

53 *Ibid.*, G C 2/157, 15 March 1940. This was nearly three months after the cabinet considered the reports on 19–21 December 1939. See NAI, DT S.10913C, memoranda and decisions on reports.

54 NAI, DF F.5/8/39, Taoiseach's Department circular on government decisions on Reports of the Economy Committee, 5 February 1940.

55 *Ibid.*

56 *Ibid.*

57 NAI, DF S.101/7/39, Economy Committee Final Report, 23 November 1939.

58 NAI, DF F.5/8/39, Taoiseach's Department circular on government decisions on Reports of the Economy Committee, 5 February 1940.

59 NAI, DT S.11466, 'Some observations on the effect of the war on the Irish economy', Smiddy, 25 September 1939.

60 *Ibid.*, p. 1.

61 *Ibid.*, p. 2.

62 *Ibid.*, pp. 2–3.

63 *Ibid.*, p. 5.

64 *Ibid.*, pp. 2–3.

65 *Ibid.*, pp. 3–4.

66 *Ibid.*, p. 4.

67 *Ibid.*, p. 5.

68 NAI, DT S.11466, 'Recommendations', 25 September 1939, pp. 1–4.

304 IRELAND IN WORLD WAR TWO

69 NAI, DT S.11466, Lemass to An Taoiseach, 7 November 1939.
70 *Ibid.*
71 *Ibid.*
72 *Ibid.*
73 *Ibid.* However, as we shall see below, a memorandum the previous April from the Taoiseach's Department did not expect this to absorb any further labour.
74 NAI, DT S.10823, Memorandum for the Government, Moynihan, 6 September 1938.
75 *Ibid.*; NAI, DT S.10823, G C 2/11/5, 7 September 1938.
76 NAI, DT S.11466, Memorandum by Department of An Taoiseach, 'Economic effects on Ireland of a European war', Moynihan, 20 April 1939.

❖ EMERGENCY LAW IN ACTION

1 *Dáil Debates*, 77, col. 2, 2 September 1939.
2 *Ibid.*, col. 5.
3 *Ibid.*, col. 19. Regarding the question of who should decide when an emergency did exist, he posed the question: 'Would it be better to leave it to a court to decide that or to the representatives of the people? I am not sure that we would be able to express it in such particular terms that a court could be permitted to decide it. After all, conditions of this sort are conditions which are best known by the Government and best appreciated, perhaps, by the representatives of the people than by any court.' See *Dáil Debates*, 77, col. 17, 2 September 1939.
4 Richard Mulcahy's amendment prohibited the imposition of taxation by Emergency Order. A suggestion that internment powers be removed was rejected, though an amendment proposed by Costello, exempting natural-born Irish citizens, was inserted.
5 Assurances were given that legislation would soon be introduced providing for such compensation.
6 The government promised there would be no conscription and that courts martial would not be established. This was not regarded as sufficient though, and the following was added to section 2: '(5) Nothing in this section shall authorise the imposition of any form of taxation or the imposition of any form of compulsory military service or any form of industrial conscription, or the making of provision for the trial by courts martial of persons not being subject to military law.'
7 *Dáil Debates*, 77, col. 42.
8 *Ibid.*, col. 50.
9 Order 42.
10 Order 74.
11 Order 305.
12 Including 443 amendment and 95 revocation orders.
13 *Dáil Debates*, 101, col. 1765–6, 11 April 1946.
14 Over 1,100 were interned during the war. 1,013 persons were tried by the Special Criminal Court by the end of 1946, 914 being convicted.
15 NAI, DT S.11543, *Dáil Debates*, 78, col. 489–566, 29 December 1939.
16 NAI, DJ file on Offences Against the State (Amendment) Act, 1940, Roche to the Minister for Justice, 8 December 1939.
17 NAI, DJ file on Offences Against the State (Amendment) Act, 1940, Roche to O'Donoghue, 28 December 1939. Roche's emphasis.
18 NAI, DT S.11577, de Valera to the Council of State, 8 January 1940.
19 [1917] AC 260.
20 [1940] IR 470, re Article 26 and the Offences Against the State (Amendment) Act, 1940.
21 In a draft memorandum Roche wrote that 'such a demand could not possibly be acceded

to as it amounted to a demand that all prisoners belonging to the [IRA] should be held in military custody, the obvious object being that they should be recognised as members of a military force, entitled to be treated as prisoners-of-war.' See (approximately 20 April 1940) A/G 19/40.

22 *Irish Times*, Gerry Boland's Story, 19 October 1968.

23 NAI, DT S.11515, inquest on John McNeela, 24 April 1940.

24 *Irish Independent*, 18 April 1940.

25 Speaking on 8 May 1940, quoted in Maurice Moynihan, *Speeches and Statements by Éamon de Valera, 1917–73* (Dublin, Gill and Macmillan: 1980), pp. 433–4.

26 J. Bowyer Bell, *The Secret Army: The IRA, 1916–1979* (Dublin, Poolbeg: 1990), p. 185.

27 UCDAD, Mulcahy Papers P7/A/210, 'The X-Summary', 5 July 1940 where he records de Valera's view of developments after May 1940; Robert Fisk, *In time of War: Ireland, Ulster and the Price of Neutrality* (London, Paladin: 1985), pp. 156–60.

28 *Irish Press*, 27 May 1940. See *Irish Times*, 29 May 1940, for some of the measures he proposed to take. He urged that 'no voice of dissension be heard'.

29 NAI, DT S.11896. See also NAI, DFA A.24, and *Irish Press*, 2 December 1944.

30 NAI, DT S.11896, Norton to de Valera, 11 June 1940.

31 UCDAD, Mulcahy Papers, P7/C/113, 1 February 1941; Fisk, *In Time of War*, p. 161.

32 NAI, DT S.11896A, internment orders issued on 3 June 1940.

33 'In the case of actual invasion, however, the Government may take whatever steps they may consider necessary for the protection of the State, and Dáil Éireann if not sitting shall be summoned to meet at the earliest practicable date.'

34 MA, Department of Defence (DD), S.205; NAI, DT S.12067, 23 May 1940.

35 NAI, DT S.11649, 24 May 1940.

36 *Ibid.*

37 NAI, DT S.11900. This was Emergency Powers (No. 27) Order, 1940. The Order was signed 4 June 1940. See also NAI, DJ S.218/40.

38 NAI, CAB, G.C. 2/172, 28 May 1940.

39 NAI, DT S.11901.

40 NAI, CAB G.C. 2/174, 31 May 1940.

41 NAI, DT S.11901, Ó Cinnéide to the Private Secretary, Minister for Justice, 4 June 1940.

42 *Seanad Debates*, 24, col. 1990–3.

43 Tim Pat Coogan, *De Valera: Long Fellow, Long Shadow* (London, Hutchinson: 1993), pp. 525–6.

44 *Dáil Debates*, 101, col. 1116, 29 May 1946.

45 For example, Michael Conway and Patrick McNeela were shot and arrested as Special Branch pressure mounted after June 1940. Gardaí, backed up by the military, arrested Denis Griffith, 5 June 1940, after a shoot out in Dunmanway, Co. Cork. J. J. Kavanagh was shot near an uncompleted tunnel as he attempted to escape from Cork prison. Gardaí arrested James Smith and Patrick McGlynn after an armed encounter on 8 November 1940. See UCDAD, McEntee Papers, P67, 'Departmental Notes', 86–86n.

46 Under the Larceny Act, 1916 for involvement in armed robbery; Uinseann Mac Eoin, *The IRA in the Twilight Years: 1923–1948* (Dublin, Argenta: 1997), pp. 526–31. In one of the cases the sentence was remitted on appeal on health grounds.

47 Bell, *The Secret Army*, pp. 182–95.

48 See Coogan, *The IRA*, p. 193.

49 Uinseann Mac Eoin (ed.), *Survivors* (Dublin, Argenta: 1980), p. 124

50 [1941] IR 85–86.

51 That same day the government made the first Order under the Emergency Powers (Amendment)(No. 2) Act, 1940.

52 [1941] IR 68.

53 See John M. Kelly, *The Irish Constitution* (Dublin, Butterworths: 1994), pp. 197–8

54 [1941] IR 77.

55 *Ibid.*, at 77–8.

56 [1941] IR at 77.

57 The main differences between the proposed order and Order No. 41 may be summarised thus:

    1. The arrangements concerning the constitution of the military courts were to be more flexible;

    2. The confirming authority would now be a commissioned officer nominated by the Government;

    3. The list of offences triable by the court was much longer (Order No. 65 contained all the offences mentioned in Order No. 41), e.g. war treason, acting as a guide for the enemy, etc.

58 *Seanad Debates*, 24, col. 1990–3, 26 June 1940; NAI, DT S.12067, 18 November 1940, Minister for Justice to the Government.

59 NAI, DT S.12067, note by the Department of Defence, 4 March 1941.

60 See NAI, DT S.12067, D/D S.205, Moynihan to Roche, 4 July 1940. For comments by Mac Mathghamhna, Defence, see NAI, DT S.11905, 31 July 1940.

61 NAI, DT S.12078, Proposals presented by the Department of Defence on 4 March 1941. The conference also advocated that there should be no clash between the adjutant and any other confirming authority, and that the officer authorised to confirm a sentence would be of the highest rank available.

62 NAI, DT S.12078, Madigan, Department of Defence, to Moynihan, 17 June 1941, with reference to a minute by Ó Cinnéide, 26 May 1941.

63 FBI memorandum to the State Department, 30 September 1943, quoted in Séan Cronin, *Washington's Irish Policy: Independence, Partition and Neutrality, 1916–1986* (Dublin, Anvil: 1987), p. 85.

64 See generally Bell, *The Secret Army*, pp. 199–212.

65 McCaughey was also convicted by the military court, but his sentence was commuted.

66 Bell, *The Secret Army*, pp. 209–12.

67 NAI, DT S.11564A.

68 Only Joseph O'Connor was found not guilty on 26 February 1942.

69 *The State (Walsh and Others) v. Lennon*, [1942] IR 112.

70 See John M. Kelly, *The Irish Constitution* (2nd ed., Dublin, Jurist Publishing: 1984), pp. 241–2.

71 [1942] IR 121–2.

72 See also Kelly, *The Irish Constitution*, p. 374.

73 [1942] IR 131.

74 NAI, DT S.12683.

75 *Dáil Debates*, 85, col. 1450, 28 January 1942.

76 *Ibid.*, col. 1483–6. The motion to annul was defeated 71–20 in the Dáil, and 35–8 in the seanad. See also speeches and notes prepared by Stephen Roche, 22 January 1942, 26 January 1942, 27 January 1942 in NAI, DJ S.14/42, and *Irish Press*, 30 January 1942, and 5 February 1942.

77 Bell, *The Secret Army*, p. 216.

78 Control of exports and imports of all kinds; regulation of keeping, treatment, storage, movement, distribution, sale, purchase, use and consumption of articles of all kinds; control of all prices, NAI, DT S.11418A.

79 Richard Dunphy, *The making of Fianna Fáil Power in Ireland, 1923–1948* (Oxford, Clarendon Press: 1995), p. 224.

80 NAI, DT S.11977.

81 *Dáil Debates*, 87, col., 2075–2175, 1 July 1942.

82 *Dáil Debates*, 91, col. 539–40, 9 July 1943.

83 *Ibid.*, col. 541.

84 *Ibid.*, col. 542.

85 *Ibid.*, col. 573.

86 *Ibid.*, col. 576.

87 *Ibid.*, col. 578.

88 NAI, DT S.12433.

89 See *Irish Times* 22 May 1946; *Irish Press* 23 May 1946. Further emphasising the government's attitude towards those classes of offences, the Special Criminal Court began to impose heavy sentences where there was systematic defiance of Emergency Powers Orders. See for example the cases of R. O'Toole and P. Follan, *Irish Times*, 21 September 1944, or the Sigal case, *Irish Times*, 27 March 1945 and 7 May 1946, where bail was set at £40,000.

90 See *Irish Times*, 19 March 1943, 30 April 1943 and *Dáil Debates*, 89, col. 1212–7, 11 March 1943. There were 17 convictions for agrarian offences.

91 *Irish Times*, 24 July 1943.

92 By December 1945, the Special Criminal Court was being described as 'a danger to liberty', see *Irish Times*, *Irish Independent*, 4 December 1945.

93 *Irish Independent*, 28 June 1944.

94 Editorial cited, for example, 'the imposition of a new rent code on the public, a thing which should have been done by a regular Act of Parliament.'

95 See also *Irish Times*, same date, for a more politic appraisal of the Emergency powers.

96 Of these 72 were Irish, 5 were German, and 1 was Dutch. Members of the German Armed Forces were interned under Emergency Powers (No. 170) Order, 1942.

97 NAI, DT S.11552B, Department of Justice memorandum, 11 May 1945, see also NAI, DT S.13667, S.11577.

98 Speaking on 4 July 1945 (*Dáil Debates*, 97, col. 1881). The 14 in question were released because 'the Government decided to give them a chance to get back to normal lives'.

99 NAI, DT S.13706, 20 June 1945.

100 NAI, DT S.11552B.

101 See NAI, DT S.13706, 15 May 1947, and also NAI, DT S.13710.

102 NAI, DT S.11552B, Department of Justice minute, 9 June 1945.

103 NAI, DT S.11552B, Roche to Moynihan, 4 July 1945.

104 See generally NAI, DT S.13667.

105 NAI, DT S.13667, 2 June 1945. To be considered was the parent act of 1939, Emergency Powers made thereunder, the three Emergency Powers (Amendments) Acts, 1940–1942 and General Elections (Emergency Provisions) Act, 1943.

106 NAI, CAB G.C. 4/83.

107 NAI, DT S.13667, MacAonghusa, Rúnaí Aire to Moynihan, 8 June 1945.

108 NAI, DT S.13667, assistant secretary of the Department of Agriculture, Seán Ó Broin to Moynihan, 9 June 1945.

109 These were in addition to those made by the Department of Supplies which particularly concerned the Department of Agriculture.

110 1. Orders introduced during the emergency, but whose importance made them indefinite necessities – those orders dealing with matters such as the production of seed, the manufacture and sale of fertilisers and compound feeding stuffs, etc., which would be expected to become part of the permanent law.

2. Orders of a temporary nature which could be revoked once normality began to return. Matters covered by such orders included pigs and bacon orders, matters relating to export of animal offal, flax, poultry, rabbits, eggs, etc. which were made because of arrangements with the British Ministry of Food. The rationing of butter and

the lack of containers, etc. would come to an end once normal trading resumed.

3. Orders concerning questions of long-term policy, i.e relating to the Dublin Milk Board, compulsory tillage, etc. which would have to be considered at some later date.

111 NAI, DT S.13667, Seán Mac Cárthaigh to Moynihan, 9 June 1945.

112 Permitted the detention of persons who were a source of infection.

113 NAI, DT S.13667, Barrington (Rúnaí Aire) to the secretary, Department of an Taoiseach, 11 June 1945.

114 NAI, DT S.13667, 11 June 1945.

115 NAI, DT S.13667, draft memorandum by the Department of an Taoiseach, 11 June 1945.

116 *Dáil Debates*, 97, col. 1879, 4 July 1945.

❖   A TALE OF WARTIME ESPIONAGE IN WARTIME IRELAND

1 David O'Donoghue, *Hitler's Irish Voices, The Story of German Radio's Wartime Irish Service* (Belfast, Beyond the Pale: 1998), p. 30.

2 MA, G2/0402, Ernstberger File.

3 MA, G2/X/0203, Bryan to Gerald Boland, 28 May 1946.

4 *Ibid.*, Schütz's microdot instructions.

5 Enno Stephan Ms, 'Die Vergessene Episode: Deutsche Agenten im irishchen Unter-grundkampf' (in possession of Enno Stephan), pp. 312–3. Captain Joseph Healy also interviewed Schütz on 18 March 1941. A linguist of note before and after the war, Healy noted that Schütz was intellectual and that confinement would be difficult on him for that reason. According to Schütz, he had withdrawn £600 of his own money from the Deutsche Bank, Berlin to make purchases in Ireland of a private nature as 'there are not many things in German [*sic*].' (MA, G2/X/0203, Healy to Bryan, 18 March 1941.)

6 MA, G2/X/0203, undated report, Healy to Archer.

7 MA, G2/0261, DMD Weekly Summary, 4 December 1939; Jan van Loon interview, May 1999. There were 28 Uhlan regiments in Imperial German service during the First World War, but none of them was based in Hamburg.

8 MA, G2/0261, Muriel Unland statement, 21 April 1941. When initially questioned by the D/Sgt Wymes, Mrs Unland responded 'I refuse to answer whether I ever entered any profession or took up any business.' For some reason, she changed her mind, add-ing to the end of her written statement, 'I now wish to say that on leaving Liverpool with my mother when I was ten years of age I was engaged as a child actress.' There is no indication as to why this confession was particularly sensitive to Mrs Unland.

9 PRO, KV 2/170, undated MI5 memo to Irish G2. Dierks was the I-M chief at Hamburg. His aliases included 'Herr Müller' and he was the notional head of Hillermann AG. An effective recruiter and a womaniser of some distinction, he was killed in a car crash while taking three England-bound agents, one of them his mistress, to their plane in 1940. See Nigel West, *MI5* (London, Triad Grafton: 1983), p. 215.

10 MA, G2/0261. The stationery letterhead from Ferrum reads: 'Ferrum (S.S.) LTD, 2 & 3 Philpot Lane, London, E. C. 3. Director: M. W. J. Dobeyn.'

11 According to Günther Schütz, Unland was not supposed to go to Ireland, but to stay in England. Schütz also volunteered that the Hamburg Ast controlled Unland (MA, G2/X/0203, Schütz interview of 10 April 1941).

12 The Gresham was a favourite site for the *Auslandsoganisation* (NSDAP overseas) Christmas celebrations held in Dublin, but Unland arrived about a year too late to participate in the last one held before the war (O'Donoghue, *Hitler's Irish Voices*, pp. 19–20).

13 MA, G2/0261, report on Phillip Bernard Richards, March 1940.

14 *Ibid.*, report of 18 October 1939, DC Walton, Metropolitan Police, Hendon Station, S

Division. Mrs Dugarde was not charged for obstructing justice, despite the clear evidence to the contrary.

15 *Ibid.*, Mrs Anna Hart, Roodborstlaan 9, The Hague to Unland, undated.

16 *Ibid.*, Hart to Unland, 26 January 1940.

17 Apparently unaware of his circumstances, Fräulein Schlattau continued to write to Unland c/o his Northern Bank address as late as 1945. When asked about these letters, Unland said he was glad the garda had intercepted them, rather than Mrs Unland, and 'was anxious that the present letter should not go on to Merrion Square.' (MA, G2/0261, Superintendent Carroll to G2, 5 June 1941.)

18 The office of the British representative in Ireland, Sir John Maffey, was also situated in Merrion Square.

19 In a post-war interrogation, Dr Praetorius of I/Wi was asked about the esoteric references in Unland's letters. He replied that they were meaningless to the Abwehr and thought that Unland included them to give his reports an air of importance (PRO, KV 2/170, MI5 memo to Irish G2). This explanation is not entirely satisfactory.

20 MA, G2/0261, undated DMD summary.

21 The Abwehr II *Kriegstagebuch* (war diary) first mentioned the possibility of a submarine insertion on 29 November 1939, some two months before Weber-Drohl was dispatched.

22 *Ibid.*, letter of 7 February 1940.

23 PRO, KV 1/173, Praetorius interview, 11 October 1946

24 MA, G2/0261, undated garda report.

25 *Ibid.*, DMD weekly summary, 5 February 1940. Hermann Görtz landed by parachute in Co. Meath in May 1940 and was on the run for some 18 months before being apprehended.

26 *Ibid.* At one point, Unland used a mail address at the National Tourist Bureau, 14 Upper O'Connell Street. When informed of this in a report, Dan Bryan scribbled 'Black list at once!' on the cover.

27 The fact that Unland would need a book on how to be a spy underscores the degree to which the Abwehr recruitment efforts had sunk. This pattern was repeated with each agent sent to wartime Ireland; c.f. Mark M. Hull, *Irish Secrets: German Espionage in Wartime Ireland, 1939–45* (Dublin, Irish Academic Press: 2002).

28 MA, G2/0265 and G2/0261, inventory of Mrs Unland's bag.

29 MA, G2/0261, Unland statement, 23 April 1941, Arbour Hill Prison. Unland was also unable to explain why he had signed his letters with the names Walsh, Peters and Green, though he admitted to doing so.

30 *Ibid.*, report of Captain J. Foley to Governor, Arbour Hill. Though this report was not dated, the subject of it would have occurred shortly after Unland was transferred to Arbour Hill on 30 April 1941. Since Unland and Schütz were detained under the Emergency Powers No. 20 Order and not on a criminal charge, it was not necessary for the government to reveal the evidence against them. Neither was aware that the microdot information had been compromised.

31 She kept the apartment on Merrion Square at the £10 per month rental. Unland was having money difficulties of his own since he no longer received monthly remittances from the Abwehr. His fellow internee Günther Schütz had to loan him £300 at one point (NAI, DFA A34, summary).

32 Costello later became the Taoiseach in the Inter-Party government that cut the final ties to Britain to create the Republic of Ireland in 1949. He was also the barrister for Stephen Carroll Held, the IRA/Abwehr courier who sheltered Hermann Görtz in 1940.

33 *Irish Independent*, 17 April 1947, p. 1; c.f. NAI, DFA A60.

34 *Evening Herald*, 25 November 1947, p. 2.

35 Enno Stephan to me, 1 September 1999. Unland declined to be interviewed for Enno Stephan's *Spies in Ireland* (London, Macdonald: 1963).

36 Information courtesy of the Office of Births, Marriages and Deaths, Dublin.

❖ BERLIN'S IRISH WAR RADIO

1 MA, G2/2473, Healy report for G2, 11 December 1939. See also *Irish Press*, 11 December 1969.

2 Of the 53 foreign languages broadcast by Nazi Germany's external radio services (54 including German itself) some 29 were European. Details of German Radio's foreign language services are contained in Werner Schwipps, *Wortschlacht im Aether* (Berlin, Deutsche Welle: 1971), p. 75; Heinz Pohle, *Der Rundfunk als Instrument der Politik: Zur Geschichte des Deutschen Rundfunks von 1923–1938* (Hamburg, Hans-Bredow Institut: 1955), p. 456. Details of the BBC's language services are in Gerard Mansell, *Let Truth be Told: 50 Years of BBC External Broadcasting* (London, Weidenfeld and Nicolson: 1982), pp. 122–3.

3 For data on licensed and unlicensed radio sets in Ireland, 1939–45, see Terence Brown, *Ireland: A Social and Cultural History 1922–1976* (London, Glasgow: 1981), p. 153; and Alacoque Kealy, *Irish Radio Data: 1926–1980* (RTÉ occasional paper series no. 1, Dublin, RTÉ: 1981).

4 My interview with Seán Ó hEochaidh, 14 January 1992. There is evidence that in 1937, Mühlhausen was on a spying mission to the north-west of Ireland. Two of his photographs of Teelin harbour, for example, turned up in a 1941 German army invasion document entitled 'Military Geographical Data on Ireland'. The document also included photographs of Sligo bay and other inlets in the north-west (see David O'Donoghue, *Hitler's Irish Voices: The Story of German Radio's Wartime Irish Service* (Belfast, Beyond the Pale Publications: 1998), pp. 14–16.

5 J. A. Cole, *Lord Haw Haw: The Full Story of William Joyce* (London, Faber: 1964), p. 149.

6 Letter to me from Seán Ó Lúing, 9 March 1993.

7 For the wavelengths, studio locations and transmitters used by the Irland-Redaktion, see O'Donoghue, *Hitler's Irish Voices*, p. 217.

8 Mahr was born in 1887 in Trent, which was then part of Austria, but the southern Tyrol was ceded to Italy in 1919 as part of the Versailles Treaty. It is thought that Mahr was attracted to the Nazi party partly because he believed that Hitler would eventually reunite the Italian Tyrol with Austria. Even after the 1938 Anschluss, however, Mahr's birthplace remained a part of Italy and does so to this day.

9 PA, R67483, 'Rundfunkpropaganda nach Irland'. For a full English translation see O'Donoghue, *Hitler's Irish Voices*, pp. 183–93.

10 For an example of Germany's secret diplomatic overtures to de Valera, see Robert Fisk, *In Time of War: Ireland, Ulster and the Price of Neutrality* (London, André Deutsch: 1983), pp. 363–4.

11 My interview with Dr Hans Hartmann, 21 October 1990.

12 The text of Hartmann's radio talk of 28 December 1941 can be found in O'Donoghue, *Hitler's Irish Voices*, pp. 71–2.

13 One explanation for Hartmann's insistence on the use of extracts from Wolfe Tone's diaries on air may be that they contained coded messages for German sympathisers in Ireland, most probably IRA operatives in Northern Ireland. The wartime papers of Col. Éamon de Buitléar (Col. Dan Bryan's deputy at G2) indicate that a cipher had been discovered by Irish Military Intelligence in a copy of Wolfe Tone's diaries. It is unclear, however, if the code was ever broken. The timing of the Wolfe Tone diary broadcasts by German Radio may be significant, particularly if they were being used to alert German agents, sympathisers or IRA units in the north. Dr Hartmann

made the first such broadcast on 28 January 1942, just two days after the arrival of US troops in Northern Ireland.

14 John O'Reilly's serialised memoirs appeared in the *Sunday Dispatch* (London) from July to December 1952.

15 From August 1939 to December 1943, a total of 12 German agents were dispatched (mainly by U-boat or parachute) to neutral Ireland. Eunan O'Halpin has also identified five other potential German agents; see *Defending Ireland: The Irish State and its Enemies since 1922* (Oxford, Oxford UP: 1999), p. 241.

16 After his release from prison in 1945, the Clare man used the reward money his father had collected, plus some counterfeit German bills, to purchase a public house in Dublin's Parkgate Street, close to army and garda headquarters. Additional information on John O'Reilly's life is contained in O'Donoghue, *Hitler's Irish Voices*, pp. 206–16.

17 For a more detailed account of Mrs Susan Hilton's peregrinations around the Third Reich and its occupied territories, see O'Donoghue, *Hitler's Irish Voices*, pp. 194–205.

18 For details of Francis Stuart's first broadcast, see Brendan Barrington (ed.), *The Wartime Broadcasts of Francis Stuart, 1942–44* (Dublin, Lilliput: 2000); see also O'Donoghue, *Hitler's Irish Voices*, p. 82.

19 For a more detailed account of Francis Stuart's 1943 election broadcasts, and the Irish government's reaction to them, see NAI, DFA A72 & 205/108; see also O'Donoghue, *Hitler's Irish Voices*, pp. 114–9.

20 O'Donoghue, *Hitler's Irish Voices*, pp. 57–8.

21 For details of Francis Stuart's 'mutiny' broadcast see MA, G2/X/0127, foreign wireless broadcasts, part 4; Fisk, *In Time of War*, pp. 400–1; O'Donoghue, *Hitler's Irish Voices*, pp. 120–1.

22 Geoffrey Elborn, *Francis Stuart: A Life* (Dublin, Raven Arts Press: 1990), p. 165; O'Donoghue, *Hitler's Irish Voices*, p. 137.

23 My interview with Francis Stuart, 17 November 1989.

24 The post-war fate of those who worked for the Irland-Redaktion is dealt with in detail in O'Donoghue, *Hitler's Irish Voices*, pp. 166–78.

❖ GUESTS OF THE STATE

1 PRO, CAB 66 WP(39) 34, Maffey, report of conversation with de Valera, 19 September 1939.

2 *Ibid.*

3 *Ibid.*

4 *Ibid.*

5 PRO, DO 35/1107, Maffey report of conversation with de Valera, 20 September 1939.

6 SPO, DFA 241/267, Regierungsrat Eric Kruger to Mrs A. Kruger, 27 August 1940.

7 SPO, DFA 241/267, Kurt Kyck to Kurt Kyck, Sr, 27 August 1940.

8 MA, DoD S.231, McNally to Adjutant General, n.d. (c. September 1940).

9 MA, CP 229, Maffey and Gray to de Valera, January 1942.

10 SPO, DFA 363/4, F. H. Boland to Liam Archer, 5 October 1940.

11 *Ibid.*

12 MA, DoD S.231, Col. Liam Archer to Adjutant General, 14 September 1940.

13 SPO, DFA 363/4, F. H. Boland to Liam Archer, 5 October 1940.

14 *Ibid.*

15 MA, DoD IC/229, Paul Mayhew to Sir Basil Mayhew, 4 January 1941.

16 Article 11 of the Hague Convention.

17 SPO, DFA 363/4, Boland to J. P. Walshe, 16 March 1942.

18 Charles Brady to me, 7 August 1978.

19 Fred Tisdall to me, 12 May 1978.

20 Ros Tees to me, 16 December 1976.

21 Bruce Girdlestone, dossier on internment, 1943, Mss, p. 3 (private source).

22 Charles Brady to me, 7 August 1978.

23 Robert Fisk, *In Time of War: Ireland, Ulster and the Price of Neutrality* (London, André Deutsch: 1983), p. 284.

24 SPO, Gray, memorandum of conversation with J. P. Walshe, 1 December 1942.

25 SPO, J. P. Walshe to David Gray, 11 December 1942.

26 Canadian Diplomatic Papers, 1841–40, John D. Kearney, Despatch 110, 12 August 1943.

27 Randolph Churchill, 'Ireland's Neutrality,' US Congressional Record, Appendix, 91: A4988.

28 PRO, DO 130/32, WP(43)88, Maffey, report of interview with de Valera, 23 February 1943.

29 PRO, DO 130/32, Maffey, report of conversation with de Valera, 9 October 1943.

30 Bruce Girdlestone, Dossier on Internment, 1943, Mss., p. 49

31 Naval Secretary to Mrs Girdlestone, 27 October 1943 (private source).

32 SPO, DFA, F. H. Boland to J. P. Walshe, 20 December 1943.

33 MA, CP 796, Parole forms signed by Mollenhauer.

34 PRO, DO 130/43, Maffey to Sir Eric Machtig, 8 January 1944.

35 MA, S/108P, Quedenfeld to Col. Sean Collins-Powell, 29 March 1944.

36 *Ibid.*

37 PRO, DO 130/43, Maffey, report of conversation with de Valera, 10 June 1944.

38 *Ibid.*

39 *Ibid.*

40 *Ibid.*

41 MA, G2/X/1270, report by Captain Lawrence Clancy to Commandant of No. 1B Internment Camp, 7 March 1945.

42 MA, G2/X/1270.

43 Interview with Voight cited in *Sunday Mirror*, 28 November 1976, p. 13.

44 *Ibid.*

Author's note: Foreign Affairs records drawn on for the writing of this article were consulted prior to the opening of the National Archives, Bishop Street, Dublin, and the general release of departmental documentation under the 30-year rule. They were consulted at the State Paper Office (SPO) by arrangement with the then foreign minister, Peter Barry. Similarly, files relating to the Department of Defence (DoD) and G2 were consulted, also with special ministerial permission, at the then Military Archives, Park Gate Street. They are now located at the Military Archives, Cathal Brugha Barracks.

❖ A MOST GREVIOUS AND HEAVY BURDEN

1 FA, de Valera papers, 1529, Walshe to de Valera, 19 January 1954. (When viewed by me, the de Valera papers resided at the Franciscan Archives, Killiney, Co. Dublin. These papers have since been transferred to the Archives Department, UCD.)

2 FA, de Valera papers, 1180, Walshe to de Valera, 1 May 1940.

3 *Ibid.*

4 *Ibid.*

5 *Ibid.*, de Valera papers, 1180, memorandum on discussions between United Kingdom and Éire ministers, 30 April 1940.

6 *Ibid.*, Walshe memorandum on 3 May 1940 meeting with Eden, 6 May 1940.

7 Joseph Lee, for example, talks of Walshe's 'tenderness towards the new masters of the continent', see Joseph J. Lee, *Ireland 1912–1985: Politics and Society* (Cambridge, Cambridge UP: 1989), p. 248. In doing so Lee is not wholly unfair to Walshe's viewpoint.

8 Maurice Moynihan (ed.), *Speeches and Statements by Éamon de Valera 1917–73* (Dublin, Gill and Macmillan: 1980), p. 435.

9 Lee, *Ireland 1912–1985*, pp. 246–7.

10 *Documents on German Foreign Policy* (DGFP), Series D, vol. IX, Doc. 310, pp. 422–4, Hempel to Foreign Ministry, 23 May 1940.

11 Franklin D. Roosevelt Library, Hyde Park, New York (FDRL), Roosevelt Papers, President's Secretary's Files, Diplomatic Correspondence, Ireland 1940, Box 40, Gray to Roosevelt, 30 April 1940.

12 National Archives of the United States (NAUS), State Department Papers, M1231, Roll 10, Gray to Roosevelt, 16 May 1940.

13 For further information on German espionage in Ireland and German–IRA links during the war see: Carole J Carter, *The Shamrock and the Swastika: German Espionage in World War II* (Palo Alto, California, Pacific Books: 1977); John P. Duggan, *Neutral Ireland and the Third Reich* (Dublin, Gill and Macmillan: 1975); Robert Fisk, *In Time of War: Ireland, Ulster and the Price of Neutrality* (London, Paladin Grafton Books: 1985); and Enno Stephan, *Spies in Ireland*, translated from the German by Arthur Davidson (Hamburg, Gerhard Stalling Verlag: 1961; trans. ed., London, Macdonald: 1963).

14 NAI, DFA , Secretary's Files, A3. This section is based on the official minutes of the meeting contained in Secretary's Files.

15 NAI, DFA, Secretary's Files, A3. 'Minutes of the First Meeting between Representatives of the Government of Éire and Representatives of the Dominions Office and Service Departments of the United Kingdom, 23 May 1940.

16 *Ibid.*

17 NAI, DFA, Secretary's Files, P3, Walshe memorandum on conversation with Hempel, 17 June 1940.

18 DGFP, Series D, vol. IX, Doc. 437, pp. 601–3, Hempel to Foreign Ministry, 17 June 1940.

19 *Ibid.*

20 DGFP, Series D, vol. IX, Doc. 506, pp. 637–40, Hempel to Foreign Ministry, 21 June 1940.

21 MacDonald had been heavily involved in the Anglo-Irish negotiation which led to the handing over of the Treaty ports to the Irish government in 1938. During these discussions he established a good working relationship with Walshe who, at the time, indicated that neutrality would be an unlikely option in time of war. MacDonald may have been hoping that Walshe could be reminded of these statements. See FA, de Valera papers, 953, Walshe to de Valera, 3 January 1938.

22 PRO, PREM 3/131/1, MacDonald memorandum, 17 June 1940. Cited by Fisk, *In Time of War*, p. 193.

23 *Ibid.*

24 PRO, PREM 3/131/1, MacDonald memorandum, 21–22 June 1940. Cited by Fisk, *In Time of War*, p. 197.

25 PRO, PREM 3/131/2, British note to the Irish government, 26 June 1940. Cited by Fisk, *In Time of War*, p. 201.

26 FDRL, Roosevelt Papers, President's Secretary's Files, Box 40, Gray to Roosevelt, 28 June 1940.

27 NAI, DFA, Secretary's Files, P13, unsigned memorandum, 'Comments of the foregoing', 1 July 1940.

28 NAI, DFA, Secretary's Files, P13, unsigned memorandum, Summary of unity proposals, 1 July 1940.

29 NAI, DFA, Secretary's Files, P13, unsigned memorandum, 'Comments of the foregoing,', 1 July 1940.

30 *Ibid.*

31 PRO, PREM 3/131/7, Maffey memorandum, 14 March 1941. Cited by Fisk, *In Time of War*, p. 305.

32 NAI, DFA, Secretary's Files, A2, unsigned memorandum (Probably written by Walshe), 'Weekend Developments in the War Situation', n.d.

33 *Ibid.*

34 *Ibid.*

35 Boland memoirs (in private possession).

36 NAI, DFA, Secretary's Files, A2, unsigned memorandum (probably written by Walshe), 11 July 1940.

37 NAI, DFA, Secretary's Files, A2, Walshe memorandum, 'The International Situation and Our Critical Position in Relation to it', 15 July 1940.

38 NAI, DFA, Secretary's Files, A3, Walshe handwritten addendum to memorandum, 'Help given by the Irish Government in relation to the actual waging of the War', n.d.

39 *Ibid.*

40 Boland memoirs.

41 NAI, DFA, Secretary's Files, A2, unsigned memorandum, 11 July 1940. Again we can see the difficulties in analysing Walshe's role. While this document is almost certainly Walshe's work it is impossible to draw a definite conclusion about this and numerous other unsigned documents contained in the archives.

42 *Ibid.*

43 *Ibid.*

44 *Ibid.*

45 *Ibid.*

46 NAI, DFA, Secretary's Files, A2, Walshe memorandum, 'The international situation and our critical position in relation to it', 15 July 1940.

47 DGFP, Series D, vol. X, Doc. 79, pp. 89–90, Hempel to Foreign Ministry, 1 July 1940.

48 DGFP, Series D, vol. X, Ribbentrop to Hempel, 11 July 1940.

49 NAI, DFA, Secretary's Files, P3, Walshe memo on conversation with Hempel, n.d.

50 *Ibid.*

51 NAI, DFA, Secretary's Files, P3, Walshe memorandum, 9 August 1940.

52 DGFP, Series D, vol. X, Hempel to Foreign Ministry, 31 July 1940.

53 Lee, *Ireland, 1912–1985*, p. 248.

54 FA, de Valera papers, 1529, Walshe to de Valera, 1933.

55 FA, de Valera papers, 1529, Walshe (writing from Cologne) to de Valera, 28 July 1933.

56 DGFP Series D, vol. X, Hempel to Foreign Ministry, 31 July 1940.

57 AHC, Laramie, Wyoming, Gray Papers, Box 3, Folder 7, Gray to Roosevelt, 13 July 1940.

58 FDRL, Roosevelt Papers, President's Secretary's Files, Diplomatic Correspondence, Ireland, Box 40, Gray to Secretary of State, 6 August 1940.

59 FDRL, Roosevelt Papers, President's Secretary's Files, Gray to Roosevelt, 7 August [1940].

60 AHC, Gray Papers, Box 3, Folder 7, Diary entries, 6 August [1940].

61 *Ibid.*

62 NAUS, State Department records, RG 84, Security Segregated records, Box 3, Gray to State Department, July 1940.

63 FDRL, Roosevelt Papers, President's Secretary's Files, Box 40, Gray to Roosevelt, 7 August 1940.

64 AHC, Gray Papers, Box 3, Folder 7, Diary entries, 6 August [1940].

65 AHC, Gray Papers, Box 3, Folder 8, Gray to Walshe, 15 August 1940.

66 FDRL, Roosevelt Papers, President's Secretary's Files, Box 40, Gray to Roosevelt, 14 August 1940.

67 *Ibid.*

68 FDRL, Roosevelt Papers, President's Secretary's Files, Box 40, Gray to Roosevelt, 25 August 1940.

69 FDRL, Roosevelt Papers, President's Secretary's Files, Box 40, Gray to Roosevelt, 8 September 1940.

70 *Ibid.*

71 *Ibid.*

72 NAI, DFA, Secretary's Files, A2, Walshe memorandum, October 1940.

73 DGFP, Series D, vol. XI, Hempel to Foreign Ministry, 29 November 1940.

74 *Ibid.*

75 DGFP, Series D, vol. XI, Doc. 455, Ribbentrop to Hempel, 5 December 1940.

76 DGFP, Series D, vol. XI, Hempel to Foreign Ministry, 10 December 1940.

77 DGFP, Series D, vol. XI, Hempel to Foreign Ministry, 17 December 1940.

❖ IRELAND, CANADA AND THE AMERICAN NOTE

1 NAI, DFA, Confidential Reports 219/49, Hearne to Department, 2 October 1939.

2 *Ibid.*

3 *Ibid.*

4 NAI, DFA, Secretary's Files, P4, Hearne to Department, 12 October 1939.

5 NAI, DFA, Confidential Reports 219/49, Hearne to Department, 24 January 1940.

6 NAC, RG25, vol. 781, file 822–39C, Kelly to Department, 15 November 1940.

7 NAC, RG25, vol. 781, file 398, Kearney to Robertson, 17 October 1941.

8 John Doherty Kearney was a lawyer and a native of Montreal. He was a Roman Catholic of Irish parentage and was married to an Irish woman. His posting in 1941 as Canadian High Commissioner in Ireland was his first diplomatic appointment.

9 NAC, RG25, vol. 1949, file 822–39C, Kearney to Robertson, 20 February 1942.

10 *Ibid.*

11 *Ibid.*

12 *Ibid.*

13 Britain had struggled to pay the huge bill for munitions and material produced for her in Canada. In an effort to ease that situation the Canadian government decided, in January 1942, to make a 'billion dollar gift' to Britain along with an interest free loan of $700 million. The 'billion dollar gift' was an undertaking by Ottawa to pay for British wartime purchases in Canada. The government later set up Mutual Aid, whereby a further one billion dollars was apportioned to buy necessary goods and to ship them to Britain and the other Allied nations. The historian C. P. Stacey outlines Canada's other efforts, 'Canada undertook the cost of equipping and maintaining all the RCAF [Royal Canadian Air Force] squadrons overseas, as well as the pay, clothing, etc., for Canadian aircrew serving with the RAF. Moreover, Canada purchased the United Kingdom's interest in Canadian war plants which the British government had financed, the cost being about $200 million, and took over certain lesser expenses which Britain had borne, including costs for camps for prisoners-of-war and internees whom Canada had accepted at Britain's request.' The British treasury calculated that by 1945 she had received $3,043,000,000 in financial assistance from Canada. See C. P. Stacey, *Canada and the Age of Conflict: A History of Canadian External Policies, Vol. 2, 1921–1945* (Toronto, University of Toronto Press: 1981), pp. 358–9.

14 NAC, RG25, vol. 1949, file 822–39C, pt. 2, Kearney to Robertson, 15 February 1943.

15 *Ibid.*

16 *Ibid.*

17 *Ibid.*

18 *Ibid.*

19 PRO, DO 35/2062, Memorandum prepared by the Dominions Office, 11 February 1943.
20 For details of the American view see T. Ryle Dwyer, 'American Efforts to Discredit de Valera during World War II' in Éire Ireland, vol. VIII, no. 2 (Summer 1973), pp. 20–33; T. Ryle Dwyer, Irish Neutrality and the USA 1939–45 (Dublin, Gill and Macmillan: 1977) and T. Ryle Dwyer, 'David Gray and the Axis Representatives to Ireland during World War II' in The Capuchin Annual (1973), pp. 108–17.
21 T. Ryle Dwyer, 'American Efforts to Discredit de Valera during World War II', p. 25.
22 NAC, RG25, vol. 781, file 398, Kearney to Robertson, 15 October 1943.
23 T. Ryle Dwyer, Irish Neutrality and the USA 1939–45, p. 175.
24 PRO, DO 35/2078, Maffey to Machtig, 8 December 1943.
25 T. Ryle Dwyer, 'American Efforts to Discredit de Valera during World War II', pp. 26–7.
26 NAC, RG25, vol. 781, file 398, 'Copy of US note to Irish Government of Feb. 21, given to Mr Robertson by Irish High Commissioner in Ottawa, Feb. 26'.
27 T. Ryle Dwyer, Irish Neutrality and the USA 1939–45, p. 185.
28 J. T. Carroll, Ireland in the War Years (Newton Abbot, David and Charles: 1975), pp. 142–3.
29 A. Nolan, 'Joseph Walshe and the management of Irish foreign policy, 1922–1946: A study in diplomatic and administrative history' (PhD Thesis, UCC, 1997), p. 283.
30 NAC, RG25, vol. 781, file 398, Kearney to Secretary of State for External Affairs, 25 February 1944.
31 NAC, RG25, vol. 781, file 398, Secretary of State for Dominion Affairs to Secretary of State for External Affairs, 23 February 1944.
32 NAC, RG25, vol. 781, file 398, Secretary of State for External Affairs to High Commissioner for Canada in Ireland, 25 February 1944.
33 NAC, RG25, vol. 5767, file 126(s), Kearney to Secretary of State for External Affairs, 28 March 1944.
34 NAC, RG25, vol. 5767, file 126(s), Robertson to Kearney, 14 April 1944.
35 NAC, RG25, vol. 781, file 398, Kearney to Secretary of State for External Affairs, 24 February 1944.
36 NAC, RG25, vol. 781, file 398, Kearney to Secretary of State for External Affairs, 25 February 1944.
37 NAC, MG26, vol. 283, 'Memorandum for the Prime Minister' initialled by NAR (Robertson), 24 February 1944.
38 Ibid.
39 Ibid.
40 NAC, MG25, D1, vol. 781, file 398, Secretary of State for External Affairs to High Commissioner for Canada in Ireland, 25 February 1944.
41 NAC, MG26, vol. 283, 'Memorandum for the Prime Minister' initialled by NAR (Robertson), 24 February 1944.
42 De Valera sought the assistance of the other dominions who were also concerned about the American note. John Dulanty, the Irish representative in London, on the instructions of de Valera approached S. M. Bruce, the Australian representative, in the hope that they would give support to the stance of the Dublin government. This effort was in vain. (T. P. O'Neill and Lord Longford, Éamon de Valera [Boston, Houghton Mifflin Company: 1971], p. 405.) This refusal led to Dr Mannix, the Irish-born Roman Catholic Archbishop of Melbourne, criticising the government's policy. While he received a lot of publicity he got little support, indicating that the Australian population was behind their prime minister's stance (NAC, RG25, vol. 3337, file 126(s), High Commissioner for Canada in Australia to Secretary of State for External Affairs, 29 March 1944). The New Zealand prime minister, Fraser, had defended Ireland's neutral stance prior to the issuing of the notes. The Canadian

High Commissioner in Wellington, W. A. Riddell, reported that Fraser sent a press release on the issuing, in which he argued that 'the New Zealand Government had felt it their duty to approve of the United States' request and had also expressed the hope that the Government of Éire would accede to the suggestions which were made' (NAC, RG25, vol. 3337, file 126(s), Riddell to Secretary of State for External Affairs, 16 March 1944).

43 NAI, DFA, Secretary's Files, A53, Hearne to Walshe, 27 March 1944.

44 NAI, DFA, Secretary's Files, A53, Hearne to Department of External Affairs, Dublin, 3 March 1944.

45 NAI, DFA, Secretary's Files, A53, Hearne to Department of External Affairs, Dublin, 3 March 1944.

46 NAC, RG25, vol. 781, file 398, 'Memorandum for the Prime Minister', 26 February 1944.

47 NAI, DFA, Secretary's Files, A53, Hearne to Department of External Affairs, Dublin, 3 March 1944.

48 Ibid.

49 NAC, MG26, J13, Mackenzie King Diary, 27 February 1944.

50 Ibid.

51 NAI, DFA, Secretary's Files, A53, Hearne to Department of External Affairs, Dublin, 3 March 1944.

52 NAC, MG26, J13, Mackenzie King Diary, 27 February 1944.

53 NAC, RG25, vol. 781, file 398, Kearney to Secretary of State for External Affairs, 28 February 1944.

54 NAC, RG25, vol. 781, file 398, Kearney to Secretary of State for External Affairs, 2 March 1944.

55 NAC, RG25, vol. 5767, file 126(s), Secretary of State for External Affairs to Kearney, 4 March 1944.

56 NAC, RG25, vol. 3188, file 4932–40, 'Mr de Valera's reply to the American note presented at Dublin on the 21 February 1944'.

57 NAC, RG25, vol. 5767, file 126(s), Canadian Embassy in Washington to Secretary of State for External Affairs, 10 March 1944.

58 NAC, RG25, vol. 781, file 398, Department of State: Confidential Future Release No. 79, 11 March 1944.

59 NAI, DFA, Secretary's Files, A53, Extract from Canadian Hansard.

60 W. S. Churchill, The Second World War, Volume 5: Closing the Ring (London, The Reprint Society: 1954), pp. 537–8.

61 NAC, RG25, vol. 781, file 398, Secretary of State for Dominion Affairs, London, to Secretary of State for External Affairs, Ottawa, 15 March 1944.

62 NAC, RG25, vol. 781, file 398, Secretary of State for External Affairs, Ottawa, to Secretary of State for Dominion Affairs, London, 20 March 1944.

63 NAC, RG25, vol. 5767, file 126(s), Robertson to Kearney, 14 April 1944. The Americans also believed that Kearney had handled the situation well. On 14 March Ray Atherton called on Mackenzie King to express gratitude for the part played by the Canadian government and Kearney regarding the American note: NAC, RG25, vol. 781, file 398, 'Memorandum – Re: Ireland' by Mackenzie King, 14 March 1944.

64 NAC, RG25, vol. 5767, file 126(s), Kearney to Secretary of State for External Affairs, 28 March 1944.

65 Ibid.

66 Ibid.

67 Ibid.

68 Shortly afterwards Walshe and a representative of the Department of Supplies accompanied Maffey to London. During the negotiations that followed, Cranborne of the

Dominion Office noted that Walshe 'was ready to accept anything which in our view was necessitated by the military situation' (PRO, DO 35/2080, Memorandum initialled C [Cranborne], 3 April 1944). It was agreed that the public telephone service was to be suspended between Ireland and Britain. Direct air services between Dublin and Liverpool were to be suspended and the Irish authorities were to undertake strict measures to ensure that civil and military aircraft were not misused in Ireland. Finally, direct shipping between Ireland and the Iberian Peninsula was to be suspended. The British undertook to ensure that Ireland would receive supplies that would otherwise have been carried via the Iberian Peninsula. Steamship services between Britain and Ireland were also to be curtailed (NAC, RG25, vol. 5767, file 126(s), Secretary of State for Dominion Affairs to Secretary of State for External Affairs, 7 April 1944). These restrictions were seen as part of the preparations for the invasion of Europe and were accepted without protest by the Irish population (NAC, RG25, vol. 3337, file 126(s), Garland to Secretary of State for External Affairs, 28 April 1944).

69 NAC, RG25, vol. 5767, file 126(s), Kearney to Secretary of State for External Affairs, 28 March 1944.

70 NAC, MG26, vol. 363, Pearson to Robertson, 6 April 1944.

71 T. Ryle Dwyer, 'David Gray and the Axis Representatives to Ireland during World War II', p. 117.

72 NAC, RG25, vol. 3300, file 7718–40, Kearney to Robertson, 28 February 1945.

❖ CON CREMIN, BERLIN AND 'DIE BILLIGE GESANDTSCHAFT'

1 NAI, DFA, 17/1, Warnock to Walshe, 12 August 1943.

2 T. Desmond Williams, 'A Study in Neutrality' in *The Leader*, 14 March 1953.

3 Patrick Keatinge, *The Formulation of Irish Foreign Policy* (Dublin, IPA: 1973), p. 111.

4 The Soviets were suspected of murdering the Swedish diplomat Raoul Wallenberg while he was serving in Budapest.

5 Correspondence with Aedeen Cremin, 16 March 2001.

6 Dermot Keogh, *Ireland and Europe, 1919–1989* (Cork and Dublin, Hibernian UP: 1990), p. 105.

7 Cremin, 'Memoirs' (in private possession), p. 24.

8 Keogh, *Ireland and Europe*, p. 105.

9 *Ibid.*, p. 139.

10 NAI, DFA, 17/1, Warnock to Walshe, 1 April 1943.

11 NAI, DFA, P12/3, Walshe to Warnock, n.d. (probably 1–11 August 1943).

12 NAI, DFA, 17/1, Warnock to Walshe, 12 August 1943.

13 *Ibid.*, Walshe to Warnock, October 1943.

14 NAI, DFA, 17/4, Walshe to Warnock, 2 June 1944.

15 NAI, DFA, 17/1, Department to Warnock, 24 November 1943.

16 Martin Gilbert, *A History of the Twentieth Century, Vol. II* (London, Harper Collins: 1998), p. 531.

17 Robert Fisk, *In Time of War, Ireland, Ulster and the Price of Neutrality, 1939–45* (London, Paladin Grafton Books: 1983), p. 371.

18 NAI, DFA, 46/14, Warnock to Department, 16 December 1943.

19 Cremin, 'Memoirs', p. 25.

20 *Ibid*, p. 25. This was the property of an Irishman, Charlie Mills, who bred trotting ponies.

21 *Ibid*, p. 26.

22 NAI, DFA, 17/1, Warnock to Walshe, 29 November 1943. Cremin's sister told me that: 'Warnock had had a breakdown, caused by nervousness and Con was sent to replace him' (Cissy Crussell interview, 10 March 2001).

23 NAI, DFA, 353/21, Warnock to Walshe, 3 December 1943.

24 Keogh, *Ireland and Europe*, p. 303.

25 NAI, DFA, 313/4, Fay to Nunan, October 1954.

26 Eunan O'Halpin, *Defending Ireland* (Oxford, Oxford UP: 1999), pp.184–5.

27 Keogh, *Ireland and Europe*, p. 311.

28 The RAF committed themselves to the 'Battle of Berlin' on 18–19 November 1943. See John Keegan, *The Second World War* (London, Hutchinson: 1989), p. 428.

29 Cremin, 'Memoirs', p. 25.

30 NAI, DFA, 19/3, Cremin to Walshe, February 1945. Cremin was also aware that the diplomatic petrol rations were constantly reduced and he had to ensure that the legation had enough fuel to leave Germany.

31 Correspondence with Aedeen Cremin, 16 March 2001.

32 Cremin, 'Memoirs', p. 40. Cremin himself recounted in his memoirs that the only time he saw Adolf Hitler was in July 1932 at a Nazi rally in Munich, where he was within three paces of him. He only once met the Nazi Foreign Minister, Joachim von Ribbentrop, in Paris in 1938.

33 Cremin, 'Memoirs', p. 28.

34 *Ibid.*, p. 29.

35 NAI, DFA, 2/10, 24 June 1944.

36 NAI, DFA, P12/3 27, Cremin to Walshe, 27 March 1944.

37 Jörg K Hoensch, *A History of Modern Hungary, 1867–1994* (London and New York, Longman: 1996), p. 157.

38 David O'Donoghue, *Hitler's Irish Voices* (Belfast, Beyond the Pale Publications: 1998), p. 155.

39 NAI, DFA, 16/1, Walshe to Cremin, 26 January 1944.

40 F. S. L. Lyons, *Ireland Since the Famine* (London, Weidenfeld and Nicolson: 1971) p. 551.

41 Keogh, *Ireland and the Vatican* (Cork, Cork UP: 1994), p. 178.

42 *Ibid.* p. 179.

43 NAI, DFA, P77, Cremin to Walshe, 20 April 1944.

44 Keogh, *Ireland and the Vatican*, p. 186.

45 NAI, DFA, P77, Cremin to Walshe, 4 June 1944.

46 Dermot Keogh, *Ireland and the Vatican*, p. 188.

47 NAI, DFA, P12/3, Cremin to Walshe, 17 April 1944.

48 *Ibid.*, Cremin to Walshe, 9 May 1944.

49 *Ibid.*

50 Len Deighton, *Overlord, D-Day and the Battle for Normandy* (London, Pan Books: 1984), p. 71.

51 Early draft of Con Cremin's memoirs compiled by Mgr Frank Cremin (in my possession).

52 NAI, DFA, P12/3, Cremin to Walshe, 14 June 1944.

53 Ian Kershaw, *Hitler, 1936–45, Nemesis* (London, Allen Lane: 2000), p. 642.

54 NAI, DFA, P12/3, Cremin to Walshe, 19 June 1944.

55 Gilbert, *A History of the Twentieth Century, Vol. II*, p. 578.

56 NAI, DFA, P12/3, Cremin to Walshe, 4 July 1944.

57 Kershaw, *Hitler Nemesis*, p. 675.

58 NAI, DFA, P12/3, Cremin to Walshe, 24 July 1944.

59 NAI, DFA, P12/3, Cremin to Department, 22 July 1944.

60 PRO, HW 1/3124. Sent on 22 July 1944, not seen by Churchill until 29 July 1944; NAI, DFA, P12/3, Cremin to Walshe, 24 July 1944.

61 Peter Grose, *Gentleman Spy, The Life of Allen Dulles* (Amherst, University of Massachusetts Press: 1996), p. 200.

62 In 1998, I came across a file reference to a personal profile of Cremin from 1944 in the PRO, Kew Gardens London. I was informed that the file was destroyed.

63 NAI, DFA, P12/3, Cremin to Walshe, 29 July 1944.

64 Major-General F. W. Von Mellenthin, *Panzer Battles* (London, Cassell: 1955), p. 194.

65 NAI, DFA, P12/3, Cremin to Walshe, 29 July 1944.

66 *Ibid.*, 11 August 1944.

67 *Ibid.*, 18 September 1944.

68 Donald S. Detwiler, *World War II, German Military Studies, Vol. 24* (New York, Garland: 1975), Appendix A.

69 PRO, HW1/3124, 21 September 1944.

70 NAI, DFA, P12/3, Cremin to Walshe, 21 September 1944. The interpolations were inserted by the telegraph operator who decoded the message.

71 PRO, HW1/3265, sent 8 October 1944 (seen on 12 October 1944).

72 NAI, DFA, P12/3, Cremin to Walshe, 19 November 1944.

73 *Ibid.*, 29 November 1944.

74 Commonly known as the Battle of the Bulge.

75 The 'colleague' was unnamed and throughout his career Cremin rarely named his colleagues. However, the colleague was probably an *Auswärtiges Amt* official.

76 *Ibid.*, 24 December 1944.

77 See Charles B. MacDonald, *Battle of the Bulge* (Phoenix, London: 1998), pp. 7–14. and Mellenthin, *Panzer Battles*, p. 406.

78 NAI, DFA, P12/3, Cremin to Walshe, 24 December 1944.

79 *Ibid.*, 14 January 1945.

80 The cases included: the Smith sisters who came from Warsaw where one of them was married to a Polish Officer (NAI, DFA, 10/14, Cremin to Walshe, 6 July 1944); May Finucane, who was repatriated (NAI, DFA, 10/1, Cremin to Walshe, 3 November 1943); and Vincent Coyle, who was killed in a air raid on Berlin (NAI, DFA, 10/2, August 1943).

81 Desmond T. Williams, 'Aspects of Neutrality', *The Leader*, 14 March 1953.

82 These were citizens who were arrested on various charges. Mary Cummins (NAI, DFA, 44/6, 1 February 1943) and Robert Vernon (NAI, DFA, 44/3, 13 September 1943) were both arrested on espionage charges.

83 O'Donoghue, *Hitler's Irish Voices*, p. 42.

84 Geoffrey Elborn, *Francis Stuart, a Life* (Raven Arts Press, Dublin: 1990), p. 126.

85 NAI, DFA, A72, Bryan to Walshe, 17 August 1945.

86 *Ibid.*

87 NAI, DFA, 2/6s, Stuart to Cremin, April 1944.

88 *Ibid.*, Walshe to Cremin, 1 June 1944.

89 J. H. Natterstad, *Francis Stuart* (London, Bucknell UP: 1974), p. 66.

90 NAI, DFA, A20, Stuart to Cremin, 24 February 1945.

91 NAI, DFA, 2/6s, Stuart to Cremin, 7 March 1945.

92 Elborn, *Francis Stuart*, p. 171. Cremin's hospitality extended further in that he enabled Stuart to travel, which he should not have (NAI, DFA, 2/6s, Walshe to Cremin, 1 June 1944).

93 Fisk, *In Time of War*, p. 406.

94 Natterstad, *Francis Stuart*, p. 66.

95 Dermot Keogh, *Twentieth Century Ireland, Nation and State* (Dublin, Gill and Macmillan: 1994), p. 155.

96 Anne McCartney, *Francis Stuart, Face to Face: a Critical Study* (Belfast, Queen's University Belfast, Institute of Irish Studies: 2000), p. 158.

97 NAI, DFA, A72, Bryan to Boland, 17 August 1945.

98 *Ibid.* He was a brother-in-law to MacBride and 'when he was director of intelligence of

the IRA he was largely responsible for their contacts with the Germans'. The second factor was that Goertz consulted with him in Berlin and he went to Stuart's house in Ireland.

99 Cremin, 'Memoirs', p. 31
100 NAI, DFA, 44/6, 29 September 1944.
101 *Ibid.*, 29 November 1944.
102 *Ibid.*, 6 and 11 December 1944.
103 *Ibid.*, 8 January 1945.
104 *Ibid.*, 16 January 1945.
105 *Ibid.*, 17 January 1945.
106 NAI, DFA, 2/12 (Berlin legation).
107 NAI, DFA, 44/6, 9 May 1945.
108 Keogh, *Ireland and Europe*, p. 105.
109 NAI, DFA, 2/12 (Berlin legation), Walshe to Cremin and Warnock, 5 January 1944.
110 *Ibid.*, Cremin and Warnock to Walshe, 10 January 1944.
111 *Ibid.*, 16 March 1944.
112 *Ibid.*, 24 March 1944.
113 *Ibid.*
114 *Ibid.*, Department II of the Foreign Ministry.
115 NAI, DFA, 2/12 (Berlin legation), Cremin to Walshe, 20 April 1944.
116 *Ibid.*, Cremin to Walshe, 22 April 1944.
117 *Ibid.*, Cremin to Walshe, 27 April 1944.
118 *Ibid.*, Cremin to Walshe, 12 May 1944.
119 *Ibid.*, Walshe to Cremin, 6 June 1944. Drancy was the notorious transit camp that the French Jews were imprisoned in until they were transported to the death camps in the east.
120 NAI, DFA, 2/12 (Berlin legation), Cremin to Department, 7 June 1944.
121 John Weitz, *Hitler's Diplomat, Joachim von Ribbentrop* (London, Phoenix Giant: 1992), p. 289.
122 NAI, DFA, 2/12 (Berlin legation), Cremin to Department, 27 August 1944.
123 *Ibid.*, 29 August 1944.
124 *Ibid.*, 5 October 1944.
125 NAI, DFA, 2/12 (Berlin legation), Walshe to Cremin, 21 October 1944.
126 NAI, DFA, 2/12 (Berlin legation), Cremin to Walshe, 27 October 1944.
127 NAI, DFA, A20 (Berlin legation), file on Frank Ryan, Cremin to Department, 21 December 1944.
128 NAI, DFA, 2/12 (Berlin legation), Cremin to Walshe, 23 December 1944.
129 Keogh, *Ireland and Europe*, p. 303.
130 NAI, DFA, P12/3, Walshe to Cremin, August 1944.
131 *Ibid*, 28 October 1944.
132 NAI, DFA, P12/3, Cremin to Walshe, 31 October 1944.
133 Cremin, 'Memoirs', p. 32.
134 *Ibid.*, 2 November 1944.
135 NAI, DFA, P12/3, Walshe to Cremin, 23 November 1944.
136 Richard Overy, *Russia's War* (London, Penguin: 1997), p. 257.
137 NAI, DFA, P12/3, Cremin to Department, 19 January 1945.
138 Fisk, *In Time of War*, p. 534.
139 NAI, DFA, P12/3, Cremin to Walshe, 31 January 1945.
140 *Ibid.*, Cremin to Walshe, 1 February 1945.
141 Cremin, 'Memoirs', p. 33. This would also have been designed to have the effect of protecting Mills and his family from the excesses of the Soviet soldiers.
142 NAI, DFA, 10/179, Cremin to Mullally, 9 March 1945.

143 Cremin, 'Memoirs', p. 35.

144 NAI, DFA, P12/3, Cremin to Walshe, 19 February 1945.

145 *Ibid.*, Cremin to Department, 23 February 1945.

146 *Ibid.*, Walshe to F. T. Cremins, 12 March 1945.

147 *Ibid.*, F. T. Cremins to Walshe, 15 March 1945.

148 *Ibid.*, Walshe to F. T. Cremins, 22 March 1945.

149 *Ibid.*, Cremin to Walshe, 30 March 1945.

150 *Ibid.*, 5 April 1945. The Swiss recommended it to the Irish legation, stating that it was too small for the Swiss legation.

151 Cremin, 'Memoirs', p. 38.

152 *Ibid.*

153 NAI, DFA, P12/3, Walshe to F. T. Cremins, 17 April 1945.

154 NAI, DFA, P12/3, Cremin to Walshe, 25 April 1945. See also James Bacque, *Crimes and Mercies, The Fate of German Civilians under Allied Occupation, 1944–50* (London, Warner Books: 1997), chap. 7.

155 NAI, DFA, P12/3, Cremin to Department, 25 April 1945.

156 Walter LaFeber, *America, Russia and the Cold War, 1945–92* (New York, McGraw-Hill Inc.: 1993), pp. 8–9; Gilbert, *A History of the Twentieth Century, Vol. II*, pp. 538–9.

157 NAI, DFA, P12/3, Walshe to F. T. Cremins, 25 April 1945.

158 Cremin, 'Memoirs', p. 39.

159 NAI, DFA, P12/3, F. T. Cremins to Walshe, 15 May 1945.

160 *Ibid.*

161 LaFeber, *America, Russian and the Cold War*, p. 24.

162 NAI, DFA, P12/3, Walshe to Cremin, 7 June 1945.

163 Keogh, *Twentieth Century Ireland*, p. 162.

❖   **KEEPING THE TEMPERATURE DOWN**

1 The latter point is highlighted by Ronan Fanning, *Independent Ireland* (Dublin, Helicon: 1983), p. 128.

2 On the propaganda role of the censorship, see Donal Ó Drisceoil, 'Censorship as propaganda: the neutralisation of Irish public opinion during the Second World War', in Brian Girvin and Geoffrey Roberts (eds), *Ireland and the Second World War: Politics, Society and Remembrance* (Dublin, Four Courts: 2000), pp. 151–64; Frank Aiken, Minister for the Co-ordination of Defensive Measures ('keep the temperature down'), *Seanad Debates*, vol. 24, col. 2614–5, 4 December 1940.

3 The party, which altered its pro-neutrality position to a pro-Allied one following the entry of the Soviet Union into the war, was now more isolated than ever. In that context, and in line with Stalinist Popular Front strategy, its members now worked within the Labour Party.

4 Hanspeter Neuhold, 'Permanent Neutrality in Contemporary International Relations: A Comparative Perspective', *Irish Studies in International Affairs*, vol. 1, no. 3, 1982, p. 26.

5 See Joseph J. Lee, *Ireland 1912–1985: Politics and Society* (Cambridge, Cambridge UP: 1989), pp. 236–7.

6 NAI, DT S.14213, correspondence in 'National Emergency 1940–1 – Views of Fine Gael', Department of an Taoiseach.

7 See Lee, *Ireland 1912–1985*, pp. 248–50; John Bowman, *De Valera and the Ulster Question 1917–73* (Oxford, Clarendon: 1982), pp. 235–9; Robert Fisk, *In Time of War, Ireland, Ulster and the Price of Neutrality, 1939–45* (London, Paladin Grafton Books: 1983), pp. 203–4; Brian Girvin, 'Politics in wartime: governing, neutrality and elections' in Girvin and Roberts, *Ireland and the Second World War*, pp. 30–1; Henry Patterson, *Ireland Since 1939* (Oxford, OUP: 2002), pp. 59–60.

8 MA, 7/58, Office of the Controller of Censorship, T. J. Coyne (assistant controller of censorship) to Maurice Moynihan, 5 July 1941.

9 See Girvin, 'Politics in wartime', pp. 31–5.

10 NLI, *Labour's Programme for a Better Ireland, General Election 1943.*

11 See Finbarr O'Shea's chapter in this volume.

12 Kieran Allen, *Fianna Fáil and Irish Labour, 1926 to the Present* (London, Pluto Press: 1997), p. 77.

13 Michael Gallagher (ed.), *Irish Elections 1922–44: Results and Analysis* (Limerick, PSAI Press: 1993), p. 245.

14 Eunan O'Halpin, 'The Origins of City and County Management' in Joseph Boland, *et al, City and County Management 1929–1990: A Retrospective* (Dublin, IPA: 1991), pp. 2–17; Mary Daly, *The Buffer State: The Historical Roots of the Department of the Environment* (Dublin, IPA: 1997), pp. 249–304; Desmond Roche, *Local Government in Ireland* (Dublin, IPA: 1982), pp. 105–8.

15 *Dáil Debates*, 86, col. 450, 15 April 1942; 87, col. 2030–40, 30 June 1942.

16 *Irish Press*, 14–31 August 1942; *Torch*, 25 July – 29 August 1942.

17 NAI, DT S.11586A, memorandum for government from Frank Aiken, 'Neutrality, Censorship and Democracy', 23 January 1940.

18 For other examples see Donal Ó Drisceoil, *Censorship in Ireland 1939–1945: Neutrality, Politics and Society* (Cork, Cork UP: 1996), pp. 265–6.

19 *Dáil Debates*, 84, col. 1481–2, 3 April 1941.

20 *Irish Press*, 8 February 1943.

21 *Irish Press*, 31 May 1943.

22 NAI, DJ, R37, wartime censorship files, 'General Election, 1942–3'; NAI, DJ, No. 165, 'Neutrality'; NAI, 'Press censorship of election speeches', Department of External Affairs memo, 15 February 1943.

23 UCDAD, P67/362, Seán MacEntee papers, MacEntee election leaflet and 'Notes for Speakers and Canvassers'; John A. Murphy, 'The Irish Party System, 1938–51' in Kevin B. Nowlan and T. Desmond Williams (eds), *Ireland in the War Years and After, 1939–51* (Dublin, Gill and Macmillan: 1969), p. 151.

24 *Irish Press*, 16 June 1943.

25 UCDAD, P67/364, MacEntee papers.

26 See Tony Varley and Peter Moser, 'Clann na Talmhan: Ireland's last farmers' party', *History Ireland*, Summer 1995.

27 Gallagher, *Irish Elections, 1922–44*, pp. 267–75.

28 Hanna Sheehy-Skeffington, 'Women in Politics', *The Bell*, vol. 7, no. 2, 1943, pp. 143–8.

29 Flanagan joined Fine Gael in 1950.

30 Maurice Manning, *James Dillon: A Biography* (Dublin, Wolfhound: 1999), p. 190.

31 Richard Dunphy, *The Making of Fianna Fáil Power in Ireland, 1923–1948* (Oxford, Clarendon: 1995), pp. 289–90; Emmet O'Connor, *James Larkin* (Cork, Cork UP: 2002), pp. 109–10; UCDAD, P67/535, MacEntee papers, William O'Brien to all LP branches, 15 January 1944. The political split was replicated in the industrial wing of the movement in April 1945 when the ITGWU and 14 other Irish-based unions disaffiliated from the 'anglified' ITUC (i.e. dominated by representatives of British-based unions, and thus suspiciously left-wing and internationalist) and formed the Catholic, nationalist, anti-communist Congress of Irish Unions, which established a corporatist relationship with the government that was effectively an alliance.

32 See O'Connor, *Larkin*, p. 110; Norton, *et al*, letter to the *Standard*, 28 April 1944; UCAD, P67/535, MacEntee papers, NLP leaflets (reprints from O'Rahilly in the *Standard*); Mike Milotte, *Communism in Modern Ireland* (Dublin, Gill and Macmillan: 1984), pp. 197–9. Reports in the MacEntee papers and released Department of

Justice files leave little doubt that MacEntee and later O'Rahilly were being 'fed' information by the special branch/Department of Justice.
33 *Irish Times*, 11 May 1944.
34 When he rebuffed Allied demands that he expel Axis diplomats. See chapter 9.
35 James Hogan, *Election and Representation* (Cork, Cork UP: 1945), p. 77.
36 *Irish Times*, 23 May 1944.
37 Another of its TDs ran as an independent. After the election, Donnellan was replaced as party leader by Mayo large farmer, Joseph Blowick.
38 Gallagher, *Irish Elections, 1922–44*, pp. 279, 300–7. Lemass had warned MacEntee of this danger at the height of his attacks on Labour in June 1943 (UCDAD, P67/363, MacEntee papers, Lemass to MacEntee, 10 June 1943).
39 See extract from FF 'General Election report – 1944' in Girvin, 'Politics in wartime', p. 45.

❖ **AILTIRÍ NA HAISEIRGHE: A PARTY OF ITS TIME?**

1 Dermot Keogh firmly labels it a fascist organisation in *Twentieth Century Ireland: Nation and State* (Dublin, Gill and Macmillan: 1994), p. 112. See also Louis de Paor, *Irish Times*, 29 March 2002.
2 Ailtirí na hAiseirghe can be translated as 'architects of the resurrection/ rising'.
3 Craobh na hAiseirghe can be translated as 'branch of the resurrection/rising'.
4 *Spectator*, July 1942. See MA, G2, Gearóid Ó Cuinneagáin file.
5 MA, G2, Gearóid Ó Cuinneagáin file, G2 intelligence report, 27 November 1943.
6 Liam Ó Laoghaire eventually went on to become an archivist in the Institute of Film in London.
7 Mac an Bheatha was a founding member of Craobh na hAiseirghe and following the split became head of Glún na Buaidhe. He continued to be a leading personality in the Irish language movement and was the author of *Téid Focal le Gaoith* (Baille Átha Cliath, Foilseacháin Náisúinta Teo: 1967) and the founder of *Inniu*, an important Irish language paper which was published between 1943 and 1984.
8 'An Orange *ceilí*'.
9 Denis Ireland was President of the Ulster Union Club.
10 Proinsias Mac Aonghusa, *Ar Son na Gaeilge, Conradh na Gaeilge 1883–1993* (Baile Átha Cliath, Conradh na Gaeilge: 1993), p. 114.
11 Ciarán Ó Nualláin continued his involvement in the Irish language movement. He was also the brother of Brian Ó Nualláin (Myles na gCopaleen) who wrote articles on Ailtirí na hAiseirghe in *Irish Times* and also wrote a recently discovered play, *An Scian*, based on the split between Ailtirí na hAiseirghe and Craobh na hAiseirghe/ Glún na Buaidhe. See Louis de Paor, *Irish Times*, 29 March 2002.
12 Mac Aonghusa, *Ar Son na Gaeilge*, p. 113.
13 *Ibid.*, p. 283.
14 This speech was later published in pamphlet form by Ailtirí na hAiseirghe as *Ireland's Twentieth Century Destiny* (1942).
15 Mac an Bheatha, *Téid Focal le Gaoith*, p. 121.
16 *Ibid.*, p. 127.
17 Glún na Buaidhe can be translated as 'triumphant generation'.
18 According to Síghle Bean Uí Chuinneagáin, it was always Ó Cuinneagáin's belief that Mac an Bheatha and his fellow civil servants were forced to leave the *craobh* by their superiors in the civil service. No evidence of this was found.
19 MA, G2, Gearóid Ó Cuinneagáin file, 24 June 1943.
20 Interview with Síghle Bean Uí Chuinneagáin, May 1998.
21 Speech given at Comhdháil Náisiúnta na Gaeilge conference in Dún Laoghaire, 22 January 1945. See MA, G2, Gearóid O Cuinneagáin file.

22 Interview with Síghle Bean Uí Chuinneagáin, May 1998.

23 This piece was stopped by the censor in accordance with the policy of preventing outrages. See MA, G2, Ailtirí na hAiseirghe, 24 January 1945.

24 Seosamh Ó Duibhghinn, *Ag Scaoileadh Sceoil* (Baile Átha Cliatha, An Clóchomar Tta: 1962).

25 Ernest Blythe's papers, which are held in the UCD archives, contain many of Ailtirí na hAiseirghe's publications and also some papers relating to the party. It is obvious from these that he took more than a passing interest in the party. Among them is a copy of Ailtirí na hAiseirghe's annual report 1942–1943 and a copy of recommendations made by Blythe on the constitution and policies of the party. This takes the form of a letter. It is however, unsigned and it is not clear whether or not Ailtirí na hAiseirghe ever received it. The question must be asked how much influence both Blythe and Walshe had on the policies of Ailtirí na hAiseirghe. British intelligence reported that 'confirmation has been obtained of previous suspicions that Cunningham is "run" by Ernest Blythe and J. J. Walsh'. See PRO, DO 121/85, Secret Reports on the situation in Ireland, 1942–1944. The answer to this question may lie in the personal papers of Gearóid Ó Cuinneagáin which are currently in the possession of his family. I, however, was unable to gain access to them.

26 MA, G2, Ailtirí na hAiseirghe file, Garda Report, 29 May 1943.

27 MA, G2, Ailtirí na hAiseirghe file.

28 Michael Gallagher, *Political Parties in Ireland in the Republic of Ireland* (Manchester, Manchester UP: 1985), p. 109.

29 In *Ireland's Twentieth Century Destiny*, Ailtirí na hAiseirghe discussed the spirituality of the Gael and explained how unification, or political freedom as they often called it, would be necessary for the building of a Gaelic Catholic/Christian Nation. 'So long as we are without political freedom we shall not be able to perform the works we desire to undertake … so long as she has her soldiers in occupation of a military bridgehead in Ireland, England will be in a position to prevent Irish progress' (p. 8). Ailtirí na hAiseirghe devoted much time to the 'partition problem' as it called it, and it was the first aim defined in the sixteen-point policy programme which was published in most of its leaflets and pamphlets. 'The securing of the independence of our country as an essential preliminary towards the establishment of a State which, in the Christian perfection of its social and economic systems, will be a model for the whole world' (p. 22).

30 Ailtirí na hAiseirghe, *An Teorann* (Dublin, 1944), p. 3.

31 *An Teorann* and *The People and Partition* (December, 1944).

32 *An Teorann*.

33 *Ibid.*

34 *Ireland's Twentieth Century Destiny*, p. 5. Ailtirí na hAiseirghe's ideas of Gaelicisation and Irish-Ireland ideology were reminiscent of those such as expressed by D. P. Moran 40 years earlier in a series of articles published by him on the theme of Irish-Ireland. 'When the people go back to their national traditions, get permeated by their own literature, create a drama, go back to their customs, develop their industries; when they have a language to bind them together and a national personality to guard, the free and full development of every individual will in no way endanger or weaken any political movement'. *The Philosophy of Irish Ireland* (Dublin, James Duffy and Co Ltd: 1905), p. 39. This is discussed both by Patrick Maume in *D. P. Moran* (Dundalk, Dundalgan Press: 1995) and Terence Brown in his chapter on Irish-Ireland in *Ireland: a Social and Cultural History, 1922–1979* (Glasgow, Fontana: 1981). In common with Ailtirí na hAiseirghe, D. P. Moran also pointed to the value of the Brehon Laws. He argued that they were the most equitable legal system of all time and in this sense they were unique. In *Nationalism in Ireland*, pp. 353–4, Boyce points

to the existence of Irish-Ireland ideology in the ideology of Fianna Fáil, which, he argues had 'a practical application in their educational policy, for example the Department of Education notes for teachers instructs them to "restore as far as practicable the characteristically Gaelic turn of mind and way of looking at life" in order to "combat the danger of Ireland becoming a hybrid people" the Gaelic attitude, encompassing "a high spirituality, a vivid awareness of the presence of God, and a deep spirit of resignation to his will" must be instilled'. Ailtirí na hAiseirghe's education policies were very similar. In its view, the function of a state education system was not merely to prepare pupils for employment, it was also to prepare them to be loyal citizens and had a large part to play in the promotion of the Irish language and of the Gaelic way of life.

35 *Ibid.*, p. 4.

36 *Ibid.*, p.12.

37 'Though paying occasional homage to Mussolini, Salazar never let it be said that the Portuguese corporative system was based on the Italian model. Features of the Italian system disturbed him, such as its populist character and Mussolini's pagan caesarism' (Tom Gallagher, *Portugal: A Twentieth-Century Interpretation* [Manchester, Manchester UP: 1983], p. 68). In its writings Ailtirí na hAiseirghe used the term corporativism. However, many of Ailtirí na hAiseirghe's supporters and detractors may not have understood the differences and similarities between the Italian and Portuguese systems and states. For a good understanding of this and of Salazar's dictatorship and corporativism in Portugal, see Antonio Costa Pinto, *Salazar's Dictatorship and European Fascism: Problems of Interpretation* (New York, Columbia UP: 1995) and Gallagher, *Portugal*.

38 Published in Dublin, 1943.

39 The Portuguese Catholic Church not only contributed to the ideological framework of the régime but was also 'one of its essential instruments, always under its political direction'. Costa Pinto, *Salazar's Dictatorship and European Fascism*, p. 66. The relationship between the Portuguese Church and the State was formalised in the 1940 Concordat which, 'crowned the commitment between the church and the regime … setting the rules for the close collaboration which was *de facto* already common practice' (*ibid.*, p. 203).

40 It has been recognised that one of Salazar's greatest achievements was keeping Portugal out of the Second World War. The Portuguese state also maintained its alliance with Britain throughout the war. In officially neutral Ireland, where the atmosphere was nonetheless pro-Allied, Portuguese corporativism would have offered a more 'palatable' alternative for those who were attracted to corporatism but did not wish to publicly associate themselves with the Axis powers. This, coupled with its abhorance of secularism, perhaps persuaded Ailtirí na hAiseirghe to 'look to Portugal', rather than Italy, or any other corporate state.

41 What was meant by 'national affairs' was never clearly defined in their writings.

42 Political actors were always conceptualised as male in Ailtirí na hAiseirghe's writings. Craobh na hAiseirghe did, however, address the women of Ireland in one pamphlet entitled *For Girls Only* (Dublin: 1942) in which they counselled the emancipated women of Ireland to support a Christian, Gaelic Ireland.

43 Ailtirí na hAiseirghe, *Aiseirghe Says*, p. 9.

44 Although Portugal was in reality a dictatorship, it maintained a veneer of democracy through its constitution. This allowed for the election, by direct suffrage, of the president of the republic and the president of the council of ministers (prime minister). However, as prime minister, Salazar was accountable only to the president of the republic. In the system of Ailtirí na hAiseirghe on the other hand, once elected, the *Ceannaire Stáit* was accountable to no-one.

45 These responsibilities were not properly outlined, it is unlikely that the parish councils would have had much power.
46 As expressed in the 1933 Portuguese constitution. One glaring difference between what was provided for in the Portuguese constitution and how the government actually operated was the failure to establish the corporations, and the forums where the managers, foremen, owners and workers would be represented. These were not set up until 1956.
47 Ailtirí na hAiseirghe, like Salazar and others advocating corporatism/corporativism, often invoked a vision of an 'organic' pre-capitalist society where a medieval guild system brought together master and artisan peacefully.
48 For a discussion on Ailtirí na hAiseirghe's policies on corporatism and Northern Ireland see *Aiseirghe Says*, pp. 9–10 and *Ireland's Twentieth Century Destiny*, p. 15.
49 The obvious exception to this would be the speech made by Oliver Flanagan in the Dáil on 9 July 1943, on the issue of the Emergency Powers Bill: 'I am very sorry that I cannot associate myself with this bill or with anything relating to the public safety measures introduced by the Cumann na nGaedheal government or by the present Fianna Fáil government because I have seen that most of these Emergency Acts were always directed against republicanism. How is it that we do not see any of these Acts directed against the Jews, who crucified Our Saviour nineteen hundred years ago, and who are crucifying us every day in the week? How is it that we do not see them directed against the Masonic Order?' *Dáil Debates*, 91. See also Robert Fisk, *In Time of War: Ireland, Ulster and the Price of Neutrality, 1939–1945* (London, Paladin Grafton Books: 1983), p. 372.
50 Ailtirí na hAiseirghe, *Aiseirghe and the Jewish Question* (Dublin: 1945), p. 1.
51 While it is not clear to whom Ó Cuinneagáin was referring, it is interesting to note that a writer in the *Official Gazette* also warned against Jews changing their names into more Irish versions. See Dermot Keogh, *Jews in Twentieth Century Ireland* (Cork, Cork UP), p. 173.
52 *Aiseirghe and the Jewish Question*, p. 2.
53 Ailtirí na hAiseirghe discussed its financial and economic policies and the presence of 'vested interests' in *Aiseirghe Says* (Dublin: 1942) and *Aiseirghe* (Dublin: 1942). See also *Aiseirghe and the Jewish Question* and *Aiseirghe for the Worker* (1944).
54 According to Dermot Keogh, George Griffin was well known to the authorities (*Jews in Twentieth Century Ireland*, p. 149). A Mr Griffin, who is probably George Griffin, is also mentioned in Fisk, *In Time Of War*, pp. 374–6.
55 MA, G2, Gearóid Ó Cuinneagáin file, 19 September 1940.
56 *Ibid.*, 30 September 1940.
57 In early 1943, British intelligence reported that Ó Cuinneagáin was still running pro-German lectures, this time however, in the premises of Ailtirí na hAiseirghe. A report written on 1 January 1943 stated that, 'The German legation porter has been seen furtively leaving 27, South Frederick Street, the address of Gerald Cunningham's Fascist Organisation. A German propaganda lantern lecture was given on the premises on 18th December. It seems probable that the porter was delivering the apparatus and material.' See PRO, DO 121/85.
58 *Ibid.*, 19 October 1940.
59 MA, G2, Gearóid Ó Cuinneagáin, 1940.
60 PRO, DO 121/85, 1 January 1944.
61 On his election, Ó Tuama's release was appealed for. However, it was refused and Ó Tuama was unable to function as president of Conradh na Gaeilge. Proinsias Mac Aonghusa believes that the anti-Fianna Fáil sentiment shown by the election of an internee soured relations between de Valera and the Conradh and contributed to the setting up, by de Valera, of An Comhdháil Náisiúnta Gaeilge in 1943. See Mac

Aonghusa, *Ar Son na Gaeilge*, p. 285.

62 MA, G2, Gearóid Ó Cuinneagáin, 28 October 1941.

63 Another group with which Ó Cuinneagáin had links was the Anti-British Propaganda Committee which included among its activities, the heckling of performer Jimmy O'Dea on stage. MA, G2, Gearóid Ó Cuinneagáin, 22 December 1941.

64 MA, G2, Gearóid Ó Cuinneagáin, 4 April 1943.

65 MA, G2, Ailtirí na hAiseirghe, 12 October 1944.

66 *Ibid.*, 5 March 1945.

67 *Ibid.*, 12 March 1945.

68 From 1943 to 1944, British intelligence reports noted some common membership between Ailtirí na hAiseirghe, Córas na Poblachta, the Green Front and the Young Ireland Association, they also claimed that these members had been attending Sinn Féin meetings. While they reported that general support for Ailtirí na hAiseirghe was low, 'the party may yet prove a dangerous factor in the event of serious post war confusion and disillusionment' (PRO, DO 121/85, 1 July 1943). The reports also suggested that Ailtirí na hAiseirghe was 'being used as a breeding ground for the IRA, and that membership of the one may in a number of cases lead to the membership of the organisation' (PRO, DO 121/85, 31 August 1944). That some members of Ailtirí na hAiseirghe were drawn to Sinn Féin is not surprising, given the strong republican policies of both parties. However, there seems to be no further evidence to suggest that the leadership or the majority of the party were seeking to align themselves with the IRA.

69 MA, G2, Ailtirí na hAiseirghe, 16 October 1942.

70 MA, G2, Ailtirí na hAiseirghe, 8 October 1945.

71 *Irish Freedom*, August 1944. It is ironic that before he established Craobh na hAiseirghe, Ó Cuinneagáin was a regular contributor (under the alias of Bruinneal gan Smal) to *An t-Eireannach*, a progressive socialist paper, during the 1930s. Eamon Ó Ciosáin, *An t-Eireannach, 1934–1937* (Dublin, An Clochomhar: 1993).

72 In this excerpt, Myles na gCopaleen mentions Glún na Buaidhe, but the sentiments expressed by the speaker he quotes were more in keeping with those usually expressed by Ailtirí na hAiseirghe. *Irish Times*, 15 March 1943.

73 These pamphlets are to be found in the National Library.

74 Michael Gallagher, *Irish Elections, 1922–1924: Results and Analysis* (Limerick, PSAI Press: 1993), p. 303.

75 Kevin Rafter, *The Clann: The Story of Clann na Poblachta* (Dublin, Mercier Press: 1995), p. 35.

76 *Ibid.*, p. 36.

77 Clann na Poblachta made a film featuring Noel Browne outlining their policies and using scenes of urban poverty as a backdrop. The making of this is described in Rafter, *The Clann*, pp. 68–9. It also recorded a series of speeches by party members which it sold to the public. While the *ceannaire* of Craobh na hAiseirghe, Ó Cuinneagáin, used the medium of film as a recruiting method and had great plans to use this and other new technologies to further the spread of the Irish language.

78 Rafter, *The Clann*, p. 29.

❖ A TALE OF TWO ACTS

1 Quoted in Maurice Moynihan (ed.), *Speeches and Statements by Éamon de Valera, 1917–73* (Dublin, Gill and Macmillan: 1980), pp. 418–19.

2 *Dáil Debates*, 77, col. 263, 27 September 1939.

3 *Dáil Debates*, 77, col. 957–71, especially col. 965–8, 8 November 1939; see Ronan Fanning, *The Irish Department of Finance 1922–58* (Dublin, IPA: 1978), pp. 315–16.

4 *Dáil Debates*, 77, col. 969, 8 November 1939.

5 *Dáil Debates*, 83, col. 44, 7 May 1941.

6 NAI, DIC, TIW 766 (W49), untitled draft DIC memorandum, March 1940; NAI, DT, S.11725A, DIC memorandum, 'Explanatory Notes on Wage Levels Before and Since the Outbreak of War', 26 July 1940.

7 NAI, DT S.11725A, DIC memorandum, 26 July 1940, paras 1–2.

8 NAI, DIC, TIW 766 (W49), DIC memorandum, March 1940, paras 2–4.

9 NAI, DT S.11725A, DIC memorandum, 26 July 1940, para. 3.

10 NAI, DIC, TIW 766 (W49), DIC memorandum, March 1940, paras 5–6. For a fuller treatment of these two memoranda, see Finbarr O'Shea, 'Government and Trade Unions in Ireland, 1939–46: The Formulation of Labour Legislation' (MA thesis, UCC, 1988), pp. 14–19.

11 Seán Redmond, *The Irish Municipal Employees Trade Union 1883–1983* (Dublin, Irish Municipal Employees Trade Union: n.d.), pp. 104–7.

12 NAI, DT S.11616A, Ó Cinnéide memorandum, 26 January 1940; see Department of Local Government and Public Health, 'Wages of Dublin Corporation Workers', 25 January 1940, for details of the wage claim.

13 ITUC, *Annual Report*, 1939–40, pp. 100–1; see also pp. 89–92.

14 For the civil service wage freeze, which took the form of prohibiting any increase in the cost of living bonus paid to civil servants irrespective of movements in the cost of living index, see O'Shea, 'Government and Trade Unions', pp. 22–3; *Dáil Debates*, 80, col. 22–4, 8 May 1940.

15 NAI, DT S.11725A, DIC 'Memorandum Relating to a Proposed Stand Still Order in Respect of Wages', 26 July 1940, para. 1; DIC memorandum, 'Explanatory Notes on Wage Levels Before and Since the Outbreak of War', 26 July 1940, paras 6–7.

16 ITGWU, *Annual Report*, 1940, pp. 7–8.

17 NAI, DT S.11725A, DIC 'Memorandum Relating to a Proposed Stand Still Order in Respect of Wages', 26 July 1940, para. 11.

18 *Ibid.*, paras 6, 3–4, 11.

19 NAI, DT S.11725A, Extract from Cabinet Minutes, 2 August 1940 (G.C. 2/192).

20 NAI, DT S.11725A, DIC 'Memorandum Supplementary to the Memorandum Relating to a Proposed Stand Still Order', 6 December 1940, para. 2.

21 NAI, DT S.11725A, Ó Cinnéide to Private Secretary to the Minister for Industry and Commerce, 19 November 1940; DIC memorandum, 6 December 1940, para. 1.

22 NAI, DT S.11725A, DIC memorandum, 6 December 1940, para. 2.

23 NAI, DT S.11725A, Ó Cinnéide to Private Secretary to the Minister for Industry and Commerce, 11 December 1940.

24 NAI, DT S.11725A, DIC 'Memorandum for the Government Regarding the Proposed Stand Still Order in Respect of Remuneration of Employees and Distribution of Profits', 4 February 1941; Extract from Cabinet Minutes, 7 February 1941 (G.C. 2/241).

25 NAI, DT S.11616A, Extract from Cabinet Minutes, 8 March 1940 (G.C. 2/154).

26 NAI, DT S.11616A, DIC memorandum, 'Measures Arising out of Dublin Municipal Strike', 8 March 1940.

27 NAI, DIC, TIW 766 (W49), MacEntee to Ferguson, 17 March 1940; all quotations in the following passage are from this minute.

28 NAI, DIC, TIW 766 (W49), 'Draft Heads of Proposed Bill to Regulate the Exercise of the Right to Strike', 2 April 1940.

29 NAI, DIC, TIW 766 (W49), Lemass to MacEntee, 23 May 1940.

30 NAI, DT S.11750A, 'Observations of the Minister for Finance', 12 April 1940.

31 NAI, DT S.11750A, Extract from Cabinet Minutes, 28 May 1940 (G.C. 2/172).

32 NAI, DIC, TIW 766 (W49), Ferguson to MacEntee, 31 May 1940; MacEntee to Ferguson, 3 June 1940; 'Draft Heads of Bill Relating to Trade Unions and Strikes in Public Utility and Industrial Undertakings', 11 June 1940. For an outline of these revised

draft heads, see O'Shea, 'Government and Trade Unions', pp. 54–6.

33 NAI, DT S.11750A, Ó Cinnéide to Industry and Commerce, 6 July 1940.

34 *Dáil Debates*, 83, col. 1547, 4 June 1941.

35 The process by which Industry and Commerce's approach to industrial relations legislation evolved from punitive in early 1940 to reformative in 1941, and in particular
the central role played by the general secretary of the ITGWU, William O'Brien, is
explored in O'Shea, 'Government and Trade Unions', pp. 61–80.

36 ITUC, *Annual Report*, 1940–1, p. 31.

37 For the campaign against the bill, see O'Shea, 'Government and Trade Unions', pp.
89–94.

38 NAI, DIC, TIW 766, Sullivan minute, 18 June 1941.

39 NAI, DIC, TIW 766, O'Moore to Sullivan, 23 June 1941.

40 *Dáil Debates*, 83, col. 1637, 5 June 1941; 84, col. 59, 24 June 1941.

41 The campaign against the bill was a victim of the internal tensions and divisions which
riddled the labour movement during the war years and which resulted in the Labour
Party splitting into two rival parties in 1944 and the ITUC splitting into two rival
congresses in 1945. The course of these events can be traced in the extensive secondary literature on the subject; see Emmet O'Connor, *A Labour History of Ireland
1824–1960* (Dublin, Gill and Macmillan: 1992), ch. 7; Charles McCarthy, *Trade
Unions in Ireland 1894–1960* (Dublin, IPA: 1977), chs 4–6; Kieran Allen, *Fianna Fáil
and Irish Labour, 1926 to the Present* (London, Pluto Press: 1997), ch. 3; O'Shea,
'Government and Trade Unions', ch. 3.

42 That is, until 1947, when the Supreme Court found the act's provisions in relation to
the tribunal to be unconstitutional. And since, in an effort to divide the opposition
to the bill in 1941, MacEntee himself had diluted the deposit requirements to such
an extent as to render them virtually meaningless, the Trade Union Act at that point
ceased to have any reforming potential.

43 See NAI, DT S.12910A; *Dáil Debates*, 88, col. 1677–9, 29 October 1942.

44 *Dáil Debates*, 88, col. 1677, 29 October 1942.

45 ITUC, *Annual Report*, 1942–3, p. 28.

46 NAI, DT S.11725B, Extract from Cabinet Minutes, 8 April 1942 (G.C. 2/351).

47 ITUC, *Annual Report*, 1941–2, p. 104; ITGWU, *Annual Report*, 1942, p. 8.

48 See, for instance, the report of the ITUC's national executive to the 1943 annual congress, which boasted of over 800 wage rate orders having been made, most of them
after hearings before tribunals and for which 'the greater credit is due to the Worker
Members'; ITUC, *Annual Report*, 1942–3, p. 25.

49 NAI, DT S.11725B, DIC memorandum, 24 February 1942.

50 NAI, DIC, IR19, Lemass to Ferguson, 13 July 1944.

51 NAI, DIC, IR19, Ferguson to Lemass, 12 October 1944; NAI, DT S.13573, Department of Finance, Memorandum for the Government, 26 October 1944.

52 NAI, DT S.13573, Extract from Cabinet Minutes, 5 December 1944 (G.C. 4/35); NAI,
DIC, IR19, Lemass to O'Shannon, 7 December 1944; NAI, DIC, IR19, O'Shannon
to Lemass, 10 January 1945.

53 NAI, DIC, IR19, Lemass memorandum on meeting with ITUC, 14 February 1945.

54 NAI, DIC, IR19, Lemass to Ferguson, 15 February 1945.

55 NAI, DIC, IR19, Lemass to Ferguson, 12 October 1944.

56 NAI, DIC, IR19, Ferguson memorandum on meeting with FUE, 26 February 1945.

57 NAI, DIC, IR19, Lemass memorandum, 'Establishment of Labour Court', December
1945.

58 NAI, DIC, IR19, Lemass to ITUC, CIU and FUE, 19 December 1945; Roberts to Lemass, 14 February 1946; O'Shannon to Lemass, 21 February 1946; DIC memoranda
on discussions with ITUC and CIU, n.d. [early March 1946]; Lemass to Williams, 8

March 1946; Draft Heads of Industrial Relations Bill, 8 March 1946.

59 NAI, DIC, IR19, Draft Heads of Industrial Relations Bill, 8 March 1946; NAI, DT S.13847A, DIC explanatory memorandum on Industrial Relations Bill, 26 April 1946.

60 NAI, DIC, IR19, O'Brien to Lemass, 6 March 1946.

61 NAI, DIC, IR19, Sullivan observations on CIU and ITUC memoranda, 27 February 1946. Sullivan at least had the merit of consistency; in July 1944, he had responded to Lemass' original idea of a commission of inquiry on wages policy with the lament that 'there will be no solution to this problem [of strikes and wages] without compulsory arbitration'. NAI, DIC, IR19, Sullivan to Ferguson, 26 July 1944.

62 NAI, DIC, IR9, Collins to Ferguson, 18 April 1946.

63 NAI, DT S.13847A, Department of Finance memorandum, 27 April 1946.

64 NAI, DIC, IR9, Sullivan to Collins, 1 May 1946.

65 *Dáil Debates*, 101, col. 2286, 25 June 1946.

66 NAI, DIC, IR19, O'Shannon to Lemass, 17 June 1946.

❖ VOCATIONALISM IN EMERGENCY IRELAND

1 See Dermot Keogh, *Ireland and Europe 1919–1989: A Diplomatic and Political History* (Cork and Dublin, Hibernian UP: 1990), p. 113.

2 Bishop Michael Browne was reluctant to serve as chairman of the commission and only agreed to do so having received an assurance from de Valera that it was 'not a mere device for shelving the question of vocational organisation' (NAI, DT, S.13550A, Memorandum, 22 May 1940). Alfred O'Rahilly suspected that the commission might be a poisoned chalice – 'set up to stultify itself, to break up into irreconcilable factions, and to lead to a triumphant justification of the *status quo*'. He decided to accept de Valera's invitation to join the commission only after Browne persuaded him to do so (Don O'Leary, *Vocationalism and Social Catholicism in Twentieth-Century Ireland: The Search for a Christian Social Order* [Dublin, Irish Academic Press: 2000], pp. 78–9).

3 The commission's terms of reference were: 'to examine and report on: (a) the practicability of developing functional or vocational organisation in the circumstances of this country; (b) the means best calculated to promote such development; (c) the rights and powers which should be conferred and the duties which should be imposed on functional or vocational bodies and, generally, the relations of such bodies to the Oireachtas and to the Government, and (d) the legislative and administrative measures that would be required' (The *Commission on Vocational Organisation Report*, 1943, para. 1).

4 For a full list of members, and their categorisation on a vocational basis, see O'Leary, *Vocationalism and Social Catholicism*, pp. 191–2.

5 NAI, DT S.13550A, Browne to de Valera, 23 September 1939.

6 O'Leary, *Vocationalism and Social Catholicism*, p. 86.

7 NAI, Papers of the Commission on Vocational Organisation, Box 1, Doc. 19, Address by Éamon de Valera to the Commission on Vocational Organisation, 5 October 1939.

8 *Dáil Debates*, 77, col. 600–601, 29 September 1939; and *Seanad Debates*, 23, col. 1255–1257, 4 October 1939.

9 NAI, Papers of the Commission on Vocational Organisation, Box 1, Doc. 19, Address by Éamon de Valera to the Commission on Vocational Organisation, 5 October 1939.

10 O'Leary, *Vocationalism and Social Catholicism*, p. 103.

11 NAI, DT S.13550A, McElligott to Moynihan, 6 February 1940.

12 Lord Glenavy (Charles Henry Gordon Campbell) was a director of the Bank of Ireland from 1 February 1943 to 30 July 1963.

13 Joseph J. Lee, 'Aspects of Corporatist Thought in Ireland: The Commission on

Vocational Organisation, 1939–1943', in Art Cosgrove and Donal McCartney (eds), *Studies in Irish History Presented to R. Dudley Edwards* (Dublin, UCD: 1979), p. 330.

14 These included the Commission on Agriculture, the Interdepartmental Committee of Inquiry regarding Shooting Rights, the Town Tenants (Occupation of Tenancies) Tribunal, the Committee on Summer-Time, and the Irish Manuscripts Commission.

15 Ronan Fanning, *The Irish Department of Finance 1922–1958* (Dublin, IPA: 1978), pp. 322–3.

16 See Lee, 'Aspects of Corporatist Thought', p. 330.

17 NAI, DT S.13550A, Browne to O'Kelly, 7 June 1940.

18 NAI, DT S.13550A, O'Kelly to de Valera, 13 June 1940.

19 NAI, DT S.11926, Handwritten postscript dated 26 June 1940 in memorandum, 10 June 1940.

20 NAI, DT S.11926, 'Submission to the Government: Suspension of Commissions and Special Inquiries During Emergency', 19 July 1940.

21 NAI, DT S.11926, 'Memorandum for the Government: Suspension of Commissions and Special Inquiries During Emergency', 19 July 1940. The Department of Finance did not press for the suspension of the Drainage Commission which had nearly completed its work. It also stated that The Committee of Inquiry into Dublin Housing should be allowed to complete its report.

22 NAI, DT S.11926, copy of the Cabinet Minutes, G.C. 2/190, item 4, 23 July 1940.

23 O'Leary, *Vocationalism and Social Catholicism*, p. 85.

24 NAI, DT S.10519A/1, untitled document, listing newspaper articles, with comments and summaries, 16 December 1939.

25 NAI, DT S.10816A, 'Parish Committees at Once: Appeal By The Taoiseach', *Irish Press*, 18 June 1940.

26 NAI, DT S.10519A/1, 'Inter-Departmental Conference on Parish Councils: 16 July 1940'; document dated 17 July 1940.

27 NAI, DT S.10519A/2, Memorandum on parish councils with covering letter to M. Ó Muimhneacháin, 19 August 1940.

28 This is an abbreviation of a longer list of functions listed in the memorandum on parish councils with covering letter to M. Ó Muimhneacháin, 19 August 1940. On 21 August 1940 John Hurson wrote to the secretaries of the county councils, enclosing an extensive list of proposed functions for parish councils, together with information about the Local Security Force, A.R.P. Services and the Red Cross. Extra copies were enclosed for circulation to parish councils (NAI, DT S.11962, letter from the secretary, Department of Local Government and Public Health, 21 August 1940, with annexed statements A, B, C, and D).

29 *Dáil Debates*, 81, col. 759, 27 November 1940.

30 See for example *Seanad Debates*, 25, col. 2150–2151, 31 July 1941.

31 *Ibid.*, col. 2167.

32 *Ibid.*, col. 2151.

33 *Dáil Debates*, 83, col. 1929, 11 June 1941.

34 *Ibid.*, col. 1971.

35 *Dáil Debates*, 81, col. 814, 27 November 1940.

36 Ruttledge was also aware of Muintir na Tíre's limitations. At his meeting with the county secretaries on 19 July he stated 'Father Hayes and others have done very good work in setting up Parish Committees throughout the country, but if we want to get things going speedily I am afraid that Father Hayes' organisation will not be able to cover the ground. What I want to discuss with you today is the organisation of these Councils' (NAI, DT S.10519A/2, Memorandum on parish councils with covering letter to M. Ó Muimhneacháin, 19 August 1940).

37 In 1942, Fr Hayes felt it necessary to emphasise that Muintir na Tíre was much more

than 'an emergency effort'. Evidently, he feared that a misunderstanding on this point would endanger the future of the organisation. See Jerome Toner, *Rural Ireland: Some of its Problems* (Dublin, Clonmore and Reynolds: 1955), p. 35.

38 *Dáil Debates*, 81, col. 813, 27 November 1940.

39 *Dáil Debates*, 83, col. 1973, 11 June 1941; and *Seanad Debates*, 25, col., 2140, 2147, 2160, 2163, 2170, 31 July 1941.

40 The *Commission on Vocational Organisation Report* (1943), para. 199.

41 NAI, DT, S.10519A/1, untitled document, 16 December 1939, in reference to an article in *Irish Independent*, 15 November 1939.

42 O'Neill to Hayes, 21 August 1940, Muintir na Tíre Archives, Canon Hayes House, Tipperary. This document was brought to my attention by J. D. Raymond O'Connor and is quoted in his MA thesis, 'The Origins, Ethos and Geographical Expansion of Muintir na Tíre: 1931–1970 (UCC, 1988), p. 112.

43 NAI, DT, S.10816A, 'Taoiseach Urges Parishes to Develop Own Organisation', *Irish Press*, 10 November 1941.

44 *Commission on Vocational Organisation Report* (1943), paras 199, 548–549.

45 This opinion of Fr Hayes is evident from NAI, DT, S.10519A/1, untitled document, 16 December 1939; in reference to a paper read by him on 'Parochial Councils in Action', at a meeting under the auspices of An Ríoghacht, on 8 November 1939.

46 NAI, DT, S.10816A, 'Taoiseach Urges Parishes to Develop Own Organisation', *Irish Press*, 10 November 1941.

47 In his address to the Commission on Vocational Organisation, at its inaugural meeting (2 March 1939), de Valera described vocational organisation as a coming together of people of similar occupations or professions who wished to promote the interests of their respective sectional organisations (*Commission on Vocational Organisation Report*, 1943, para. 4).

48 See note 3.

49 NAI, DT, S.10813, 'Seán Lemass on Bureaucracy and Politicians', transcript of a speech reported in *Irish Press*, 29 October 1943.

50 O'Leary, *Vocationalism and Social Catholicism*, pp. 110–2.

51 See J. H. Whyte, *Church and State in Modern Ireland 1923–1979* (2nd ed., Dublin, Gill and Macmillan: 1984), p. 108.

52 FA, de Valera papers, 1410/1, 'Recasting Economy For Full Employment: Mr Lemass Outlines Programme', *Irish Press*, 28 March 1945.

53 O'Leary, *Vocationalism and Social Catholicism*, pp. 140–1.

54 The anonymous author of 'Muintir na Tíre: A Brief Sketch of its History' wrote 'mushroom growths are apt to enjoy only mushroom existence; many of the emergency parish councils were formed hurriedly – I know of an instance in which three were formed by a county official in an afternoon' (p. 4). Document in Muintir na Tíre archives, Canon Hayes House, Tipperary.

55 NAI, DT, S.10519B/2, 'The Parish Council: Its Place in Irish Rural Development', *Limerick Leader*, 26 August 1944.

56 NAI, DT, S.10519A/2, 'Department of Local Government and Public Health: Notice of Motion in Seanad on 28th August' (1940), pp. 3–7.

57 O'Leary, *Vocationalism and Social Catholicism*, pp. 147–8.

❖ BLUEPRINTS FROM BRITAIN

1 *Irish Press*, 18 January 1957.

2 The NHS, while originally proposed and endorsed by the wartime coalition, was the product primarily of Aneurin Bevan, the Minister for Health of the Labour Government (1945–51). The story of Irish health reform in the 1945 to 1951 period is detailed elsewhere. Education was even more neglected. De Valera did express

concern in 1944 about the lack of planning for education in Ireland in comparison with Britain. A report on expanding secondary education was produced in 1947 but was never implemented and Ireland retained the poorest funded second-level education system in the developed world. The Church's control of education went unchallenged by successive governments. No attempt was made to provide more than elementary education for children by government. In 1932, 93% of children received no secondary education due to the refusal of the state to provide free secondary education or provide an adequate supply of scholarships. This figure was nearly 80% in the early 1960s. Henry Patterson, *Ireland since 1939* (Oxford, Oxford UP: 2002), p. 166 and Joseph J. Lee, *Ireland 1912–85: Politics and Society* (Cambridge, Cambridge UP: 1989), p. 132.

3 Mark Mazower, *Dark Continent* (Penguin, London, 1999), p. 186.

4 See Paul Addison, *The Road to 1945* (London, Pimlico: 1994) especially pp. 130–2. Revisionists and dissenters from Addison's interpretation would include from a centre-left perspective: Kevin Jeffreys, *The Churchill Government and Wartime Politics* (New York, St Martins: 1991) and Stephen Brooke, *Labour's War: The Labour Party during the Second World War* (Oxford, Clarendon Press: 1992). Brooke (p. 342) argues that consensus was forged after the war, i.e. by the Labour government from 1945 to 1951, not during it. From the right, Corelli Barnett in *The Audit of War* (London, Macmillan: 1986), particularly chapters 1–2, is scathing about the negative impact of Beveridge on Britain's post-war economic performance. He trains his sights on the post-war Labour government in *The Lost Victory* (London, Macmillan: 1996). It should be said that both Brooke and Barnett have drawn considerable criticism for, among other reasons, their use of hindsight.

5 *The Beveridge Report in Brief* (HMSO, 1942), para. 17.

6 José Harris, *William Beveridge* (Oxford, Oxford UP: 1998), p. 415.

7 This was on the advice of John Maynard Keynes. See José Harris, *William Beveridge*, p. 410.

8 See the arguments among Churchill, Cherwell and Wood about releasing the plan, in Barnett, *The Audit of War*, especially pp. 26–8.

9 This paragraph is based on Addison, *The Road to 1945*, pp. 220–5.

10 In 1908 the old age pension was introduced which provided pensions for those over 70, subject to a means test. Three years later, a state-aided and state-organised scheme – the National Health and Unemployment Insurance Scheme – came into being. This spread the risks over the general population and was financed by a combination of general taxation and contributions from employees and employers. These Acts were extended after the transfer of power in 1922, most notably with the Unemployment Assistance Scheme of 1933 and the Widows and Orphans' Pensions (Non Contributory) Scheme of 1935.

11 Mel Cousins, 'The Introduction of Children's Allowances in Ireland 1939–44', *Ir. Econ. Soc. Hist.* XXVI (1999), pp. 35–53 provides a recent study of the matter.

12 This rather bizarre notion was later put forward by Alexis Fitzgerald in his reservation to the *Commission on Emigration 1956*.

13 Lee, *Ireland 1912–85*, pp. 226–7.

14 *Ibid.*, pp. 229–30.

15 It is described as 'vulgar political fear' by Paul Bew and Henry Patterson, *Seán Lemass and the Making of Modern Ireland* (Dublin, Gill and Macmillan: 1982) p. 27. See also Richard Dunphy, *The Making of Fianna Fáil Power in Ireland* (Oxford, Oxford UP: 1995), pp. 231–2 for a discussion of the responses to the Beveridge Report in Ireland.

16 NAI, DT S.13053A, Flinn to de Valera, 13 December 1942.

17 *Irish Times*, 4 December 1942.

18 NAI, DT S.11109B, Inter-Departmental Committee on Social Services, Departmental Views, 12 December 1945.

19 NAI, DT S.12117B, Finance Memo, 1 March 1943. This receives lengthy treatment in Lee, *Ireland, 1912–85*, pp. 280–3.

20 NAI, S491, Department of the Environment Secretary Files, Childers to the Minister for Local Government and Public Health, and to the Inter-Departmental Committee on Employment Schemes, 17 March 1945.

21 James Deeny, *To Cure and to Care* (Dublin, Glendale: 1989), p. 78.

22 The speech is quoted at length in Dermot Keogh, *Twentieth Century Ireland* (Dublin, Gill and Macmillan: 1994), pp. 133–4.

23 UCDAD, P67/261, MacEntee papers, Department of Industry and Commerce Memorandum for the Information of the Members of the Government on Social Insurance Schemes in Great Britain and the Estimated Cost of Adopting them in this Country, Appendix 5, n.d. It should be noted that a Department of Industry and Commerce Memo of 19 April 1945 (NAI, DT S.13053) has lower estimates for the implementation of Beveridge and the White Paper.

24 *Labour's Programme for a Better Ireland – General Election 1943.*

25 Beveridge at the same time published *Full Employment in a Free Society, A Report by William H. Beveridge* (London, Liberal Publications Dept: 1944). Coincidentally, one of the advisers to Beveridge was Frank Pakenham (Lord Longford) later biographer of de Valera. Harris, *William Beveridge*, p. 435. Pakenham was of the opinion that Beveridgism was not suitable to Ireland either. See his comments to the Magnificat Society of UCD reported in *Irish Press*, 16 May 1945.

26 It is reproduced in full in Peter Hennessey, *Never Again* (London, Vintage: 1993), pp. 186–7.

27 Cited in Addison, *The Road to 1945*, p. 245.

28 NAI, DT S.11852B, Department of External Affairs memo on Emigration, 30 December 1947. This memo describes the failings of agriculture as a means of solving unemployment.

29 NAI, DT S.13101A, Finance memo, 31 October 1944.

30 NAI, DT S.13101A, Observations by the Minister for Industry and Commerce on Memorandum circulated to Cabinet Committee by Department of Finance on the British White Paper on Employment Policy, 22 November 1944.

31 NAI, DT S.13101A, Industry and Commerce Memo, 17 January 1945.

32 NAI, DT S.13101A, Memorandum by the Minister for Agriculture, 14 May 1945.

33 There is a reference in R. J. Raymond, 'Irish Economic Development', in John A. Murphy and Paddy O'Carroll (eds.), *De Valera and His Times* (Cork, Cork UP: 1983), p. 128, to 'detailed notes' written by McElligott which conclude: 'To a layman these proposals suggest that the "vicious spiral" which was so unpopular a few years ago has lost its terrors. The authorities cited in support of this policy (Keynes, Beveridge and Kaldor) all appear to belong to the escapist school of economics.' I have been unable to identify these notes on the file cited: NAI, D, S.13101A.

34 Lee, *Ireland 1912–85*, p. 232.

35 A full copy of the speech is in NAI, DT S.13221A. It is also covered in *Irish Press*, 19 November 1944. Significantly, de Valera was in attendance at the reading of this paper. This quotation was highlighted in the *Irish Press* report presumably so the readership could be in no doubt about the key message. See also Bew and Patterson, *Seán Lemass*, p. 32. Does this suggest that he was not as enthusiastic about his paper as is made out? It might be another case of Lemass, the enigmatic patriot.

36 *Irish Times*, 8 May 1944.

37 Fredrich von Hayek, *The Road to Serfdom* (London, Routledge: 1944) had been recently published with its argument that freedom and collectivism were incompatible. In 1944 he was a voice in the wilderness: Mazower, *Dark Continent*, pp. 206–7. There appears to be no direct reference to the book in any of MacEntee's papers but the

similarity of the language would suggest that he had at least read reviews of it. Hayek's work was published some months before Beveridge's. Interestingly while Beveridge disliked Hayek's book (Harris, *Beveridge*, pp. 440–1), John Maynard Keynes was more favourable but nonetheless dismissed its central thesis that all planning was inevitably bad. It was a question of 'drawing the line' according to Keynes. Robert Skidelsky, *John Maynard Keynes Vol. III* (London, Macmillan: 2000), pp. 284–5. Friedman was the founder of the Chicago School of Economics, which was very pro-free market.

38 UCDAD, P67/270, MacEntee papers. The speech is reported in *Irish Press*, 14 March 1945. MacEntee began with a by now routine flagellation of the Dignan plan. He made a similar attack on Beveridge at the inaugural meeting of the UCD Commerce Society. Some of his comments were extraordinarily conservative to say the least. See *Irish Press*, 9 May 1945; Tom Feeney, 'The Road to Serfdom: Seán MacEntee, "Beveridgism" and the development of Irish Social Policy', *The History Review*, XII (2001), pp. 69–71 makes a similar point about MacEntee's conservatism in this speech and the influence of Hayek.

39 As reported in *Irish Press*, 28 March 1945.

40 Richard Dunphy, *The Making of Fianna Fáil Power in Ireland* (Oxford, Clarendon Press: 1995), p. 247.

41 *Dáil Debates*, 97, col. 38–39, 2 May 1945.

42 The representatives of the Department of Local Government and Public Health dissented from the Report of the Inter-Departmental Committee on Social Services. They did 'not consider that the proposals in the majority report would warrant the establishment of a separate Department of State to administer the Income Maintenance Services as defined in the Majority Report'. NAI, DT S.11109B Inter-Departmental Committee on Social Services, Departmental Views.

43 J. H. Whyte, *Church and State in Modern Ireland 1923–1979* (Dublin, Gill and Macmillan: 1980), pp. 132–4, 141.

44 Lee, *Ireland 1912–85*, pp. 301–13 provides an interesting critique.

45 Some of MacEntee's 1943 election speeches are preserved in UCDAD, P67/364, MacEntee papers. The Lemass complaint is in UCDAD, P67/363 MacEntee papers, Lemass to MacEntee, 10 June 1943. MacEntee's resignation letter, one of a number he drafted during his career, is offered in UCDAD, P67/366, MacEntee papers, MacEntee to Taoiseach, 28 June 1943.

46 UCDAD, P67/257, MacEntee papers, contains a large series of files on the MacEntee/Dignan clash.

47 Lee, *Ireland 1912–85*, p. 285.

48 UCDAD, P67/257(1), MacEntee papers, T. J. Barrington to Mr J. Kennedy TD, 19 October 1945.

49 NAI, S491, Department of the Environment, Secretary Files, Memorandum submitted by the Parliamentary Secretary (Mr Erskine Childers) to the Minister for Local Government & Public Health to the Inter-Departmental Committee on Employment Schemes, 17 March 1945. I suspect that this was never submitted to the interdepartmental committee judging by the files in the Taoiseach Department. As Mary Daly, *The Buffer State – The Historical Roots of the Department of the Environment* (Dublin, IPA: 1997), pp. 250–1 notes, MacEntee kept close interest in all local government submissions to other departments or the government.

50 UCDAD, P67/261, MacEntee papers, Local Government and Public Health Memorandum for the Minister on the problems of extending social insurance in Ireland with special reference to the rural community, 9 July 1945.

51 UCDAD, P67/293, MacEntee papers, Childers to MacEntee, 1947. In fact Fianna Fáil's percentage share of the vote in 1948 bares comparison with the Conservatives in

1945. The Conservatives received just over 39% of the vote, Fianna Fáil 41.9%. The British Labour party won a landslide in terms of seats with just under 50% of the vote. In Ireland, Fianna Fáil, thanks to the divided nature of the opposition, still had twice as many seats as any other party.

52 UCDAD, P67/299, MacEntee papers, Childers to MacEntee, February 1948.

53 See in particular NAI, DT S.11852B, Department of External Affairs memo on Emigration, 30 December 1947.

54 NAI, DT S.13101B, Department of Finance Memo, Dilemma of Full Employment Policy in Scandinavia, 6 April 1953.

55 NAI, DT S.15536A, Cabinet Committee on the Provision of Employment, Observations of Minister for Finance, 31 July 1953 on Memorandum of Minister for Industry and Commerce, 28 July 1953.

56 Cormac O'Gráda, A Rocky Road: The Irish Economy since the 1920s (Manchester, Manchester UP: 1997), p. 69. As regards Health and Social Welfare, where he ministered from 1957 to 1966, MacEntee remained on his guard against do-gooders such as Fine Gael's Tom O'Higgins' proposals for an expansion of Health Services and health insurance in 1963. UCDAD, P67/336 and P67/337, MacEntee papers.

57 John Horgan and Brian Girvin outline Lemass' growing frustration, between 1945 and 1948, with the failure of protectionism, but note his utter failure to take any serious action. John Horgan, Seán Lemass (Dublin, Gill and Macmillan: 1997), pp. 117–20; Brian Girvin, Between Two Worlds: Politics and Economy in Independent Ireland (Dublin, Gill and Macmillan: 1989), pp. 164–8.

58 See NAI, DT S.14818, B/2 Department of Industry and Commerce Memo for Government, 7 October 1952, Report of American Experts engaged by Coras Trachtála. This report made for some grim reading about the dollar export potential of Irish industry in the early 1950s.

59 As noted in Mazower, Dark Continent, p. 297

60 See the report in Irish Independent, 31 July 1957 quoting the Central Statistics Office reservation from the Commission on Emigration which noted that 'despite the fact that the national income per head in Ireland is only half that of Britain, the wage structure is similar in the two countries'.

61 Kevin Myers makes some acute observations in Irish Times, 13 July 2001.

62 Tom Garvin, 'Political Power and Economic Development in Ireland' in Maurice R. O'Connell (ed.), People Power (Dublin, Gill and Macmillan: 1993), p. 36.

63 The highest Fianna Fáil vote, under de Valera, was 689,000 in 1933, the lowest being 554,000 in 1948. Using the average net emigration figures cited for the census in Enda Delaney, Demography, State and Society (Liverpool, Liverpool UP) pp. 40, 162, 231, would suggest that 699,785 people emigrated, the vast majority of them to England, in the period from 1932 to 1959. The figure is actually probably higher as the highest rate of emigration was recorded in the period 1957–59 (well over 50,000 emigrants a year) while the figure for 1932–36 is considerably lower than the average figure due to the depression in England. Ireland had one of Europe's most restrictive franchises for non-residents.

64 NAI, DT S.13831C, Department of Finance Memo for the Government, 7 February 1952.

❖ THE BELFAST BLITZ, 1941

1 PRONI COM 17/3/1 and COM17/3/2.

2 Brian Barton, The Blitz: Belfast in the War Years (Belfast, The Blackstaff Press: 1989), pp. 27, 43, 57; Robert Fisk, In Time of War: Ireland, Ulster and the Price of Neutrality 1939–45 (London, André Deutsch: 1983), p. 478.

3 Daily Express, 13 January 1938.

4 Barton, The Blitz, p. 40.

5 J. W. Blake, *Northern Ireland in the Second World War* (Belfast: HMSO, 1956), p. 168.
6 Ronnie Munck and Bill Rolston, *Belfast in the Thirties: An Oral History* (Belfast, The Blackstaff Press: 1987), p. 66; Jonathan Bardon, *A History of Ulster* (Belfast, The Blackstaff Press: 1992), pp. 532–4.
7 Munck and Rolston, *Belfast in the Thirties*, pp. 70–7; Bardon, *The Blitz*, p. 531.
8 Barton, *The Blitz*, p. 36; Bardon, *A History of Ulster*, p. 563.
9 Fisk, *In Time of War*, pp. 102–3.
10 Brian Barton, *Brookeborough: The Making of a Prime Minister* (Belfast, Institute of Irish Studies: 1988), p. 152.
11 *Ibid.*, *Brookeborough*, pp. 153 and 168.
12 Fisk, *In Time of War*, p. 476.
13 Blake, *Northern Ireland*, p. 168.
14 Barton, *The Blitz*, p. 107.
15 *Ibid.*, *The Blitz*, p. 129.
16 Douglas Carson, 'The Blitz', BBC Northern Ireland schools radio programme (22 November 1973) in the series *Modern Irish History: People and Events*.
17 Fisk, *In Time of War*, p. 495.
18 Carson, 'The Blitz'.
19 Tape recorded interview by pupils for *Ulster and the World Wars* learning resource pack (Northern Ireland Council for Educational Development, Belfast, 1983).
20 PRONI D/2109/13.
21 Barton, *The Blitz*, p. 178.
22 Fisk, *In Time of War*, p. 500.
23 Barton, *The Blitz*, p. 202.
24 Tape recorded interview for *Ulster and the World Wars*, *op. cit.*
25 PRONI D/2109/13.
26 Jonathan Bardon, *Belfast: an Illustrated History* (Belfast, The Blackstaff Press: 1982), p. 239.
27 Barton, *The Blitz*, p. 166.
28 PRONI CAB/4/473, Memorandum by the Minister of Public Safety.
29 PRONI CAB/4/473, Memorandum by the Minister of Commerce.
30 PRONI CAB/4/473, Memorandum by the Minister of Home Affairs.
31 *Belfast Newsletter*, 3 June 1941.
32 James McConville, '1935 and All That' (unpublished memoir, Belfast: 1977).
33 *Parliamentary Debates* (Northern Ireland House of Commons), 24, col. 828.
34 PRONI CAB/4/480 and CAB/4/482.

❖ NEUTRALITY, IDENTITY AND THE CHALLENGE OF THE 'IRISH VOLUNTEERS'

1 Thomas Hennessey, *Dividing Ireland: World War I and Partition* (London, Routledge: 1998), especially pp. 235–9.
2 By 'identity' I mean individual and collective self-definitions of place in the world and of relationships with other groups and individuals. For a broad discussion and exploration of identity in the Irish context see P. O'Mahony and G. Delanty, *Rethinking Irish History: Nationalism, Identity and Ideology* (London, Macmillan: 1998).
3 Figures derived from Richard Doherty's estimates in his 'Irish Heroes of the Second World War' in Brian Girvin and Geoffrey Roberts (eds), *Ireland and the Second World War* (Dublin, Four Courts: 2000). See also Aiden McElwaine's chapter on 'The Politics of Numbers' in his MPhil thesis: 'The Forgotten Volunteers: Irish Service in the British Armed Forces during the Second World War', UCC, 1998.
4 David Fitzpatrick, 'The Logic of Collective Sacrifice: Ireland and the British Army,

1914–1918', *The Historical Journal*, Vol. 38, no. 4, 1995. Fitzpatrick's theme is that individuals volunteered mainly because of social pressures emanating from the groups and organisations to which they belonged. In a critical review of Richard Doherty's *Irish Men and Women in the Second World War* (Dublin, Four Courts: 1999), Fitzpatrick argues that 'in order to explain military enlistment, it is necessary to examine the differential impact of both official and unofficial propaganda, the agencies which translate propaganda into personal decisions, and the economic and social inhibitions which discourage enlistment in certain classes or communities more than in others'. Later he speaks of the need 'for a systematic analysis of the backgrounds most favourable to Irish enlistment, and hence of the complex factors influencing that momentous decision' (*Irish Review* 26 (2000) pp. 140–1). Obviously, there are various social pressures, circumstances and influences which impact on individual decisions, and these need to be fully explored, but the problem with the sociological reductionism advocated by Fitzpatrick is that it cannot adequately explain either the action of those who joined up or that of those who did not (despite maybe fitting into the same social category as those who volunteered). A full explanation requires reference to an individual's reasons for volunteering, including a recognition and respect for the autonomy of that person's rationality. This is particularly important in the case of Irish volunteers during the Second World War, most of whom defy sociological and situational pigeon-holing.

5 210,000 is David Fitzpatrick's figure, cited by Keith Jeffery, *Ireland and the Great War* (Cambridge, Cambridge UP: 2000), p. 6. However, as the latter points out, the Fitzpatrick calculation does not include the Irish who joined up in Britain and elsewhere. Adjusting Fitzpatrick's figure upwards suggests that the rate of volunteering during the Second World War was about half that of the First World War.

6 Terence Brown, *Ireland: A Social and Cultural History 1922–1985* (London, Fontana: 1985), ch. 6. See also S. N. Eisenstadt's interesting comparative analysis of national identity formation 'World Histories and the Construction of Collective Identities' in P. Pomper, *et al*, *World History: Ideologies, Structure and Identities* (Oxford, Blackwell Publishers: 1998).

7 See the collection of de Valera's speeches in his *Ireland's Stand* (Dublin, Gill: 1946).

8 *Ibid.*, p. 18.

9 Saul Friedlander, *Pius XII and the Third Reich: A Documentation* (New York, Octagon Books: 1980), pp. 48–9.

10 Aengus Nolan, 'Joseph Walshe and the Management of Irish Foreign Policy, 1922–1946', PhD thesis, UCC, 1997, p. 119.

11 See Geoffrey Roberts, 'Three Narratives of Neutrality: Historians and Ireland's War' in Girvin and Roberts, *Ireland and the Second World War*. See also the relevant chapters in Maurice Manning's *James Dillon: A Biography* (Dublin, Wolfhound Press: 1999).

12 Donal Ó Drisceoil, 'Censorship as Propaganda: the Neutralisation of Irish Public Opinion during the Second World War' in Girvin and Roberts, *Ireland and the Second World War*.

13 Brian Girvin, 'Politics in Wartime: Governing, Neutrality and Elections' in Girvin and Roberts, *Ireland and the Second World War*.

14 John M. Regan, *History*, April 2001, p. 285. These formulations appear in a review by Regan of the Girvin and Roberts volume and are his gloss on John A. Murphy's 'Irish Neutrality in Historical Perspective' in Girvin and Roberts, *Ireland and the Second World War*.

15 Cited by H. Patterson, *Ireland since 1939* (Oxford, Oxford UP: 2002), p. 58.

16 James Hogan, *Election and Representation* (Cork, Cork UP: 1945), pp. 33–5.

17 J. B. O'Brien, 'Ireland's Departure from the British Commonwealth', *The Round Table* (1988), 306, pp. 179–94.

18 Alvin Jackson, *Ireland 1798–1998: Politics and War* (Oxford, Blackwell: 1999), p. 303.

19 See T. Connolly, 'Irish Workers in Britain during World War Two' in Girvin and Roberts, *Ireland and the Second World War*.

20 Brian Girvin, *From Union to Union: Nationalism, Democracy and Religion in Ireland – Act of Union to EU* (Dublin, Gill and Macmillan: 2002), p. 101.

21 However, according to Maurice Manning, whatever he might have said during the war, James Dillon's retrospective view was that not even the pope and Éamon de Valera combined could have led the Irish people away from neutrality!

22 Girvin, *From Union to Union*, pp. 100–1. See also Geoffrey Roberts, 'The British Offer to End Partition, June 1940', *History Ireland*, vol. 9, no. 1, Spring 2001.

23 PRO, DO 121/85/81626.

24 OSS, 'Report on the Present State of Éire', 27 January 1943. I am grateful to Aengus Nolan for a copy of this and other OSS reports from the National Archives in Washington DC.

25 Elizabeth Bowen, *The Mulberry Tree: Writings of Elizabeth Bowen*, selected and introduced by Hermione Lee (London, Vintage: 1999), pp. 30–5. For a sample of Elizabeth Bowen's reports to the British authorities during the war see Elizabeth Bowen, *'Notes on Éire': Espionage Reports to Winston Churchill, 1940–2* (Aubane, Aubane Historical Society: 1999).

26 Brown, *Ireland: A Social and Cultural History 1922–1985*, ch. 6.

27 Cited by Thomas Hennessey, *A History of Northern Ireland 1920–1996* (Dublin, Gill and Macmillan: 1997), p. 92.

28 The Volunteers Project was set up by members of the History Department, UCC, in 1995, with a view to examining the role and experience of Irish volunteers in the British armed forces during the Second World War. One of the main results of the project's work has been the collection of a large number of taped interviews with Irish veterans of the war.

29 Jack White, *Minority Report: The Protestant Community in the Irish Republic* (Dublin, Gill and Macmillan: 1975), pp. 109–11; B. Inglis, *West Briton* (London, Faber and Faber: 1962), pp. 59–60; and Eunan O'Halpin, *Defending Ireland* (Oxford, Oxford UP: 1999), p. 167.

30 This generalisation is based on the data collected by the Volunteers Project. See also the evidence contained in Richard Doherty, *Irish Men and Women in the Second World War* (Dublin, Four Courts: 1999) and *Irish Volunteers in the Second World War* (Dublin, Four Courts: 2001).

31 See the summary of the oral history evidence presented by Aiden McElwaine in 'The Oral History of the Volunteers' in Girvin and Roberts, *Ireland and the Second World War*. Commenting on Richard Doherty's argument that people volunteered for noble reasons, Cormac Ó Gráda states: 'a colder reading of the evidence suggests that residual loyalism, bleak economic prospects in the Irish Free State, and conscription of Irishmen already resident in Britain are more convincing reasons for the higher southern numbers in 1939–1945' (review of *Irish Men and Women in the Second World War* in *English Historical Review*, June 2000, p. 774). However, Ó Gráda offers no evidence himself, save a presumption that Irish volunteering must have been the result primarily of adverse circumstances of one kind or another.

32 Cited by Clair Wills, '"Scrap 'me'; scrap my wretched identity": The Aesthetics of Neutrality during the Second World War', *Boundary 2*, vol. 31, no. 1, Spring 2004. However, as Wills points out, it was only when Johnston reached the Buchenwald concentration camp in 1945 that he became fully convinced of the righteousness of the Allied cause. It is difficult to believe that many other volunteers would have had such a troubled conscience.

33 In the sense of being based on concrete values rather than essentialist, romantic or

mystical notions of nationality. See C. Cronin, 'Democracy and Collective Identity: In Defence of Constitutional Patriotism', *European Journal of Philosophy*, vol. 2, no. 1 2003.

34 R. M. Smyllie, 'Unneutral Neutral Éire', *Foreign Affairs*, vol. 2, no. 24, 1946.

35 Peadar O'Donnell, 'Our Mythical Fascism Again', *The Bell*, vol. 15, no. 1, October 1947. I am grateful to Donal Ó Drisceoil for this reference.

36 See Cormac Kavanagh, 'Neutrality and the Volunteers: Irish and British Government Policy towards the Irish Volunteers' in Girvin and Roberts, *Ireland and the Second World War*.

37 See Roberts, 'Three Narratives of Neutrality' in Girvin and Roberts, *Ireland and the Second World War*.

38 On 11 December 1999, J. P. Duggan wrote to *Irish Times* complaining that 'Kevin Myers's jingoistic tunnel vision relegates to second class the thousands of young patriotic Irishmen who answered the de Valera-Cosgrave "call to arms" in 1940, believing that their first duty was to defend their own country in accord with the overwhelming will of the people'. Presumably Duggan would be particularly critical of the 5,000–7,000 members of the Irish army who deserted during the war and joined the British armed forces.

39 Another oft made point about the war years is that Fine Gael's support for neutrality led to the dissolution of *en bloc* southern unionist/loyalist support for the party.

40 Kurt Bowen, *Protestants in a Catholic State: Ireland's Privileged Minority* (Montreal, McGill–Queen's UP: 1983), p. 195. I am grateful to Andrew Bielenberg for the reference to this book.

41 *Ibid.*, p. 33 provides data which indicates a significant net migration during the war of Protestants in the military service age-range, although, of course, many young Protestants, like their Catholic counterparts would have left for economic reasons, i.e. gone to work in the British war economy. The evidence is also clear that the bulk of Irish war workers in Britain settled in the country after the war, thereby laying the foundations of the substantial Irish community in post-war Britain. See the essay by Connolly and others in Andrew Bielenberg (ed.), *The Irish Diaspora* (London, Longman/Pearson Education: 2000).

42 'Epochal narrative' refers not to a coherent text or a series of texts but to the somewhat disparate discourse on the nation's past, present and future in the press and other mass media, in political speeches and official pronouncements, in popular attitudes and folk myth, as well as in the works of historians. I tried to capture some aspects of it in my 'Three Narratives of Neutrality'.

43 Dennis Kennedy, *The Widening Gulf: Northern Attitudes to the Independent Irish State, 1919–1949* (Belfast, Blackstaff Press: 1988), p. 220.

44 J. Leonard, 'The Twinge of Memory: Armistice Day and Remembrance Sunday in Dublin since 1919' in Richard English and G. Walker (eds), *Unionism in Modern Ireland* (London, Macmillan: 1996). Note also Leonard's comment (p. 108) that during 'the Second World War, the British Legion encouraged its southern Irish members to join the regular Irish army or the Local Defence Force'.

45 The changing attitude to the volunteers can be traced in newspaper coverage of the various war anniversaries from the 1970s onwards.

46 For Myers' defence of Irish neutrality see 'An Irishman's Diary', *Irish Times*, 13 November 1999.

47 Kevin Myers, 'An Irishman's Diary', *Irish Times*, 4 November 1999.

48 Cited by Leonard, 'The Twinge of Memory', p. 111.

49 *Irish Times*, 29 April 1995. Bruton's figures on enlistment and casualty rates were wildly exaggerated. According to Richard Doherty, Irish war dead in the Second World War was about 4,500. This compares to 25,000– 35,000 during the First World War

(see Jeffery, *Ireland and the Great War*, p. 35). See also Y. T. McEwen, *Irish Volunteers and Volunteer Deaths in Irish Regiments 1939–1945*, MSc thesis, Edinburgh University, 2003.

50 A more recent example of changing attitudes was media coverage of the death and funeral of Lance-Corporal Ian Malone, killed in action in Iraq in April 2003 while serving in the Irish Guards: 'Ian Malone – UK soldier, Irish hero', ran the headline in the *Sunday Independent*, 27 April 2003.

❖ CONCLUDING THOUGHTS

1 Cited in Robert Fisk, *In Time of War: Ireland, Ulster and the Price of Neutrality 1939–45* (London, Paladin Grafton Books: 1985), p. 165.

2 Documents on German Foreign Policy, series D, vol. 7, docs 428 and 484.

3 See Seosamh Ó Longaigh, chapter 2 of this volume.

4 Joseph J. Lee, *Ireland 1912–1985: Politics and Society* (Cambridge, Cambridge UP: 1989), p. 242.

5 See Finbarr O'Shea's essay in this volume.

6 J. J. Lee, *Ireland, 1912–1985*, p. 237.

7 See Fisk, *In Time of War*, p. 524.

8 David Day, *The Politics of War: Australia at War, 1939–45: From Churchill to MacArthur* (Australia, HarperCollins Publishers: 2003).

9 All the American agents sent to Ireland by the Office of Strategic Services (OSS) drew these conclusions. See Martin S. Quigley, *A U.S. Spy in Ireland* (Dublin, Marino: 1999), pp. 19, 98–100.

10 R. F. Foster, *Modern Ireland, 1600–1972* (London, Penguin: 1990), p. 561.

11 See O'Driscoll, *Ireland, Germany and the Nazis*; Mervyn O'Driscoll, 'Inter-war Irish–German diplomacy: continuity, ambiguity and appeasement in Irish foreign policy' in Michael Kennedy and Joseph M. Skelly (eds.), *Irish Foreign Policy, 1919–1969: from independence to internationalism* (Dublin, Four Courts: 2000).

12 Cited in Fisk, *In Time of War*, p. 538.

13 *Ibid.*, p. 539.

SELECT BIBLIOGRAPHY

Allen, Trevor, *The Storm Passed By: Ireland and the battle of the Atlantic, 1941–2* (Dublin: 1996).

Alvarez, D., 'No immunity: Sigint and the European neutrals, 1939–45', *Intelligence and National Security*, vol. 12, no. 2 (April 1997).

Anon., 'The days of Emergency', *An Cosantóir* (November 1979) (copies of letters in *Irish Times*).

Balfour, Michael, *Propaganda in War, 1939–1945: organisations, policies and publics in Britain and Germany* (London: 1979).

Bardon, Jonathan, *A History of Ulster* (Belfast: 1992).

Barton, Brian, 'The Impact of the War in Northern Ireland', in Brian Girvin and Geoffrey Roberts (eds), *Ireland and the Second World War* (Dublin: 1999)

Bartlett, Thomas and Jeffery, Keith (eds.) *A Military History of Ireland* (Cambridge: 1996).

Bell, J. Bowyer, *The Secret Army: the IRA, 1916–1979* (Dublin: 1989).

Bennett, G. H. and R., *Survivors: British Merchant Seamen in the Second World War* (London: 1999).

Bewley, Charles (ed.: W. J. McCormack), *Memoirs of a Wild Goose* (Dublin: 1989).

Blake, John W., *Northern Ireland in the Second World War* (Belfast: 1956).

Bowman, John, *De Valera and the Ulster question, 1917–1973* (Oxford: 1982).

Brennan, Robert, 'Secret war documents', *Irish Press*, 23–30 August, 1958.

Bromage, Mary C., *Churchill and Ireland* (Indiana: 1964).

Burdick, Charles, 'Gruen, German Military Plans and Ireland, 1940', *An Cosantóir* (March 1974).

Brunicardi, Daire, 'The Marine Service', *Irish Sword*, vol. XIX, no. 75–8 (1993–5).

Bryan, Col. Dan, 'The Germans' Transmitter in Dublin', *Irish Times*, 26–7 October, 1981.

Butler, Hubert, *Independent Spirit: essays* (New York: 1996).

Buttimer, John 'The Treaty Ports', *An Cosantóir* (July 1978).

Canning, Paul, *British Policy Towards Ireland 1921–41* (Oxford: 1985).

— 'Yet another failure for appeasement? The case of the Irish ports', *International Historical Review*, 4:3 (1982).

Carroll, Joseph Thomas, *Ireland in the War Years, 1939–1945* (Newton Abbot: 1975).

Carter, Carolle J., *The Shamrock and the Swastika* (California: 1977).

— 'The Spy who Brought his Lunch', *Éire-Ireland*, vol. 10, Spring 1975.

Cassidy, Lt. Col. M., 'A Short History of the Irish Air Corps', *An Cosantóir* (May 1980).

Churchill, Winston S., *The Second World War, vols I–VI* (London: 1948–54).

Colville, J., *The Fringes of Power: Downing Street Diaries, vol. I, 1939–1941* (London: 1985).

Coogan, Tim Pat, *The IRA: A History* (London: 1987).

— *De Valera: Long Fellow, Long Shadow* (London: 1993).

Cooney, John, *John Charles McQuaid: ruler of Catholic Ireland* (Dublin: 1999).

Cox, C., 'Wir Fahren Gegen Irland', *An Cosantóir* (May 1974 and March 1975).

— 'Militar Geograpahische Angaben uber Irland', *An Cosantóir* (March 1975).

Cronin, Mike and Regan, John M. (eds.), *Ireland: The Politics of Independence, 1922–49* (Basingstoke: 2000).

Cronin, Seán, *The McGarrity Papers: revelations of the Irish revolutionary movement in Ireland and America, 1900–1940* (Tralee: 1972).

— *Frank Ryan, the search for the Republic* (Dublin: 1980).

— *Washington's Irish policy, 1916–86* (Dublin: 1987).

Cullingford, Elisabeth, *Yeats, Ireland and Fascism* (London: 1981).

Davis, Troy, *Dublin's American Policy: Irish–American relations, 1945–1952* (Washington D.C.: 1998).

Day, David, *The Politics of War: Australia at war, 1939–45: From Churchill to MacArthur* (Australia: 2003).

Delaney, Enda, *Demography, State and Society: Irish migration to Britain, 1921–1971* (Liverpool: 2000).

Ditchburn, Robert W., 'The refugee problem', *Studies*, vol. 28 (June 1939).

Doherty, Richard, *The War Years, Derry, 1939–1945* (Derry: 1992).

— *Clear the way! A history of the 38th Irish Brigade, 1941–47* (Dublin: 1993)
— *Irish Men and Women in the Second World War* (Dublin: 1999).
— *Irish Volunteers in the Second World War* (Dublin: 2002).
Dickel, H., *Die Deutsche Aussenpolitik und die Irische Frage von 1932 bis 1944* (Wiesbaden: 1983).
Drudy, P. J., *Ireland and Britain since 1922* (Cambridge: 1986).
Duggan, John P., *Neutral Ireland and the Third Reich* (Dublin: 1989).
— *A History of the Irish Army* (Dublin: 1991).
— *Herr Hempel at the German Legation in Dublin, 1937-1945* (Dublin and Portland Oregon: 2003).
— 'Celtic Cloaks and Teutonic Daggers', *An Cosantóir* (May 1978).
— 'The German Threat – myth or reality', *An Cosantóir* (September 1989).
— 'Germany and Ireland in World War II', *The Irish Sword*, vol. XIX no. 75–8 (1993–5).
Dukes, Jim, 'The Emergency Services', *The Irish Sword*, vol. XIX, no. 75–8 (1993–5).
Dungan, Myles, *Distant Drums: Irish soldiers in foreign armies* (Belfast: 1993).
Dunphy, Richard, *The Making of Fianna Fáil in Ireland* (Oxford: 1995).
Dwyer, T. Ryle, *Irish Neutrality and the USA, 1939–47* (Dublin: 1977).
— *Éamon de Valera* (Dublin: 1980).
— *Strained Relations Ireland at peace and the USA at war 1941-45* (Dublin: 1988).
— *Guests of the State the story of allied and axis servicemen interned in Ireland during World War II* (Dingle: 1994).
— 'The mad escape', *An Cosantóir* (August 1979).
Elborn, Gaffney, *Francis Stuart: A Life* (Dublin: 1990).
Falls, Cyril, *Northern Ireland as an Outpost of Defense* (Belfast: 1952).
Fanning, Ronan, *The Irish Department of Finance, 1922–58* (Dublin: 1978).
— 'Irish Neutrality – an historical review', *ISIA*, vol. 1, no. 3 (1982).
— *Independent Ireland* (Dublin: 1983).
— '"The Rule of Order": Éamon de Valera and the IRA, 1923-40' in John P. O'Carroll and John A. Murphy (eds.), *De Valera and his Times: Political Development in the Republic of Ireland* (Cork: 1983).
— 'Anglo-Irish relations: partition and the British dimension in historical perspective', *ISIA*, vol. 2, no. 1 (1985).
— 'The Politics of Irish Neutrality during World War II' in Louis-Edward Roulet (ed.) *Les Etats Neutres Européens et la Seconde Guerre Mondiale* (Neuchatel: 1985).
— 'The Anglo–American alliance and the Irish Application for Membership of the United Nations, 1945–46', *ISIA*, vol. 2, no. 2 (1986).
— 'Irish Neutrality' in *UNESCO Yearbook on Peace and Conflict Studies 1985* (Paris: 1987).
— 'Irish Neutrality' in Bo Huldt and Atis Lejins (eds.), *Neutrals in Europe: Ireland* (Stockholm: 1990).
— 'Small States, Large Neighbours: Ireland and the United Kingdom', *ISIA*, vol. 9 (1998).
— 'Raison d'État and the Evolution of Irish Foreign Policy' in Michael Kennedy and Joseph Morrison Skelly (eds.), *Irish Foreign Policy 1919–1966* (Dublin: 2000).
— 'Dublin: The View from a Neutral Capital' in Arnold A. Oftner and Theodore Wilson (ed.), *Victory in Europe 1945: from World War to Cold War* (Kansas: 2000).
— 'The Anglo–American Alliance and the Irish Question in the Twentieth Century' in Howard Clarke and Judith Devlin (ed.) *Encounters with Europe: Essays in Honour of Albert Lovett* (Dublin: 2003).
Fanning, Ronan, Michael Kennedy, Dermot Keogh and Eunan O'Halpin, *Documents on Irish Foreign Policy, vol. I, 1923–1925* (Dublin: 2000), *vol. II, 1923–1925* (Dublin: 2000), *vol. III, 1926–1932* (Dublin: 2002), *vol. IV, 1932–1936* (Dublin, October 2004).
Farrell, T., 'The "Model Army": Military imitation and the enfeeblement of the army in post-revolutionary Ireland, 1922–42', *ISIA*, vol. 8 (1997).
Fleming, Peter, *Operation Sea Lion* (New York: 1957).
— *Invasion 1940* (London: 1957).
Fisk, Robert, *In Time of War: Ireland, Ulster and the Price of Neutrality, 1939–45* (London: 1983).

FitzGerald, Garrett, 'The Origins, Development and Present Status of Irish "Neutrality"', *ISIA*, vol. 9 (1998).

Forde, Frank, *The Long Watch: The History of the Irish Mercantile Marine in World War II* (Dublin: 1981).

Gaffney, Phyllis, 'Why was Ireland given special treatment? The awkward state of Franco-Irish diplomatic relations, August 1944–March 1945', *Études Irlandaises*, no. 24 (1999).

Gageby, Douglas, *The Last Secretary General: Sean Lester and the League of Nations* (Dublin: 1999).

Gallagher, M. (ed.), *Irish Elections, 1922–1944: results and analysis* (Limerick: 1993).

Geary, F. and Johnson, W., 'Shipbuilding in Belfast, 1861–1986', *Irish Economic and Social History*, vol. XVI (1989).

Geiger, T. and Kennedy, Michael, *Ireland, Europe and the Marshall Plan* (Dublin: 2004).

Girvin, Brian, *Between Two Worlds: politics and economy in independent Ireland* (Dublin: 1989).

— 'The Politics of War in Ireland: Elections, neutrality and governing' in B. Girvin and G. Roberts (eds), *Ireland and the Second World War* (Dublin, 1999).

Girvin, Brian and Roberts, Geoffrey (eds.), *Ireland and the Second World War: politics, society and remembrance* (Dublin: 2000).

Glynn, Seán, 'Irish Immigration to Britain, 1911–1951: Patterns and Policy', *Irish Economic and Social History*, vol. VIII (1981).

Goertz, Hermann, 'Mission to Ireland', *Irish Times*, 25 August–10 September, 1970.

Goldring, Maurice, '"The Bell" Pendant la Seconde Guerre Mondiale', *Études Irlandaises*, no. 10 (December 1985).

— 'Belfast Ouvrier Pendant la Seconde Guerre Mondiale', *Études Irlandaises*, no. 14 (1989).

Goldstone, Katrina, '"Benevolent Helpfulness"? Ireland and the international reactions to Jewish refugees, 1933–39' in M. Kennedy and J. M. Skelly (eds), *Irish Foreign Policy, 1919–66* (Dublin: 2000).

Gray, Tony, *The Lost Years: the emergency in Ireland, 1939–45* (London: 1997).

— *Mr Smyllie Sir* (Dublin: 1991).

Harkness, David, *The Restles Dominion: the Irish Free State and the British Commonwealth* (London: 1969).

Harrison, Richard S., *Irish Anti-war Movements, 1824–1974* (Dublin: 1986).

Hayes, Stephen, 'My Strange Story', *The Bell*, vol. XVII, no. 4 (July 1951).

Hayes-McCoy, G. A., 'Irish Defence Policy, 1938–51' in K. B. Nowlan and T. D. Williams (eds), *Ireland and the War Years and After* (Dublin: 1969).

Harrison, Henry, *The Neutrality of Ireland: Why it was inevitable* (London: 1940).

Hawkins, R., '"Bending the Beam": Myth and reality in the bombing of Coventry, Belfast and Dublin', *The Irish Sword*, vol. XIX, nos. 75–8 (1993–5).

Hennessey, T., *A History of Northern Ireland, 1920–1996* (Basingstoke: 1997).

Holmes, Michael, Rees, Nicholas, and Whelan, Bernadette (eds.), *The Poor Relation: Irish foreign policy and the Third World* (Dublin: 1993).

Horgan, John, *Seán Lemass: the enigmatic patriot* (Dublin: 1997).

— 'Irish Foreign Policy, Northern Ireland, Neutrality and the Commonwealth: the historical roots of a current controversy', *ISIA*, vol. 10 (1999).

Howard, Constance, 'Eire, The War and the Neutrals' in Arnold and Veronica Tonybee (eds.) *Survey of International Affairs, 1938–1946*, vol. IX (London: 1956).

Hull, Mark, *Irish Secrets: German espionage in Ireland, 1939–45* (Portland, Oregon and Dublin: 2003).

Joannon, Pierre (ed.), *De Gaulle and Ireland* (Dublin: 1991).

Keatinge, Patrick, 'Ireland and the League of Nations', *Studies*, vol. 59 (1970).

— *The Formulation of Irish Foreign Policy* (Dublin: 1973).

— *A Place Among the Nations: Issues of Irish Foreign Policy* (Dublin: 1978).

— *A Singular Stance: Irish neutrality in the 1980s* (Dublin: 1984).

Kennedy, Michael, *Ireland and the League of Nations, 1919–1946: International relations, diplomacy and politics* (Dublin: 1996).

— 'Principle Seasoned by the Sauce of Realism: Joseph Walshe, Sean Lester and Irish policy at the League of Nations towards the Japanese invasion of Manchuria', *ISIA*, vol. 6 (November 1995).
— 'Prelude to Peacekeeping: Ireland and the Saar 1934–1935', *Irish Historical Studies*, May 1997.
— 'Our Men in Berlin: some thoughts on Irish diplomats in Berlin, 1929–39', *ISIA*, vol. 10 (1999).
— 'In Spite of all Encumbrances, the Development of the Early Irish Foreign Service', History Ireland, Spring 1999.
— '"It is a disadvantage to be represented by a woman": the experiences of women in the Irish diplomatic service', *ISIA*, vol. 12, 2002.
— '"Nobody knows and ever shall know from me that I have written it": Joseph Walshe, Éamon de Valera and the execution of Irish foreign policy, 1932–8', *ISIA*, vol. 14, 2003.
Kennedy, Michael and Skelly, Joseph M. (eds.), *Irish Foreign Policy, 1919–1966: From independence to internationalism* (Dublin: 2000).
Keogh, Dermot, *Ireland and Europe, 1919–1948* (Dublin: 1988).
— *The Vatican, the Bishops and Irish Politics* (Cambridge: 1986).
— *Twentieth Century Ireland: Nation and State* (Dublin: 1994).
— *Ireland and the Vatican: The Politics and Diplomacy of Church and State, 1922–1960* (Cork: 1995).
— *Jews in Twentieth Century Ireland: Refugees, Anti-Semitism and the Holocaust* (Cork: 1998).
— 'Ireland, de Gaulle and World War II' in Pierre Joannon (ed.), *De Gaulle and Ireland* (Dublin: 1991).
— 'Irish Department of Foreign Affairs' in Zara Steiner (ed.), *The Times Survey of Foreign Ministries of the World* (London: 1982).
— 'Jewish refugees and Irish Government Policy in the 1930s and 1940s' in *Proceedings of Conference – Remembering for the Future*, vol. I (Oxford: 1988).
— 'Ireland, Vichy and de Valera, de Gaulle' in Bernard Tricot, *Charles de Gaulle* (Paris: 1991).
— 'The Irish Free State and the Refugee Crisis, 1933–1945' in Paul Bartrop (ed.), *False Havens: The British Empire and the Holocaust* (New York: 1995).
— 'Ireland and the Holocaust' in David S Wyman (ed.), *The World Reacts to the Holocaust* (Baltimore: 1996).
— 'Éamon de Valera and Hitler: an analysis of international reaction to the visit to the German Minister, May 1945', *ISIA*, vol. 3, no. 1 (Autumn 1989).
— 'Profile of Joseph Walshe, Secretary of the Department of Foreign Affairs 1922–46', *ISIA*, vol. 3, no. 2 (Autumn 1990).
— 'L'Irlande et de Gaulle', *Espoir, revue de L'Institut Charles de Gaulle*, no. 80 (Mars 1992).
— 'An Eye Witness to History: Fr Alexander J. McCabe and the Spanish Civil War, 1936–1939', *Breifne – Journal of Cumann Seanchais Bhreifne* (Cavan: 1994).
Keogh, Dermot and Nolan, Aengus, 'Anglo-Irish Diplomatic Relations and World War II', *The Irish Sword*, vol. XIX, no. 75–8 (1993-5).
Kehoe, Emmanuel, 'The Life and Times of Francis Stuart', *Sunday Press*, 23 July 1978.
Kilbride-Jones, H. E., 'Adolf Mahr', *Archaeology Ireland*, vol. 7, no. 3 (Autumn 1993).
Knowlson, James, *Damned to Fame: the life of Samuel Beckett* (London: 1997).
Lee, Joseph J., *Ireland, 1912–1985: politics and society* (Cambridge: 1989).
Longford, Earl of, and O'Neill, Thomas P., *Éamon de Valera* (London: 1971).
Longford, Earl of, *Peace by Ordeal* (London: 1972).
Lowry, Donal, 'New Ireland, Old Empire and the Outside World, 1922–1949: the strange evolution of a "dictionary republic"' in Mike Cronin and John M. Regan (eds.), *Ireland: the Politics of Independence, 1922–49* (Basingstoke: 2000).
MacCarron, Donal, *"Step Together!" Ireland's emergency army 1939–46 as told by its veterans* (Dublin: 1999)
McCarthy, Denis J., 'Armour in the war years', *An Cosantóir* (March 1975).
MacEoin, Uinseann, *The IRA in the Twilight Years, 1923–1948* (Dublin: 1997).
McIvor, A., *A History of the Irish Naval Service* (Dublin: 1994).

McMahon, Deirdre, 'Ireland, the dominions and the Munich crisis', *ISIA*, vol. 1, no. 1 (1981).

— 'A "transient apparition": British policy towards the de Valera government', *Irish Historical Studies*, vol. 22, no. 88 (September 1981).

— *Republicans and Imperialists: Anglo-Irish relations in the 1930s* (New Haven: 1984).

— 'Ireland and the Empire-Commonwealth, 1900–1948', in Judith M. Brown and William Roger Louis (eds.), *The Oxford History of the British Empire, vol. IV, The Twentieth Century* (Oxford: 1999).

Maguire, Maria, *A Bibliography of Published Works on Irish Foreign Relations, 1921–1978* (Dublin: 1981).

McMahon, Seán, 'The men who caught the German ambassador spying', *Sunday Tribune Magazine*, 3 January 1982.

Mangan, Colm, 'Plans and operations', *The Irish Sword*, vol. XIX, no. 75–8 (1993-5).

Manning, Maurice, *The Blueshirts* (London: 1970).

— *James Dillon: a biography* (Dublin: 1999).

Mansergh, Nicholas, *Documents & Speeches on British Common Affairs, 1931-1952, vol. I* (Oxford: 1953).

— *The Unresolved Question: the Anglo-Irish settlement and its undoing, 1912–1972* (New Haven: 1991).

— *Nationalism and Independence: selected Irish papers* (Cork: 1997).

Maye, Brian, *Fine Gael, 1923–87* (Dublin: 1993).

Molohan, Cathy, *Germany and Ireland, 1945–1955: Two Nations' Friendship* (Dublin: 1999).

Monsarrat, Nicholas, *The Cruel Sea* (London: 1951).

Mulcahy, Risteárd, *Richard Mulcahy (1886–1980): a family memoir* (Dublin: 1999).

Murphy, John A., *Ireland in the Twentieth Century* (Dublin: 1975).

Natterstad, J. H., *Francis Stuart* (London: 1974).

Nowlan, Kevin B., and Williams, T. Desmond (ed.), *Ireland in the War Years and After, 1939–51* (Dublin: 1969).

Ó Broin, Leon, *Just Like Yesterday: an autobiography* (Dublin: 1985).

O'Brien, Conor Cruise, 'Ireland in international affairs', in Owen Dudley Edwards (ed.), *Conor Cruise O'Brien introduces Ireland* (Dublin: 1969).

O'Callaghan, Seán, *The Jackboot in Ireland* (New York: 1958).

O'Carroll, Donal, 'The emergency army', *The Irish Sword*, vol. XIX, no. 75–8 (1993–5).

O'Connell, Col. J. J., 'The Vulnerability of Ireland in War', *Studies* (March 1938).

O'Donoghue, David, *Hitler's Irish Voices: The story of German radio's wartime Irish service* (Belfast: 1998).

Ó Drisceoil, Donal, *Censorship in Ireland, 1939–1945: neutrality, politics and society* (Cork: 1996).

— 'Moral neutrality: censorship in emergency Ireland', *History Ireland*, vol. 4, no. 2 (Summer 1996).

— 'Censorship and Irish perceptions of the war, 1939–45', in B. Girvin and G. Roberts (eds), *Ireland and the Second World War* (Dublin: 1999).

— *Peadar O'Donnell* (Cork: 2001).

O'Driscoll, Mervyn, 'Irish–German Relations 1929–32: Irish Reaction to Nazis', *Cambridge Review of International Affairs*, vol. XI, no 1 (Summer/Fall 1997).

— 'Irish–German Commerce, 1932–39: Irish Foreign Trade Policy, the Economic War and the Anglo–Irish–German Diplomatic Triangle', *ISIA*, vol. 10 (1999).

— 'Inter-war Irish–German Diplomacy: continuity, ambiguity and appeasement in Irish foreign policy', in M. Kennedy & J. M. Skelly (eds.), *Irish Foreign Policy, 1919–1966: From independence to internationalism* (Dublin: 2000).

— '"To Bring Light Unto the Germans": Irish Recognition-Seeking, the Weimar Republic and the British Commonwealth, 1930–2', *European History Quarterly*, vol. 33, no. 1 (2003).

— *Ireland, Germany and the Nazis 1919–39: People, Policy and Diplomacy* (Dublin: 2004).

— 'The "Jewish Question", Irish Refugee Policy and Charles Bewley, 1933–39' in G. Halfdanarson (ed.), *Racial Discrimination and Ethnicity in European History* (Pisa: 2004).

O'Halloran, Clare, *Partition and the Limits of Irish Nationalism* (Dublin: 1987).

O'Halpin, Eunan, *Defending Ireland: the Irish state and its enemies since 1922* (Oxford: 1999).
— *The Geopolitics of Republican Diplomacy in the Twentieth Century* (Dublin: 2001).
— *MI5 and Ireland 1939–1945: the official history* (Dublin: 2003).
— 'Intelligence and security in Ireland, 1922–45', *Intelligence and National Security*, 5:1 (1990).
— 'Ireland in Spy Fiction' [with Keith Jeffery], *Intelligence and National Security* 5:4 (1990).
— 'Army, Politics and society, 1923–1945', in T. G. Fraser and Keith Jeffery (eds.), *Men, Women and War: Historical Studies XVIII* (Dublin: 1993).
— 'Aspects of intelligence', *The Irish Sword*, Vol. XIX (1994/5).
— '"According to the Irish Minister in Rome": British decrypts and Irish diplomacy during the second world war', *ISIA*, 6 (1995).
— 'The Army in Independent Ireland' in Thomas Bartlett and Keith Jeffrey (eds), *A Military History of Ireland* (Cambridge: 1996).
— 'The Politics and Practice of Anglo-Irish security co-operation, 1939–45' in B. Girvin and G. Roberts (eds), *Ireland and the Second World War* (Dublin: 1999).
— 'MI5's Irish Memories: fresh evidence on Anglo-Irish relations during the Second World War' in Brian Girvin and Geoff Roberts (eds.), *Ireland and the Second World War: politics, economy and remembrance* (Dublin: 2000).
— '"Toys" and "whispers" in "16-land": SOE and Ireland, 1940–42', *Intelligence and National Security*, 15, no. 4 (Winter 2000).
— 'Irish–Allied relations and the "American Note" crisis: new evidence from British records', *ISIA*, 11 (2000).
— 'Irish Neutrality in the Second World War' in Neville Wylie (ed.), *European Neutrals and Non-belligerents during the Second World War* (Cambridge: 2002).
— 'Small States and Big Secrets: understanding sigint cooperation between unequal powers during the Second World War', *Intelligence and National Security*, vol. 17, no. 3 (Autumn 2002).
— 'British Intelligence, the Republican Movement and the IRA's German links, 1935–45' in Fearghal McGarry (ed.), *Republicanism in Modern Ireland* (Dublin: 2003).
O'Leary, Don, *Vocationalism and Social Catholicism in Twentieth-Century Ireland : the search for a Christian social order* (Dublin: 2000).
Ó Lúing, Seán, *Celtic Studies in Europe and other essays* (Dublin: 2000).
Ottonello, Paola, 'Irish–Italian diplomatic relations in World War II: The Irish perspective', *ISIA*, vol. 10 (1999).
Parsons, D., 'Mobilisation and Expansion, 1939–1940', *The Irish Sword*, vol. XIX, no. 75–8 (1993–5).
Patterson, Henry, *The Making of Fianna Fáil Power in Ireland, 1923–1948* (Oxford: 1995).
Patterson, Robert, 'Ireland, Vichy and Post-liberation France, 1938–50' in M. Kennedy and J. M. Skelly (eds), *Irish Foreign Policy, 1919–1966* (Dublin: 2000).
Phelan, Jim, *Ireland – Atlantic Gateway* (London: 1941).
Quigley, A., 'Air Aspects of the Emergency', *The Irish Sword*, vol. XIX, no. 75–8 (1993–5).
Quigley, Martin S., *A US Spy in Ireland* (Dublin: 2000).
Quinn, Owen, 'The Coastwatching Service', *The Irish Sword*, vol. XIX, no. 75–8 (1993–5).
Raymond, Raymond J., 'American Public Opinion and Irish Neutrality, 1939–45', *Éire-Ireland*, vol. 18, no. 1 (1983).
— 'Irish Neutrality: Ideology or Pragmatism?', *International Affairs*, vol. 60 (1984).
— 'David Gray, the Aiken Mission and Irish Neutrality', *Diplomatic History*, vol. 9 (1985).
Roberts, Geoffrey, 'Revising Neutrality: Historians and Ireland's War' in B. Girvin and G. Roberts (eds), *Ireland and the Second World War* (Dublin: 1999).
Rosenberg, J. L., 'The 1941 Mission of Frank Aiken to the United States: an American Perspective', *Irish Historical Studies*, vol. 22, no. 86 (1980).
Roth, Andreas, *Mr Bewley in Berlin: Aspects of the career of an Irish diplomat, 1933–1939* (Dublin: 2002).
Ryan, John, *Remembering How We Stood* (Dublin: 1975).
Salmon, Trevor, *Unneutral Ireland: An ambivalent and unique security policy* (Oxford: 1989).
Schutz, Gunther, 'My secret mission to Ireland' as told to John Murdoch, *Sunday Press*, 24 May–24 June, 1970.

Share, Bernard, *The Emergency: Neutral Ireland, 1939–1945* (Dublin: 1975).
Shields, L. (ed.), *The Irish Meteorology Service: the first 50 years, 1936–1986* (Dublin: 1987).
Sloan, G. R., *The Geopolitics of Anglo-Irish Relations in the Twentieth Century* (London: 1997).
— 'Geopolitics and British strategic policy in Ireland: issues and interests', *ISIA*, vol. 8 (1997).
Smith, M. L. R., *Fighting for Ireland? The military strategy of the Irish republican movement* (London: 1995).
Smyllie, Robert M., 'Unneutral Neutral Éire', *Foreign Affairs*, vol. 24, no. 2 (January 1946).
Stephan, Enno, *Geheimauftrag Irland* (Hamburg: 1961).
— *Spies in Ireland* (London: 1963).
— *Die Deutsche Keltologie und ihre Berliner Gelehrten bis 1945* (Berlin: 1999).
Stuart, Francis, *Black List – Section H* (London: 1996).
Sturm, Hubert, *Hakenkreuz und Kleebatt: Irland, die Allierten und das Dritte Reich, 1933–1945* (Frankfurt: 1984).
Sweeney, O., 'The Coast Watching Service', *The Irish Sword*, vol. XIX, no. 75–6 (1993–4).
Toynbee, Arnold and Veronica (eds.), *The War and the Neutrals* (London: 1964).
Whelan, Bernadette, *Ireland and the Marshall Plan, 1947–57* (Dublin: 2000).
Williams, T. Desmond, 'Study in Neutrality', *The Leader*, January–April 1953.
— 'Neutrality!', *Irish Press*, 6 June–17 July 1953.
— 'Ireland and the war' in K. B. Kowlan and T. D. Williams (eds), *Ireland in the War Years and After* (Dublin: 1969).
— 'Conclusion' in K. B. Kowlan and T. D. Williams (eds), *Ireland in the War Years and After* (Dublin: 1969).
Young, Peter, 'Defence and the new Irish state, 1919–1939', *The Irish Sword*, vol. XIX, no. 75–6 (1993–5).
Young, Peter, 'Pageantry and the Irish Defence Forces', *An Cosantóir*, vol. 45, no. 9 (September 1989).
Young, Peter, 'The Way We Were', *An Cosantóir* (September 1989).
Walsh, J. J., *Recollections of a Rebel* (Tralee: 1944)
Wylie, Paula L., *Diplomatic Recognition in Irish Foreign Policy, 1949–1963* (Dublin: 2005).

INDEX